A FILMOGRAPHY
OF THE
THIRD WORLD

An Annotated List of 16mm Films

by

HELEN W. CYR

The Scarecrow Press, Inc.
Metuchen, N.J.   1976

Library of Congress Cataloging in Publication Data

Cyr, Helen.
 A filmography of the Third World.

 Includes index.
  1. Underdeveloped areas--Film catalogs. 2. Under-
developed areas--Social conditions--Film catalogs.
I. Title.
HC59. 7. C97   016. 909'09'724   76-22584
ISBN 0-8108-0940-0

FOREWORD

In preparing this filmography my intent is to provide film background for students, scholars and others about unfamiliar peoples and lands. As I feel that the typical North American may be just as limited in his or her view of "developed" nations, such as Turkey or Japan, as about the less well-known places, such as Bolivia, or Nigeria, and has little knowledge of the traditions and life experience of Afro-Americans, Native Americans and other ethnic groups at his own doorstep, I have used the most extensive definition of "Third World," among the variety currently in use, to include all non-Western nations--that is, all except the United States, Europe and the Soviet Union--and the ethnic minorities of North America and Europe.

With the use of this book the public can find relatively easy access to many of the important 16mm films on this subject. The range from short to feature-length films covers subjects such as customs, geographic features, history, science, politics, fine arts, religion, sports, technology, and travel. Fictional films are also listed as a means to reflect some of the self-expression of peoples and nations and to demonstrate the cinematic achievement of specific cultures. Inclusion in my film list does not in any way constitute endorsement of a film's content or point of view, however.

The reader will find the majority of films cited herein to have release dates of the late 1960s or the 1970s, proof that film producers have been interested in Third World subjects in recent years. Unfortunately, production coverage is irregular. Although films about Afro-Americans or Native Americans, Japan, or Brazil exist, for example, few items are available on Latinos, Asian Americans, or countries such as Bolivia, Paraguay, or certain African nations. For this reason I have tried to supply these gaps with older films which can at least illustrate geographic features or the sociology, anthropology, or politics of former years. In addition, I deliberately added old films that are critically acclaimed classics of ageless appeal and importance.

For the purpose of clarity, geographers' terminology is used to group various countries of the world. Thus "Near East" (or its alternate, "Middle East") here has become "Southwest Asia." "Far East" is supplanted by "East Asia," and so on.

Not all the titles selected for this list are films of the highest quality. Some of them were added only to illustrate specific topics that seemed to warrant attention. On the other hand, certain genres of feature films are omitted, or at the most, are lightly represented. "Exploitation" films--those which exploit a popular theme or fad without care for depth of treatment, or which demonstrate reverse stereotyping--have been excluded.

Availability was yet another factor in the selection of films for this book. All titles cited herein are distributed in the United States and/or Canada for sale or rental, or, if out of print, are at least available for rental from university film depositories. Some foreign films had to be left out for lack of North American distribution. But I hope that such omission will not be construed as lack of film activity in certain countries. Indeed, international film festivals of the last few years have brought a number of fine cinematic efforts from the Third World to worldwide attention and acclaim. And, in addition, there are a few covertly made films, shot under the threat of censorship, oppression, and physical torture, which would be of great interest to many persons, if we could only lay hands on them. Recent frightening reports of the kidnapping and torture of several Chilean filmmakers are a case in point.

The reader is cautioned that distributors referred to in the film descriptions may, or may not, be the current sources for the films. Certain vagaries of the film world preclude the reliability of any film list. There are no Books in Print or Cumulative Book Index equivalents for films to lead the way, and precise details about films are hard to pin down sometimes. The situation is further complicated by the frequent reassignment of films by their producers to new distributing agencies, or unexpected deletions from commercial sales lists.

The table of contents presents the basic geographical outline for this filmography. It can be seen that films for some areas are listed nation by nation (South America, East Asia), whereas in other cases, film titles are given in one grouping without further subdivision by country (Southwest Asia, Northern and Southern Africa). This variation in treatment was largely determined by the measure of generality or specificity of available films.

Each film description includes the following information: title; alternate title, if any; production company, producer, or filmmaker; release or copyright date; running time; color; code(s) for distributor(s); a brief descriptive annotation. In the case of feature-length theatrical films, additional data are given: foreign language; English subtitles, if any; directory; credits for screenplay, music, photography, production; cast. An alphabetical list of distributors' codes, along with their names and addresses, is provided at the back of the book.

My description of this work wouldn't be complete without an expression of thanks to the people who helped directly or indirectly with this project: above all to Margot Kernan, Antioch College, who expanded my awareness of film activity in South America and Africa, and to the numerous U. S. and Canadian film distributors who provided needed information.

H. W. Cyr
Baltimore, Maryland

v

TABLE OF CONTENTS

PART I

FILMOGRAPHY OF THE THIRD WORLD

1

AFRICA

Africa/General

AFRICA: AN INTRODUCTION. Wayne Mitchell, 1967. 18 min.
    color. BFA
An introduction to the geography of Africa and the many different
people who live there.

AFRICA AWAKENS. United Nations, 1968. 29 min. b/w. UN
An overview of the changes and problems of emerging nations in
Africa--economic, political, social.

AFRICA DANCES. United Nations, 1967. 28 min. color. MGH,
    CINL
A performance of Les Ballets Africains in the General Assembly
Hall at the United Nations Headquarters. With introduction by the
permanent representative of Guinea to the United Nations, whose remarks are translated by Alistair Cooke.

AFRICA, EAST AND WEST. Henry Strauss, 1967. 28 min. color.
    ASF, PAN
A travelogue designed to promote tourism in Africa. Shows attractive locales throughout the continent.

AFRICA: HISTORICAL HERITAGE. Encyclopaedia Britannica Edu-
    cational Corporation, 1972. 9 min. color. EBEC
Historical research on the evolution of sophisticated nation-states
such as Kush, Ghana, Mali, and Songhai.

AFRICA: LIVING IN TWO WORLDS. Visual Education Centre, 1971.
    (The African Scene Series.) 16 min. color. EBEC, UWY
Contrasts old tribal communities and new African nations, with emphasis on the people's interest in mechanization and education.

AFRICA ON THE BRIDGE. World Wide, 1960. 58 min. color.
    Directed by Dick Ross. ROAF, MUND
A documentary about Billy Graham's 17,000-mile trip through Africa.
Shows scenes of many new nations.

AFRICAN CONTINENT: AN INTRODUCTION. Coronet, 1962. (Afri-
    can Continent Series.) 16 min. color. COR, UWY
About the emergence of peoples of new, independent nations and the
physical, historical and cultural factors of the regions in which they
live.

3

AFRICAN FAUNA. Hoefler, Disney, 1957. Rev. version. 11 min.
        color. UCA, UUT.
Shows African animals at home in their natural environment.

AFRICANS ALL. International Film Foundation, 1963. 22 min.
        color. EFD, IFF, IFP, UCA
Begins with film animation to parody misconceptions about Africa.
Then reveals the beauties and diversity of Africa in live action
footage. Includes authentic African music and sounds. Animation
by Philip Stapp.

THE ANCIENT AFRICANS. International Film Foundation, 1969.
        27 min. color. EFD, IFF, UUT
An overview of the grandeur of ancient African kingdoms, revealing
their arts and their archaeological artifacts. Kingdoms included are
Kush, Axum, Ghana, Mali and Songhai.

ANIMALS OF AFRICA. ABC, 1968. 14 min. color. MGH, UCA
African animals are viewed in terms of African ecology and the effect of human encroachments in primitive areas.

AWAKENING AFRICA. Hearst, 1960. 11 min. b/w. UCO
Covers Nigeria's 1960 voting, a major step toward independence,
and the unrest that divided Algeria also in 1960.

BLACK GENESIS: THE ART OF TRIBAL AFRICA. Pyramid, 1970.
        5 min. color. PYR
Hundreds of masks, carvings, drawings, jewelry and other African
art examples are presented against a background of black African
rhythms and songs.

CONTINENT OF AFRICA. Encyclopaedia Britannica Educational
        Corporation, 1962. (Africa in Change Series.) 22 min. color.
        EBEC, UCO
A description of Africa's revolutions--causes and effects. Discusses
problems of new nations in establishing stable societies, and gives a
general introduction to the African continent.

THE CONTINENT OF AFRICA. ACI, 1966. (Africa Series.) 15
        min. color. MGH, UUT
Examines the land forms, industrial and agricultural development,
and the people of Africa.

THE ECONOMY OF AFRICA. ACI, 1966. (Africa Series.) 13 min.
        color. MGH
An account of the African economy from colonial days through the
new era of independent countries.

EDUCATION: AFRICA'S ROAD TO THE FUTURE. CCM, n.d.
        (Africa Series.) 14 min. b/w. AIM, MAC
About the urgent need for education in Africa to bring economic
growth.

HEALTH AND EDUCATION: KEYS TO AFRICAN DEVELOPMENT.
ABC, 1968. 14 min. color. UCA, MGH
Examines the indigenous diseases of Africa and the shortage of doctors. Also shows examples of folk medicine, such as a Yoruba rite to ward off illness.

I TOOK MY WOMEN TO AFRICA. CCM, 1972. (Africa Series.)
13 min. color. MAC
A tour of the 6,000 miles from northern to southern Africa. Among the locales highlighted are Victoria Falls and Mount Kilimanjaro.

IN AFRICAN HANDS. Texture, n.d. 14 1/2 min. color. TEX
A study of newly formed African countries, such as Zambia, Ghana, Tanzania, Guinea, Senegal, with details of influences, counter-influences, economic status, and technological developments.

IN THE NAME OF ALLAH. NET, 1970. 76 min. b/w. IND
A visit to the Muslim community of Fez, Morocco to study the history and religious practices of Islam.

INDUSTRY IN AFRICA. Frank Gardonyi and Clifford Janoff, 1970.
11 1/2 min. color. BFA
Describes the growth of local industries to replace the importation of goods that was typical of colonial Africa. Shows African people at work in textile mills, oil refineries and automotive plants.

KWANZAA. Nafasi Co-Operative, n.d. 30 min. color. AFR
Presents the Nguzo Saba (Seven Principles of Blackness) and describes the Kwanzaa as an African holiday with its own special ceremony.

MODERN AFRICA: SPORTS AND ENTERTAINMENT. ABC, 1968.
14 min. color. MGH
About the modern and traditional elements of African amusement. Shows scenes of African people at leisure.

THE NEW AFRICA: PEOPLES AND LEADERS. ABC, 1968. 15
min. color. MGH
Explores how African leaders are building new nations in a variety of ways, how much outside help they are accepting, and to what degree they are helping themselves.

OUR TRIP TO AFRICA. Peter Kubelka, 1966. 13 min. color.
MAC
One of filmmaker Peter Kubelka's best films--a record of a businessmen's safari to Africa, contrasting the European and African worlds.

THE PEOPLES OF AFRICA. ACI, 1966. (Africa Series.) 16
min. color. MGH
Shows the diversity of peoples and cultures that comprises present-day Africa.

YOU HIDE ME. Kwate Nee-Owoo, 1972. 20 min. b/w. TRI
Ghanaian filmmaker Kwate Nee-Owoo expresses his reaction to his
discovery of African art treasures in the British Museum and his
concern for the African people's lack of awareness of their rich
artistic heritage, much of which was carted off to foreign countries.

Northern Africa

> (includes Algeria, Cameroon, Central African Republic, Chad,
> Dahomey (Benin), Egypt (United Arab Republic), Ethiopia,
> Gambia, Ghana, Guinea-Bissau, Ivory Coast, Liberia, Libya,
> Mali, Mauritania, Morocco, Niger, Nigeria, Senegal, Sierra
> Leone, Somali Republic, Spanish Sahara, Sudan, Togo, Tun-
> isia, Upper Volta)

AN ADVENTURER RETURNS. Argos, 1972. 34 min. color. MGH
A reverse study of stereotyping--in this case a Nigerian student
returns home from the United States, bringing cowboy outfits for
his friends as symbols of American life.

AFRICA IS MY HOME. Atlantis, 1961. 22 min. color, ATL,
    BOSU
A Nigerian woman tells her life story and the meaning of African
nationalism for her.

AFRICAN CARVING: A DOGON KANAGA MASK. Film Study
    Center of Harvard University, 1975. 19 min. color. PHO
A detailed study of the actual carving of a Kanaga mask used by
the Dogon people of Mali in their sacred rituals--in this case a
sacred dance performed on the death of one of their men.

AN AFRICAN CITY: CONTRASTING CULTURES. Frank Gardonyi
    and Clifford Janoff, 1970. 11 min. color. BFA
Shows the various cultures and life styles to be found in African
cities, such as Abidjan, Ivory Coast.

AFRICAN CONTINENT: NORTHERN REGION. Coronet, 1962.
    (African Continent Series.) 13 1/2 min. color. COR
The Arabic culture, the lack of water, and the European influence
--factors which affect northern African life.

AFRICAN CRAFTSMEN: THE ASHANTI. Frank Gardonyi and
    Clifford Janoff, 1970. 11 min. color. BFA
A close look at the crafts of the Ashanti people of West Africa.

AFRICAN VILLAGE. Theodore Holcomb, 1960. 17 min. color.
    IFB, UNE
Customs and daily life in a village of the Kissi tribe in Guinea, a
nation which was granted independence from France.

ALGERIA, BIRTH OF A NATION. Hearst, 1962. 9 min. b/w.
    UCO

The history of Algeria from the Roman colonial period to 1962, the date of independence.

ALGERIA, TEN YEARS LATER. Richard Marquand, n. d. 60 min. color. ITC
How Algeria, now the tenth largest country in the world, struggles for survival after an eight-year war and ten years of attempted recovery.

ALGERIA: WHAT PRICE FREEDOM? NET, 1966. 54 min. b/w. IND.
Algerian people are shown in their struggle for stability and a higher standard of living. Includes a visit with a family whose life style is partly European and partly traditional. Shows the changing role of women and efforts to overcome illiteracy.

ANANSI, THE SPIDER. Landmark, 1969. 10 min. color. TEX
An African parable about the origin of the moon and a spider who is a trickster-hero of the Ashanti people of Ghana. A cartoon animation.

ANCIENT EGYPT. Coronet, 1952. 10 1/2 min. color. COR, UCO, UUT, UWY
Studies the contribution of Egyptian civilization to Western culture and artifacts of ancient Egypt.

ANCIENT EGYPT: DIGGING UP HER RICH PAST. Brian Blake, n. d. 51 min. color. TL
Explores the magnificent pyramids, temples and tombs of Egypt. Includes interviews with Egyptologists and archaeologists and a discussion of the history of Egyptology.

THE ANCIENT EGYPTIAN. International Film Foundation, 1963. 27 min. color. EFD, IFF, UCA
How the ancient Egyptians lived; their arts and artifacts. With live action footage and animation by Philip Stapp. An award-winning film.

ANCIENT EGYPTIAN IMAGES: ART OF ANCIENT EGYPT. Cloche, 1953. 13 min. b/w. MAC
The culture of the ancient Egyptian people from the earliest period to the decline of their civilization, as traced through art works in the Louvre.

ANNUAL FESTIVAL OF THE DEAD. International Film Foundation, 1967. (The African Village Life Series.) 14 min. color. EFD, IFF, UCA
A clear view of the Dogon Tribe's unusual festival that uses war game reenactments, offerings, a parade, dancing and beer drinking to commemorate those who died in the past year.

ART OF ISLAM. ACI, 1970. 10 min. color. ACI
Shows the religion-based craftsmanship of Arabian arts in metal and wood as preserved in the Museum of Islamic Art in Cairo, Egypt.

ARTS AND CRAFTS IN WEST AFRICA.   Wayne Mitchell, 1969.
        10 1/2 min.   color.   BFA
The heritage and general background of West Africa's arts and
crafts.   Shows present-day craftsmen creating foods from leather,
cloth, metal, clay, gourds and rattan.

ATLANTIC SLAVE TRADE.   University of Minnesota, 1973.   (West
        Africa: An Introduction to the Peoples and Cultures Series.)
        17 min.   color.   UMN
A departure from films which carelessly misrepresent African his-
tory and culture, this one explores in depth the elements of the
Atlantic slave trade and its effect on Africa and its people.

A BACKWARD CIVILIZATION: THE BERBERS OF NORTH AFRI-
        CA.   Encyclopaedia Britannica Educational Corporation, 1937.
        21 min.   b/w.   EBEC, UCO, UUT, UWY
Presents a rare look at the Berber people of northern Africa who
live completely isolated because of natural barriers.   Although old,
still valuable as a film, even though the 1930s point of view evaluates "primitive" peoples in terms of the technological civilization
around them.

BAMBARA OF MALI.   University of Minnesota, 1973.   (West Afri-
        ca: An Introduction to the Peoples and Cultures Series.)
        10 min.   color.   UMN
An in-depth study of the Bambara people who live in Mali.   Shows
scenes of family life, customs, dance and feasts.   Poses questions
about self and ethnic identity.

BATTLE OF ALGIERS.   Antonio Musu and Yacef Saadi, 1966.
        123 min.   b/w.   In French and Arabic with English
        subtitles.   Directed by Gillo Pontecorvo; screenplay by
        Franco Solinas; based on a story by Gillo Pontecorvo and
        Franco Solinas; photography by Marcello Gatti; music by
        Ennio Morricone and Gillo Pontecorvo.   With Jean Martin,
        Yacef Saadi, Brahim Haggig, Tommaso Neri.   MAC
About the Algerian revolt against the French between 1954 and 1957.
Winner of eleven international awards, including Best Picture Award
at the Venice Film Festival.

BLACK GIRL.   (LA NOIRE DE...)   Actualités Françaises of Paris
        and Films Domirev of Dakar, 1969.   60 min.   b/w.   In
        French with English subtitles.   Directed by Ousmane Sem-
        bene; written by Ousmane Sembene, based on Ousmane Sem-
        bene's novel "La Noire de..."   With Mbissine Therese Diop,
        Anne-Marie Jelinck, Robert Fontaine, Momer Nar Sene.
        NC, NYF
Ousmane Sembene's first feature film and the first black African
feature-length film.   A young girl from Dakar is maneuvered into
working for a typical middle-class French family.   A virtual prisoner, she commits suicide.   Sembene won a Prix Jean Vigo for
Best Direction.

BLOODY SCHEMES.   Statens Filmcentral, Denmark, 1972.   15
    min.   color.   TRI
A cartoon animation (part of a historical series made in Denmark)
about the development of slavery, the founding of towns and forts
along Africa's coasts, and black slave-hunters selling their fellow
countrymen.   A witty approach to history.   American version has
soundtrack recorded by the San Francisco Mime Troupe.

BLUE MEN OF MOROCCO.   Walt Disney, 1968.   28 min.   color.
    ASF, UUT
About the strange nomadic tribe of Arabs who live in the desert
and whose skin acquires its color from the dye in their clothing.

BOROM SARRET.   Ousmane Sembene, 1964.   20 min.   b/w.   NYF
A critical view of black life in Dakar, where the male protagonist
of the story earns a meager living with his horse and cart.   Directed by Ousmane Sembene.

BRONZE CASTING: VINCENT KOFI. Leo Steiner, 1972.   18
    min.   b/w.   PIC
A famous sculptor and teacher from Ghana shows how he creates a
bronze-cast figure in the method used centuries ago.

BUILDING A BOAT ON THE NIGER.   International Film Founda-
    tion, 1967.   (The African Village Life Series.)   8 min.   color.
    EFD, IFF
The skillful conversion of hard lumber to finely constructed boats,
performed by members of the Bozo tribe, who live near the Niger
River.

BUILDING A HOUSE ON THE NIGER.   International Film Founda-
    tion, 1967.   (The African Village Life Series.)   7 min.
    color.   EFD, IFF
A study of how the people of the Bozo tribe in Africa build a house
with skill and in harmony with one another.

BUMA: AFRICAN SCULPTURE SPEAKS.   Encyclopaedia Britannica
    Educational Corporation, 1952.   9 min.   color.   EBEC, PAR,
    UCO
A dramatic presentation of the sculpture--statues and masks--of
the Central and West African people.   With authentic African music.

CENTRAL AFRICAN REPUBLIC.   Universal Education and Visual
    Arts, 1968.   (The Peoples of Africa Series.)   15 min.
    b/w.   UEVA
What investment and technology have supposedly done for an African emerging nation.   A study of social and economic problems
faced by the Central African Republic in its growth in the modern
world.

CHILDREN IN THE BALANCE: THE TRAGEDY OF BIAFRA.
    NET, 1969.   60 min.   b/w.   IND
Tells of the desperate need for food by the people of Biafra, aris-
ing from their war with Nigeria.

CHILDREN OF THE WORLD: DAHOMEY. NET, 1968.   29 min.
     color. IND
A boy from a West African country discusses his country, his
tribe and his present life.

CHILDREN OF THE WORLD: SOMALIA. NET, 1968.   28 min.
     color. IND
A boy from a nomadic camel herder's community shows how he
lives always traveling and hunting for pasture.

CITY BOY OF THE IVORY COAST. Visual Education Centre,
     1970. (The African Scene Series.) 16 min. color. EBEC,
     VEC
A typical teen-age boy is shown getting an education that prepares
him for a white collar job despite his country's need for manual
labor.

COTTON GROWING AND SPINNING.   International Film Foundation,
     1967. (The African Village Life Series.) 6 min. color.
     EFD, IFF
How the Dogon people of Africa grow cotton and prepare the fiber
for spinning in the traditional way.

THE COWS OF DOLO KEN PAYE: RESOLVING CONFLICT
     AMONG THE KPELLE. Holt, Rinehart and Winston, 1970.
     32 min. color. BFA
A study of tradition and Western influences in the Liberian village
of Fokwele.

DAILY LIFE OF THE BOZO PEOPLE. International Film Founda-
     tion, 1967. (The African Village Life Series.) 16 min.
     color. EFD, IFF, UCA
The members of the Bozo people near the Niger River in Mali
perform their daily activities--fishing, weaving, cooking, and
milling. Without narration.

DESERT CARAVAN. NBC, 1971. 13 min. color. FI
A shortened version of an NBC television documentary on the trip
of a nomad boy with his family on a camel caravan in the Sahara.

DISCOVERING THE MUSIC OF AFRICA. Bernard Wilets, 1967.
     22 min. color. BFA
A master drummer of Ghana and associates demonstrate bells,
rattles and drums while telling of their use in African music.
Also, includes discussion of the use of drums for communication.

DOGON OF MALI: CLIFF DWELLINGS OF BANDIAGARA. Uni-
     versity of Minnesota, 1973. (West Africa: An Introduction
     to the Peoples and Cultures Series.) 10 min. color. UMN
A study of the reasons why the Dogon people have come to live on
the cliffs of Mali. Shows the use of caves as graves and as storage centers for religious items, such as masks.

DURO LADIPO. NET, 1967. 30 min. b/w. IND, UCA
A close look at the playwright-composer-actor-founder of the Duro
Ladipo Travelling Theatre Company of Oshogbo, Nigeria and his
travels to small villages by bus to present his African folk operas.

EGYPT, A COUNTRY IN TRANSITION. International Film Bureau,
    1961. 10 min. color. UCA, UUT
Shows ancient tombs and temples as contrast to the present life of
Egypt which combines old and new ideas.

EGYPT: CRADLE OF CIVILIZATION. Encyclopaedia Britannica
    Educational Corporation, 1962. 12 min. color. EBEC,
    UCA, UWY
About ancient Egypt's contributions to Western civilization.

EGYPT: LAND OF ANTIQUITY. Paul Hoefler, 1964. 17 min.
    color. UCO, UWY
A visit to Egypt which includes the Nile Valley, Aswan, Nubia,
temples of Karnak and Luxor, and Cheops' tomb at Giza.

EGYPT, LAND OF THE NILE. Dudley Pictures, 1962. 17 min.
    color. UEVA
A view of the old and new elements in the ancient nation of Egypt.
Includes scenes of tombs and pyramids and a discussion of the
economic importance of the Nile River.

AN EGYPTIAN VILLAGE. Gouldsou, 1964. 18 1/2 min. color.
    BFA
A visit with an Egyptian farmer in one of the many farming villages
along the Nile. Stresses the continuity of old ways with those of
the present-day.

EGYPTIAN VILLAGERS. Visual Education Centre, 1969. 14 min.
    color. FI, VEC
One day in the life of an Egyptian villager and his family.

EMITAI. (LORD OF THE SKY.) Films Domirev, 1972. 101 min.
    color. In Wolof and French with English subtitles. Directed
    by Ousmane Sembeno. NYF
The elders in a Senegalese village during World War II must yield
their sons to war but balk at having to surrender their rice to the
French army. A story of conflict with colonials and with traditional
African beliefs. The first color epic made in Africa by an African.

ETHIOPIA: AFRICA'S ANCIENT KINGDOM. Hoefler-Disney, 1962.
    (Far Places Series.) 17 min. color. UCA, UUT
About the 3,000-year history and present problems of Ethiopia.

ETHIOPIA: CULTURES IN CHANGE. National Geographic Society,
    1971. 21 min. color. FI, VEC
The contrasts of Ethiopia: feudal lords and peasants, skyscrapers
and mud huts, plus rich highlands and hot deserts.

ETHIOPIA 9.   CCM, n.d.   (Africa Series.)   14 min.   b/w.   AIM,
    MAC
The Ethiopian government's program to educate doctors and nurses
in an atmosphere of conflict with traditional beliefs.

ETHIOPIA: THE HIDDEN EMPIRE.   National Geographic Society,
    1970.   52 min.   color.   FI, VEC
Shows a medieval monastery on a mesa-top; Addis Ababa; Bume
tribesmen; professional hunters; and a four-day Ethiopian Easter
celebration.

ETHIOPIA: THE LION AND THE CROSS.   CBS, 1963.   (Africa
    Series.)   52 min.   b/w.   MAC
About the only African nation that has never been a colony.

ETHIOPIAN MOSAIC.   National Film Board of Canada, 1967.   10
    min.   color.   IFB
A close look at the history and contemporary life of the people of
Ethiopia.   Without narration.

FAMILY OF GHANA.   National Film Board of Canada, 1958.   30
    min.   b/w.   UCO, UUT
Shows village life in Ghana, where some community members strive
to find new and more productive ways of fishing.

A FAMILY OF LIBERIA.   Visual Education Centre, 1970.   (The
    African Scene Series.)   17 min.   color.   EBEC, VEC
Contrasts two groups of people, a family in a mining town and people in a village.

FINCHO.   Sam Zebba, 1958.   75 min.   color.   Directed by Sam
    Zebba; music by Alexander Laszlo.   With Patrick Akponu,
    Comfort Ajilo, Gordon Parry-Hobroyd.   Introduction by Harry
    Belafonte.   MAC[1]
In an African village the people begin to do business with a white
man and gradually adjust to automated equipment, even going so
far as to build their own sawmill.   Shot in Nigeria with a non-
professional cast.

FIRST WORLD FESTIVAL OF NEGRO ARTS.   UNESCO, 1968.
    20 min.   color.   MGH
About a symposium held in Dakar designed to affirm the value of
African art.   Shows music performances, dance, sculpture, painting
and various influences on and from the Western world.

FISHING ON THE NIGER RIVER.   International Film Foundation,
    1967.   (The African Village Life Series.)   18 min.   color.
    EFD, IFF
An account of the Bozo tribe's ingenious methods of fishing on the
Niger River as performed individually and in small groups.

THE FORGOTTEN KINGDOM.   BBC, 1971.   (PART 12.   The Glory
    That Remains Series.)   30 min.   color.   TL

Shows the ruins of the temples, pyramids and other objects representing the isolated and strange kingdom of Kush in the Sudanese desert.

FREE PEOPLE IN GUINEA-BISSAU.   Axel Lohman and Rudi Spee, 1970. 50 min. b/w. With English narration and subtitles.
    TRI
A Swedish film made to describe the background of the independence movement in Guinea-Bissau, otherwise known as "Portuguese Guinea." Directed by Axel Lohman and Rudi Spee.

FULBE OF M'BANTOU. University of Minnesota, 1973. (West Africa: An Introduction to the Peoples and Cultures Series.) 10 min. color. UMN
A look at the daily routines of the Fulbé people, nomadic herdsmen who live near the Senegal River. Shows three social classes--the nobles, the rimbe, and the neybe.

GHANA. ABC, 1968. 14 min. color. MGH
About the efforts of the Ghanaian military forces to alter the situation created by Kwame Nkrumah's one-man rule.

HERDING CATTLE ON THE NIGER. International Film Foundation, 1967. (The African Village Life Series.) 7 min. color.
    EFD, IFF
About the Fulani (or Peul) tribe of Mali, black nomads who move with their cattle from one grazing spot to another. In this case, they are seen driving their herds across the Niger River.

HUNTING WILD DOVES. International Film Foundation, 1967.
    (The African Village Life Series.) 8 min. color. EFD, IFF
How the Dogon tribe scales steep cliffs to hunt for doves. Shows how the handwoven rope used comes from tree bark.

IN SEARCH OF MYSELF. United Nations, 1965. (Africa Series.) 15 min. b/w. AIM, MAC
Several young authors at the Mbari Art Center in Nigeria discuss their country's cultural life and tell how Africa's traditional art forms are being adapted to the needs of modernization.

ISLAMIC REPUBLIC OF MAURITANIA. Universal Education and Visual Arts, 1967. 20 min. color. UEVA, UMN
A report on the country that must rely on its mineral resources for future development, because its land is not suited to agriculture on a large scale.

JACKPOT IN LIBYA. CBS, 1966. 26 min. b/w. MAC
What happened when a poor Arab country struck oil--its effect on the culture.

JAGUAR. Pierre Braunberger for Les Grandes Films Classique Sitac/Les Films de la Pleiade, 1955. 93 min. color. In

French with English subtitles.   Directed by Jean Rouche.
MGH
Explores West African people of the 1950s in a mixture of fiction
and fact using a non-professional cast.

LEOPOLD SEDAR SENGHOR. NET, 1967.   30 min.   b/w.   IND,
   UCA
A portrait of the first president of Senegal, who is also a poet
laureate.   Includes his early life and his later attitudes toward the
development of Africa.

LIFE IN THE NILE VALLEY.   Coronet, 1952.   10 1/2 min.
   color.   COR, UCO, UUT
A study of a family in the Nile Valley where for thousands of years
Egyptians have worked the land as farmers.

LIFE IN THE OASIS: NORTH AFRICA.   Coronet, 1962.   11 min.
   color.   COR, UUT
How the North African oasis environment affects daily life: the
struggle with wind and sand, irrigation farming, house construction with mud bricks.   Also shows man-made oases.

LIFE IN THE SAHARA.   Clifford Kamen, 1953.   15 min.   color.
   UCO
Describes the way people live in the desert, their customs, search
for food and use of the camel.

THE LION HUNTERS.   (LA CHASSE AU LION A L'ARC.)   Pierre
   Braunberger, 1958-1965.   68 min.   color.   MGH, PEN
Made by Jean Rouch, a filmmaker who has spent most of his adult
life in Africa, this is a documentary study of the people of Nigeria.

LION OF JUDAH: HAILE SELASSIE.   BBC, 1972.   50 min.   color.
   TL
A profile of Haile Selassie, long-time, former Emperor of Ethiopia
and symbolic African leader.

THE LIVING DESERT OF LIBYA.   (LIBYE, DESERT VIVANT.)
   Explo-Mundo, n.d.   52 min.   color.   RAY
Filmmaker Freddy Tondeur traveled across the Sahara Desert to
record its people and natural life.   French version available.

MADINA BOE.   Jose Massip, n.d.   40 min.   b/w.   TWN
A Cuban film about life in Guinea-Bissau, the Republic and the liberated Portuguese territories, with emphasis on guerrilla camp
activities.

MAGIC RITES: DIVINATION BY ANIMAL TRACKS.   International
   Film Foundation, 1967.   (The African Village Life Series.)
   7 min.   color.   EFD, IFF
Describes the method of the Dogon tribe's shaman to determine the
future from animal tracks in the sand.

MAGIC RITES: DIVINATION BY CHICKEN SACRIFICE. International Film Foundation, 1967. (The African Village Life Series.) 7 min. color. EFD, IFF
A brief view of the Dogon tribe's religious practice of sacrificing a chicken to divine forces.

MAGICIANS OF THE BLACK HILLS. BBC and Odyssey, 1968. 25 min. color. TL
About the Matakam people of Cameroon. Shows their arts of smelting iron, toolmaking and jewelry making handed down through the sons of blacksmiths, who consider their work magic. Narrated by Lowell Thomas.

MALI: THE DESERT AND THE RIVER. CCM, n. d. (Africa Series.) 11 min. b/w. AIM, MAC
One West African nation's attempt to use natural resources efficiently for farming, fishing and trading.

MAN CHANGES THE NILE. Visual Education Centre, 1969. 13 min. color. VEC, FI
How modern man has built dams, power plants and factories to provide energy and fertilizer for progress.

MANDABI. Domirev, 1969. 90 min. color. In Wolof dialect with English subtitles. Directed by Ousmane Sembene. GRO
Best Foreign Film at the Atlanta Festival, 1970. Made by "the first truly African filmmaker of international standing." Shows in a humorous way how an ancient civilization copes with change. A man who receives a money order consequently finds his way of life threatened. A Senegalese film.

MARINKA VILLAGES IN TRANSITION. University of Minnesota, 1973. (West Africa: An Introduction to the Peoples and Cultures Series.) 15 min. color. UMN
A study made during a week's residence in various villages of Senegal and Mali. Shows farming, housing for a polygamous family, differences of ritual and social status.

THE MARKET'S EDGE: GLIMPSES OF THE HAUSA WORLD. C. E. Hopen, 1971. 28 min. color. PEN
Illustrates the adjunct social functions of Hausa markets in Nigeria in addition to their economic role in the community.

MASKED DANCES. International Film Foundation, 1973. (The African Village Life Series.) 6 min. color. EFD, IFF
About the ritual dances of the Dogon people of West Africa--a study in body movement filmed to convey the authentic features of their art.

A MATTER OF LIFE AND DEATH. (PART 10. The Glory that Remains Series.) BBC, 1969. 30 min. color. TL
The story of how the ancient Egyptians lived as traced from extant paintings, models and reliefs found in tombs.

MEDINA. Ron Stevenson, 1973. 15 min. color. SERB
A poetic, lyrical documentary by filmmaker Scott Bartlett and a
fine work of film art. Filmed in Morocco. Uses footage of the
people, the architecture, and street scenes.

MEDITERRANEAN AFRICA. Clifford Kamen, 1952. 12 min.
        color. UGO, UUT, UCA
An account of the past and present cultures and geography of the
north African region bordering on the Mediterranean.

MODERN EGYPT. Audio, 1965. 18 min. color. MGH
A tribute to Egypt's tremendous growth in recent years and its contributions to civilization.

MUSIC OF AFRICA. NET, 1963. 59 min. b/w. IMP, IND
An African musicologist and composer demonstrates with a group
of Nigerian musicians how contemporary African music has blended
traditional and Western idioms. Shows the function of the talking
drum for musical purposes and message communication.

MYTH OF THE PHARAOHS. ACI, 1971. 13 min. color. ACI
Uses animation to describe Egyptian tomb paintings and the symbolic and complete life of a typical Pharaoh.

NEGRO KINGDOMS OF AFRICA'S GOLDEN AGE. Atlantis, 1968.
        17 min. color. UCA, UAR, SYR
Describes the rich cultural heritage of Africa's ancient kingdoms
of Songhai, Mali and Ghana.

A NEW DAWN. Statens Filmcentral, Denmark, 1972. (The His-
        tory Book Series.) 15 min. color. TRI
A cartoon animation film (part of a history series made in Denmark) about the Portuguese colony, Guinea-Bissau, which is involved in a struggle for independence. A witty approach to history.
American version contains a soundtrack recorded by the San Francisco Mime Troupe.

NEW HORIZONS: MOROCCO, KENYA. Pan American World Air-
        ways, 1961. 13 min. color. ASF, PAN
A tourist travelogue about two African countries--one in the north,
the other in the south.

THE NEW NORTH AFRICA. Stanton, 1971. 16 min. color. EFD,
        STAN
Provides historical background (including the Roman occupation)
and modern views with emphasis on the Republic of Tunisia, one
of Africa's "Big Three."

NIGER: IRON-MAKING THE OLD WAY. Texture, n.d. 18 min.
        color. TEX
Shows people of the Niger area involved in iron-making with the
use of a simple blast furnace and great skill.

NIGER: WATER ON THE SAVANNA.   Texture, n. d.   20 min.
    color.   TEX
Nomads are shown in the traditional search for water.   In contrast, the Niger government is shown providing deep wells which
lead to the formation of villages.

NIGERIA: A SCHOOL FOR JACOB.   NET, 1965.   30 min.   b/w.
    IND
Explores the thwarted educational ambitions of a Nigerian boy in
contrast with the needs of a U. S. boy in Appalachia, to raise the
question of U. S. support for both.

NIGERIA: BIAFRA.   CBS, 1970.   30 min.   color.   CAR
Mike Wallace and Harry Reasoner in an on-the-scene report recount Nigerian history and describe the factors in Biafra's succession after the attacks on the Ibos.   Considers the implications of
this war as indicator of other developments in Africa.

NIGERIA: GIANT IN AFRICA.   National Film Board of Canada,
    1960.   52 min.   b/w.   MGH
Explores Nigeria's quiet development as a nation.   Describes the
ancient African cultures in Nigeria.   Includes views of Queen Elizabeth II, Prime Minister Harold Macmillan, Dr. Nmamdi Azikiwe,
and Prime Minister Abubakar Tafawa Balewa.

NIGERIA: NIGERIA ONE.   Facts Africa, n. d.   54 min.   b/w.
    TWN
An edited version of a longer film, made by a film team, FACTS
AFRICA, during the Nigerian Civil War and post-war period, which
attempts to tell what actually happened.

NIGERIA: PROBLEMS OF NATION BUILDING.   Atlantis, 1967.
    Rev. ed.   21 min.   color.   ATL, BOSU, NYU
Nigeria is treated as an example of the interrelationship between nationalism and tribalism in Africa.

THE NILE IN EGYPT.   Gateway Educational Films, 1966.   10
    min.   color.   COR, UCO
Old methods of irrigation and modern developments, such as the
Aswan dam, are contrasted.

THE NILE VALLEY AND ITS PEOPLE.   Encyclopaedia Britannica
    Educational Corporation, 1962.   16 min.   color.   EBEC, UCO
Why the Nile is regarded as the "Lord of All Rivers" by the people
of the various countries through which it flows.

NORTHERN AFRICA: WATER AND MAN.   ACI, 1966.   (Africa
    Film Series.)   16 min.   color.   MGH
The people of North Africa viewed in terms of an advancing technology and its possible effect on their future.

THE NUER.   Robert Gardner and Hilary Harris, 1970.   75 min.
    color.   MGH

A sensitive study of the culture of the Nuer people of Ethiopia and
the Sudan who call themselves "Nath" ("the real people"). Made
for the Film Study Center of the Peabody Museum at Harvard University.

OASIS. Encyclopaedia Britannica Educational Corporation, 1965.
    11 min. color. EBEC.
About the importance of the date palm for oasis dwellers. Shows
their activities and life style.

OASIS IN THE SAHARA. Visual Education Centre, 1969. 16 min.
    color. VEC, FI
A study of water, date crops, and other factors in the life of oasis
dwellers.

OIL IN LIBYA. Visual Education Centre, 1969. 15 min. color.
    FI, VEC
Explores Libya's transformation since her growth as oil producer.
Shows impact on the people.

THE OLD AFRICA AND THE NEW: ETHIOPIA AND BOTSWANA.
    ABC, 1968. UCO, UCA
Africa's oldest independent country, Ethiopia, is studied in contrast
with the newly independent Botswana.

OLD SOLDIERS NEVER DIE. (PART 9. The Glory That Remains
    Series.) BBC, 1969. 30 min. color. TL
A study of the policy of Rome's Third Legion which controlled the
province of Numidia--what is now modern Algeria. Follows the
life of a Roman legionnaire from barracks to retirement in Numidia
in 100 A. D. under the rule of Emperor Trajan.

THE OLIVE TREES OF JUSTICE. (LES OLIVIERS DE LA JUS-
    TICE.) Georges Derocles, 1961. 90 min. b/w. Directed
    by James Blue in collaboration with Jean Pelegri; adapted
    from the novel by Jean Pelegri; music by Maurice Jarre.
    With Pierre Prothon and Jean Pelegri. In French with Eng-
    lish subtitles. MGH
A study of the conflict between French colonists and Algerian na-
tionalists as revealed in a story about a young man who returns to
Algeria, his native land, to see his dying father.

OMOWALE: THE CHILD RETURNS HOME. NET, 1965. (History
    of the Negro People Series.) 30 min. b/w. IND, UCA,
    UCO
A visit by Black American novelist John Williams to Badagary,
Nigeria, the port from which his ancestors left for America as
slaves.

ONION FARMING. International Film Foundation, 1967. (The Af-
    rican Village Life Series.) 7 min. color. EFD, IFF
A close-up of black Africans--in this case the Dogon people working
on their onion crop.

THE PASSENGERS. Centre Algerian de Documentation et d'Information, 1968-71. 90 min. b/w. In French with English subtitles. TRI
Follows a young Algerian from his departure from Algeria through his two-year stay in metropolitan Paris to his return home. Gives a probing examination to the problems of language, culture, racism, and oppressive regulations barring job training and access to certain jobs. Directed by Annie Tresgot.

THE PROBLEM OF NIGERIAN UNITY. ABC, 1968. 19 min. color. UCA, UCO
Studies the problem of Nigeria's 150 tribes, intertribal warfare, and the Biafran secession. Narration by Gregory Peck.

RAINY SEASON IN WEST AFRICA. Visual Education Centre, 1969. 14 min. color. FI, UMN, VEC
Tells how an African tribe waits for the monsoons after a period of drought; shows rainmaker's ritual; effect of rain on the land. Treats superstition as obstacle to "progress."

RAMPARTS OF CLAY. Jean-Louis Bertucelli, 1970. 85 min. color. In Arabic with English subtitles. Directed by Jean-Louis Bertucelli; screenplay by Jean Duvignaud; director of photography, Andreas Winding; Berber songs collected and sung by Taos Amrouche. With Leila Schenna and the villagers of Tehouda in Algeria. CF
A sensitive study of a woman in a desert village who refuses to accept the typical role of subservience determined by tradition. Her conflict is paralleled by her people's growing awareness of exploitation. Based on an actual incident.

REOU-TAKH. Ousmane N'Diaye, 1971. 60 min. color. In French with English subtitles. Directed by Mahama Traore; written by Mahama Traore and Pathe Diagne; photographed by Baidy Sow. With Alain Christian Plenet and N'Dack Gueye. TRI
Mahama Traore, one of Africa's new directors, made this feature film to reveal life in Senegal through the eyes of an Afro-American visitor. The camera looks realistically at details of poverty and neo-colonial factors, as well as the fashionable tourist spots in this "independent" country.

REPUBLIC OF CHAD. Universal Education and Visual Arts, 1967. 20 min. b/w. UEVA, UMN
About the struggle of Chad to develop its resources and its way of life.

REPUBLIC OF NIGER. Universal Education and Visual Arts, 1967. 20 min. b/w. UEVA, UMN
Tells what life is like in a land on the edge of the Sahara that desperately needs water. Shows new irrigation and pesticide projects.

REPUBLIC OF THE IVORY COAST.   Universal Education and Visu-
      al Árts, 1967.   20 min.   b/w.   UEVA, UMN
About the life in this West African country; its favorable natural resources and good climate.

RETURN TO ETHIOPIA.   Thames Television, n. d.   (This Week
      Series.)   30 min.   color.   RIT
A follow-up report on the famine discussed in the earlier film,
THE UNKNOWN FAMINE.   Shows how action accomplished results
in Ethiopia despite ignorance and indifference that had existed
among officials.

RIVER JOURNEY ON THE UPPER NILE.   Visual Education Centre,
      1969.   18 min.   color.   VEC, FI
Covers a trip of riverboats, lashed together, that made the 500-
mile journey between Malakal and Juba.   Includes various adventures: a visit to a Shilluk village, rescue by a tug, storms, wild
animals.

RIVER NILE.   McGraw-Hill, 1962.   34 min.   color.   UCA, UCO
An adaptation of a longer, award-winning documentary by Lou Hazam
which follows the Nile along its course over 4,000 miles.   Narration by actor James Mason in which he describes the Nile's 5,000-
year history.

RIVER PEOPLE OF CHAD.   Visual Education Centre, 1969.   20
      min.   color.   FI, VEC
Follows the people of Kotokos, a village on the Shari River, in
building boats and houses, cooking, eating, fishing, plus trading at
Fort Lamy, Chad's capital.

RIVERS OF SAND.   Robert Gardner, 1974.   83 min.   color.   PHO
About the Hamar people of Southwestern Ethiopia who live a traditional way of life which happens to include male supremacy.   In
this culture the men are masters, women are slaves.

THE ROOTS OF CHANGE.   CBS, n. d.   30 min.   color.   NACC
A report on the latest changes in Ghana and the self-help projects
in Accra and Kumasi where the Ashanti customs are threatened by
change.

SAHARA FANTASIA: A DESERT FESTIVAL.   International Film
      Foundation, 1970.   9 min.   color.   EFD, IFF
Nomadic desert tribes gather in Southern Morocco to celebrate the
Mousseum, a festival with dancing, music, trade, and traditional
pageantry, including the "fantasia" which combines musketry with
horsemanship.

SAHARA: LA CARAVANE DU SEL.   NBC, 1969.   52 min.   color.
      FI
Follows a camel caravan in the salt trade as it makes its four-
week, 1,000-mile journey across the desert from the salt mines in
Bilma to the market place in Agades.

SENEGAL.   Universal Education and Visual Arts, 1967.   20 min.
    b/w.   UEVA, UMN
Tells how Senegal is trying to develop its natural resources while
coping with economic problems.

SOLEIL-O.   Med Hondo, 1972.   106 min.   b/w.   In French with
    English subtitles.   Directed by Med Hondo.   Credits and
    cast unlisted.   NYF
The first feature film by a black Mauritanian--the story of a black
African seeking work and acceptance in Paris.

SORO.   H. K. Davis, C. E. Hoppen, 1968.   25 min.   color.   PEN
Shows how nomads, the Fulani people of Nigeria, set up a campus
during the wet season near a Hausa town.   The Hausa provide musicians and an audience for dancing.   Some boys demonstrate
"soro," a flogging of the right pectoral muscle by which they prove
their ability to stand pain.

SPREADING THE WORD.   CCM, n. d.   (The Africa Series.)   13
    min.   b/w.   AIM, MAC
A study of the literacy program in Ghana and one black American
woman's efforts to help.

THE STORY OF GHANA.   BBC, 1969.   20 min.   b/w.   TL
Explores the exploitation of Ghana, British colonization, the 1940s
independence movement, the rise and fall of Kwame Nkrumah.

THE STORY OF MODERN EGYPT.   BBC, 1969.   20 min.   b/w.
    TL
Covers the British rule of Egypt until 1922, the British installation
of King Faud, the succession of King Farouk, and the emergence
of Gamul Abdul Nasser, and the War of June, 1967 against Israel.

SUBMERGED GLORY: A STUDY IN STONE.   United Nations, 1961.
    28 min.   b/w.   MGH, UCA, UUT
Examines Abu Simbel, the pair of temples carved from Nubian rock
over 3,000 years ago, significant as a treasure and as a symbol of
the meeting place of inner African and Mediterranean cultures.
Narrated by Alistair Cooke.

SUGAR IN EGYPT.   Visual Education Centre, 1969.   13 min.   FI, VEC
Shows how Egyptian farmers still use old methods of plowing in the
same region where machines do similar work in government-super-
vised plantations.

THE SWAMPDWELLERS.   Wole Soyinka, 1973.   40 min.   b/w.
    PHO
A film adaptation of Nigerian playwright Wole Soyinka's play, The
Swampdwellers, which won international praise in 1958 during its
first production in London.   The story concerns a young man who
returns from the city to his village too sophisticated for the ignorance, superstition and corruption he sees in his home environment.

THE TALKING DRUMS. CCM, n. d. 14 min. color. AIM, MAC
The role of the drum as instrument of communication in rural
Ghana. Shows the selection of tree trunks and the carving and
tuning.

TAUW. National Council of Churches, 1970. 27 min. color. In
      Wolof with English subtitles. NACC, NYF, TRI
In Dakar a poor man searches for work on a dock where even a
gate-pass costs a hundred francs, which he doesn't have. A close
look at all-black street life.

A THOUSAND AND ONE HANDS. Souhel Ben Barka, 1972. 80
      min. color. In French with English subtitles. Directed by
      Souhel Ben Barka. TRI
A much-awarded protest film about a poor Moroccan family of rug-
makers, typical of the hardworking, exploited people who suffer at
the hands of wealthy exporters. The father, in this case, suffers
injuries on the job but dies because his son cannot obtain medical
help for him.

THE THOUSAND-YEAR WALK. BBC, 1970. (PART 11. The
      Glory That Remains Series.) 30 min. color. TL
A visit to the famous Egyptian Temple of Karnak with its reliefs
and inscriptions which record the political events of a thousand
years from 1800 B. C.

TRADE AND MARKETS IN WEST AFRICA. University of Minne-
      sota, 1973. (West Africa: An Introduction to the Peoples
      and Cultures Series.) 15 min. color. UMN
A review of indigenous trading systems of West Africa.

TREASURES FROM THE VALLEY OF THE KINGS. (TRESORS DE
      LA VALLEE DES ROIS.) Explo-Mundo, n. d. 52 min. color.
      RAY
A reverent view of the Egypt of the Pharaohs, showing the artifacts
of their rich culture contrasted with contemporary customs that often reflect ancient times.

TUTANKHAMUN: THE IMMORTAL PHARAOH. University of
      Houston, 1968. 12 min. color. ACI
Gives an unusual view of the artifacts found in King Tutankhamun's
tomb and discusses their significance.

TWILIGHT FOREST. British Information Service, 1958. 27 min.
      color. MGH
Shows the rich Nigerian rain-forest which supplies trees for West
Africa and the West in general.

TWO BOYS OF ETHIOPIA. Visual Education Centre, 1971. (The
      African Scene Series.) 20 min. color. EBEC, UWY
One youth, who lives in the mountains and shares the work of adults,
is contrasted with a city boy who lives like other modern youth of
Addis Ababa.

TWO FAMILIES: AFRICAN AND AMERICAN.   John H. Secondari,
    1974. 22 min. color.   LEC
Contrasts two families--one, Central West African; one, American
of New York City--to provide a sympathetic view of the humanistic
characteristics of African tribal life.

TWO WEST AFRICAN FISHING VILLAGES.   University of Minne-
    sota, 1973. (West Africa: An Introduction to the Peoples
    and Cultures Series.) 10 min. color.   UMN
A discussion of rural Africans of two widely separated villages:
Sussex in Sierra Leone and Ganvie in Dahomey. Shows live fishing
methods of the Sherbo people (Sussex) and fish farming (Ganvie).

THE UNKNOWN FAMINE.   Thames Television, London, n.d.
    (This Week Series.) 30 min. color.   RIT
A report on the terrible famine in the Wollo province, Ethiopia,
which at first was kept hidden from the outside world.

VISIT TO A SMALL VILLAGE.   United Nations, 1969. (Africa
    Series.) 12 min. color.   AIM, MAC
An account of how Ghana is trying to strengthen village communities rather than continue to absorb people who move from villages
to the cities. Narrated by Alistair Cooke.

WALLS THAT SPEAK.   (PART 13.   The Glory That Remains
    Series.) BBC, 1964. 30 min. color.   TL
A survey of four centuries of Leptis Magna, the Roman city on the
Libyan coast.

WEST AFRICA: ANOTHER VIETNAM?   Granada International,
    1968. 40 min. b/w.   IMP
An interview with the late Amilcar Cabral, leader of the independence movement in Guinea-Bissau (formerly Portuguese Guinea),
and a photographic record of one guerrilla unit's struggle.

WEST AFRICA: NIGERIA.   Encyclopaedia Britannica Educational
    Corporation, 1963. (Africa in Change Series.) 22 min.
    color.   EBEC, UCA, UCO, UUT, UWY
How Nigeria has tried to pull its diverse people together to face the
problems of a new nation.

WEST AFRICA: TROPICAL LOWLANDS.   ACI, 1966. (Africa
    Film Series.) 15 min. color.   MGH
Describes the many new nations of West Africa and the many physical barriers that contribute to isolation of groups.

WEST AFRICA: TWO LIFE STYLES.   Frank Gardonyi and Clifford
    Janoff, 1970. 17 1/2 min. color.   BFA, AAI
A farmer and a wealthy businesswoman of different parts of West
Africa are compared in life styles and goals.

WHEN THE BRIDES DO THE CHOOSING.   BBC and Odyssey, n.d.
    25 min. color.   TL

In a valley in the Atlas Mountains of Morocco, tents are pitched
and the would-be brides look over the bachelors. The rejected
ones are consoled with entertainment. Narrated by Lowell Thomas.

WOMEN OF THE TOUBOU. Anne Balfour-Fraser, 1974. 25 min.
        color. PHO
Examines the culture of the Toubou people of the Sahara, once described by Herodotus. Their elegance and nomadic life style, in
which women are treated as equals with men, are portrayed with
sensitivity. Includes discussion of a recent drought which threatens
the Toubous.

WOMEN UP IN ARMS. United Nations, 1966. 29 min. b/w.
        MGH
Explores the life styles and point of view of three generations of
Tunisian women. Narration by a 15-year-old girl.

THE WORLD SAVES ABU SIMBEL. UNESCO, 1969. 28 min.
        color. MGH
How the two temples of Abu Simbel, carved in rock in Upper Egypt,
were removed stone by stone to higher ground when threatened with
destruction by the Aswan Dam.

XALA. Ousmane Sembene, 1974. 135 min. color. In French
        and Wolof with English subtitles. Directed by Ousmane Sem-
        bene. Cast and credits unlisted. NYF
A theatrical feature film about a fifty-year-old polygamous man who
is struck by an evil spell (xala) on his wedding night with his third
wife. A study of the effects of Europeanization on Africa.

YOU DON'T BACK DOWN. National Film Board of Canada, 1966.
        28 min. b/w. SEF
How a doctor and his teacher-wife work in the village of Itu in
Nigeria. An interesting study of intercultural exchange.

Southern Africa

        (includes Angola, Botswana, Burundi, People's Republic of
        Congo, Equatorial Guinea, Gabon, Kenya, Lesotho, Malagasy
        Republic (Madagascar), Malawi, Mozambique, Rhodesia,
        Rwanda, South Africa, South-West Africa, Swaziland, Tan-
        zania, Uganda, Zaire, Zambia.)

A LUTA CONTINUA. (THE STRUGGLE CONTINUES.) Robert Van
        Lierop and Robert Fletcher, 1971. 32 min. color. TRI
A film made by an Afro-American film crew that lived and marched
for six weeks with the Mozambique Liberation Front's guerrilla
army in 1971. Shows scenes of combat with the Portuguese and
what life is like in the areas now held by the guerrillas. Directed
by Robert Van Lierop.

AFRICA CHANGES: A YOUNG LEADER IN A YOUNG NATION.
  Frank Gardonyi and Clifford Janoff, 1970. 13 min. color.
  BFA
A young African commissioner tours his East African district and
reveals the goals and problems of his people.

AFRICA SPEAKS. Columbia, 1930. 70 min. b/w. FICE, THUN
The cinematic record of the Colorado expedition across Equatorial
Africa in 1928-29. Records the noises of the jungle and shows the
local people, including Ubangis and pygmies, as well as animal
life.

AFRICA: THE HIDDEN FRONTIERS. NET, 1964. 60 min. b/w.
  IND
Shows attempts to unify the many tribal groups plus Europeans and
Asians who live in Kenya. Traces Eurasian influences and compares
life in Nairobi with rural life.

AFRICAN ADVENTURE. Marty Stouffer, n.d. 93 min. color.
  MAC[1]
A report on the Botswana area of Central Africa by filmmaker
Marty Stouffer which records the wildlife and the customs of the
Kalahari Bushmen.

AN AFRICAN COMMUNITY: THE MASAI. Frank Gardonyi and
  Clifford Janoff, 1969. 16 min. color. BFA
How the nomadic Masai in East Africa live and how their environ-
ment affects what they do.

AFRICAN CONTINENT: SOUTHERN REGION. Coronet, 1962. 10
  min. color. COR
The variety of people--Bantu, Dutch, English and Asians--who live
in the rich southern part of Africa with its gold and diamond fields,
ranches and fruitlands, are shown in their respective life styles.

AFRICAN CONTINENT: TROPICAL REGION. Coronet, 1962. 13
  min. color. COR
A view of the great social change and potential wealth of Africa's
Eastern Highlands, grassy Savanna and rain forests of the Congo
Basin and Guinea Coast.

AFRICAN MUSICIANS. Gérard de Boe, 1957. (Africa Series.)
  14 min. b/w. MAC[1]
Shows through African sculpture and actual performances of music
of the Congo region the relation of "man's breath in his musical
instruments" to his world harmony.

AFRICAN ODYSSEY: THE RED BICYCLE. ACW, 1971. 13 min.
  color. LEC
Follows a red bicycle built in Nairobi from city to village to countryside to village as it passes through a succession of owners.

AFRICAN ODYSSEY: THE TWO WORLDS OF MUSEMBE.   ACW,
    1971.   15 min.   color.   LEC
A young boy of Kenya, a city resident, returns home to his family's
village.

AFRICAN SAFARI.   Ron Shenin, n.d.   98 min.   color.   ASF, CPC
Filmmaker Ron Shenin made this dramatic documentary on Eastern
and Central Africa after 5-1/2 years of work and 25,000 miles of
travel.

AFRICAN TRIBES.   Paul Hoefler, 1942.   10 min.   color.   UCA,
    UUT
A study of four groups--the Ubangi, the pygmies, the long-headed
people (Mangbettu), and the nomadic pagans (Rendilli).

AFRIKANER.   BBC, 1971.   40 min.   color.   TL
A study of South Africa, and the contradictions in present-day Boer
society.

AN ARGUMENT ABOUT A MARRIAGE.   J. Marshall, 1966.   18
    min.   color.   PEN
Two Bushmen bands argue about a child born out of wedlock.   They
also contest the legitimacy of a marriage.   Gives background of
customs before presenting details of the incident.

AZANIA: A CHANGING ORDER OF AFRICA.   International Film
    Bureau, 1968.   11 min.   color.   UUT
A study of the Republic of Kenya, an area once called Azania by
Herodotus.

BAKUBA: PEOPLE OF THE CONGO.   Gérard de Boe, 1957.   (Af-
    rica Series.)   19 min.   b/w.   MAC
A brief view of the Bakuba people who have produced excellent
crafts, woven mats, embroidery, ceremonial costumes, ritual tools
and drums, statuary, tattooing.   Includes a royal court in session,
dances following a typical mourning period.

BEHIND THE LINES.   Contemporary Films, 1971.   32 min.   color.
    IMP
A close look at the guerrilla forces of the Liberation Front and
their war against the Portuguese.   Includes newsreel footage for
background and historical context of the struggle.

BITTER MELONS.   J. Marshall, 1966.   (The !Kung and G/wi
    Bushmen Series.)   30 min.   color.   PEN
How the G/wi Bushmen of the Kalahari desert area must find their
liquids in the food they gather.   Shows games, dances and music in
performance.

BOESMAN AND LENA.   Ross Devenish, 1973.   102 min.   color.
    NYF
A film based on the play by Athol Fugard which attacks South Africa's
apartheid policy.   The playwright plays Boesman.

BORAN HERDSMEN. Norman N. Miller, 1974. 17 min. color.
FF
A study of the Boran people of Northern Kenya as they confront
modernization and its effect on their life style.

BORAN WOMEN. Norman N. Miller, 1974. (Faces of Change
Series.) 18 min. color. FF
How educational opportunity and modernization are affecting Boran
women in Kenya.

BOY OF BOTSWANA. Visual Education Centre, 1971. (The African Scene Series.) 17 min. color. EBEC, UWY
The long journey home of two boys who tend cattle 70 miles away.

BOY OF CENTRAL AFRICA. Kevin Duffy, 1969. 13 1/2 min.
color. BFA
Follows a youth of a Zambia village as he works as wood carver to
pay for correspondence courses.

BUSHMEN OF THE KALAHARI. ABC, 1968. 12 min. color.
UCA
Anthropologist Dr. George Silverbauer narrates this study of the
nomadic Bushmen who have resisted outside influences in their
self-contained society.

BUSHMEN OF THE KALAHARI: PARTS I-II. National Geographic
Society, 1975. (The !Kung and G/wi Bushmen Series.) 50
min. color. NGS, PEN
Anthropologist and filmmaker John Marshall goes back to see the
!Kung Bushmen he filmed some years earlier. He traces the
changes of life style observed. Includes much evidence of gradual
acculturation.

BWANA TOSHI. (BWANA TOSHI NO UTA.) Toho, 1965. 115
min. color. In Japanese with English subtitles. Directed
by Susumu Hani; screenplay by Hani and Kunio Shimzu;
photography by Monji Kanau; music by Toru Takemitsu. With
Kiyoshi Atsumi, Hamisi Salehe, Tsutomu Shimomoto. MAC^1,
AAI
A Japanese engineer arrives in East Africa to deliver and complete
construction on a prefabricated house. Unfortunately, Bwana Toshi
speaks no Swahili and the local people speak no Japanese. A wry
treatment of racial prejudice. Photographed in East Africa.

CENTRAL AFRICA. ABC, 1968. 20 min. color. UCA
A study of Angola, the Congo, Mozambique, Rhodesia, and Zambia,
including interviews with leaders, some of whom are white supre-
macists.

COFFEE PLANTERS NEAR KILIMANJARO. Visual Education Centre, 1969. 14 min. color. FI, VEC
A Tschaga tribesman raises coffee plants and his son goes to a
modern school. A view of present-day rural life near Kilimanjaro

where black and white people are working together for improved
conditions.

COME BACK, AFRICA. Lionel Rogosin, 1959. 83 min. b/w.
    Directed by Lionel Rogosin; script by Lionel Rogosin with
    Lewis N'Kosi, Bloke Modisane; photographed by Emil Knebel,
    Ernst Artaria; music editor, Lucy Brown. With Miriam
    Makeba and cast of non-professionals. MGH, IMP, GRO
A much awarded film made in secret in Johannesburg, Sophiatown
and in restricted areas of South Africa. Follows Zachariah, a
Zulu, who is forced to leave his village because of famine to seek
work in the gold mines. Captures the frustration and depravity of
the apartheid way of life.

CONGO DOCTOR. CCM, n.d. (Africa Series.) 13 min. b/w.
    AIM, MAC
Describes efforts to cope with the shortage of doctors in the Congo,
where under former Belgian rule no Congolese could qualify as a
doctor. The situation is viewed from the first-hand report of a
man who at age 40 completed his medical studies.

THE CONGO, THE TROUBLED LAND. Hearst, 1965. 10 min.
    b/w. UCO
A brief review of the Congo's post-independence experiences, including the mutiny of the Congolese army, Tshombe's attempt to
remove Katanga, the U.N. intervention, and guerrilla campaigns
against the government.

CONGO: THE WAY AHEAD. United Nations, 1962. (Africa
    Series.) 11 min. b/w. AIM
The United Nations' activities in the Congo, including the training
of Congolese in specialized technical and professional fields: doctors, mechanics, technical workers, and transportation workers.

CRY, THE BELOVED COUNTRY. United Artists, 1952. 105 min.
    color. Directed by Zoltan Korda; screenplay by Alan Paton,
    adapted from his novel; produced by Zoltan Korda. With
    Canada Lee, Sidney Poitier, Charles Carson. BUDG, MAC[1],
    READ
About a black minister from a small village who goes to Johannesburg and is disgusted by the miserable life and racial tension of the
city. Partly filmed in Natal and in Johannesburg.

A CURING CEREMONY. J. Marshall, 1966. (The !Kung and G/wi
    Bushmen Series.) 8 min. b/w. PEN
A young woman of a !Kung group, who is about to have a miscar-
riage, is cured by a Bushman who goes into a trance.

DANCES OF SOUTHERN AFRICA. A. G. Zantzinger, 1973. 55
    min. color. PEN
Various tribal groups who work in South African mines perform
dances for recreation--the Xhosa shaking dance, high-kicking
Ndlamu dance, and tumbling Ndau dance.

DEBE'S TANTRUM.   J. Marshall, 1966.   (The !Kung and G/wi
     Bushmen Series.)   9 min.   color.   PEN
A scene in the life of a !Kung youngster, his mother and his aunt.
When his mother plans to leave him behind on her berry-gathering
expedition, he has a temper tantrum.

DIAMOND MINING IN EAST AFRICA.   Visual Education Centre,
     1969. 9 min. color. FI, VEC
A view of a well-guarded diamond mine site near Lake Victoria.
Shows the life of the workers.

DINGAKA.   Embassy, 1965. 96 min. color. Directed by Jamie
     Ulys; also written and produced by Jamie Ulys. With Stanley
     Baker, Juliet Prowse, Ken Gampu, Gordon Hood, Paul Mak-
     goba. MAC[1], PFS
A theatrical film which tells the story of two contrasting ways of
life.   A Masai warrior leaves his African village to hunt his
daughter's murderer in the city, where he runs into problems with
the white man's legal system in his quest for justice.   The filmmaker is South African.

DISCOVERING THE MUSIC OF AFRICA.   Film Associates, 1969.
     22 min. color. UCA, UCO
A drummer of Ghana, Robert Ayitee, demonstrates the complexities
and sophistication of African traditional music.

EAST AFRICA.   Encyclopaedia Britannica Educational Corporation,
     1962. 21 min. color. EBEC, UCA, UCO, UUT, UWY
How the people of Kenya, Tanganyika and Uganda coped with developments in their transition into independent nations.

EAST AFRICA: ENDS AND BEGINNINGS.   NET, 1970.   48 min.
     b/w.   IND
Describes political, economic, and social aspects of Kenya, with
its considerable foreign investment and control, and Tanzania, with
the people working toward socialism.

EAST AFRICA: TROPICAL HIGHLANDS.   ACI, 1966.   (Africa
     Film Series.)   15 min. color. MGH
Describes life and physical factors in Kenya, Tanzania, Uganda,
Rwanda, and Burundi.

EAST AFRICA: TWO LIFE STYLES.   Frank Gardonyi and Clifford
     Janoff, 1970. 18 1/2 min. color. BFA
A fisherman and a herder-farmer from two different parts of Tanzania are compared to show their successful use of natural environ-
ments.

END OF THE DIALOGUE.   (PHELA-NDABA.)   American Document-
     ary Films, 1970. 42 min. color. MAY
A documentary, made secretly by Africans, to show what apartheid
is like in South Africa.

FAMILY OF THE BUSH: SON OF WARRIORS. McGraw-Hill and
    Pan American World Airways with Vision Associates, 1971.
    11 min. color. MGH
Shows Kenya's Masai people and their children going about their
daily routines, tending cattle, training themselves as warriors,
mastering skills.

FAMILY OF THE CITY: ADVENTURE IN NAIROBI. McGraw-Hill
    and Pan American World Airways with Vision Associates,
    1971. 11 min. color. MGH
A portrait of two small boys who live in Nairobi, a busy African
city. Narrated by one of the boys.

GENTLE WINDS OF CHANGE. Marshall H. Segall, 1961. 33
    min. color. PEN
The life style of the Banyankole people of Uganda.

A GIANT PEOPLE: THE WATUSI. Encyclopaedia Britannica,
    1939. 11 min. b/w. EBEC, UCA
About the daily life and customs of the Watusi, people noted for
their advanced culture. Includes a ceremonial dance.

A GROUP OF WOMEN. J. Marshall, 1966. (The !Kung and G/wi
    Bushmen Series.) 5 min. b/w. PEN
A group of women of the !Kung Bushmen group are seen talking
and nursing a baby while resting under the shade of a baobab tree.

THE HADZA. London School of Economics and Political Science,
    1966. 40 min. b/w. UCA
How the little known Hadza people of East Africa hunt food. A co-
operative venture between filmmaker Sean Hudson and anthropologist
Dr. James Woodburn.

HARAMBEE. (PULL TOGETHER.) Norman N. Miller, 1974.
    (Faces of Change Series.) 19 min. color. FF
How formerly isolated peoples face the prospect of a united country. With sounds and snatches of dialogue picked up while filming
in Kenya, Tanzania, Lebanon and Tanganyika.

THE HEART OF APARTHEID. BBC, 1970. 39 min. b/w. TL
South Africa's black people speak out about segregation.

THE HUNTERS. Film Study Center, Harvard University, 1958.
    72 min. color. MGH
A close look at the bushmen of the northern Kalahari desert in
Southwest Africa and the Bechuanaland Protectorate during a 13-day
hunt. Winner of many awards.

INDUSTRIAL WORKER IN KENYA. Films Incorporated, n. d. 12
    min. color. FI
A look at the life of a plant supervisor who lives in the city with
his family but maintains contact with his relatives in a country village.

A JOKING RELATIONSHIP. J. Marshall, 1966. (The !Kung and
  G/wi Bushmen Series.) 13 min. b/w. PEN
Shows a flirtatious episode between a young wife and her great
uncle. Explains the psychological meaning of this important part
of institutionalized kinship behavior.

JOURNEY TO MAGIC VALLEY. BBC and Odyssey, 1968. 25 min.
  color. TL
The Matakams are contrasted with the Bushmen of Kalahari in their
lives and relationship to magic and the supernatural. Narrated by
Lowell Thomas.

KATUTURA. U. Schweizer, 1974. 37 min. color. PHO
An award-winning film about Katutura (the total insecurity) of the
black people who live in South Africa. Traces South Africa's history from the time of the first Dutch settlers.

KENYA BORAN, I. Norman N. Miller, 1974. (Faces of Change
  Series.) 33 min. color. FF
KENYA BORAN, II. Norman N. Miller, 1974. (Faces of Change
  Series.) 33 min. color. FF
Isolated people of the desert are threatened by growth of a town
and its roads. Two films show two fathers and sons facing the
situation.

KENYA: MOMBASA. BBC, 1974. (People of Many Lands Series.)
  20 min. color. TL
A visit to Kilindini, an old harbor, and a modern port in Kenya.

KENYA: THE MULTI-RACIAL EXPERIMENT. ABC, 1968. 19
  min. color. MGH
Explores Kenya in the course of coping with problems of education
and equal work opportunities for her multi-racial population.

KENYATTA. Anthony-David, 1973. 28 min. color. FI
The interrelated history of Kenya and the life of Jomo Kenyatta with
emphasis on his contributions to stability and continuity with the
past.

THE KING'S ACCORDION. Paul and Odile Martin, 1971. 22 min.
  NYF
Contrasts traditional, ritualistic Madagascar with new, contemporary
influences.

!KUNG BUSHMEN HUNTING EQUIPMENT. J. Marshall, 1966.
  (The !Kung and G/wi Bushmen Series.) 37 min. color.
  PEN
How Bushmen construct a hunting kit from a collection of raw mate-
rials. Includes the search for poisonous larvae and plants to serve
as coating for arrow shafts.

LION GAME. J. Marshall, 1966. (The !Kung and G/wi Bushmen
  Series.) 4 min. color. PEN

A young !Kung bushman plays a lion game with a group of boys in which they simulate hunting and killing.

THE LION HAS SEVEN HEADS. (DER LEONE HAVE SEPT CABE-
    ZAS.) Polifilm, 1970. 97 min. b/w. In French and Por-
    tuguese with English subtitles. Directed by Glauber Rocha;
    screenplay by Glauber Rocha and Gianni Amico. With Rade
    Rassimov, Gabriele Tinit, Jean-Pierre Leaud. NYF
The multi-lingual title represents the various imperial nations as-
saulted in this political allegory set in the Congo. The story is
concerned with a black revolutionary a Portuguese mercenary, an
American CIA agent, a French missionary and a nude woman called
the Golden Temple of Violence.

LOBOLA. Contemporary, 1954. 26 min. b/w. MGH, UCA
A young man, whose father does not give the "lobola," or bridal
gift, to his girl friend's father, is forced to go to Johannesburg
to work for the money himself. Written, directed and photographed
by Jan M. Perold in South Africa.

THE MAGIC TREE. Gerald McDermott, 1970. (African Folklore
    Series.) 10 min. color. TEX
A boy in the Congo discovers a magic tree which brings forth a
princess, who in turn transforms him into a prince and marries
him--with the warning that he is not to tell his mother. An animated film by artist Gerald McDermott. Narrated by Athmani
Magoma.

MALAWI: THE WOMEN. Churchill, 1971. 20 min. color. UMN
Examines the life of women in a village that is already somewhat
westernized, in a city office and in a suburban home.

MALAWI: TWO YOUNG MEN. Churchill, 1971. 20 min. color.
    UMN
An account of two men who are rebuffed in the city and who, there-
fore, try to find a use for their skills in a lakeside village.

MAN, BEAST AND THE LAND. NBC, 1968. 52 min. color.
    MGH
An ecological study of the Serengeti-Mara plains of East Africa.
Narrated by Dr. and Mrs. Lee Talbot of the Smithsonian Institution.

MAN OF THE SERENGETI. National Geographic Society, 1972.
    52 min. color. FI, VEC
Leslie Nielsen narrates this report on the land and Masai people of
Serengeti National Park in northern Tanzania, where self-sufficient
men and wildlife live in harmony.

MASAI IN TANZANIA. Public Media, 1969. 13 min. color. FI,
    PEN, VEC
About the life style of the Masai people in Tanzania: their clothing, tasks, trading and customs.

MASAI WARRIOR: BETWEEN TWO WORLDS. National Geographic
    Society, 1972. 25 min. color. FI, VEC
Over four hundred years ago Masai warriors moved from the Upper
Nile to the Serengeti Plains; and now they fight the problem of
change. Focuses on one Masai who is breaking away from his
roots.

MAU MAU, PARTS I AND II. Films Incorporated, 1973. (Black
    Man's Land Series.) 52 min. color. FI, UIO
A documentary on the "Mau Mau," the name given by whites to the
Land and Freedom Army fighting repression and armed aggression
in Kenya.

MEN BATHING. J. Marshall, 1966. (The !Kung and G/wi Bush-
    men Series.) 14 min. color. PEN
How !Kung Bushmen wash clothes and bathe. Shows the bathing
men joking about sex.

MODERN EAST AFRICAN WOOD CARVER. Minerva Films, 1968.
    8 min. color. MGH
A Makonde wood carver reveals his thoughts on the commercial
market for his creations while he works. Filmed near the capital
of Tanzania.

NAWI. D. and J. MacDougall, 1969. 22 min. color. PEN
Shows the drive of cattle to Uganda's dry season camps (nawi) by
the Jie people. Presents conversations they have while working and
playing. With English subtitles.

THE NEW AND THE OLD. CCM, n. d. (Africa Series.) 15 min.
    b/w. AIM, MAC
A school teacher tries to question old beliefs in face of the village
elder's displeasure in this study of transition from old to new in
the Malagasy Republic.

NEW HORIZONS: MOROCCO, KENYA. Pan American World Air-
    ways, 1961. 13 min. color. ASF, PAN
A tourist travelogue about two African countries--one in the north,
the other in the south.

THE 1973 MGODO WA MBANGUZI. Gei Zantzinger and Andrew
    Tracey in cooperation with the Museum of the University of
    Pennsylvania, 1974. 48 min. color. PEN
Shows dancers, music (both vocal and instrumental) in performance
by the Chopi people in southern Mozambique. Also presents a
similar performance by people of a different village in the film,
THE 1973 MGODO WA MKANDENI.

THE 1973 MGODO WA MKANDENI. Gei Zantzinger and Andrew
    Tracey in cooperation with the Museum of the University of
    Pennsylvania, 1974. 48 min. color. PEN
Shows dancers, music (both vocal and instrumental) in performance
by the Chopi people in southern Mozambique. Also presents a

similar performance by people of a different village in the film,
THE 1973 MGODO WA MBANGUZI.

N!OWA T'AMA: THE MELON TOSSING. J. Marshall, 1966. (The
!Kung and G/wi Bushmen Series.) 15 min. color. PEN
Shows the Bushmen of Nyae Nyae playing one of their games--the
melon tossing game.

N/UM TCHAI: THE CEREMONIAL DANCE OF THE !KUNG BUSH-
MEN. J. Marshall, 1966. (The !Kung and G/wi Bushmen
Series.) 20 min. b/w. PEN
Shows a curing ritual--a medicine dance of the !Kung people.

NZURI: EAST AFRICA. Summit, 1970. 28 min. color. AIM,
SUM
A much-awarded film which combines biblical themes with sounds
and imagery to trace the progress of civilization in East Africa.
Shot in Kenya, Tanzania and Uganda.

THE OLD AFRICA AND THE NEW: ETHIOPIA AND BOTSWANA.
ABC, 1968. 17 min. color. UCA, UCO
Africa's oldest independent country is studied in contrast with the
newly independent Botswana, a nation of southern Africa.

PEOPLE OF THE CONGO: THE MANGBETU. Encyclopaedia
Britannica Educational Corporation, 1939. EBEC, UCA,
UCO, UUT, UWY
A brief introduction to the culture of the Mangbetu people of the
Congo.

PLAYING WITH SCORPIONS. J. Marshall, 1966. (The !Kung and
G/wi Bushmen Series.) 4 min. color. PEN
How !Kung children, living in an environment not easily excited by
threatening circumstances, play with scorpions.

POWDER KEG IN THE CONGO. Hearst, 1961. 11 min. b/w.
UCO
An old film, useful for its historical coverage of the Congo under
Belgian rule, the activities of Lumumba, Kasavubu, the Congolese
Army, and Tshombe, entry of U.N. forces, and Russia's attack on
Secretary General Hammarskjold at a U.N. session.

PYGMIES OF AFRICA. Encyclopaedia Britannic Educational Corporation, 1939. 20 min. b/w. PEN
An old film showing practices of the pygmies, such as bow and arrow making, hunting, food preparation, shelter construction, eating,
dying, rituals.

THE PYGMIES OF THE ITURI FOREST. Jean-Pierre Hallet, 1974.
19 min. color. EBEC
Describes the physical precociousness of the pygmies--crawling at
two months, and full maturity at nine or ten years. Also shows
life style, rituals and hunting practices. Includes scenes of a

wedding and a birth. Filmed in northeast Zaire and narrated by Belgian anthropologist Jean-Pierre Hallet.

RECONCILIATION AND JUSTICE.   CBS, n.d.   30 min.   color.
      NACC
About the Kimbanguist church in Zaire, founded in recent years by an African prophet. Located in an area usually dominated by the Catholic Church.

REMNANTS OF A RACE.   Kalahari Films, 1952.   18 min.   color.
      EBEC
Describes the life of the Kalahari desert's bushmen, whose chief concern is the search for food.

THE REPUBLIC OF SOUTH AFRICA: ITS LAND AND ITS PEO-
      PLE.   Encyclopaedia Britannica Educational Corporation,
      1956.   Rev. ed.   17 min.   color.   EBEC, UCA, UCO, UUT
Compares three life styles: that of traditional tribes; Boer farms; and mining communities and cities.

RHYTHM OF AFRICA.   François Villiers, 1947.   17 min.   b/w.
      MAC[1]
Presents the arts and ceremonial ritual of the Chad people in French Equatorial Africa.   With commentary by black baritone, Kenneth Spencer with African music.   Based on an idea by Jean Cocteau.

RICHES OF THE VELD: SOUTH AFRICA.   Louis de Rochemont,
      1948.   20 min.   b/w.   UEVA
About the cultivation of the grassy plain into rich land, which is also a source for mineral deposits.   Stresses the significance of gold and diamonds in South Africa.

A RITE OF PASSAGE.   J. Marshall, 1966.   (The !Kung and G/wi
      Bushmen Series.)   14 min.   color.   PEN
A !Kung ceremony to celebrate the importance of hunting is performed when a young boy shoots his first wildebeest.

SALIMA IN TRANSITION.   Churchill, 1970.   28 min.   b/w.   REI
A non-narrated film about life in the town of Salima in Malawi centered around young people in a secondary school.

SAMBIZANGA.   Sarah Maldoror, 1972.   102 min.   color.   In
      Portuguese with English subtitles.   Directed by Sarah Maldor-
      or; screenplay by Mario de Andrade and Maurice Pons from
      a novel of the same title by Laundino Viera.   With Domingos
      Oliviera, Elisa Andrade and Dino Abelino.   NYF
A prize-winning film that has sometimes been called "the black African Z."   The story concerns a woman who searches for her missing husband, a laborer thought to be part of the Angolan national liberation movement.   It turns out that he has been put in jail, relocated several times, and finally tortured to death.   Filmed by a French crew in the Congolese republic of Brazzaville.

SHE SHALL BE CALLED WOMAN. Gérard de Boe, 1954. 14
   min. b/w. MAC
About the role of women in the Belgian Congo, as depicted through
native sculpture. Narrated by Flora Robson.

SOUTH AFRICA. ABC, 1968. 27 min. color. UCA, UCO
White and black people of South Africa voice their opinions and
concerns about their country's serious problems.

SOUTH AFRICA: INDUSTRY AND AGRICULTURE. ACI, 1966.
   (Africa Film Series.) 15 min. color. MGH
A look at the people and resources of Africa's most developed in-
dustrial area.

SOUTH AFRICAN ESSAY: FRUIT OF FEAR. NET, 1965. 59
   min. b/w. IND
A study of contrasts between South Africa's white and black societies.

SOUTH AFRICAN ESSAY, II: ONE NATION--TWO NATIONALISMS.
   NET, 1965. 59 min. IND
A documentary on South Africa's Nationalist Party and apartheid.
Includes interviews with leaders.

TANZANIA: LIFE ON KILIMANJARO. BBC, 1974. (People of
   Many Lands Series.) 20 min. color. TL
Shows the step-by-step process of coffee cultivation in Tanzania
from plant care to seed removal, crushing and drying.

TANZANIA: PROGRESS THROUGH SELF-RELIANCE. Minerva,
   1969. 20 min. color. MGH
Examines three areas of Tanzania--the Kilimanjaro district, the
southern highlands, and the area south of Lake Victoria--to show
cooperative socialism in Africa.

TANZANIA: THE QUIET REVOLUTION. NET, 1965. 60 min.
   b/w. IND
How Tanzania's people try to cope with their problems, including
the very fragile bond between two of Tanzania's states: Tanganyika
and Zanzibar.

TROPICAL AFRICA. International Film Foundation, 1961. 30
   min. color. EFD, IFF, UCA, UCO
A broad view of the tropical area which comprises approximately
three-fourths of the African continent. Shows urban development,
new industrialization, attempts at self-rule, educational development and the evolving relationship between blacks and whites.
With original music by Norman Lloyd.

UGANDA: FISHING VILLAGE. BBC, 1974. (People of Many
   Lands Series.) 20 min. color. TL
Shows Murchison Falls, wildlife on the banks of the River Nile, and
daily life in the village of Wanseko on the shores of Lake Albert.

UNDER THE BLACK MASK. (SOUS LE MASQUE NOIR.) Paul
Haesaerts, Belgium, 1958. 50 min. color. MAC, UNE
An award-winning film which studies artifacts of various peoples,
such as the Ba-Kuba, Ba-Mbala, Ben Lulua, and Ba-Yaka, in the
Congo. (Also available in three parts ranging from 14 min. to 17
min. in length: PART I. BIRTH OF THE WORLD AND OF MAN;
PART II. STYLES AND INFLUENCES IN AFRICAN ART; PART III.
THE POWER OF ROYALTY AND THE POWER OF SORCERY.)

UNDER THE MEN'S TREE. David MacDougall, 1974. 15 min.
b/w. RAD
Under the men's tree Jie tribesmen get together to talk and par-
ticipate in their daily crafts of leather thong and spear making.
Their conversation reveals their feelings about the automobile and
man. Filmed in Uganda.

VICTORIA FALLS: THE SMOKE THAT THUNDERS. Paul Hoefler,
1958. 10 min. color. UCA
A visit to Victoria Falls on the Zambesi River and to the town
Livingstone, named for the man, David Livingstone, who discovered
the Falls.

VIVA FRELIMO. Dutch Kenmark TV, 1969. 30 min. color. In
Portuguese with English subtitles. IMP, TRI
A report on the activities of the Mozambique Liberation Front
(Frelimo), including their national reconstruction program for lib-
erated areas.

VOLUNTEERS. NET, 1968. 55 min. b/w. IND
Shows the British equivalent of the U.S. Peace Corps at work in a
few Malawi villages.

THE WASP NEST. J. Marshall, 1966. (The !Kung and G/wi
Bushmen Series.) 20 min. color. PEN
Shows !Kung women gathering wild foods: berries, roots. Includes
baiting a nest of wasps.

WHITE AFRICA. BBC, 1970. 40 min. b/w. TL, UMN
A documentation of the policy of apartheid in South Africa. Gives
the white African's arguments in defense of what is now referred
to as "separate development."

WHITEMAN'S COUNTRY. Films Incorporated, 1973. (Black Man's
Land Series.) 51 min. color. FI, UIO
Traces the history of the white man's rule in what is now known
as Kenya. Includes steps to independence.

WILD GOLD. New York Zoological Society, n.d. 25 min. color.
UCA
A study of the economic importance of East Africa's wildlife in
Tanganyika, Kenya and Uganda.

WITNESSES. Knight, 1971. 30 min. color. TRI
A British film which takes a frank look at apartheid in South Africa.
Gives specific details of oppressive conditions and their impact on
the black population. Includes a reenactment of the Sharpeville
massacre of 1960.

WOODEN GIRAFFE. Kevin Duffy, 1967. 26 min. color. EFD,
   UCA
Follows a young Barotse man as he selects a tree and demonstrates
his heritage of wood carving. Gives a history of wood carving in
Zambia.

YOUTH BUILDS A NATION IN TANZANIA. Visual Education Centre, 1971. (The African Scene Series.) 18 min. color.
   EBEC, UWY
How girls of a secondary school help to build a higher standard of
living for their people.

ZANDE ELEPHANT MEN AND ZANDE WOMEN'S DANCES. Machris, 1968. 10 min. color. silent PEN
Scenes of Zande people taking care of their elephants and performing dances, men and women together.

ZANZIBAR: THE GATEWAY TO AFRICA. Henry Steiner for Fotosonic, n.d. 8 min. color. PIC
The history of Zanzibar, now part of Tanzania, from the Arab
colonization in the eighth century to the present.

ZULU. Cy Endfield and Stanley Baker, 1964. 138 min. color.
   Directed by Cy Endfield; screenplay by Cy Endfield and John
   Prebble; based on a story by Prebble; photography by Stephen
   Dade; music by John Barry. With Stanley Baker, Jack Hawk-
   ins, Uela Jacobsson, Michael Caine, James Booth, Nigel
   Green, Patrick Magee. With a foreword spoken by Richard
   Burton. MAC[1]
A recreation of the Zulu War of 1879 and the Battle of Rorke's
Drift in which Zulus attacked a British company of soldiers. Shows
the cultural background of the Zulu people. Set in the Natal area
of South Africa.

ZULU CHRISTIAN DANCES: PART 1, CHURCH OF SHEMBE.
   Machris, 1968. 21 min. color. silent. PEN
Scenes of Zulu villagers performing daily routines, such as hair
styling, attendance at church services, food gathering, crafts,
dancing.

ZULU COUNTRY DANCES. Machris, 1968. 16 min. color.
   silent. PEN
Zulu villagers perform a mock battle dance and a bridal dance,
sing, and play a musical bow.

ASIA

General

ASIA: A CONTINENTAL OVERVIEW. Coronet, 1964. 16 min.
color. COR
Gives a review of the geography, history and present living conditions of principal regions in Asia.

ASIA: AN INTRODUCTION. Wayne Mitchell, 1970. 20 min.
color. BFA
A study of each major region in Asia: geography, life styles, economic factors.

BUDDHISM. National Film Board of Canada, 1962. (The Great
Religions Series.) 27 min. b/w. MGH
How Buddhism was founded and how it is practiced today through-
out Asia. Illustrates with scenes of Southeast Asia, India, Burma,
Ceylon, Thailand, Japan and China.

BUDDHISM, PART 1. International Communications, 1968. (Religions of the Eastern World Series.) 16 min. color. DOU
How Buddhism was founded in India and grew to its large following
today. Shows daily life of a young monk.

THE BUDDHIST WORLD. Coronet, 1963. 10 1/2 min. color.
COR
Filmed in India, Thailand, Japan and Tibet. An examination of the
roots of Buddhism, the life and work of Gautama Buddha and the
influence of Buddhism on certain countries today.

THE HINDU WORLD. Coronet, 1963. 11 min. color. COR
A survey of the history and cultural aspects of Hinduism. Explains
the basic beliefs of the Hindus.

HINDUISM. Films Inc., 1973. 28 min. color. FI
About the far-flung reach of Hinduism. Shows a new temple in
Toronto, Canada where Hindus worship and discuss their religious
beliefs and Indian roots.

HINDUISM. International Communications, 1968. (Religions of the
Eastern World Series.) 20 min. color. DOU
Examines the wide range of three hundred million persons who practice Hinduism. Illustrates objects of worship, the caste system,
and influence on society.

HINDUISM.   National Film Board of Canada, 1962.   (The Great Re-
     ligions Series.)   19 min.   b/w.   MGH, UCA
Describes the world's oldest living religion with details of ritual,
essential beliefs.

ISLAM.   International Communications, 1968.   (Religions of the
     Eastern World Series.)   16 min.   color.   DOU
Discusses the details of the five pillars of Islam and the influence
of Mohammed and the Koran.

ISLAM.   National Film Board of Canada, 1962.   (The Great Reli-
     gions Series.)   19 min.   b/w.   MGH
Traces the history of Islam and the Islamic way of life.

ISLAM: THE PROPHET AND THE PEOPLE.   RAI-Texture, n. d.
     34 min.   color.   TEX
Presents the scope of Mohammed's life, a history of Islam, and a
discussion of the basic beliefs and practices of the religion in relation to their significance in the Middle East today.

ISLAMIC MYSTICISM: THE SUFI WAY.   Elda Hartley, 1971.   28
     min.   color.   HARP, UMN
An MIT philosophy professor studies Islam and its mystical base,
Sufism.   Discusses the Koran, Muslim ritual dervish dancing.
Covers Islam from Morocco to India.

THE MOSLEM WORLD: BEGINNINGS AND GROWTH.   Coronet,
     1965.   10 1/2 min.   color.   COR
A view of Mohammedan history, religion, politics, language and
art.   Filmed in Moslem centers, such as Baghdad, Mosul, Damas-
cus, Cairo and old Jerusalem.

ODYSSEY IN ASIA.   BBC and Odyssey, 1968.   (Asia Series.)   25
     min.   color.   TL
Follows the adventures of two men who travel from Turkey to Japan
passing along the Mediterranean across Syria, Iran, Afghanistan,
India to the Himalayas, then on to Bangkok, Hong Kong and Mount
Fumi.   Narrated by Lowell Thomas.

THE ORIENT: TOWARDS A BETTER LIFE.   McGraw-Hill, 1969.
     19 min.   color.   MGH
An overview of Asia and its weak points of food, industry and education.   Gives specific examples in various Asian countries.

RICE.   McGraw-Hill, 1965.   25 min.   b/w.   PEN, MGH
A documentary covering all the steps involved in the cultivation and
preparation of rice for food as practiced throughout the "rice bowl"
of Asia.   Includes rituals performed to help the rice crop.

Southwest Asia (Middle East)

     (includes Bahrein, Cyprus, Iran, Iraq, Israel, Jordan, Kuwait,

Lebanon, Oman, People's Democratic Republic of Yemen, Qatar, Saudi Arabia, Syria, Trucial States, Turkey, Yemen Arab Republic.)

ALKHALIJ: THE GULF. Rayant, 1974. 28 min. color. ASF
Examines the history and life of people who live in countries of the Persian Gulf area--Bahrain, Qatar, and the United Arab Emirates.

ANCIENT MESOPOTAMIA. Coronet, 1953. 10 min. color. UCO,
    UNE, UUT, UWY
Shows Iraq of the 1950s with views of ruins of Babylon and Ur. Discusses the Sumerians, Semites, Assyrians, Chaldeans and others who once lived there.

ANCIENT SARDIS. Lyman, 1969. 28 min. color. LYM
Summarizes ten years of archeological work in Sardis, Turkey. Shows burial mounds being excavated.

ARAB ISRAELI DIALOGUE. Impact, n. d. 40 min. color. IMP
Two old friends, an Israeli journalist and a Palestinian poet, discuss the Mid-East situation frankly and with understanding.

ATATURK. Sim, 1971. 26 min. b/w. SIM
Discusses Ataturk's life, including the fall of the Ottoman Empire and the War for Independence that established the Turkish republic in 1928.

ATATURK, FATHER OF MODERN TURKEY. CBS, 1960. 25 min.
    b/w. MGH, UMN
A portrait of Mustapha Kemal Ataturk, Turkish leader who ruled his country after the close of World War I.

THE BAKHTIARI MIGRATION; PARTS I AND II. Films Inc., 1973.
    52 min. color. FI, UIO
About the largest annual movement of people in the world--the expedition of 500,000 persons plus millions of animals 200 miles across the Zagros mountains into Southern Iran, from winter to summer pasture--a move that has been repeated for 2,500 years.

THE BEDOUINS OF ARABIA. Films Inc., 1969. 20 min. color.
    FI, VEC
A close look at the Bedouin tribesmen of southern Arabia.

BEHIND THE VEIL. Eve Arnold, 1972. 50 min. color. IMP
A visit inside a harem where women live in isolation and servitude to their husbands under the edict of the Koran. Written and directed by Eve Arnold. Nourma's voice is narrated by Janet Suzman.

THE BIG DIG. Televisual, 1974. 22 min. color. EBEC
An award-winning film about the archeological excavations at Tel Gezer, site of 140 generations of residents.

BRIDE OF IRAN. Iran, 1960. 20 min. b/w. UUT
An Iranian film of the third marriage of the Shah of Iran. Gives a
revealing look at Iranian royalty and customs.

BUILDING A NATION. De Rochemont, 1950. 20 min. b/w.
    UEVA
Studies post-World War II developments in Israel: immigrants ar-
riving to work on farmlands, growth in industry, new architecture.

CAST A GIANT SHADOW. Mirisch-Llenroc-Batjac, 1966. 139
    min. color. Directed by Melville Shavelson; adapted and
    produced by Melville Shavelson from the book by Ted Berk-
    man. With Kirk Douglas, Senta Berger, Angie Dickinson,
    Haym Topol, Luther Adler, John Wayne, Gary Merrill, Frank
    Sinatra, James Donald, Ruth White, Yul Brynner, Stathis
    Giallelis. UNAR
The story of Colonel David (Mickey) Marcus, the New York lawyer-
soldier who helped form the modern state of Israel.

THE CHANGING MIDDLE EAST. International Film Foundation,
    1975. 25 min. color. IFF, EFD
This is an up-date of THE MIDDLE EAST with emphasis on two
important contemporary matters: conflict and oil.

CHILDREN OF BET ALPHA. Krosney, 1974. 27 min. color.
    PHO
How children are raised in the kibbutz--a communal approach to
"education in life."

CHILDREN OF ISRAEL. International Film Foundation, 1967.
    (How We Live Series.) 13 min. color. EFD, IFF
Young Israelis of a variety of ages are examined as they go about
their daily lives. No narration. Background of authentic Israeli
music.

CHRISTMAS IN THE HOLY LAND. National Council of Churches,
    n.d. 28 min. color. NACC
An account of all the Christian groups that converge on the Holy
Land in celebration of Christmas--the Roman Catholics, Greek
Orthodox, Copts, Armenians and Protestants from many foreign
countries.

CLOUDS OVER ISRAEL. Mati Raz and Harold Cornsweet, 1962.
    85 min. b/w. In Hebrew and Arabic with English subtitles.
    Directed by Ivan Lengyel; screenplay by Moshe Hadar. With
    Yiftach Spector, Ehud Banal, Dina Doronne. MAC[1]
Set in Sinai where the Israelis beat the Egyptians in 1956, the
story concerns an Israeli pilot who bails out of his plane behind
enemy lines. He finds that he has destroyed a Bedouin encamp-
ment except for a woman with two children, who later conceals his
whereabouts from the Egyptians.

A COMMON HOUSE. (Original Title: TWENTY YEARS.) Y.
Yoresh, Jerusalem, 1968. 14 min. color. MIR
Examines Israel's history in terms of her existence side by side
with Arab nations and her role in the United Nations. Uses children's drawings in animation.

THE CROSSROADS OF THE WORLD: 1. SUN, SAND AND SEA.
National Film Board of Canada, 1965. 29 min. b/w.
NFBC
Discusses the origins of Islam, the extent of the Arab conquest,
and the decline of Islam.

THE CROSSROADS OF THE WORLD: 2. THE IMPACT OF THE
WEST. National Film Board of Canada, 1965. 29 min.
b/w. NFBC
Describes the Western expansion into Islamic lands and the emergence of nationalism.

THE CROSSROADS OF THE WORLD: 3. THE ROUGH ROAD TO
FREEDOM. National Film Board of Canada, 1965. 30 min.
b/w. NFBC
About the impact of Western colonization in North Africa and the
Middle East and the development of new revolutionary leaders.

THE CROSSROADS OF THE WORLD: 4. THE CONTEST FOR
POWER. National Film Board of Canada, 1965. 29 min.
b/w. NFBC
A look at a variety of countries in the Middle East and North Africa in each of which the desire for change is expressed differently.

THE CROSSROADS OF THE WORLD: 5. ASPIRATIONS. National
Film Board of Canada, 1965. 29 min. b/w. NFBC
About the efforts of oppressed nations of North Africa and the Mid-
dle East to be liberated from colonial rule.

THE CROSSROADS OF THE WORLD: 6. NEW VOICES. National
Film Board of Canada, 1965. 29 min. b/w. NFBC
A look at the leaders of the Islamic world expressing themselves
at the United Nations and other international gatherings.

DHOFAR: GUERRILLA WAR ON THE ARABIAN GULF. James
Vaughan, n.d. 40 min. color. IMP
About the revolution that has been going on in Dhofar since 1965.
Gives examples of life under rebel occupation.

A DIFFERENT PATH. Jerry Blustein, 1973. 28 min. color.
UCA
Life in several kibbutz communities with discussions of founders.
Includes interviews with residents and visitors.

DISCOVERING THE MUSIC OF THE MIDDLE EAST. Bernard
Wilets, 1968. 21 min. color. BFA
The impact of Mohammedanism as Middle Eastern music is dis-
cussed and typical instruments demonstrated.

DISCOVERY GOES TO ISRAEL.   International Film Bureau, n. d.
    21 min.   color.   EFD
An Arab family is shown living in an Israeli village, and the people
of Ramah, near Haifa, protect their traditions and language.

THE DYBBUK.   Ilan Eldad, 1970.   95 min.   color.   In Hebrew
    with English subtitles.   Directed by Ilan Eldad; screenplay
    by Shraga Friedman, based on the play by Sholom Anski;
    photography by Goetz Neumann; music by Noam Sheriff.   With
    David Opatoshu, Peter Frye, Tina Wodetsky.   MAC[1]
A classic drama about two lovers pledged to marriage from childhood.   Unfortunately, the girl's father gives her to another and the
young man drops his study of the Talmud to take up an unholy alliance with the Kabala and its teachings.   Filmed in Israel.

THE ECONOMY: OIL, WATER AND ASPIRATIONS.   National
    Film Board of Canada, 1963.   (The Middle East Series.)
    24 min.   b/w.   MGH
A detailed study of contrasts--new developments, new industry
within sight of artifacts and mud villages.   Includes some discussion of North Africa.

THE EMPTY QUARTER.   Public Media, 1968.   48 min.   color.
    FI, VEC
About one of the expeditions of Wilfred Patrick Thesinger, an Englishman, who was the first white man to explore the "Empty Quarter," a desert area in Southern Arabia.   A study of the Bedouin
people.

FALL OF CONSTANTINOPLE.   BBC, 1970.   34 min.   color.   TL
Explores the historical roots of Constantinople on the site of present-day Istanbul.

FAREWELL ARABIA.   NET, 1968.   53 min.   b/w.   IND
The impact of wealth from the oil market on a small Arabian sheik-
dom, Abu Dhabi.

GOLDA MEIR OF ISRAEL.   Time-Life, 1973.   52 min.   color.
    TL
Premier Golda Meir's life and career as seen in documentary footage and interviews.

THE GOLDEN CRESCENT.   California-Texas Oil Corporation, 1963.
    28 min.   color.   MAC
A brief history of Turkey with scenes of cities such as Istanbul
and Ankara, plus rural areas.

GOREME.   Pierre Levie, 1968.   13 min.   color.   RAD
Explores the history of labyrinthian grottos in a ravine of Goreme,
Turkey.   Includes the story of the refugee monks who came and
stayed for centuries.   Also shows today's residents--peasants, who
still herd their livestock in the traditional way.

GRASS.   Merian C. Cooper and Ernest B. Schoedsack, 1925.   66
    min.   b/w.   silent.   UCA
A classic silent film documentary, made by the men who later
made KING KONG, about the effort of the Baktyari tribe of Persia
to secure grass for their flocks and herds via a semi-annual trip
across difficult terrain.

THE GREAT SOPHY.   (PART 3. The Glory That Remains Series.)
    BBC, 1969.   30 min.   color.   TL
A visit to the great 16th century city of Isfahan. Includes views
of the mosque, Khaju Bridge and the Chihil Sutun.

HISTORY AND CULTURE: PART 1.   National Film Board of Can-
    ada, 1964.   (The Middle East Series.) 28 min.   b/w.   MGH
Explores the cultural background of the Middle East and some of
North Africa, including origins and decline of Islam and the Arab
conquest.

HISTORY AND CULTURE: PART 2.   National Film Board of Can-
    ada, 1964.   (The Middle East Series.) 28 min.   b/w.   MGH
Covers the Western colonization of the Middle East and the rise of
nationalism.

THE HOLY LAND.   Boulton-Hawker, England, 1962.   10 min.
    color.   EFD, IFB
A tour of the Holy places in Palestine with attention to geographical
setting.

IMPOSSIBLE ON SATURDAY.   Meroz Films, Tel Aviv, and Athos
    Films, Paris, 1965.   105 min.   b/w.   Directed by Alex
    Joffe; story and screenplay by Jean Ferry, Pierre Levy-
    Corti, Shebati-Tevet, and Alex Joffe. With Robert Hirsch,
    Mischa Asherov, Dahlia Friedland, Geula Noni.   MAC[1]
Robert Hirsch plays eight parts in this story about an 83-year-old
conductor who can't get into heaven because the ghost of his de-
ceased father says his indiscretions are a barrier. For atonement
the conductor must arrange for his son and six illegitimate children
to come to Israel and be married. Includes excellent views of the
Holy Land.

THE INCREDIBLE TURK: KEMAL ATATURK.   CBS, n. d.   26
    min.   b/w.   MAC
Covers the contributions of the Turkish leader who led his country
into twentieth century life.

INVADERS AND CONVERTS.   (PART 2: The Glory That Remains
    Series.) BBC, 1969.   30 min.   color.   TL
An account of Persia's flourishing art which persisted despite invasions of Mongol hordes in ancient times.

IRAN.   Aria, 1972.   18 min.   color.   PYR
Filmmaker Claude Lelouch provides visual contrasts to compare the
old and the new, the natural life and the man-made objects of Iran.

Winner of many film awards, including Venice Film Festival, Tehran Film Festival, Sydney Film Festival.

IRAN, BETWEEN TWO WORLDS. Encyclopaedia Britannica Educational Corporation, 1954. 14 min. b/w. UCA, UUT
A brief discussion of Iran's geography and history. Shows modern cities, industrialization efforts and oil developments.

IRAN: THE STRUGGLE TO INDUSTRIALIZE. Jules Power, 1967. (Middle Eastern World Series.) 17 min. color. MGH, UWY
Explains the several land and climatic conditions under which Iranians live in contrast to the new industrial developments. Predicts the future importance of Iran's oil resources.

IRAN TODAY. NBC, 1974. 25 min. color. FI
The efforts of Iran to progress in its "Shah People Revolution" to develop the economy and educational levels of the people.

ISRAEL. AV-ED, 1961. 10 min. color. AVE
A brief survey of Israel's growth after it became a nation in 1948.

ISRAEL. International Film Foundation, 1965. 31 min. color. EFD, IFF
An introduction to Israel. With animation and documentary footage to show 4,000 years of history as well as the contemporary scene.

ISRAEL: A NATION IS BORN. Dudley, 1963. 17 min. b/w. UEVA
Tells the story of Israel as an emerging nation built by displaced persons. With scenes of Jerusalem and Tel Aviv.

ISRAEL: EXODUS TO INDEPENDENCE. Metromedia, 1972. 29 min. color. FI
Discusses the roots of Zionism in terms of the history of oppression and the creation of Israel as a nation by the United Nations in 1947.

ISRAEL, ITS HISTORY AND PEOPLE. J. Michael Hagopian, 1974. 17 min. color. ATL, SYR, USC
Gives background history of the Jewish people and the state of Israel with particular emphasis on the Arab-Israeli tension.

ISRAEL: MAKING A LAND PRODUCTIVE. Jules Power, 1967. 17 min. color. MGH
Focuses on one Dutch family--emigrés to Israel. Examines life in collective communities and the Arab-Jewish conflict.

ISRAEL: MIDDLE EAST NEIGHBOR. Ed Lark, 1962. 16 min. color. BFA
Shows many details of life and physical background--Roman ruins, modern buildings, schools, farms, cities in the fast-growing nation of Israel.

ISRAEL: THE LAND AND THE PEOPLE.   Coronet, 1970.   13 1/2
    min.   color.   COR
A tour of modern Israel that shows how Israel has planned its
economy, redeveloped neglected land.

ISRAEL TODAY.   Martin Murray, 1965.   23 min.   color.   ROT
Covers the industrial development and history of Israel.

THE ISRAELIS.   CBS, 1974.   36 min.   color.   CAR
The relationship of Jews and Arabs is examined along with the current status of the people and their culture in Israel.

ISTANBUL AND IZMIR.   International Film Bureau, 1961.   11
    min.   color.   IFB
An account of the old and present-day aspects of certain cities in
Western Turkey, such as Istanbul, Izmir.

JERUSALEM AND ITS CONTRIBUTIONS.   Atlantis, 1970.   16 min.
    color.   ATL, BOSU, UAR
Illustrates the significance of the three major religious groups in
the Holy City.

JERUSALEM: CENTER OF MANY WORLDS.   Atlantis, 1969.   29
    min.   color.   ATL, SYR, NYU
A study of Jerusalem's history and the modern city with ruins of
ancient cultures.

JEWISH DIETARY LAWS.   Lew Ayres, 1968.   (The Religions of the
    Eastern World Series.)   7 min.   color.   DOU
Gives instruction in preparation of meat and wines.   Also describes
the origins of dietary laws in the Old Testament and in interpreta-
tions by rabbis.

JUST ANOTHER DAY.   United Israel Appeal, 1971.   27 min.   color.
    UIA
Shows how daily life in Israel goes on despite threats of war.
Children are seen sleeping in bomb shelters and people are searched
for explosives.

THE KIBBUTZ.   Camera International, 1966.   20 min.   color.
    PER, VEC
Contrasts two kibbutzim, one a fairly prosperous operation and the
other, a typical farming kibbutz.   Shows the work and social activities of the people.

KIBBUTZ KFAR MENACHEM: CROSSROADS.   Lawrence Levy,
    n. d.   26 min.   color.   EBEC
Tells what's on the minds of a young generation growing up on a
kibbutz who are fascinated by the outside world and self-determina-
tion.   Conjectures on the future of the kibbutz system.

LAWRENCE OF ARABIA.   Columbia, 1962.   221 min.   color.
    Directed by David Lean; screenplay by Robert Bolt.   With

Peter O'Toole, Alex Guinness, Jack Hawkins, Anthony Quinn, Jose Ferrer, Omar Sharif, Claude Rains, Anthony Quayle. AST, COLU, CPC
The story of T. E. Lawrence, the Englishman who served as a guerrilla leader of Arabian tribesmen during World War II against the Turks.

MAMBUSH, TAPESTRY MAKER.   International Film Foundation, 1975.   13 min.   color.   EFD, IFF
Isracli tapestry maker Yitzhak Mambush (also ceramist and printer of serigraphs) works in the village of Ein Hod in Israel, a community inhabited and governed by artists and artisans.

THE MIDDLE EAST.   Encyclopaedia Britannica Educational Corporation, 1954.   14 min.   color.   UCA, UCO, UNE, UUT, UWY
A survey of the development of a culturally and geographically rich area with importance to the rest of the world.

THE MIDDLE EAST.   International Film Foundation, 1959.   28 min.   color.   IFP, EFD, UCO, UUT, UCA
Examines the problems and changes of the people of the Middle East.   Early scenes include film animation to portray 4,000 years of Middle Eastern history.

MIDDLE EAST: CROSSROADS OF THREE CONTINENTS.   Coronet, 1955.   13 1/2 min.   color.   COR, UCO, UUT
How the Middle East, a crossroads of cultures and trade, uses its major resource, oil, in its relations with the rest of the world.

THE MIDDLE EAST: THE NEED FOR WATER.   Jules Power, 1967.   (Middle Eastern World Series.)   16 min.   color.   MGH, UCO, UWY
A survey of the many problems of the Middle East, including the major need of an adequate water supply.

THE MOSLEMS AND THE WEST: CRISIS IN IRAN.   March of Time, 1951.   18 min.   b/w.   UUT
Modern cities, ancient ruins, oil refineries, and nomadic tribesmen are contrasted to show the economic and political conditions that brought on the 1949-50 crisis.

NOW THEIR HOME IS ISRAEL.   Hadassah, 1972.   27 min.   color.   HAD
Tells how young people from all over the world develop self-identity in their new land, Israel.

AN OLD WOMAN IN ROSH PINA.   Yehuda Azaba, 1970.   13 min.   b/w.   In Hebrew with English subtitles.   FMCO
A poetic treatment of an old pioneer woman in a deserted Israeli town who will not leave despite the fact that she is the last resident.

PROBLEMS OF THE MIDDLE EAST.   Atlantis, 1968.   2nd ed.
    22 min.   color.   ATL, UCA
An account of the Middle East from ancient times to the present
with discussion of four major problems of today.' Uses authentic
ethnic music.

REVOLUTION IN DHOFAR.   Jimmy Vaughn, 1973.   55 min.
    color.   TWN
Shows the changes wrought in Dhofar, Oman by the Popular Front
Organization for the Liberation of the Occupied Arab Gulf. This
is an area where the ruling Sultan had prohibited the use of medicine, wearing glasses or shoes, and eating certain fruits.

REVOLUTION UNTIL VICTORY.   Cine News, 1973.   52 min.
    b/w.   TWN, TRI
Presents the situation of the Palestinian people after years of
struggle against the Turks, the British, and Zionism. Uses old
footage to explore the theory of Zionism's role in undermining
Jewish resistance to Nazism and in making Israel "an extension of
Western imperialistic interests."

SALLAH.   Sallah Limited, 1965.   105 min.   b/w.   In Hebrew with
    English subtitles.   Directed by Ephraim Kishon; written by
    Ephraim Kishon; produced by Menachem Golam.   With Haym
    Topol, Geula Noni, Gila Almogor, Arik Einstein, Shraga
    Friedman, Zaharira Harifai.   BUDG, MAC[1], MOSP, SWA,
    WECF, WIL, INTF
A comedy about an unschooled Oriental Jew who immigrates to
Israel where he manages to overcome Israeli bureaucracy and
custom.

THE SEVEN SPLENDORS OF PERSIA.   CCM, n. d.   18 min.
    color.   MAC
Present-day Iran with its traces of old Persia alongside new
sophistication and wealth.

SEVEN WIVES OF BAHRAM GUR.   A-V Center, Indiana Univer-
    sity, 1961.   (Arts of the Orient Series.)   19 min.   color.
    IND
An account of the Persian hero of legend.   Adapted from the epic
poem by Nizami and filmed from 15th and 16th century Persian
miniatures.

SHALOM.   Sherwood Price, 1971.   74 min.   color.   MAC[1]
Narrated by Robert Vaughn.   A tour of modern Israel combined
with the history of early Zionism.

SHALOM OF SAFED: THE INNOCENT EYE OF A MAN OF
    GALILEE.   Arnold Eagle, 1967.   28 min.   color.   EAG
Studies the art and life of self-taught painter Shalom of Safed.
Discusses stylistic similarities among native artists.

SHUSHA. Anthony David, 1972. 27 min. color. FI
An Iranian folk singer presents songs of her native land against a
visual background of Southern Iran.

SINAI. NBC, 1973. 36 min. color. FI
A look at the Bedouins, the nomadic people of Sinai, the peninsula
taken by Israel from Egypt in 1967 during the Six Day War. Narrated by John Dancy.

SPEAKING OF ISRAEL. Baruch Dienar, Tel Aviv, 1969. 28 min.
     color. ALD
Shows how Israel's residents view their country, its culture, heritage, its intellectual life.

THE SUDDEN EMPIRE. (PART 1. The Glory That Remains
     Series.) BBC, 1969. 30 min. color. TL
The rise and fall of the Persian Empire told with footage of archeological remains.

THE SUEZ CANAL. Gateway, 1966. 11 min. color. COR
Traces the history of the dream to have a canal through the
Isthmus of Suez from ancient times. Discusses Ferdinand de
Lesseps and shows an English ship going from Port Said to the
Indian Ocean via the canal.

TERRA SANCTA: A FILM OF ISRAEL. University of Arizona,
     1969. 31 min. color. EFD, IFB
A personal view of Israel as one Israeli citizen examines his country in terms of its history, religions, customs and people.

THE THIRD TEMPLE. Jewish National Fund, 1967. 40 min.
     color. JNF
Examines the variety of backgrounds from which people of several
ethnic groups have come to live in Israel.

TURKEY. International Film Foundation, n.d. 27 min. color.
     IFP
A study of Turkey, its visual beauties and its important role in the
Middle East.

TURKEY: A NATION IN TRANSITION. International Film Founda-
     tion, 1962. 27 min. color. EFD, IFF
A survey of the developments in Turkey's industry and agriculture
from the regime of Kemal Ataturk in 1923 on.

TURKEY: A STRATEGIC LAND AND ITS PEOPLE. Coronet,
     1959. 11 min. b/w. COR, UMN
Traces the beginnings of Westernization introduced by Ataturk and
shows geographical features of Turkey.

TURKEY: EMERGENCE OF A MODERN NATION. Encyclopaedia
     Britannica Educational Corporation, 1963. 17 min. b/w.
     EBEC

A summary of Turkey's history with emphasis on changes in the
last half century.

TURKEY: YESTERDAY'S TOMORROW.   Neil Douglas, 1966.   95
    min.   color.   silent.   DOUG
About Turkey's history and culture.

THE UPSURGE OF NATIONALISM.   National Film Board of Canada,
    1964.   (The Middle East Series.)   26 min.   color.   MGH
How revolutionary leaders reorganized society, restored national
pride and developed technology in the Middle East.

A WALL IN JERUSALEM.   (UN MUR A JERUSALEM.)   EYR Pro-
    grams, 1972.   92 min.   b/w.   EYR
An exhaustive history of Israel from 1896 through the Six Day War
in 1967.

South Asia

    (includes Afghanistan; Bangladesh; Himalayan States of Nepal,
    Sikkim and Bhutan; India; Pakistan; Sri Lanka [Ceylon])

Afghanistan

AFGHAN NOMADS: THE MALDAR.   Norman N. Miller, 1974.
    (Faces of Change Series.)   21 min.   color.   FF
Shows a caravan of nomads descending on Aq Kupruk and studies
their relationship with the townspeople.

AFGHAN VILLAGE.   Norman N. Miller, 1974.   (Faces of Change
    Series.)   45 min.   color.   FF
A view of daily life in Aq Kupruk.

AFGHAN WOMEN.   Norman N. Miller, 1974.   (Faces of Change
    Series.)   FF
Women's role in an Afghan rural community.

AFGHANISTAN.   Hungarofilm, 1972.   15 min.   color.   AC
Emphasis on visual beauty of exotic Afghanistan with authentic music as background.   Shows tribesmen traveling on camels, farmers
at work and horsemen using their skills in violent games.

BAKING BREAD.   International Film Foundation, 1973.   (The
    Mountain Peoples of Central Asia Series.)   10 min.   color.
    EFD, IFF
A rare view of a remote nomadic people, the Pushtu, of Badakhstan
in northeastern Afghanistan.   In this case, a woman is seen preparing and kneading dough to make bread.

BOYS' GAME.   International Film Foundation, 1968.   (The Mountain
    Peoples of Central Asia Series.)   5 min.   color.   EFD, IFF,
    PEN

Pushtu boys test their physical superiority in an ancient game.

BUILDING A BRIDGE.   International Film Foundation, 1968.   (The
    Mountain Peoples of Central Asia Series.)   10 min.   b/w.
    EFD, IFF
In three days of construction, one hundred Tajik men and boys construct a cantilever span bridge--their only contact with the outside
world.

BUZKASHI.   International Film Foundation, 1968.   (The Mountain
    Peoples of Central Asia Series.)   8 min.   color.   EFD, IFF,
    PEN
Buzkashi, one of the toughest sports in the world, is performed on
horses by Afghan tribesmen in honor of their king.

CASTING IRON PLOW-SHARES.   International Film Foundation,
    1968.   (The Mountain Peoples of Central Asia Series.)   11
    min.   b/w.   IFF, PEN
Shows the Tajik people casting plow-shares in wet sand with the
traditional methods.

GRINDING WHEAT.   International Film Foundation, 1968.   (The
    Mountain Peoples of Central Asia Series.)   7 min.   b/w.
    EFD, IFF, PEN
A close look at the Tajik people grinding wheat into flour in the
traditional manner.

ISTALA MASHI: MAY YOU NEVER BE TIRED.   UNICEF, 1960.
    10 min.   b/w.   UCO
Follows the nomadic tribes of Afghanistan who move their herds to
Pakistan when winter comes.

MAKING BREAD.   International Film Foundation, 1968.   (The
    Mountain Peoples of Central Asia Series.)   11 min.   b/w.
    EFD, IFF, PEN
How the Tajik people of Badakhstan, Northeastern Afghanistan, prepare their flat unleavened bread by slapping it to the walls of their
clay oven.

MAKING FELT.   International Film Foundation, 1968.   (The Moun-
    tain Peoples of Central Asia Series.)   9 min.   color.   EFD,
    IFF, PEN
How the nomadic Pushtu people make felt mats--the shearing of the
sheep, the pounding and separating of the wool fibers.

MAKING GUN POWER.   International Film Foundation, 1968.
    (The Mountain Peoples of Central Asia Series.)   10 min.
    b/w.   EFD: IFF, PEN
A Tajik tribesman makes gunpowder using an ancient technique.
With authentic musical background.

MEN'S DANCE.   International Film Foundation, 1968.   (The Moun-
    tain Peoples of Central Asia Series.)   11 min.   color.   EFD,
    IFF, PEN

Traditional dances serve the nomadic Pushtu people as entertainment and recreation.   Here a dance portraying man's combat with evil is performed.

NAIM AND JABAR.   Norman N. Miller, n. d.   (Faces of Change
    Series.)   50 min.   color.   FF
Reflects the adolescent aspirations of two Afghan boys.

POTTERY MAKING.   International Film Foundation, 1972.   (The
    Mountain Peoples of Central Asia Series.)   15 min.   b/w.
    IFF, PEN
Shows the Tajik people in Badakhstan, Northeastern Afghanistan, making pottery.   Without narration.

SHEARING YAKS.   International Film Foundation, 1968.   (The
    Mountain Peoples of Central Asia Series.)   9 min.   b/w.
    IFF, PEN
How Tajik tribal people of Afghanistan shear yaks with scissors. Shows yaks being brought down from the mountains to the village for shearing and what is done with the yaks hair afterward.

STONES OF EDEN.   William Furman, 1965.   25 min.   color.
    MGH
About one year in the life of a farmer in Central Afghanistan.   An award-winning film written, directed and photographed by William A. Furman.

THRESHING WHEAT.   International Film Foundation, 1968.   (The
    Mountain Peoples of Central Asia Series.)   9 min.   b/w.
    IFF, PEN
Shows the Tajik people of Northeastern Afghanistan threshing wheat using traditional methods.

WEAVING CLOTH.   International Film Foundation, 1968.   (The
    Mountain Peoples of Central Asia Series.)   9 min.   color.
    EFD, IFF, PEN
The practical and essential art of weaving performed by the Pushtu women on looms similar to those of Genghis Khan's days.

WHEAT CYCLE.   Norman N. Miller, 1974.   (Faces of Change
    Series.)   16 min.   color.   FF
About the relationship between the people and the sowing and harvesting of wheat in Afghanistan.

Bangladesh

BANGLADESH.   Authentic, 1975.   7 min.   color.   MGH
One of the newest films on Bangladesh, the new state.   Shows how climate affects crops, which in turn influence the life and economy. Also covers Bangladesh's history and beginnings of industrialization. Excerpt from PAKISTAN: A TWO-PART NATION, which is now out of print.

BANGLADESH NATIONHOOD: SYMBOLS AND SHADOWS. South
    Asian Center, University of Wisconsin, n. d.   49 min.   color.
    UWI
An account of the feelings of the Bangladesh people about their society, filmed just before the assassination of Sheik Mujib, "Father
of the Nation."

BANGLADESH PLOWMAN.   Mennonite Central Committee, n. d.
    20 min.   color.   MEN
A documentary about the new country of 75 million people who must
cope with disease, hurricanes, floods, and hunger.   Shows the
need for better equipment, good fertilizers and other help.

Himalayan States/Nepal, Bhutan, Sikkim

CHILDREN OF THE WORLD: NEPAL. NET, 1968.   28 min.
    color.   IND
A youth from Nepal, one of the oldest cultures in the world, shows
the conflict between his religious beliefs and his scientific knowledge.

GURKHA COUNTRY.   John and Patricia Hitchcock, 1967.   19 min.
    color.   EFD, IFB
How a cultural anthropologist studies the life of a village in the
Bhuji River Valley of Nepal.

HIMALAYA: LIFE ON THE ROOF OF THE WORLD.   Atlantis,
    1958.   22 min.   b/w.   UCA
Emphasizes Kashmir, Sikkim, Nepal and Assam in this study of
Himalaya Mountain civilization.

HIMALAYA: LIFE ON THE ROOF OF THE WORLD.   Atlantis,
    1968.   Rev. ed.   21 min.   color.   ATL, NYU, USC
Discusses the strategic importance of the Himalaya Mountains
where diverse cultures live.

HIMALAYAN FARMER.   John and Patricia Hitchcock, 1968.   16
    min.   color.   EFD, IFB, UCA
How a farmer of Bhuji Khola must survive on the basis of his
skills and energy.

HIMALAYAN SHAMAN OF NORTHERN NEPAL.   John and Patricia
    Hitchcock, 1967.   15 min.   color.   EFD, IFB, UCA
The role of the powerful Shaman in his community.

HIMALAYAN SHAMAN OF SOUTHERN NEPAL.   John and Patricia
    Hitchcock, 1967.   14 min.   color.   EFD, IFB, UCA
Shows a Shaman at work in the more Hinduized southern portion of
the Nepalese Himalaya.

LETTER FROM THIMPU.   BBC, n. d.   40 min.   color.   TL
Describes the almost inaccessible Buddhist kingdom, Bhutan,

through the letters of a 15-year-old Bhutanese boy to a friend in the West. A view of a country that only in recent times learned of the wheel and that conducts trade by barter.

THE SHERPAS OF EVEREST. BBC, 1971. 51 min. color. TL
A study of the Sherpa people of the highest Himalayan villages who live and work at twelve to fifteen thousand feet above sea level and without whom mountain climbing expeditions would not easily succeed.

SHIMBUK: A TIBETAN VILLAGE. John Friedman, 1974. 42 min. color. EDC
About the family life and work of the Tibetan people of an isolated agricultural community in Nepal.

India

THE ADVENTURES OF GOOPY AND BAGHA. (GOOPY GYNE BAGHA BYNE.) Satyajit Ray, 1969. 117 min. b/w and color. With English subtitles. Directed by Satyajit Ray; also written and designed by Satyajit Ray. With Tapan Chatterjee, Robi Ghose. NC, JAN
A musical fairy tale for adults about two outcasts who are given three wishes which lead to misadventure.

THE ADVERSARY. (PRATIDWANDI.) Satyajit Ray, 1971. 110 min. b/w. In Bengali with English subtitles. Directed by Satyajit Ray; screenplay by Satyajit Ray, based on a story by Sunil Ganguli; photography by Soumendu Roy; music by Satyajit Ray. With Dhritiman Chatterjee, Joyshree Roy, Krishna Bose, Kalyan Chatterjee. MAC[1]
A young man grows in spirit as he suffers the loss of his medical studies, the death of his father and the realization that he must make his own way in the world.

APARAJITO. (THE UNVANQUISHED.) Satyajit Ray, 1957. 108 min. b/w. In Bengali with English subtitles. Directed by Satyajit Ray; screenplay by Satyajit Ray, based on the novel "Pather Panchali" by Bibhuti Banerji; photography by Subrata Mitra; music composed and played by Ravi Shankar. With Pinkai Sen Gupta, Smaran Ghosal, Karuna Banerji, Kanu Banerji, Ramani Sen Gupta, Charu Ghosh, Subodh Ganguly, Kali Charan Ray. MAC[1]
Apu's family arrives in Benares. The father dies, the mother goes to work, and Apu tries Brahman priesthood training only to find his interests are in going to the University of Calcutta. A magnificent sequel to PATHER PANCHALI; the second part of the Apu Trilogy.

THE APU TRILOGY see PATHER PANCHALI; APARAJITO; THE WORLD OF APU

ASIAN EARTH. Atlantis, 1954. 22 min. color. UCA
How a middle class peasant family lives in northern India.

ASSIGNMENT: INDIA. NBC, 1967. 57 min. b/w. FI, PEN,
    VEC
Covers the problems facing the Indian people, their aspirations, and
attitudes.

AT FIVE PAST FIVE. Vimal Ahuji, n. d. 66 min. b/w. With
    English dialogue. Directed and written by Kamar Vasudev;
    based on a play by Lalit Sehgal; photography by Kamal Bose,
    music by Vasent Desai. MAC[1]
Five past five on January 30, 1948 was the time of Mahatma Gandhi's assassination and is the subject for filmmaker Vasudev's fictional film which traces the actions of the conspirators before the
event.

AUTOBIOGRAPHY OF A PRINCESS. Merchant-Ivory, 1975. 57
    min. color. Directed by James Ivory; produced by Ismail
    Merchant; written by Ruth Prawer Jhabvala; photographed by
    Walter Lassally. With James Mason and Madhur Joffrey.
    CF
Archive footage of India in the 1920s through the 1940s shows the
life style at the Maharajas' courts and provides the setting for a
fictional story about two survivors of the old way of life--an old
English tutor and a princess in exile.

BHARATA NATYAM. Government of India Information Services,
    n. d. 10 min. b/w. UCA
A demonstration of the gesture language, known as "madras," as
it is connected with a traditional South Indian dance.

BISMILLAH KHAN. NET, 1968. (Creative Person Series.) 29
    min. b/w. IND, UCA
A look at India's great musician, Bismillah Khan, who plays the
shenia, an oboe-like instrument used for temple processions and
marriages.

BOMBAY TALKIE. Ismail Merchant, 1971. 112 min. color.
    With English dialogue. Directed by James Ivory; screenplay
    by James Ivory and R. Prawer Jhabvala; photography by
    Subrata Mitra; music by Shankar-Jaikishan. With Shashi
    Kapoor, Jennifer Kendal, Zia Mohyeddin, Aparna Sen. MAC[1]
The conflict of three people who are working together on a musical
in a Bombay movie studio--a woman novelist, an Indian movie
star, and his scriptwriter friend. A social satire by American director James Ivory, a frequent collaborator with the producer and
screenplay writer of this film.

BOY OF BOMBAY. Yehuda Tarmu, 1969. 16 min. color. BFA
A visit with a twelve-year-old boy of Bombay who is poor and has
no skills or training.

CALCUTTA. Louis Malle, 1968. 105 min. color. NC, PYR
French filmmaker Louis Malle's documentary on a city that is over-
crowded with poor, starving people.

CHARULATA, THE LONELY WIFE. Satyajit Ray, 1964. 115 min.
b/w. In Hindustani with English subtitles. Directed by Satyajit Ray; screenplay by Satyajit Ray from a story by Rabindranath Tagore; photographed by Subrata Mitra; music by
Satyajit Ray. With Soumitra Chatterji, Madhabi Mukherji,
Sailen Mikherji, Shymal Ghoshal, Geetali Ray. MGH
A story set in nineteenth century Bengal about a man who devotes
all his time to promoting freedom through his journalistic enterprises but badly neglects his wife.

THE CROSS IN THE LOTUS. Broadcasting and Film Commission,
National Council of Churches, 1972. 23 min. color. NACC
The story of Christianity in India from 52 A.D. to the present, told
with intercuts of documentary footage and dance-drama.

THE DAM AT NAGARJUNASAGAR. Gene Searchinger, 1972. 9
min. color. CAR, PEN
Ossie Davis narrates this film about the construction of the largest
masonry dam ever erected near Hyderabad in Central India. Examines one typical work day with workers singing, eating a skimpy
allotment of rice, and receiving a few coins for their labor.

DANCES OF INDIA. Serisawa Brothers, n.d. 20 min. color.
IFP
Two famous dancers, Sujota and Asoka, perform four basic Indian
dances from specific parts of India.

DAYS AND NIGHTS IN THE FOREST. Nepal Dutta and Ashim Dutta for Priya, 1970. 120 min. b/w. In Bengali with English subtitles. Directed by Satyajit Ray; screenplay by Satyajit Ray, from a story by Sunil Ganguly; photography by Soumendu Roy; art direction by Bansi Chandragupta; music by
Satyajit Ray. With Soumitra Chatterjee, Subhendu Chatterjee,
Samit Bhanja, Robi Ghose, Sharmila Tagore, Kaberi Bose,
Simi, Aparna Sen, and Pahari Sanyal. MGH
Four men drive off to the country for a holiday with a variety of
results: a drunken spree, quarrels, love affairs, games.

DECCAN VILLAGE. J. Arthur Rank, 1967. 10 min. color.
UEVA
A view of India's attempts to achieve a place in the modern world
of technological and educational advances.

THE DELHI WAY. James Ivory, 1964. 45 min. color. RAD
A visit to Delhi with the help of art, architecture, old photographs,
film footage, and present-day views of streets, homes, religious
shrines.

DEVI. (GODDESS.) Satyajit Ray, 1961. 96 min. b/w. In Ben-
    gali with English subtitles. Directed by Satyajit Ray; screen-
    play by Satyajit Ray; music by Alik Akbar Khan. With
    Chhabi Biswas, Soumitra Chatterjee, Sharmila Tagore. MAC[1]
This film was withheld for awhile from international distribution because of protests by fundamentalist Hindus. The story concerns a
father who believes his daughter-in-law is a reincarnation of a
goddess and promotes her to the people as a deity--with tragic results.

DISCOVERING THE MUSIC OF INDIA. Bernard Wilets, 1969. 22
    min. color. BFA
The instruments of north and south India, such as the sitar, flute,
tabia, mridangam, and tamboura, are demonstrated along with details of melody and rhythm. Also gives examples of dance gestures
performed with music.

DISCOVERY: A VISUAL IMPRESSION OF INDIA. Anthony Kent,
    n.d. 30 min. color. TL
A young American filmmaker shows the ritual of daily life in India
with every act, every gesture regarded as a form of worship.

DISTANT THUNDER. Satyajit Ray, 1973. 100 min. color. In
    Bengali with English subtitles. Directed by Satyajit Ray;
    screenplay by Satyajit Ray, based on the novel of Bibhuti
    Bhusan Bannerji; photography by Soumendu Roy; music by
    Satyajit Ray. With Soumitra Chatterji, Babita. CF
A drama about a young Brahmin who settles into his new life in a
village when his world is shattered by the Second World War. Considered to be one of Ray's finest works.

FABLE OF THE PEACOCK. Jo Schaeffer, 1950. 14 min. color.
    MAC
A view of Indian culture through music and dance. Lakshimi Wana
Singh dances a fable and explains movements.

FAMILY LIFE IN INDIA: TEN OF US. George Stoney, 1969.
    (Family Life Around the World Series.) 13 min. color.
    MGH
A portrait of a large, typical family which includes relatives, such
as cousin, grandmother and uncle. Follows two children and some
activities of the rest of the family as seen through the eyes of the
children.

FARM VILLAGE OF INDIA: STRUGGLE WITH TRADITION. Phil-
    lips Foster, 1971. 21 min. color. COR, UUT
On the northern Ganges Plain a farmer and his family cope with
present-day problems in order to keep their small farm going.

THE FLUTE AND THE ARROW. (EN DJUNGELSAGA; A JUNGLE
    SAGA.) Arne Sucksdorff, 1958. 78 min. color. Directed,
    written and photographed by Arne Sucksdorff; music by Ravi
    Shankar. Narrated in English by Arthur Howard. MAC[1]

During two years spent among the Murias, a tribe said to be India's
original inhabitants, documentary filmmaker Arne Sucksdorff directed, wrote and photographed this film.   The flute is a Muria's
symbol of love and the bow and arrow are his weapon against tigers
and lions.

FOUR MEN OF INDIA.   Lever Brothers, 1969.   30 1/2 min.
    color.   BFA
A study of modern Indian life with emphasis on overpopulation,
poverty, the caste system, variety of languages, and poor transportation.

GANDHI.   CBS, 1958.   27 min.   b/w.   MGH
Mohandas Gandhi's life from his involvement in political activity
to his assassination in 1948.

GANDHI.   David Wolper, 1964.   26 min.   b/w.   MGH
The story of Mohandas Gandhi who gained India's independence
through non-violent methods.

GANDHI'S INDIA.   BBC, 1969.   (World History from 1917 to the
    Present Series.)   20 min.   b/w.   IND, TL
Discusses India in the late 1800s, Gandhi's life work to obtain home
rule, and the birth of India and Pakistan as independent nations.

GANGES: SACRED RIVER.   NBC, 1965.   Edited version.   27
    min.   color.   EBEC, UCO
A prize-winning film which follows the Ganges River from the
mountains through the center of India to Calcutta and shows the
river's effect on the people's way of life.

THE GREAT MOGUL.   (PART 6.   The Glory That Remains Series.)
    BBC, 1969.   30 min.   color.   TL
The rule of Akbar, third of India's Mogul rulers and how he built
Fathepur-Sikri and the fort of Agra.

HARVEST OF MERCY.   CBS, 1966.   41 min.   color.   CAR
CBS correspondents Winston Burdett and Charles Kuralt describe
how the U.S. has fed the starving people of India with shipments
of wheat.   Shows grim conditions in India.

HELEN: QUEEN OF THE NAUTCH GIRLS.   Ismail Merchant, 1973.
    30 min.   color.   Directed by Anthony Korner; screenplay by
    James Ivory.   NYF
"Nautch" girls are professional dancing girls in India.   Helen is a
Bombay movie goddess who is viewed on and off stage and as she
prepares for a big production number.

HINDU FAMILY.   Encyclopaedia Britannica Educational Corporation,
    1952.   11 min.   b/w.   UCO, UUT, UCA
Describes the marriage of a young girl in Gujaret, India and important aspects of Hindu daily life.

HINDUISM AND THE SONG OF GOD.   Hartley, 1975.   30 min.
     color.   HARP
Uses the beauty of India as background to discuss some of Hindu-
ism's basic tenets as expressed in the Bhagavad Gita, or Song of
God.

HOW DEATH CAME TO EARTH.   National Film Board of Canada,
     1972.   15 min.   color.   NFBC
A film animation by an Indian filmmaker about a legendary story
that concerns gods and men.

IMMINENT DEITIES.   (PART 4.   The Glory That Remains Series.)
     BBC, 1969.   30 min.   color.   TL
A view of the Hindu religion as manifested in early rock carvings
and chola bronzes.

THE IMPACT OF INDIA.   Koplin and Grinker, n.d.   26 min.
     color.   PIC
Charles Blair traces the grim problems of India and the progress
that has been made in the fight against disease and illiteracy despite many setbacks.

IN INDIA THE SUN RISES IN THE EAST.   Richard Kaplan, 1969.
     14 min.   color.   MGH
Without narration or dialogue the scenes provocatively reveal the
people and places of India.   An award-winning film.

IN SEARCH OF PARADISE.   Gita Mehta, n.d.   45 min.   color.
     ITC
Written, narrated and directed by Gita Mehta, a young native Indian who explores the present generation, which has grown up in a
time of economic depression.

INDIA.   Gateway, 1960.   22 min.   color.   IFB, UCA, UUT
A documentary on life of the Indian people today.   Shows the under-
privileged masses contrasted with the comfortable upper classes.

INDIA: A BETTER TOMORROW.   Bailey, 1962.   16 min.   color.
     BFA, UUT
About India's efforts to overcome the caste system, to achieve
equal rights and to educate the people.

INDIA: CRAFTS AND THE CRAFTSMAN.   Richard Kaplan, 1968.
     15 min.   color.   ACI
Presents a variety of old and new techniques for traditional crafts.
Uses music representative of the many locations shown.

INDIA: INTRODUCTION TO ITS HISTORY.   Encyclopaedia Britan-
     nica Educational Corporation, 1957.   16 min.   color.   UCA
A brief survey of India's history from 2,000 B.C. until the de-
claration of independence in 1947.

INDIA! MY INDIA! PART I: AFTER 17 YEARS.   Current Affairs,
   England, 1968.   26 min.   b/w.   MGH, UCO
Yavar Abbas, a native Indian, returns to his homeland after an
absence of seventeen years.

INDIA! MY INDIA! PART II: AS IN MY TIME.   Current Affairs,
   England, 1968.   26 min.   b/w.   MGH
Yavar Abbas, a native Indian, reflects on life in his homeland as
he knew it before his absence for a period of seventeen years.

INDIA! MY INDIA! PART III: SINCE MY TIME.   Current Affairs,
   England, 1968.   26 min,   b/w.   MGH
A native Indian observes the changes that have taken place in India
during the almost two decades since he left.

INDIA! MY INDIA! PART IV: YET ANOTHER HARVEST.   Current
   Affairs, England, 1968.   26 min.   b/w.   MGH
When a native Indian returns to his homeland after a long absence,
he observes the changes independence has brought.

INDIA: PAKISTAN AND THE UNION OF INDIA.   Encyclopaedia
   Britannica Educational Corporation, 1952.   17 min.   b/w.
   UCA
An old film that gives an account of the role of tradition and geo-
graphic factors in shaping the life of Indian and Pakistani people.

INDIA: SUB-CONTINENT OF ASIA.   United World, 1964.   17 min.
   color.   UEVA
Visits India's important cities to study their attempts at industrialization.

INDIA: THE BEWILDERED GIANT.   BBC, n. d.   38 min.   color.
   TL
Poet-author Dom Moraes, born in India, returns to find his homeland reverting back to old pre-colonial ways: fighting among small
states, contempt for race or caste, and other disturbing conditions.

INDIA: THE LAND AND THE PEOPLE.   Murl Deusing, 1958.
   11 min.   color.   IFB, UUT
The heritage, the topography and climate, and present-day problems
of India.

THE INDIA TRIP.   National Film Board of Canada, n. d.   50 min.
   color.   MGH
About the spiritual mecca of Pondicherry in India where Europeans
and North Americans go to live a contemplative life.   Narrated by
a professor from Sir George Williams University, Montreal.

INDIA: WRITINGS ON THE SAND.   NET, 1965.   (Population Problem Series.)   60 min.   color.   IND
A study of issues and factors in India's population problem.   This
film is also available in Spanish, Portuguese and French language
versions.   Also available in 30 min. version (English or Spanish).

INDIAN HOLY MEN. (DARSHAN.) Satyam Shivan Sandaram and
    Florence Davey, n.d. 28 min. color. NLC
Four Indian holy men illustrate the varieties of Indian spirituality.

AN INDIAN PILGRIMAGE: RAMDEVRA. South Asia Area Center,
    University of Wisconsin, 1975. 25 min. color. UWI
Studies an Indian folk pilgrimage of cultists devoted to Ramdev, a
hero and saint of the Middle Ages, whose worship is spread by
folk music telling stories of him. The songs figure prominently
in the film.

INDIA'S HISTORY: BRITISH COLONY TO INDEPENDENCE. Coro-
    net, 1956. 10 1/2 min. color. COR, UCA
Follows India from the days of the British East India Company to
her independence with coverage of Gandhi's contribution.

INDIA'S HISTORY: EARLY CIVILIZATIONS. Coronet, 1956.
    10 1/2 min. color. COR, UCA
The cultural contributions of India's people throughout her long history. Covers original inhabitants, invaders and leaders up to the
beginnings of Buddhism and Hinduism.

INDIA'S HISTORY: MOGUL EMPIRE TO EUROPEAN COLONIZA-
    TION. Coronet, 1956. 10 1/2 min. color. COR, UCA
Traces the rule of India from 13th century Delhi Sultans to the
Moguls, including the competition between Britain and France over
Indian trade.

INDIRA GANDHI OF INDIA. BBC, 1973. 60 min. color. TL
An autobiographical interview with Mrs. Gandhi, who describes her
rise to political power.

JAWAHARLAL NEHRU. NBC, 1958. 30 min. b/w. FI, VEC
A TV portrait of the late Prime Minister of India who discusses
his life, his work and his country's problems with Chester Bowles,
former U.S. Ambassador to India.

JUGGERNAUT: A FILM OF INDIA. National Board of Canada,
    1968. 28 min. color. LEC
How a tradition-oriented people struggles to cope with today's
problems; told with a "juggernaut" (nuclear reactor) used as ironic
symbol.

KALEIDOSCOPE ORISSA. Pilgrim, England, 1967. 37 min. color.
    EFD, IFB, UCA, UUT
About the beautiful art and crafts of Orissa, one of India's poorest
states. An award-winning film.

KANCHENJUNGHA. Satyajit Ray, 1962. 102 min. color. In
    Bengali with English subtitles. Directed, written by Satyajit
    Ray; musical arrangement and title paintings by Satyajit Ray;
    photography by Subrata Mitra. With Chhabi Biswas, Karuna
    Banerji, Nilima Roy Chowdhury, N. Vis Wanathan. MAC[1]

This is the first color film of Satyajit Ray, the distinguished Indian filmmaker. A rich family from Calcutta falls apart within a few hours. The father tries to dominate but fails; his wife and children are unhappy because they must follow the old ways: arranged marriages, docile roles of women, political conservatism.

KHAJURAHO ETERNAL. Amin Chaudhri, 1966. 11 min. color.
    ART
One thousand-year-old sculptures of Khajuraho temples are used to present an expression of the creation-destruction cycle.

KRISHNAMURTI. BBC, n. d. 25 min. color. TL
An interview with Krishnamurti, known as the World Teacher, who has traveled widely to encourage the liberation of minds from "systems" and to preach his concept of meditation.

LIFE IN RURAL INDIA. Visual Education Centre, n. d. 13 min. color. VEC
Contrasts primitive agricultural methods of the farmers of Sokhodera, a small village in the Central Indian Plateau, with their needs for greater food yield that can only come through education and use of new methods.

THE LONG CHAIN. Pea Holmquist, 1971-72. 20 min. b/w.
    TRI
Discusses the exploitation of Indian workers at starvation wages for the construction of overseas branches of foreign corporations in India. Shows how the people are stranded in the slums after the job is completed.

MAHANAGAR. (THE BIG CITY.) Satyajit Ray, 1964. 122 min.
    b/w. In Bengali with English subtitles. Directed by Satyajit Ray; screenplay by Satyajit Ray, based on a short story by Ivarenda Mitra; photography by Subrata Mitra; music by Satyajit Ray. With Anil Chatterji, Madhabi Mukherjee, Vicky Redwood, Haradhan Banerjee, MAC[1]
A young married couple struggle with poverty in an inflexible society. When the wife gets a job, tensions mount with husband and relatives.

MAHATMA GANDHI. Encyclopaedia Britannica Educational Corporation, 1955. 19 min. b/w. UCA, UCO, UUT, UWY
The life story of Mohandas Karamchand Gandhi.

MAHATMA GANDHI: SILENT REVOLUTION. Pilgrim, 1970. 38 min. color. EFD, IFB, UUT
An account of Gandhi's theory for basic education that included preparation for agricultural reform, handicrafts, and industrial training.

MRS. INDIRA GHANDI. CBS, n. d. 26 min. b/w. MAC
A visit with India's Prime Minister, the daughter of the late Jawaharlal Nehru.

MOTHER TERESA OF CALCUTTA.   BBC, 1971.   51 min.   color.
    TL
Malcolm Muggeridge's interview with an Indian nun who has drawn
a following of fellow Christians as well as Hindus, Muslims and
Parsees.

MUNNA.   (THE LOST CHILD.)   K. A. Abbas, 1955.   86 min.
    b/w.   In Hindi with English subtitles.   Directed by K. A.
    Abbas; music by Anil Biswas.   With Romi; rest of cast un-
    listed.   MAC[1]
About a seven-year-old orphan who is not adopted because his caste
and background are unknown.   Before being rescued he falls in with
a street gang.   An example of an Indian film influenced by the
Italian neorealist style.

THE MUSIC ROOM.   Satyajit Ray, 1959.   95 min.   b/w.   In Ben-
    gali with English subtitles.   Directed by Satyajit Ray; screen-
    play by Satyajit Ray, based on a novel by Narshankar Baner-
    jee; photography by Subrata Mitra.   With Chhabi Biswas,
    Padma Devi, Pinaki Sen Gupta.   MAC[1]
A once wealthy and music-loving landowner becomes a relatively
poor and despondent hermit after his wife's and son's deaths.
When a neighbor plans an elaborate music festival, the man im-
prudently tries to raise money for a musical soirée of his own.
A perceptive study of a vanishing way of life.

NAYAK, THE HERO.   R. D. Bansal and Saran Kumari Bansal,
    1966.   120 min.   b/w.   Direction, screenplay and music by
    Satyajit Ray; photography by Subrata Mitra.   With Uttam Ku-
    mar Chatterji, Sharmila Tagore.   With English subtitles.
    MGH
A successful actor on his way via train to Delhi for an award, encounters a variety of people during his journey.

NEHRU.   Drew and Time-Life, n. d.   54 min.   b/w.   TL
Nehru as he looked at 73, when President of the world's largest
democracy.

NEHRU: MAN OF TWO WORLDS.   CBS, 1966.   25 min.   b/w.
    MGH
An account of Jawaharlal Nehru's life-long efforts to build a new
India, an independent and stable nation.

NEW HORIZONS: INDIA.   Pan American Airways, n. d.   13 min.
    color.   ASF, PAN
A travelogue designed to promote tourism in India.

NON-VIOLENCE: MAHATMA GANDHI AND MARTIN LUTHER
    KING, THE TEACHER AND THE PUPIL.   Koplin and Grink-
    er, n. d.   (The Turning Points: America in the 20th Century
    Series.)   15 min.   color.   PIC
Explores the parallels between the two leaders who used non-violent methods in fighting oppression.

India   65

NORTH INDIAN VILLAGE.   Patricia Hitchcock, 1959.   32 min.
    color.   EFD, IFB
Examines the village of Khalapur, the customs, the religion, the
ceremony, the roles of men and women.

PATHER PANCHALI.   (SONG OF THE ROAD.)   Satyajit Ray, 1954.
    112 min. b/w.   In Bengali with English subtitles.   Directed
    by Satyajit Ray; screenplay by Satyajit Ray, based on the
    novel by Bibhuti Banerji; photography by Subrata Mitra; music
    composed and played by Ravi Shankar.   With Kanu Banerji,
    Karuna Benerji, Subir Banerji, Uma Das Gupta, Chunibala
    Devi, Reva Devi.   MAC[1]
One of the great films of all time and the first Bengali film shown
widely outside West Bengal.   The story is a profound study of a
boy's family, each member of which struggles to survive in their
ancestral village.   Over the hard life depicted the director manages
to sustain humor and joy.   This is the first part of the Apu Trilogy.

PHANTOM INDIA.   (INDES FANTOMES.)   Louis Malle, 1967-8.
    364 min. color. In 7 segments.   NYF
One of the best documentaries on India.   In six parts edited from
50 hours of film made by a small crew with a minimum of equipment.
PART 1.   THE IMPOSSIBLE CAMERA.   Shows a country of beautiful landscapes and hungry people.
PART 2.   THINGS SEEN IN MADRAS.   Contrasts the government's
methods with the religious and tradition-rooted peasants.
PART 3.   THE INDIANS AND THE SACRED.   The religious search
for immortality.
PART 4.   DREAM AND REALITY.   The city of Kerala, a community of contrasts and springboard for the future.
PART 5.   A LOOK AT THE CASTES.   The rigid system of social
distinction.
PART 6.   ON THE FRINGES OF INDIAN SOCIETY.   A look at
minorities--the Christians, Jews and outcast tribes.
PART 7.   BOMBAY: THE FUTURE INDIA.   The city capable of
change--India's springboard for the future.
All seven parts can be shown at one program or presented separ-
ately.

THE PINK CITY.   (PART 7.   The Glory That Remains Series.)
    BBC, 1969.   30 min.   color.   TL
An account of Jaipur's three famous maharajas, Man Singh, Jai
Singh, and Sawai Jai Singh.

RAGA.   Howard Worth, n.d.   With Ravi Shankar, Yehudi Menuhin
    and George Harrison.   NLC
Filmed in India and in Europe and the U.S.A.   Studies Ravi Shankar's music and its impact on Europe and the U.S.

SATYAJIT RAY.   B. C. Garga, n.d.   13 min.   b/w.   MAC[1]
The famous Indian filmmaker discusses his approach to filmmaking.
Includes scenes of Ray at work.

SATYAJIT RAY. NET, 1967. 28 min. b/w. IND
The Indian filmmaker discusses the philosophy that influences his
film production and his views on Western culture.

SERMONS IN STONE. (PART 5. The Glory That Remains Series.)
     BBC, 1969. 30 min. color. TL
How King Asoka encouraged the spread of Buddhism, told through
references to the beautiful reliefs, reliquaries, and sculpture that
remain.

THE SITAR. Hungry Mind Enterprises, 1973. 17 min. color.
     UCA
A report on the history, philosophy and ritual involved in Indian
classical music performed on the sitar.

TAGORE. India, 1961. 54 min. b/w. Direction and screenplay
     by Satyajit Ray; photography by Soumendu Roy; music by
     Iyotirindra Gangophyay. Narration in English by Satyajit
     Ray. MGH
A documentary on the late Dr. Rabindranath Tagore, educator,
writer, and winner of the Nobel Prize for Literature.

URVASI. Amin Q. Chaudri, 1972. 11 min. color. Directed by
     Amin Q. Chaudri; music by Ragunath Seth. With Preeti Nad-
     karni, Stephen Creado. ART
A reenactment of the legend about a disciple of Buddha who is
tempted by the dancing girl, Urvasi.

VILLAGE MAN, CITY MAN. South Asian Area Center, University
     of Wisconsin, n. d. 40 min. color. UWI
Follows a young mill worker in Delhi on a visit to his village.
Compares the Western life style with the Indian situation.

VINOBA BHAVE: WALKING REVOLUTION. Pilgrim, 1970. 39
     min. color. IFB, UUT
About Gandhi's disciple, Vinoba Bhave, and his efforts through a
"walking revolution" to revive Indian village life.

WELTHY FISHER. NET, 1967. 30 min. b/w. IND
A visit with Welthy Fisher, an educator who lives and works in India where she has founded training institutes and has promoted
learning with lectures, books, puppet shows.

WHERE ARE WE GOING? NET, 1968. 29 min. b/w. IND
A talk by Krishnamurti, Indian spiritual leader and writer about the
world crisis in terms of his spiritual beliefs.

THE WORLD OF APU. (APU SANSAR.) Satyajit Ray, 1959. 103
     min. b/w. In Bengali with English subtitles. Directed by
     Satyajit Ray; screenplay by Satyajit Ray, based on the novel
     "Aparajito" by Bibhuti Banerji; photography by Subrata Mitra;
     music composed and played by Ravi Shankar. With Soumitra
     Chatterjee, Sarmilla Tagore, Alok Chakravarty, Swapan

Mukherji. MAC[1]
The concluding part of Satyajit Ray's Apu Trilogy. Apu, now living in poverty in Calcutta, leaves school, tries to write a novel
and marries a beautiful Hindu girl. When his wife dies, he falls
apart, deserting his son.

Pakistan

DAY SHALL DAWN. Century, 1958. 100 min. b/w. In Urdu
  with English subtitles. Directed by Aejay Kardar; photographed by Walter Lasally; sound by John Fletcher; music
  by Timir Bahan Rahat, Nauman Taseer. With Triptri Mitra,
  Anees Ama, Maina Latif, Zurain Rakshi, Kazi Khaliq, and
  the people of Shaitnol. MGH
Not a condemnatory picture of poverty but an attempt to portray
the passive life of the poor people of Shaitnol, a village in Pakistan.

INDUSTRIAL BEGINNINGS IN WEST PAKISTAN. Films Inc., 1972.
  15 min. color. FI, VEC
Tells how the West Pakistani people, mostly Moslems, face a future that demands adaptation to the needs of an industrial society.

LAND OF BUDDHA. Armin Chaudhri, 1965. 17 min. color.
  ART
Some two hundred-year-old sculptures in Pakistan are used to tell
the story of Gautama Buddha.

PAKISTAN. Authentic, 1975. 12 min. color. MGH
An up-to-date account of the economic, social, and climatic aspects
of Pakistan.

PAKISTAN. Encyclopaedia Britannica Educational Corporation,
  1955. 14 min. color. UCO, UUT, UWY
Contrasts hot, humid East Pakistan with West Pakistan's desert regions and shows the unity achieved through the Moslem faith.

Sri Lanka (Ceylon)

CEYLON AND BALI: SOUTHEAST ASIAN ISLANDS. United World,
  1964. (Our World of the 60's Series.) 17 min. color.
  UEVA
Shows customs and daily life of the people of two islands, Ceylon
and Bali.

CEYLON, THE RESPLENDENT LAND. AV-ED, 1961. 13 min.
  color. AVE
The historical heritage of Ceylon and contemporary life of the people. With details of coconut harvesting, farming and fishing.

GEMS FROM A RICE PADDY. ACI, 1970. 11 min. color. ACI
A discussion of traditional mining and processing methods of pre-
cious gems, e.g. , sapphires, rubies, topazes and moonstones in
Ratnapura and Columbo. Also shows Ceylon as a modern country
with highways and the usual facilities of advanced technology, such
as telephones and telegraphs.

LAND OF THE BUDDHA. Delux, n. d. 20 min. color. UCA
Shows the art treasures found on Ceylon in castles and temples of
Buddha.

THE PEARL OF THE EAST. BBC and Odyssey, 1967. (Asia
    Series.) 25 min. color. TL
A trip to Ceylon with views of the Temple of Kandy, Buddhist and
Hindu ceremonies and other sites. Narrated by Lowell Thomas.

SONG OF CEYLON. John Grierson for Ceylon Tea Propaganda
    Board, 1934. 40 min. b/w. Directed by Basil Wright;
    commentary from Robert Knox's 17th-century account of
    Ceylon read by Lionel Wendt; music by Walter Leigh. PAR
Considered one of the finest documentaries ever made for its sensitive mood and camera movements. A view of Ceylon's traditional
culture contrasted with modern commerce circa 1934.

SRI LANKA: COASTAL VILLAGES AND TOWNS. BBC, 1974.
    (People of Many Lands Series.) 20 min. color. TL
A report on the varied and colorful life of a people who live off
the fish of the sea in addition to fruit, vegetables and rice.

SRI LANKA: LIFE IN THE HILLS. BBC, 1974. (People of Many
    Lands Series.) 26 min. color. TL
A visit to the Ratwatta tea estate in the low foothills between Kandy
and Matale. Shows detail of operation plus the life style of the
Sinhalese who live in the environs.

East Asia

    (Includes China, Japan, Korea, Ryukyu Islands, Taiwan [For-
    mosa])

General

ANCIENT ORIENT: THE FAR EAST. Coronet, 1957. 14 min.
    b/w. UCA
An account of the early Oriental civilizations in China, Japan and
India using reenactments and actual locales. Traces their heritage
from ancient times to the present.

LIFE IN THE FAR EAST. Gateway, 1969. 17 min. color. COR,
    UWY
The westernization of the Far East's great cities and their cultural
links to China.

ORIENTAL BRUSHWORK. Encyclopaedia Britannica Educational
     Corporation, 1951. 16 min. color. EBEC
Reveals the essential characteristics of Oriental painting, the materials used, the use of space and line. Includes work by Chinese
and Japanese artists.

TREASURES OF TIME: ORIENTAL ART. Horizon, 1963. 15
     min. color. UCA
A comparison of Chinese and Japanese art treasures, including the
influence of religion on both, plus contrasts in other aspects of
life. Shows furniture, ornaments, scrolls, porcelain, sculpture
and screens.

China

AGONIES OF NATIONALISM, 1800-1927. Films Inc., n. d. 23
     min. b/w. VEC, FI
Background of China's myths of power and how they crumbled in
the face of invasion, crushing of the Manchu Dynasty, and civil
war. Discusses Sun Yatsen and Chiang Kai-shek as well as the
communists.

THE ANCIENT CHINESE. International Film Foundation, 1974.
     24 min. color. EFD, IFF
A look at the Chinese people in their daily life. Emphasis on
artists, artifacts, and arts.

AT HOME IN CHINA: THE MODERN FAMILY. Jens Bjerre, n. d.
     13 min. color. PIC
The story of how Chinese young and old live together as a family
unit under one roof--on one hand adhering to tradition, and yet in-
corporating new ideas into daily life.

AN AWAKENING GIANT. PART I. CHINA: AN OPEN DOOR.
     Oxford, 1973. 20 min. color. OXF
The ideals and principles of Mao Tse-tung and major historical developments involving China during the twentieth century.

AWAY WITH ALL PESTS. Blue Bus, 1972. 60 min. b/w. TRI
Dr. Joshua Horn, the British surgeon who worked in China from
1954 to 1969, talks about his experiences there and, in particular,
about the sociological aspects of medical practice and research in
China.

BAREFOOT DOCTORS OF CHINA. Jens Bjerre, n. d. 13 min.
     color. PIC
About China's paramedics, or "barefoot doctors," who go into remote areas to set up clinics.

BATTLE OF CHINA. U. S. Signal Corps, 1944. (Why We Fight
     Series.) 67 min. b/w. PAR
One film of a motivational series that Frank Capra was asked to

make for the armed forces in World War II. Describes the Japanese plans for conquest, reviews Japanese attacks on China, and
shows China's cultural and industrial contributions. A propaganda
film that won a New York Film Critics Award.

BEHIND THE GREAT WALL OF CHINA. Leonardo Bonzi, 1959.
    96 min. color. English narration. Directed by Carlo Liz-
    zani; written and adapted for AromaRama by Sidney Kaufman.
A travelogue of modern China by Italian filmmaker Leonardo Bonzi.
Narrated by Chet Huntley. Includes scenes of Hong Kong.

BORN CHINESE: A STUDY OF THE CHINESE CHARACTER.
    BBC, 1969. 57 min. b/w. TL
A fresh approach to the study of the Chinese, this time as people,
not as political entities. Includes their culture, daily routine and
why they believe they are superior.

BUDDHISM IN CHINA. Wan-go Weng for the China Institute in
    America, n. d. 30 min. color. PIC
An award-winning film that surveys the basic ideas and evolution
of Chinese Buddhism.

CHINA! Felix Greene, 1965. 65 min. color. GRO, IMP
Felix Greene traveled thousands of miles to photograph the country, the people and conditions of communist China. Although now
superseded by later films, this documentary still comes off as a
powerful statement. Winner of many awards.

CHINA: A PORTRAIT OF THE LAND. Magnum, 1967. 18 min.
    color. EBEC, UCO, UWY
Covers economic progress in six regions: Manchuria, North China,
South China, Inner Mongolia, Sinkiang Province, and Tibet.

CHINA: A REVOLUTION REVISITED. Metromedia, 1971. 82
    min. b/w. EFD, FI
A new look at the Chinese Revolution in terms of its significance
in twentieth century history. Uses archival footage to cover the
fall of the Manchu Dynasty plus rare scenes of interviews and
events; also President Nixon's official visit.

CHINA: AN END TO ISOLATION. Filmfact Educational Produc-
    tions, England, 1972. 23 min. color. ACI, EFD
Mao Tse-tung's credo to "live simply, work hard" is traced for its
role in China's accomplishments.

CHINA: AN OPEN DOOR SERIES see AN AWAKENING GIANT
    (PART I); THE PAST IS PROLOGUE (PART II); TODAY AND
    TOMORROW (PART III)

CHINA AND ITS AGRICULTURE. Coronet, 1969. 16 min. color.
    COR
About China's efforts to produce enough food to feed its enormous
population.

CHINA AND ITS INDUSTRY. Coronet, 1969. 15 min. color. COR
How China has become one of the major industrial nations in Asia.

CHINA AND ITS PEOPLE. Coronet, 1969. 15 1/2 min. color.
    COR, UWY
A view of modern China, the most populous nation on earth, and
how it is trying to work for change.

CHINA AND THE WORLD. BBC, 1969. (Revolution in China
    Series.) 20 min. b/w. TL
Surveys the invasions of China by foreign powers, China's involvement in Korea, and the breakdown in relations with Russia after
1955.

CHINA: FEEDING ONE-FOURTH OF THE HUMAN RACE. (Alter-
    nate Title: CHINA: FEEDING ONE QUARTER OF THE
    HUMAN RACE.) Sandler/Wald, 1967. (China Series.) 16
    min. color. MGH
How China copes with the challenge of feeding her enormous population.

CHINA: MAO TSE-TUNG'S SYSTEM. BBC, 1971. 35 min. color.
    TL
A documentary on life and politics in contemporary China. Shows
the "classless" society, the improvements of health, literacy, agriculture.

CHINA: ROOTS OF MADNESS. Xerox, 1966. In 2 parts. PART
    I, 38 min.; PART II, 41 min. b/w. UUT, VEC, FI
Covers the fall of the Manchu Dynasty, the rise of Mao Tse-tung,
the resentment of foreign intervention. Includes interviews with
Burton Holmes and Pearl Buck.

CHINA: THE AWAKENING GIANT. Sandler/Wald, 1967. (China
    Series.) 17 min. color. MGH
Moves from a survey of China's geographical features to a study
of the achievement and plans of this country for industrial growth.

CHINA: THE INDUSTRIAL REVOLUTION. Sandler/Wald, 1967.
    (China Series.) 16 min. color. MGH, UCO, UUT
Focuses on problems which China must solve to become a major
industrial nation.

CHINA: THE LAND AND THE PEOPLE. Coronet, 1955. 14 min.
    color. COR
Shows the centuries-old, close relationship between the people of
China and the land.

CHINA: THE OLD AND THE NEW. Sandler/Wald, 1967. (China
    Series.) 16 min. color. MGH, UWY
Contrasts urban and rural China as well as old and new ways.

CHINA: THE RED SONS. Roger Whitaker, 1968. 52 min. color.
    MGH
A searching documentary made by two young Australians who show
candid interviews with workers, visits to six major cities without
censorship, even though the film was processed in Peking. (Also
available in two parts: PART I, 27 min.; PART II, 25 min.)

CHINA: THE SOCIAL REVOLUTION. Sandler/Wald, 1967. 17
    min. color. UCO, UUT, MGH
A history of Chinese society from the fall of the Manchu Dynasty
in 1911 to the revolution of 1949.

CHINA TODAY. NBC, 1972. 22 min. color. FI, VEC
Uses up-to-date footage to give a report on China, where participation is valued over efficiency.

CHINA UNDER COMMUNISM. Encyclopaedia Britannica Educational
    Corporation, 1962. Rev. ed. 22 min. color. EBEC,
    UCA, UUT, UWY
The report of the first U. S. newsman allowed into China to photograph new developments in the life style.

CHINA'S INDUSTRIAL REVOLUTION. Magnum, 1967. 16 min.
    color. EBEC, UCA, UCO, UWY
The struggle of the Communists to transform traditional China into
a modern industrial nation.

CHINA'S VILLAGES IN CHANGE. Magnum, 1967. EBEC, UCA,
    UCO, UWY
Description of modern improvements by the village people of south
China, north China, and Inner Mongolia, filmed by a Swiss camera-
man.

CHINESE BRONZES OF ANCIENT TIMES. Wan-go Weng, n. d.
    20 min. color. PIC
About the development and influence of ancient Chinese bronze ceremonial vessels representing an unusual and unique art.

CHINESE CERAMICS THROUGH THE AGES. Wan-go Weng, 1952.
    20 min. color. PIC
A presentation on the origin of porcelain ("chine") and its meaning
in the interdependence of various cultures.

CHINESE FIRECRACKERS. Wan-go Weng, 1950. 10 min. color.
    PIC
Shows the historical and cultural background, as well as the actual
making of "exploding bamboos" which symbolize festivity for the
Chinese people.

CHINESE FOLK DANCES. Wan-go Weng, n. d. 10 min. color.
    PIC
Describes the revival of interest in folk dancing among the Chinese
people. Shows a marriage and funeral drum dance plus a dance
taken from a drama from Southwest China.

CHINESE JADE CARVING. Wan-go Weng, 1950.   10 min.   color.
   PIC, UCA
About the beauty and symbolism of jade in the Chinese culture as
demonstrated by a master artist of jade carving.

CHINESE JOURNEY.   BBC and Odyssey, 1967.   (Asia Series.)
   25 min.   color.   TL
A journey up the Yangtze River from Shanghai to Peking, then beyond the Great Wall to Mongolia and the Gobi Desert.   Narrated
by Lowell Thomas.

CHINESE PAINTING THROUGH THE AGES.   Wan-go Weng, 1952.
   PIC
The evolution of Chinese painting, its unique features.

CHINESE PEASANT GOES TO MARKET.   Gateway, 1949.   10 min.
   b/w.   UCA
A view of a typical peasant-farmer of Yunnan Province at work.

CHINESE SCULPTURE THROUGH THE AGES.   Wan-go Weng, 1965.
   20 min.   color.   PIC, UCA
Traces the philosophical and religious roots of functional Chinese
sculpture in stone, bronze and jade.

CHINESE SHADOW PLAY.   Wan-go Weng, 1947.   10 min.   color.
   MGH, UCA
An account of an art that developed in the tenth century with characters of donkey skin parchment painted in transparent color which
perform behind an illuminated screen.

LA CHINOISE.   Productions de la Gueville, 1967.   95 min.   color.
   In French with English subtitles.   Directed and written by
   Jean Luc Godard.   With Anne Wizemsky, Jean-Pierre Leaud,
   Juliet Berto, Michel Semeniako.   NYF
Considered one of Jean-Luc Godard's best films, this is a study of
the Chinese cultural revolution and its implications.   In Paris five
pro-Chinese students discuss how to bring about a similar revolu-
tion in the West through terrorism.

CITIES OF CHINA.   Jens Bjerre, n. d.   13 min.   color.   PIC
A visit in China's most important cities: Peking, the cultural center, Shanghai, the largest and most industrialized, and Canton, the
most modern and westernized.

CIVIL WAR AND INVASION, 1927-1941.   David Wolper, 1967.
   (China: Century of Revolution Series.)   22 min.   b/w.   FI,
   UCA
The story of the factors that led to the ousting of Chiang Kai-shek
and the growing strength of Chinese Communists.

COMMUNIST CHINA.   McGraw-Hill, 1965.   22 min.   b/w.   MGH,
   UCO
A look at the present Communist regime in China and its goals for
economic and military power.

CONFUCIANISM.   NET, 1955.   (Religions of Man Series.)   30 min.
    b/w.   IND, UCA
A portrait of Confucius as a teacher and statesman who searched
for a way people could live together in harmony.

THE EAST IS RED.   East Is Red Enterprises, 1967.   130 min.
    color.   In Chinese with English subtitles.   MGH
An example of Chinese filmmaking in which the Chinese Communists tell of Chinese history, contemporary life and China's role in
international affairs.   Based on a theatrical spectacle that celebrated the fifteenth anniversary of the People's Liberation and the
withdrawal of Chiang Kai-shek.   The first Communist Chinese feature film released in the U.S.

EIGHT OR NINE IN THE MORNING.   Felix Greene, 1973.   (Felix
    Greene's China Series.)   25 min.   color.   TL
A study of education in China during the post-cultural revolution.
The title reflects Mao Tse-tung's likening of youth in the bloom of
life to "the sun at eight or nine in the morning."   British journalist Felix Greene went to China for five months in 1972 to make
this film series.

ENEMIES WITHIN AND WITHOUT, 1927-1944.   Films Inc., n.d.
    25 min.   b/w.   FI, VEC
Chiang Kai-shek and the Nationalists are discussed, along with
Chiang's failure to defeat the Communists, and his eventual alli-
ance with the Communists against Japan.

FACE OF RED CHINA.   CBS, 1958.   54 min.   b/w.   UCA, UCO
A report made inside Communist China in 1958.   Shows urban and
rural life.

THE FALL OF CHINA.   CBS, 1959.   27 min.   b/w.   MGH, UCO
Begins with 1945, the time of civil war in China, to the capture of
Nanking, Shanghai and Canton by the Communists.   Presents a vari-
ety of explanations for the Communist victory.

FARMING IN SOUTH CHINA.   United World, 1949.   (The Earth and
    Its Peoples Series.)   UCA, UUT
Shows a boy and his farmer family working in the fields and selling
their vegetables on their sampan.

FELIX GREENE'S CHINA SERIES   see   THE PEOPLE'S COM-
    MUNES; EIGHT OR NINE IN THE MORNING; SELF RELI-
    ANCE; THE PEOPLE'S ARMY; ONE NATION, MANY PEO-
    PLES; MEDICINE IN CHINA; FRIENDSHIP FIRST, COMPETI-
    TION SECOND

THE FORBIDDEN CITY.   NBC, 1973.   43 min.   color.   FI
A look at the 78 palaces in Kai Kung, the fortress that served as
home for the emperors of China from 1421 to 1911.

FRIENDSHIP FIRST, COMPETITION SECOND.   Felix Greene, 1973.
(Felix Greene's China Series.)   25 min.   color.   TL
British journalist Felix Greene, who released an earlier film on
China (see CHINA!) in the 1960s, returned to China for five months
in 1972 to make a series.   This part shows the Chinese performing
in various sports, including many Western ones, in the spirit which
emphasizes hospitality over competition.

FROM WAR TO REVOLUTION.   BBC, n.d.   (Revolution in China
     Series.)   20 min.   b/w.   TL
Covers Chinese history in the 19th century as prelude to the development of the Chinese Republic in 1911, its fall, Civil War,
Chiang Kai-shek and the Nationalist Party, the Japanese invasion
and Chiang's defeat by Mao Tse-tung.

THE GOOD EARTH.   Encyclopaedia Britannica Educational Corpo-
     ration, 1937.   40 min.   b/w.   UCA
An edited version of Pearl Buck's story, produced as a film by
Metro-Goldwyn-Mayer, about a Chinese family in poverty-ridden
China of the 1930s.   With Luise Rainer and Paul Muni.   Directed
by Sidney Franklin.

THE GOOD EARTH.   MGM, 1937.   138 min.   b/w.   Directed by
     Sidney Franklin; screenplay by Talbot Jennings, Tess Slesing-
     er and Claudine West; based on the novel by Pearl Buck and
     the stage adaptation by Owen Davis and Donald Davis.   With
     Paul Muni, Luise Rainer, Walter Connolly, Soo Yong, Keye
     Luke.   FI
The story of the House of Wang Lung, the farmer, who finds tragedy
when he neglects his land.

GROWING UP IN CHINA.   Jens Bjerre, n.d.   13 min.   color.   PIC
A look at the schools of China and the young people who attend
them.

IMPRESSIONS OF CHINA.   Don McWilliams, 1974.   22 min.
     color.   MAR
What the first high school students to visit China since 1949 saw
and thought during their visit.

INDUSTRIAL CHINA.   Jens Bjerre, n.d.   13 min.   color.   PIC
China's phenomenal industrial and technological advances in the
twentieth century.

INSIDE RED CHINA.   CBS, 1966.   51 min.   color.   CAR
Filmed for CBS by a West German production team inside Red
China.   Shows daily life in the cities and rural areas.   Includes
comments by Hans Konigsberger, Robert Guillan and Dr. Han
Suyin.

INSIDE RED CHINA.   NBC, 1965.   45 min.   b/w.   MAC, UCA
A tour of China in 1957 by NBC newsreel cameraman Robert Cohen.
Includes an updated narration of the filmmaker.

A JOURNEY FORWARD: CHESTER RONNING IN CHINA. Crawley,
    n. d. 50 min. color. CRA
Canada's retired Ambassador returned to China after 20 years' absence and traveled extensively to study changes and developments.

LIFE IN A CHINESE COMMUNE. Jens Bjerre, n. d. 13 min.
    color. PIC
The Chinese commune, like the Israeli kibbutz, is an economic,
political and social unit run by the people who live in it. This is
a study of a large commune near a metropolitan area and a small
one in a rural area.

LIFE IN NORTH CHINA. Public Media, 1971. 18 min. color.
    FI, VEC
Shows rural and urban workers of northeast China celebrating National Liberation Day in the streets of a city.

MADAME CHIANG KAI-SHEK. David Wolper, 1965. 27 min.
    color. SEF
Uses newsreel footage to tell the story of the dynamic woman who
fought for social, medical and technological advances in her country before leaving it during the Communist revolution.

MAO TSE-TUNG. David Wolper, 1963. 26 min. b/w. MGH
The full life story of China's political leader from his birth in 1893
to the modern period.

MAO VS. CHIANG. Metromedia, n. d. 25 min. b/w. VEC
The story of the 25-year conflict between the two men who each
aspired to be China's ruler. Covers Mao's victory in 1949. Narrator: Edmond O'Brien.

MAO'S CHINA. Peter Gettinger, 1971. 77 min. color. MAC
A major documentary about The People's Republic of China and the
effects of Mao Tse-tung's cultural revolution.

MAO'S CHINA. Canadian Broadcasting Corp. , n. d. 21 min.
    color. VEC
About the emergence of China as a major power through application
of Mao Tse-tung's doctrine.

MEDICINE IN CHINA. Felix Greene, 1973. (Felix Greene's China
    Series.) 25 min. color. TL
British journalist Felix Greene, who released an earlier film on
China (see CHINA!) in the 1960s, returned to China for five months
in 1972 to make a series. This part is a study of the dramatic
improvements in Chinese medicine and the health of the Chinese.

MISSION TO YENAN. Films Inc. , 1972. 32 min. color. FI,
    VEC
An account of the U. S. relationship to Communist China in the
1940s and the fate of members of a U. S. mission to China.

MISUNDERSTANDING CHINA, PARTS I AND II. CBS, 1972. 51
   min. UIO
A concise history of Chinese and American relations, showing how
public communications media built racist and inaccurate ideas about
this country and its people.

THE NEW CHINA. BBC, n. d. (Revolution in China Series.) 20
   min. b/w. TL
Studies 20 years of Mao Tse-tung's rule: the attack on landlords,
establishment of farm cooperatives, equality for women and the
Red Guard inquisitions of 1966-7.

ONE FOURTH OF HUMANITY. Edgar Snow, 1968. 74 min.
   color. IMP
The late Edgar Snow, who knew Mao Tse-tung and Chou En-lai for
35 years, made this film out of footage accumulated through three
decades of visits to China. Includes the only existing footage of
the Long March, plus early pictures of historic personages in the
Revolution.

ONE NATION, MANY PEOPLES. Felix Greene, 1973. (Felix
   Greene's China Series.) 25 min. color. TL
British journalist Felix Greene, who released an earlier film on
China (see CHINA!) in the 1960s, returned to China for five
months in 1972 to make a series. This part is a report on the
wide variety of ethnic groups, not all of whom are Chinese, such
as Mongolians, Uighurs, who live in China.

THE OTHER HALF OF THE SKY: A CHINA MEMOIR. Shirley
   MacLaine, 1975. 74 min. color. PPC
Covers the first American Women's Delegation to The People's Republic of China. The delegation, led by Shirley MacLaine, included
women of diverse racial and socio-economic backgrounds.

PAINTING THE CHINESE LANDSCAPE. Wan-go Weng, 1952. 10
   min. color. PIC
Four steps in Chinese landscape painting are illustrated: layout,
brushwork, shading, and retouching. Emphasizes the philosophical
and cultural aspects of Chinese art as contrasted with Western art.

THE PAST IS PROLOGUE. PART II: CHINA: AN OPEN DOOR.
   Oxford, 1973. 20 min. color. OXF
Newsman John Roderick covers international relations with China
and gives his personal view of Mao Tse-tung and Chou En-lai as
leaders.

PEIPING FAMILY. International Film Foundation, 1948. 21 min.
   b/w. EFD, IFF
A family prepares to survive during the siege of Peiping by Red
Army. A historic view of traditional Chinese life before the present regime.

PEKING: MARCO POLO'S WONDER. Athena, 1950. (Land of China

Series.) 10 min. color. UCA
A brief overview of Peking as China's perennial capital.

PEKING OPERA. Peking Film Studio, 1968. 32 min. color.
    GRO, IMP
A film from Communist China of an actual performance of the Peking Opera, a sophisticated blend of dance and music describing in
this case the "Dance of the Warriors," a seventh century tale of a
revolt against despotic government. Directed by Tzen Fan.

PEKING REMEMBERED. CCM, n. d. 40 min. color. MAC
A sensitive re-creation of pre-Communist Peking with carefully
researched art, folklore and history. Directed by Dave Butler;
narrated by Paul Henreid.

THE PEOPLE OF PEOPLE'S CHINA. David Jayne, Art Holch,
    1973. 50 min. color. XER
A five-part film on the People's Republic of China made on a journalistic expedition to study the daily life of the Chinese.

THE PEOPLE'S ARMY. Felix Greene, 1973. (Felix Greene's
    China Series.) 25 min. color. TL
British journalist Felix Greene, who released an earlier film on
China (see CHINA!) in the late 1960s, returned to China for five
months in 1972 to make a series. This part is the first inside
view of the Chinese Army which is revealed as more than a fighting force--a school of politics, engineering, agriculture, and an
informal organization in which officers and men share similar uni-
forms, quarters, food.

THE PEOPLE'S COMMUNES. Felix Greene, 1973. (Felix Greene's
    China Series.) 25 min. color. TL
British journalist Felix Greene who released an earlier film on
China (see CHINA!) in the late 1960s, returned to China for five
months in 1972 to make a series. This part describes the daily
life of the Chinese peasants.

RED CHINA. NBC, 1962. 54 min. b/w. MGH, UCA
Swiss photographer Fernand Gigon made this film inside China to
show changes under the Communist regime.

RED CHINA DIARY WITH MORLEY SAFER. CBS, 1968. 54 min.
    color. BFA
Two CBS newsmen managed to film the first documentary of Red
China by a U. S. television network. Explores the life of modern
China.

RED CHINA: MAO TSE-TUNG'S SYSTEM. BBC, n. d. 50 min.
    color. TL
About the single purpose, single direction of Mao Tse-tung's China.
Shows the flourishing industry, people hard at work and propagand-
ists hostile to the U. S. Winner of 1971 New York International
Film Festival award.

RED CHINA: PEKING AND THE COMMUNE.   Universal Education
and Visual Arts, 1968.   22 min.   color.   UEVA
A team of Australian filmmakers photographed scenes of city and
country life in modern China.

RED CHINA: YEAR OF THE GUN?   ABC, 1967.   51 min.   color.
MGH
Discusses China's relationship to Vietnam and its possible impact
on the rest of the world.

RED DETACHMENT OF WOMEN.   People's Republic of China, n. d.
105 min.   color.   TWN
A story told through Chinese ballet about a peasant woman who es-
capes her master and joins the Red Army.

REPORT FROM CHINA.   Unijapan Films, 1967.   90 min.   color.
RAD, VEC
Concentrates on agricultural and industrial development of north-
eastern China.   A study of the effects of the Cultural Revolution.
Photographed by a Japanese team during 1966.

REQUIEM FOR A FAITH.   Hartley, 1968.   14 min.   color.   NACC
Houston Smith narrated and wrote this documentary on the fast dis-
appearing Buddhism in Tibet.

RISE OF COMMUNIST POWER, 1941-1967.   Films Inc., 1967.
(China: Century of Revolution Series.)   29 min.   b/w.   UCA
Traces the events in China that led to the Communist take-over in
1949 and subsequent developments.

SAMPAN FAMILY.   International Film Foundation, 1949.   16 min.
b/w.   EFD, IFF, UCA, IFP, UCO, UUT
One of the last films made in China before the 1949 Revolution.   A
work day in the life of a Chinese family near Foochow in Fukien
province.

SEARCH FOR NATIONAL UNITY, 1800-1927.   David Wolper, 1967.
(China: Century of Revolution Series.)   29 min.   b/w.
UCA
Traces China from the Opium War, the Boxer Rebellion, the Man-
chu Dynasty's corruption, to Sun Yat-sen's nationalism and the
eventual development of the communist state.

SELF RELIANCE.   Felix Greene, 1973.   (Felix Greene's China
Series.)   25 min.   color.   TL
British journalist Felix Greene, who released an earlier film on
China (see CHINA!) in the late 1960s returned to China for five
months in 1972 to make a series.   This part describes China's
goals in developing industrialization: to decentralize, to encourage
rural involvement in small-scale efforts.

SHANGHAI: THE NEW CHINA.   CBS, 1974.   33 min.   color.
BFA

An American reporter comments on his observations during a visit to Shanghai. Shows government leaders talking about Shanghai's future, people discussing their reactions to Shanghai's changes in recent times.

THE STORY OF CHINESE ART.   Wan-go Weng, 1952.   20 min. color.   PIC
Not only the beauty of the art works selected, but also their significance in culture, history, philosophy and religion is stressed in this basic survey of Chinese art.

TAOISM.   NET, 1955.   (Religions of Man Series.)   30 min.   b/w. UCA
An account of Lao-tzu, his work, "The Way of Life" and the creative quiet favored by Taoism.

TIBET.   Almanac, 1955.   20 min.   b/w.   ALM, PEN
Follows an expedition to the Himalayas.   Shows the Plateau of Tibet and the city of Lhasa along with customs and ceremonies.

TIBETAN TRADERS.   Atlantis, 1957.   27 min.   b/w.   PEN
Tibetan traders purchase items such as rice and sugar at the foot of the mountains in India, then goats carry the goods over perilous trails to high markets in Tibet, where bartering is done for salt and wool.

TIBETAN TRADERS.   Atlantis, 1968.   2nd ed.   22 min.   color. ATL, SYR, USC
The life style and bartering methods of nomadic traders who journey from the lower slopes of the Himalayas to meet traders of the Mongolian Plateau.

TODAY AND TOMORROW.   Oxford, 1973.   (China: An Open Door Series.)   15 min.   color.   OXF
Contrasts the old and new China.   The life style of the typical Chinese citizen is discussed along with the effect of admission of the People's Republic of China to the United Nations.

A TOWN BY THE YANGTZE.   Wan-go Weng, n. d.   10 min.   color. PIC
A visit to Changshu, a medieval Chinese town near Shanghai, for centuries the home of famous artists, scholars, poets, and philosophers.

A TRIP TO MODERN CHINA.   King Screen, 1973.   26 min.   color. BFA
The narrator, a man who hasn't seen China since 1949, travels throughout rural and urban China of today and draws comparisons between the past and the present.

TWO CHINESE DANCES.   Athena, 1948.   10 min.   color.   UCA
Dancer Tai Ai-lien, who has traveled extensively in China, demonstrates ceremonial dances and dance drama of the Chinese Southwest.

THE TWO FACES OF CHINA.   René Burri/Magnum, 1970.   50
   min.   color.   PIC
A contemporary view of China and its people as seen through the
eyes of René Burri, a Swiss visitor.   An award-winning film.

A VILLAGE IN CHINA TODAY.   Sandler/Wald, 1966.   17 min.
   MGH, UCO
A visit to Mei Jung, a small village in southeast China which typi-
fies the life and farming methods of the Chinese rural people elsewhere.

WAR IN CHINA: 1932-1945.   CBS, 1957.   27 min.   color.   MGH,
   UCO
The Chinese resistance to the Japanese invasion attempt just prior
to World War II.

YIN HSIEN.   Michael Whitney, 1974.   8 min.   color.   PYR
Using a computerized optical printer, the filmmaker presents the
real and non-real as if through a mist.   Yin Hsien (meaning ap-
pear-disappear) describes the treatment of the subject--in this
case the Chinese martial arts of T'ai-chi Chuan and Kung Fu.

Hong Kong

ACHIEVEMENT IN HONG KONG.   International Film Bureau, 1958.
   15 min.   color.   IFB
An account of the resettlement of the many Chinese who fled to
Hong Kong, from their early makeshift quarters to their later improved housing.

CHINA COAST FISHING.   Norman N. Miller, 1974.   (Faces of
   Change Series.)   19 min.   color.   FF
A study of modernization and its effect on the Chinese who fish
in the China coast area (Hong Kong) in large junks.

HONG KONG, CROSSROADS OF THE ORIENT.   United World,
   1964.   (Today's People in Our Changing World Series.)   17
   min.   color.   UEVA
About the problems of Hong Kong as a center for refugees from
China.

HONG KONG: FREE PORT.   LeMont, 1961.   21 min.   color.
   LMF
About the problems of a free port to which Chinese refugees immi-
grate.   Shows British projects to help refugees.

HONG KONG: PEARL OF THE ORIENT.   CCM, 1972.   (Thirteen
   from Asia Series.)   15 min.   color.   MAC
Written and filmed by Asians about the present-day life and background of Hong Kong.

HOY FOK AND THE ISLAND SCHOOL. Norman N. Miller, 1974.
(Faces of Change Series.) 32 min. color. FF
A visit with a fourteen-year-old boy who resides on a fishing junk
in the Hong Kong territory.

THE ISLAND FISHPOND. Norman N. Miller, 1974. (Faces of
Change Series.) 13 min. color. FF
How Hong Kong is attempting to increase productivity on the island
of Tai a Chau.

ISLAND IN THE CHINA SEA. Norman N. Miller, 1974. (Faces
of Change Series.) 33 min. color. FF
Shows a typical fisherman and a farmer of Tai a Chau, an island
in the China Sea.

THE OPIUM TRAIL. Independent Television Corporation, n.d.
60 min. color. ITC
A probing survey of the opium-smuggling industry that operates
from Burma to Hong Kong. Describes the enormous profits at the
expense of the growers, the despair of addicts and the corruption
in Southeast China and elsewhere.

OUR MAN IN HONG KONG. NBC, 1961. 54 min. b/w. MGH
A comprehensive tour of Hong Kong. Narrated by David Brinkley.
An NBC "Special Reports" film made for television.

A PIER ON THE CONTINENT. CCM, 1972. (Thirteen from Asia
Series.) 15 min. color. MAC
Written and filmed by Asians about the present-day life and back-
ground of Kowloon, Hong Kong.

SOUND OF A CITY. CCM, n.d. 12 min. color. MAC
An "Education Come Alive" film about Hong Kong, the British crown
colony that serves as door to mainland China.

THREE ISLAND WOMEN. Norman N. Miller, 1974. (Faces of
Change Series.) 17 min. color. FF
Three women of different ages and walks of life compare life today
with the situation in the past.

Japan

AN AUTUMN AFTERNOON. (SAMMA NO AJI.) Yasujiro Ozu,
1962. 112 min. color. In Japanese with English subtitles.
Directed by Yasujiro Ozu; screenplay by Kogo Noda and Yasujiro Ozu. With Chishu Ryu, Shima Iwashita, and Keiji Sada.
NYF
This is Ozu's last film. A widower attempts to marry off his only
daughter in this revealing study of modern Japan where old ways
clash with the new culture.

BAD BOYS. (FURYO SHONEN.) Susumu Hani, 1960. 90 min.
b/w. In Japanese with English subtitles. Directed by Susumu
Hani; screenplay by Susumu Hani, based on the book "Pinioned
Wings"; photography by Mitsuji Kanou; music by Toru Takemitsu. With Yukio Yamada, Hirokozu Yoshitake, Kochiro
Yamazaki, Yasuo Kurokawa, Masayuki Ito. MAC1
The grim story of delinquent boys made on actual locales with non-
professional actors (former reform school inmates). One boy who
eventually succeeds in earning probation is the film's subject.

THE BAD SLEEP WELL. (WARUI YATSU HODO YUKU NEMURU.)
Tomiyuki Tanaka and Akira Kurosawa, 1960. 135 min.
color. cinemascope. In Japanese with English subtitles.
Directed by Akira Kurosawa; screenplay by Akira Kurosawa,
Hideo Oguni, Eijiro Hisaita, Ryuzo Kikushima, and Shinobu
Hashimoto; photography by Yuzuru Aizawa; music by Masaru
Sato. With Toshiro Mifune, Takeshi Kato, Masayuki Mori,
Takashi Shimura, Akira Nishimura. MAC1
A tale of revenge set in a milieu of corrupt executives in a govern-
ment housing corporation.

THE BAILIFF. (SANSHO DAYU. SANSHO, THE BAILIFF.)
Masaichi Nagata, 1954. 125 min. b/w. In Japanese with
English subtitles. Directed by Kenji Mizoguchi; screenplay
by Juli Yahiro and Yoshikata Yoda, based on the novel by
Ogai Mori; photography by Kezuo Miyogawa; music by Fumio
Hayasaka. With Kinuyo Tanaka, Yoshiaki Hanayagi, Kyoko
Kagawa, Eitaro Shindo. MAC1
A story with a folk-legend quality set in 11th century Japan about
a mother and children separated and sold into slavery when they
were to join their banished father. A tyrannical bailiff is the one
to whom the children are sold. A poetic film of great moral power
and beauty.

BAMBOO: PLANT OF A THOUSAND USES. Sterling S. Beath and
Robert Lang, 1967. 14 min. color. BFA
A study of bamboo and its uses in modern Japanese life.

THE BOMB. Thames Television, 1973. (The World at War.) 60
min. color. RAY, RIT
The dropping of the bomb on Hiroshima and Nagasaki and the effect
on World War II. Lord Laurence Olivier narrates.

BONSEKI: THE JAPANESE ART OF ROCK PAINTING. Leo
Steiner for Fotosonic, n.d. 5 min. color. PIC
How the Japanese create land and sea scapes with sand and stone
in the oldest of Japanese arts dating back to the seventh century.

BOY. Sozasha-A.T.G., 1969. 97 min. color. In Japanese with
English subtitles. Directed by Nagisa Oshima; screenplay by
Tsutomu Tamura. With Tetsuo Abe, Fumio Watanabe, Akiki
Koyama, Tsuyoshi Kimoshita. GRO
A study of a child's fantasy and sense of reality in conflict. A

young boy is forced by his parents to throw himself in the path of
automobiles.

BUDDHA. Daiei, 1965. 134 min. color. Dubbed in English.
    Directed by Kenji Misumi; screenplay by Fuji Yahiro. With
    Kojiro Hongo, Charito Solis, Shintaro Katsu, Machiko Kyo.
    UNAR
An ornate life portrait of Gautama, the Enlightened One.

BUDDHISM, PART 2. International Communications, 1968. (Re-
    ligions of the Eastern World Series.) 15 min. color. DOU
A discussion of Japanese Buddhist sects, including Zen.

BUNKA. Classroom Film Distributors, n. d. 12 min. color.
    UCA
An introduction to Japanese culture, including its arts of dance,
music and flower arrangement.

BUNRAKU PUPPET. NHK Japan, 1968. 35 min. b/w. FI
A visit with the Bunraku puppet handlers and makers of Japan and
with the traditional stage art of Bunraku that involves Tayu chant-
ers, Shamisen players and puppets.

THE BURMESE HARP. (BIRUMA NO TATEGOTO.) Masayuki
    Takagi for Nikkatsu, 1956. 116 min. b/w. In Japanese
    with English subtitles. Directed by Kon Ichikawa; screenplay
    by Natto Wada, based on a story by Michio Takeyama;
    photography by Minoru Yokoyama; music by Akira Ifukube.
    With Shoji Yasui, Rentaro Mikuni, Tatsuya Mihashi, Taniye
    Kitabayashi, Yenosuke Ito. MAC[1]
A young private, using a harp as signal, serves as advance scout
for a Japanese unit trying to escape from Burma to Thailand at
the end of World War II. Eventually he is separated from his
comrades and experiences a number of grim encounters. A film
about war guilt and people under stress.

CAPTIVE'S ISLAND. (SHOKEI NO SHIMA. PUNISHMENT ISLAND.)
    Shintaro Ishihara, 1966. 87 min. color. cinemascope. In
    Japanese with English subtitles. Directed by Mashiro Shin-
    oda; written by Shintaro Ishihara, based on a story by Taijun
    Takeda; photography by Tatsuo Suzuki; music by Toru Take-
    mitsu. With Akira Nitta, Rentaro Mikuni, Shima Iwashita,
    Kei Sato, Kinzo Shin. MAC[1]
Evil, its nature and effect on those it touches, is the theme of this
revenge drama about a man who returns to an island where he was
cruelly treated by a reform school guard.

CENTURY OF IMPERIALISM. Metromedia, n. d. (The Japan
    Series.) 30 min. b/w. VEC
Describes Japan from 1850 through 1945 and the rise and fall of
her imperialism in particular.

CERAMIC ART: POTTERS OF JAPAN. Richard E. Peeler, 1968.
16 min. color. MGH
Five Japanese potters demonstrate the traditional methods of Japanese pottery making.

CITY LIFE IN THE NEW JAPAN. University of California, 1961.
29 min. b/w. IND
The ways of a westernized "new" family and a traditional "old" family are contrasted to show the rate of change and the influence of the city Tokyo.

COLLISION WITH JAPAN, 1931-1941. ABC, 1966. (Roosevelt
Years Series.) 22 min. b/w. UCA
The relations of Japan with other countries before Pearl Harbor, the factors that led to the Japanese invasion of Manchuria and the events of December 7, 1941.

COLORFUL NIKKO. Alfred T. Palmer, n.d. 14 min. color.
UCA
A visit to some of Japan's shrines, the tomb of Leyasu, Cryptomeria Avenue and the village of Nikko.

COMMUNIST PARTY IN JAPAN. NET, 1961. (Japan: Changing
Years Series.) 29 min. b/w. IND, UCA
Discusses the growth of the Communist Party in Japan from pre-World War II days to the 1961 date of this kinescope.

CONSPIRACY IN KYOTO. University of Indiana, 1953. (Arts of
the Orient Series.) 21 min. color. IND, UCA
Uses narrative scrolls of the 12th, 13th and 14th centuries, predecessors of today's motion pictures, for its material. The story is about an innocent man, accused of burning the Imperial Gate, who is eventually vindicated. Based on the "Ban Dainagon."

DEATH BY HANGING. Sozosha, 1968. 117 min. b/w. In
Japanese with English subtitles. Directed by Nagisa Oshima; music by Hikaru Hayashi; photography by Yasuhiro Yoshioka. With Undo-Yun, Akiko Koyama, Kei Sato, Fumio Watanabe, Toshiro Ishido. Narrated by Jagisa Oshima. GRO
A much-acclaimed masterpiece which studies law and guilt in an expressionistic manner. A condemned man must be executed a second time and the police, in acting out his crime to convince him of his guilt, also commit rape and murder.

DEMOCRACY AND POLITICS. NET, 1961. (Japan: Changing
Years Series.) 29 min. b/w. IND, UCA
Explores the political history of Japan from early times to the formation of a democratic government in 1945.

DIARY OF YUNBOGI BOY. Nagisa Oshima, n.d. 24 min. b/w.
NYF
The diary and still shots of Yunbogi, a ten-year old deserted Korean boy, who roams the streets, a victim of Asian politics. Directed by Japanese director Nagisa Oshima.

DISCOVERING THE MUSIC OF JAPAN. Bernard Wilets, 1967.
    22 min. color. BFA
Provides historical background for the musical instruments--the
shakuhachi, the koto and the samisen--and examples of singing,
dancing, and musical performance.

DODES 'KA-DEN. Akira Kurosawa, 1972. 140 min. color. In
    Japanese with English subtitles. Directed by Akira Kurosawa;
    screenplay by Akira Kurosawa, Hideo Oguni and Shinobu
    Hashimoto, based on "The Town Without Seasons" by Shugaro
    Yamamoto; photography by Tawao Saito and Yasumichi Fuku-
    zawa; music by Toru Takemitsu. With Yoshitaka Zushi, Jun-
    zaburo Ban, Kiyoko Tange. JAN
The title means "clickety-clack" and represents the theme that begins and ends the short stories on which the film is based--a de-
mented youth, who believes he is a train motorman running a line
in the garbage dump near where his mother and other poor people
live, is seen driving his imaginary train back and forth.

DRUNKEN ANGEL. (YOIDORE TENSHI.) Toho, 1948. 102 min.
    b/w. In Japanese with English subtitles. Directed by Akira
    Kurosawa; screenplay by Akira Kurosawa and Keinosuke Veg-
    usa; photography by Tukeo Ito; music by Fumio Hayasaka.
    With Toshiro Mifune, Takashi Shimura, Reizaburo Yamamoto,
    Michivo Kogure, Chieko Nakakita. MAC[1]
A postwar film about one doctor's attempt to bring about the moral
recovery of the human wrecks around him. Set in a squalid neighborhood dominated by young gangsters. This was Director Kurosawa's first award-winning film.

EDUCATION IN THE NEW JAPAN. University of Michigan, 1961.
    29 min. b/w. IND
Highlights of Japan's past and present educational systems.

EMOTION. Nobuhiko Ohbayashi, n.d. 40 min. color. MAC[1]
Filmmaker Nobuhiko Ohbayashi's experimental film made in homage
to French director Roger Vadim. A series of special effects reflecting the dream life of a girl.

THE EMPEROR AND A GENERAL. Toho, 1967. 29 min. b/w.
    IND
An excerpt from a Japanese feature film of the same name about
the events in 1945 when the Japanese decided to surrender to the
Americans.

FAMILY LIFE IN JAPAN: REMEMBER, I'M ME. McGraw-Hill
    and George Stoney, 1969. 10 min. color. MGH
Follows two Japanese girls to examine their life style in Tokyo
with their immediate family, and by contrast, also gives a view of
life in the country. Includes religious practices, grave sites,
temple gardens.

FANTASY CITY. Tatsuo Shimamura, n. d. 6 min. color. MAC[1]
An animated film by Tatsuo Shimamura describing the complex life
of the city with silhouettes, abstract shapes, surrealistic settings.

FISHING ON THE COAST OF JAPAN. International Film Founda-
tion, 1963. 13 min. color. IFF
Authentic Japanese music accompanies this photographic study of
Japanese people fishing in their unique way.

GARDENS OF JAPAN. Japan, n. d. 10 min. color. CGJ
Discusses gardens of Japan in terms of the Japanese love of nature. A film produced by the Japanese government.

GATE OF HELL. Masaichi Nagata, 1954. 86 min. color. In
Japanese with English subtitles. Directed by Teinosuke Kinu-
gasa; screenplay by Teinosuke Kinugasa; based on a play by
Kan Kikuchi. With Kazuo Hasegawa, Machiko Kyo. SWA,
TWY, NC
A thirteenth century legend about a samurai who loves a Japanese
lady whom he rescues during a palace revolt, only to find out later
that she is already married. A much-awarded film.

HARVEST IN JAPAN. International Film Foundation, 1964. 11
min. color. EFD, IFF
Daily life on a farm in Okayama province with details of rice cut-
ting, making rope, and the Harvest Feast celebrated in the farmer's home.

HIROHITO. David Wolper, 1963. 26 min. b/w. MGH
A portrait of Japan's Emperor Hirohito whose life time has spanned
periods of defeat and recovery in Japan.

HIROSHIMA. CBS, n. d. 26 min. b/w. AIM
About the U. S. bomber crew that dropped the first atom bomb on
Hiroshima, Japan.

HIROSHIMA, MON AMOUR. Alain Resnais, 1959. 88 min. b/w.
In French with English subtitles. Also English dubbed version
available. Directed by Alain Resnais; screenplay by Marguerite Duras; photography by Sacha Vierny and Michio Takahashi; music by Giovanni Fusco and Georges Delerue. With
Emmanuelle Riva, Eiji Okada. MAC[1], MGH, CPC
A French actress and a Japanese architect meet and fall in love
in Hiroshima. Both have suffered in the War, he in Japan, she
in Europe. Director Resnais' expressionistic treatment of two
anguished people has been called "a landmark in the history of the
film form."

HIROSHIMA, NAGASAKI. Erick Barnouw and Paul Ponder, 1969.
16 min. b/w. IMP
Made of footage by Japanese cameramen on the U. S. Air Force's
bombing of Hiroshima and Nagasaki.

HOODLUM SOLDIER.   (HEITAI YAKUZA)   Yasuzo Masumura,
    1965. 103 min. b/w. Cinemascope. In Japanese with
    English subtitles.   Directed by Yasuzo Masumura; screenplay
by Ryuzo Kikushima, based on a story by Yoriyoshi Arima;
photography by Setsuo Kobayashi; music by Naozumi Yamamoto. With Shintaro Katsu, Takahiro Ramura, Keiko Awaji,
Eiko Taki, Mikio Narita. MAC[1]
A powerful anti-war film about two Japanese soldiers at the Rus-
sian border during World War II. One hates the war, and the
other finds it useful for personal reasons--yet they manage to become friends.

HOP SCOTCH.   Kenji Kanesaka, n. d.   10 min. b/w.   MAC[1]
Confrontations between police and demonstrators are interposed with
episodes of a child playing, a couple making love, and other
events--all taking place on a hopscotch court.

THE IMMACULATE EMPEROR.   BBC, 1972.   60 min.   color.
    TL
A documentary on the life of Emperor Hirohito, including his years
as the Son of Heaven, the center of his country's religious cult.

IYOMANDE: THE AINU BEAR FESTIVAL.   University of Califor-
    nia, 1935.   Re-edited with sound in 1971.   26 min. b/w.
    UCA
A British doctor, Neil Gordon, studied the Ainu people of non-
Japanese stock who live on Hokkaido Island, Japan as they were
in the 1930s.   Illustrates the role of animism in their lives.   Includes a festival and examples of daily life.

JAPAN.   International Film Foundation, 1958.   27 min.   color.
    EFD, IFF
An introduction to modern Japan showing a new nation built on the
roots of tradition.   An award-winning film.

JAPAN.   Walt Disney, 1958.   (People and Places Series.)   27
    min.   color.   ASF
A report on the unique culture of the Japanese people.

JAPAN.   Thames Television, 1973.   (The World at War Series.)
    60 min.   color.   RIT, RAY
A documentary study using historic footage of the Japanese experience during World War II.   Lord Laurence Olivier narrates.

JAPAN: A NEW DAWN OVER ASIA.   Wolper, 1965.   50 min.
    b/w.   VEC, FI
Describes Japan of the immediate post-World War II period in her
effort to build a modern industrialized state.   Narration by Richard
Baseheart.

JAPAN: AN HISTORICAL OVERVIEW.   Coronet, 1964.   14 min.
    color.   COR, UWY
The outstanding events in Japan's history from 800 B. C. to the
present.

JAPAN: AN INTRODUCTION. Wayne Mitchell, 1968. 16 1/2
    min. color. BFA
An overview of Japan, an interesting country of traditional and industrial contrasts.

JAPAN: ANSWER IN THE ORIENT. NET, 1965. (Population
    Problem Series.) 60 min. color. IND, UCA
How the Japanese cope with the balance between births and deaths,
via late marriage, fertility control measures and legalized abor-
tion. Also available in Spanish, Portuguese and French language
versions.

JAPAN: EAST IS WEST. NBC, 1963. 23 min. color. MGH
The impact of Western culture on Japanese life. Shows the ancient
capital Kyoto in contrast to westernization of Japan's large cities.

JAPAN: HARVESTING THE LAND AND THE SEA. Encyclopaedia
    Britannica Educational Corporation, 1963. EBEC, UCA,
    UCO, UUT
How 100 million people manage to survive in Japan's small land
area.

JAPAN HARVESTS THE SEA. Walt Disney, 1958. (People and
    Places Series.) 29 min. color. ASF, DIS, UUT
The role of the ocean in meeting the Japanese people's food re-
quirements.

JAPAN: ITS CUSTOMS AND TRADITIONS. Walt Disney, 1964.
    27 min. color. DIS
The traditional culture of the Japanese people in a technological
world.

JAPAN: LAND OF THE KAMI. Horizon, 1964. 27 min. color.
    SEF
A survey of modern Japanese religions that have evolved since the
religious revival of 1949.

JAPAN: MIRACLE IN ASIA. Encyclopaedia Britannica Educational
    Corporation, 1963. 30 min. color. EBEC, UCA, UCO,
    UUT
A close look at Japan's rapid rise as a formidable industrial nation.

JAPAN: PACIFIC NEIGHBOR. Justin and Geraldine Byers, 1962.
    16 min. color. BFA
How the Japanese have adapted to their environment to meet the
challenges of growing population, climatic extremes, and a varied
topography.

JAPAN: THE COLLECTIVE GIANT. Canadian Broadcasting Cor-
    poration, n. d. 20 min. color. VEC
An account of the lives of the Japanese people in a corporate society based on the old imperial system.

JAPAN: THE LAND AND THE PEOPLE.   Coronet, 1965.   12
   min.   color.   UCA
Examines the geography and present-day problems of the relatively
new Japanese democracy.

THE JAPANESE.   CBS, 1970.   52 min.   color.   CAR, UCO
A survey of Japan by Harvard professor and former Ambassador
Edwin O. Reischauer in which he tries to relate the interesting
parallels to Western social goals.

JAPANESE ECONOMY.   University of Michigan, 1961.   29 min.
   b/w.   IND
About Japan's World War II economy and post-war rise from the
ashes.

JAPANESE FAMILY.   International Film Foundation, 1950.   23
   min.   b/w.   EFD, IFF, UCA
A visit with a family of silk-weavers in Kyoto, Japan with special
interest given to the activities of two children.

JAPANESE FARMERS.   Films Inc., 1969.   (Man and His World
   Series.)   17 min.   color.   FI, VEC
Shows rural Japanese at work raising crops but stresses Japan's
dependence on others for much of her food.

THE JAPANESE GARDEN.   Japan, n. d.   10 min.   color.   CGJ
A study of beautiful gardens in Japan.   Shows details of creativity
and maintenance.

JAPANESE HANDICRAFTS.   Wayne Mitchell, 1968.   11 min.
   color.   BFA
A look at Japanese crafts of straw hat weaving, wood carving, pottery making and glazing, wood-block carving and printing, doll
making, paper lantern construction, and painting on silk.

JAPANESE MOUNTAIN FAMILY.   Wayne Mitchell, 1966.   15 min.
   color.   BFA
How a woodcarver's family lives in the forested mountains of Japan.
A view of rural life in modern Japan.

JAPANESE PRINT MAKING.   Cine-Pic, 1953.   11 min.   color.
   IFP, UCA
The eldest son of the Yoshida family of print makers works before
the camera to complete a color woodblock print.   Accompanied by
two koto instruments.

JAPANESE VILLAGE LIFE.   Frederik Lek, 1963.   15 min.   color.
   MGH
A survey of Japanese villages from those whose farmers grow rice
to the communities where fishing is the major interest.

JAPAN'S ART: FROM THE LAND.   Metro-Goldwyn-Mayer, 1962.
   10 min.   color.   SEF

A visit with Japanese artist Shuson Kono as he works on a landscape. With music performed by chorus and bamboo flutes.

JAPAN'S CHANGING FACE. CBS, 1960. 52 min. b/w. MAC
How the youth of Japan are changing the values and customs in
their search for new ones.

JAPAN'S NEW FAMILY PATTERNS. Metro-Goldwyn-Mayer, 1962.
15 min. color. SEF
A psychological study of a middle-class family in Kyoto, Japan
and their adjustment to new ideas and methods.

JUDOKA. National Film Board of Canada, 1965. 19 min. b/w.
MGH
A profile of an athlete in Japan, who has become an expert at
judo, appearing at the Tokyo Olympics and at the Pan-American
Games.

KASHIMA PARADISE. Benie Deswarte and Yanh le Lasson, 1974.
110 min. color. In Japanese with English subtitles. Directed by Benie Deswarte and Yanh le Lasson; photography
by Yanh le Masson; music by Hirashi Hara. TRI
A French documentary on the effects of industrialization on a rural
community. Unobtrusive camera work conveys the waste and destruction of technological "progress."

KAZE. (THE WIND.) NHK Japan, 1968. 26 min. b/w. FI
How the Japanese use the wind to best advantage in their daily life,
from rattan blinds to capture breezes in hot weather, to special
roofing and windbreakers to combat the storms.

THE KOUMIKO MYSTERY. Sofracima, 1965. 47 min. color.
Directed, written, photographed and edited by Chris Marker;
music by Toru Takemitsu. With Kumiko Muraoka. MGH,
NYF
A lyrical documentary about a modern Japanese girl and a reveal-
ing view of youth and individuality.

KYUDO: JAPANESE CEREMONIAL ARCHERY. ACI, 1970. 10
min. color. ACI
The ancient discipline of archery as taught in the classes of master
Kyonobu Ogasawara. Includes a special annual ceremony still
practiced at the Toshogu Shrine in which archers ride galloping
horses and shoot with extraordinary skill and style.

LATE AUTUMN. (AKIBIYORI.) Yasujiro Ozu, 1960. 127 min.
b/w. In Japanese with English subtitles. Directed by Yasujiro Ozu; screenplay by Kogo Noda and Yasujiro Ozu; photography by Yushun Atsuta; music by Takanobu Saito. With
Setsuko Hara, Yoko Tsukasa, Chishu Ryu, Mariko Okada,
Keijo Sada. NYF
A woman at first accepts then rebels against an arranged marriage
in this study of Japanese family life.

LATE SPRING.   (BANSHUN.)   Shochiku, 1949.   107 min.   b/w.
In Japanese with English subtitles.   Directed by Yasujiro
Ozu; screenplay by Yasujiro Ozu and Kogo Noda; photography
by Yuharu Atsuta.   With Chisu Ryu, Setsuko Hara, Haruka
Sugimura.   NYF
A professor, who is a widower, lives with his unmarried daughter
whom he tries to help find a life of her own not dependent on him.

LEAP ACROSS TIME.   NET, 1961.   (Japan: Changing Years
Series.)   29 min.   b/w.   IND, UCA
Traces Japan's move from a medieval culture to a modern society
in 70 years.

THE LIFE OF O-HARU.   (SAIKAKU ICHIDIA ONNA.)   Shintoho,
1952.   133 min.   b/w.   In Japanese with English subtitles.
Directed by Kenji Mizoguchi; screenplay by Kenji Mizoguchi
and Yoshikata Yoda after the novel by Ibara Saikaku (17th
century); photography by Yoshimi Hirano.   With Toshiro
Mifune, Kinuyo Tonaka, Ichiro Sugai, Tsukie Matsura.   NYF
Considered one of the greatest pictures of all time in a 1961 International Critics' Poll and ranked by its director as his masterpiece.   The decline of a 17th century court lady into the life of a
prostitute is treated sympathetically as symptomatic of the situation
of women in a feudal society.

MADE IN JAPAN.   BBC, n. d.   52 min.   b/w.   TL
Examines the motives and background that have made Japan a major
force in world trade.

THE MEN WHO TREAD ON THE TIGER'S TAIL.   (TORA NO O O
FUMU OTOKOTACHI.)   Toho, 1945.   60 min.   b/w.   In
Japanese with English subtitles.   Directed by Akira Kurosawa;
screenplay by Akira Kurosawa, based on the Kabuki drama
"Kanjincho"; photography by Takeo Ito; music by Tadasha Hattori.   With Hanshiro Iwai, Susumu Fujita, Kenichi Enomot,
Denjiro Okochi.   MAC[1]
Director Kurosawa took a popular Kabuki drama, added a comic
porter to the fable, and created a satire on militarism.   The film
was banned by wartime Japan and by the occupation government that
followed.   The story concerns a clan lord of the 17th century who
eludes the cruel sovereign, his brother, by fleeing with six follow-
ers disguised as monks.

THE MOOD OF ZEN.   Hartley, 1967.   13 min.   color.   NACC
Beautiful scenes of Japan with koto music, monks chanting and a
discussion of the basic teachings of Zen by Alan Watts.

MUDDY WATERS.   (NIGORIE.   PORTRAITS OF SHAME.)   Tadashi
Imai, 1953.   104 min.   b/w.   In Japanese with English subtitles.   Directed by Tadashi Imai; based on three short stories
by Ichiyo Higuchi; photography by Shunichiro Nakao; music by
Ikuma Dan.   With Ken Mitsuta, Akiko Tamura, Susumu Tat-
suoka, Teruoko Nagoka, Noboru Nakaya, Yoshiko Kuga,

Noboru Nakamura, Chikage Awashima, So Yamamura, Seiji
Miyaguchi.   MAC[1]
Three stories about the decaying feudal society of Japan at the end
of the 19th century.   "The Thirteenth Night": a woman is forced
to marry above her status and her husband turns out to be a phil-
anderer.   "On New Year's Eve": a maid who works in a well-to-
do house steals money from her mistress to provide funds for her
uncle to pay his debtors.   "Muddy Waters" concerns a prostitute
killed by a jealous customer just as she plans to escape her plight.

A NATION TRANSFORMED.   Metromedia, n. d.   (The Japan Series.)
      30 min.   b/w.   VEC
Covers the history of Japan from 1945 through her unparalleled
rise from defeat to economic importance.

NEW HORIZONS: JAPAN.   Pan-American World Airways, n. d.
      13 min.   color.   ASF, PAN
A travelogue designed to promote tourism in Japan by featuring the
most scenic sights.

NOH.   Toho, n. d.   45 min.   color.   In Japanese with English sub-
      titles.   TOH
A study of the theatrical and musical elements of Japan's classical
music drama.

OCCUPATION OF JAPAN.   University of Michigan, 1961.   (Japan:
      the Changing Years Series.)   29 min.   b/w.   IND
The failures and successes of the U. S. occupation of Japan from
1945 to 1942.

OHAYO.   (GOOD MORNING.)   Shochiku, 1959.   93 min.   color.
      In Japanese with English subtitles.   Directed by Yasujiro
      Ozu; screenplay by Yasujiro Ozu and Kogo Nada; photography
      by Yusun Atsuta.   With Koji Shidora, Masahiko Shimazu,
      Chishu Ryu, Kuniko Mujake.   MAC[1]
The internecine relations of a middle class family who live in a
crowded development near Tokyo.   A view of life as it really is
by one of Japan's greatest directors.

1,000 CRANES: THE CHILDREN OF HIROSHIMA.   Fleetwood,
      1968.   24 min.   b/w.   MAC
About the old Japanese belief that folding 1,000 paper cranes will
protect against illness and the horrible heritage of Hiroshima's
children, in the hope of warding off after-effects of radiation exposure.

THE OPEN CITY.   CCM, n. d.   13 min.   color.   MAC
A tour of the interesting people and sites in the world's biggest
city, Tokyo.

PEARL IS BORN.   Alfred T. Palmer, n. d.   20 min.   color.   UCA
A view of the step-by-step activities involved in the pearl culture
of Ise-Shima National Park area of Japan.

PEASANTS OF THE SECOND FORTRESS.   Shinsuke Ogawa, n. d.
143 min.   b/w.   In Japanese with English subtitles.   Directed by Shinsuke Ogawa; photographed by Masaki Tamura.
TRI
A report on the five-year struggle of Japanese residents in Narita,
Japan who protested when the government wanted to build a new
airport for Tokyo on their land.

PERSONALITY IN CULTURE.   University of Michigan, 1961.
(Japan: The Changing Years Series.)   29 min.   b/w.   IND,
UUT
Probes the paradoxical Japanese character as a complex of contra-
dictory qualities.

PRINCESS YANG KWEI FEI.   (YOKIHI.)   Daiei, 1955.   91 min.
color.   In Japanese with English subtitles.   Directed by Kenji
Mizoguchi; screenplay by To Chin, Matsutaro Kawaguchi,
Yoshikata Yoda and Masahige Narisawa; photography by Kohei
Sugiyama.   With Machiko Kyo; Masayuki Mori and Saskae
Ozawa.   NYF
One of Mizoguchi's last films, an experiment with wide screen,
color and change of locale.   Always sensitive to the social and
psychological problems of women in his films, Mizoguchi here reveals the love story of an Emperor of the T'ang Dynasty who loves
a servant girl but, due to a turn of events, becomes a prisoner of
rebels and loses his mistress through her death in the rebellion.
Finally they are reunited in a ghostly scene in a graveyard.

RASHOMON.   Daiei, 1951.   87 min.   b/w.   In Japanese with Eng-
lish subtitles.   Directed by Akira Kurosawa; screenplay by
Akira Kurosawa and Shinobu Hashimoto; based on the novel
"In the Forest" by Ryunosuke Akutagawa; produced by Jingo
Minodra.   With Toshiro Mifune, Machiko Kyo and Masayuki
Mori.   JAN
A tale of many centuries ago about three Japanese wanderers who
ponder the circumstances of a brutal act that worries them.   Various versions of the incident are shown from the victim's, the wife's
and the bandit's point of view as well as the perspective of one of
the three men who says he is an eye witness.   Winner of the grand
prize at the Venice Film Festival.

RECORD OF A TENEMENT GENTLEMAN.   (NAGAYA SHINSHI
ROKU.)   Yasujiro Ozu, 1947.   72 min.   b/w.   In Japanese
with English subtitles.   Directed by Yasijiro Ozu.   Credits
unlisted.   With Choko Iida, Chishu Ryu.   NYF
After World War II an orphan goes to live with a middle-aged
woman.   The story concerns the difficulties of their lives, the
hostility of the woman and the awkwardness of the child.

RED BEARD.   (AKAHIGE.)   Toho-Kurosawa, 1965.   185 min.
b/w.   In Japanese with English subtitles.   Directed by Akira
Kurosawa; screenplay by Masato Ide, Hideo Oguni, Ryuzo
Kikushima, and Akira Kurosawa; photography by Asaichi Nakai

and Takao Saito; music by Masaru Sato.   With Toshiro Mifune, Yuzo Kayama, Yoshio Tsuchiya, Reiko Dan, Kyoko
Kagawa, Terumi Niki.   MAC[1]
Set in the 19th century, the story concerns an eager young doctor
who goes to work at a slum clinic where the hospital's chief doc-
tor-administrator rules in dictatorial fashion.

A RICE FARMER OF JAPAN.   McGraw-Hill, 1964.   14 min.
color.   MGH
A portrait of the Asiatic farmers who devote their lives to rice
cultivation.

RICE GROWING IN JAPAN.   NHK International, 1969.   17 1/2
min. color.   BFA
Explores the modern and traditional methods of rice planting and
harvesting.

RITE OF LOVE AND DEATH.   (YUKOKU.)   21 min.   b/w.   Yukio
Mishima, n. d.   21 min.   b/w.   Directed by Yukio Mishima.
GRO
The only film written and directed by Japan's famous novelist before he committed hara-kiri.   Based on one of Mishima's short
stories "Patriotism" concerning an officer asked by the Emperor
to execute his fellow officers after an uprising.   Mishima also plays
the part of the young lieutenant.

ROMANCE OF SILK.   Alfred T. Palmer, 1955.   14 min.   color.
UCA
A close look at silk production from leaf to textile production in
Japan.

THE SAGA OF ANATAHAN.   Josef von Sternberg, 1953.   92 min.
b/w.   Directed and photographed by Josef von Sternberg;
written by von Sternberg from a news story in Life Magazine;
music by Akira Hukube; Japanese dialog by Asono; English
narration written and spoken by von Sternberg.   With Akemi
Negishi, Tadashi Suganuma, Hiroshi Kondo.   MGH
Based on an actual story about Japanese sailors isolated on a jungle
island who continued for years to believe that World War II was
not yet over and killed one another over a young woman.

SAGA OF THE CRUCIFIED LOVERS.   (CHIKAMATSU MONOGAT-
ARI.)   Daiei, 1955.   100 min.   color.   In Japanese with Eng-
lish subtitles.   Directed by Kenji Mizoguchi; screenplay by
Yoshikato Yoda and Masutaro Kwaguchi, after a kabuki drama
by Chikamatsu Monzemon; photographed by Kazuo Miyagawa.
NLC
Cited as one of the director's greatest films.   Set in 17th century
Kyoto with a story about a scrollmaker who falls in love with his
master's wife.

SALES TRAINING, JAPANESE STYLE.   NBC, 1969.   5 min.   color.
FI

A humorous, tongue-in-cheek report on a training session for Japanese salesmen involving yoga, Freud, Zen and Dale Carnegie.

SAMURAI. (MUSASHI MIYAMOTO.) Toho, 1954. 92 min. color. In Japanese with English subtitles. Directed by Hiroshi Inagaki; screenplay by Tokuhei Wakao and Hiroshi Inagaki; adaption by Hideji Hojo, based on the novel by Eiji Yoshikawa; photography by Jun Yasumoto; music by Ikuma Dan. With Toshiro Mifune, Kaoru Yachigusa, Rentaro Mikuni, Mariko Okada, Kuroemon Onoe, Mitsuko Mito, Eiko Miyoshi. MAC[1]
One of the few Japanese movies to win an Academy Award as Best Foreign Language Film and one of the earliest color films made in Japan. A 16th century samurai is wounded in battle, finds refuge with a widow, goes to his native village, kills some guards, flees and ultimately becomes a missionary.

SANJURO. Toho, 1962. 96 min. b/w. cinemascope. In Japanese with English subtitles. Directed by Akira Kurosawa; screenplay by Ryuzo Kikushima, Hideo Oguni, and Akira Kurosawa; music by Masaru Sato. With Toshiro Mifune, Yuzo Kayama, Tatsuya Nakadai, Reiko Dan. TOH
A humorous story about a group of samurai who seek the aid of a surly, rough ronin to help them reform their clan.

SAPPORO WINTER OLYMPICS. Toho, 1972. 166 min. color. cinemascope. In Japanese with English subtitles. TOH
A documentary on the winter Olympics international competitions. Directed by Masahiro Shinoda.

SCIENCE OF ZAZEN. Orient Electrical Industries, 1967. 30 min. b/w. UCA
Two Japanese psychiatrists study Zen masters during meditation to determine physical changes during their contemplation.

SEVEN SAMURAI. (SHICHININ NO SAMURAI.) Shojiro, Motoki, 1954. 141 min. b/w. (also 208 min. version.) In Japanese with English subtitles. Directed by Akira Kurosawa; photography by Asaichi Nakai; music by Fumio Hayasaka. With Takashi Shimura, Toshiro Mifune, Yoshio Inaba, Seiji Miyaguchi, Minoru Chiaki, Daisuke Kato, Ko Kimura, Keiko Tsushima. AST, MAC[1], CPC
An epic set in 16th century Japan about some villagers who hire seven unemployed samurai to protect them from marauder bandits. A dramatic adventure in the American Western tradition. Venice Film Festival winner.

SHE AND HE. (KANOJO TO KARE.) Iwanami, 1963. 110 min. b/w. In Japanese with English subtitles. Directed and written by Susumu Hani; photography by Juichi Nagano; music by Toku Takemitsu. With Sachiko Hidari, Kikuji Yamashita, Eiji Okada, Mariko Igarashi. MAC[1]
A middle class housewife--a Manchurian refugee who resides in an apartment complex--becomes involved in the lives of squatters

living next door when a fire destroys their shacks. Her involvement with reality makes her ponder her existence.

SILK MAKERS OF JAPAN.   Sterling S. Beath and Robert Lang,
    1964. 16 min. color. BFA
The making of silk from caterpillars to cocoons to factory processing of thread and silk exportation.

SPIRIT OF ZEN.   Orient Electrical Industries, 1967. 35 min.
    color. UCA
A detailed view of two Zen training centers in Japan whose traditions are based on over 700 years of Buddhist practice.

THE STONECUTTER.   International Film Foundation, 1965.   6
    min. color. EFD, IFF
An abstract animation by artist Gerald McDermott telling an ancient
tale of greed--the story of Tasaku, the stonecutter.

STRAY DOG.   (NORA INU.) Toho, 1949. 122 min. b/w. In
    Japanese with English subtitles. Directed by Akira Kurosawa;
    screenplay by Akira Kurosawa and Ryuzo Kikushima; music by
    Fumio Hayasaka; photography by Asakazu Naka. With Toshiro
    Mifune, Keiko Awaji, Takashi Shimura, and Reisaburo Yama-
    moto. MAC[1]
A young detective hunts for his stolen gun in the Japanese world of
criminals, drug addicts, prostitutes.

STREET OF SHAME.   (AKASEN CHITAI. RED-LIGHT DISTRICT.)
    Masaichi Nagata, 1956. 85 min. b/w. In Japanese with Eng-
    lish subtitles. Directed by Kenji Mizoguchi; screenplay by
    Masahige Narusawa. With Machiko Kyo, Aiko Mimasu, Ayako
    Wakao, Michiyo Kogure, Hiroko Machida, Yasuko Kowakami,
    Eitaro Shinde. MAC[1]
This is direct Mizoguchi's last work and, true to form, a film ex-
ploring woman's lot and her relationship to man. The story concerns four prostitutes, each for various reasons living a life without love and human involvement.

TALE OF TWO CITIES.   Du Art, 1949. 12 min. b/w. UCA
A U. S. Army film about the destructive effect of atomic warfare
on Hiroshima and Nagasaki.

TALES OF THE TAIRA CLAN.   Daiei, 1947. 120 min. color.
    In Japanese with English subtitles. Directed by Kenji Mizo-
    guchi; written by Yoshikata Yoda, Masahige Narusawa and
    Kyuichi Tsuji, after the novel by Eiji Yoshikawa; photographed
    by Kazuo Miyagawa; Music by Fumio Hayasaka. NLC
The Yoshikawa historical novel ("The Heike Story") recreates the
disturbed world of 1137 A. D. before a conflict between powerful
monasteries and the samurai families.

TOKYO INDUSTRIAL WORKER.   Films Inc. , 1969. 17 min. color.
    FI, VEC

A visit with the O-ga family of modern Tokyo who alternate between traditional and modern customs as they go through their daily lives.

TOKYO OLYMPIAD. Organizing Committee for the Games of the XVIII Olympiad, 1964. 93 min. color. MAC[1]
Despite the influence of Leni Riefenstahl and Sergei Eisenstein, director Kon Kchikawa created a personal and technically dazzling commentary on the human endeavors of the world's greatest athletes. English narration by Jack Douglas.

TOKYO STORY. (TOKYO MONOGATORI.) Yasujiro Ozu, 1953. 134 min. b/w. In Japanese with English subtitles. Directed by Yasujiro Ozu; screenplay by Kogo Noda and Yasujiro Ozu. With Chishu Ryu, Chiyeko Higashiyama and Setsuko Hara. NYF
This is Ozu's favorite film and one nominated by some international critics as one of the ten best films of all time. The story is a study of the generation gap in a Japanese family, in this case a couple who visit their married children.

TOKYO: THE FIFTY-FIRST VOLCANO. BBC, 1971. 30 min. color. TL
About the crisis of urban living in Tokyo, the world's largest city, located in a country that also has fifty active volcanoes.

TWO FACTORIES: JAPANESE AND AMERICAN. Learning Corporation, 1971. 22 min. color. LEC
A comparison of a U.S. Sylvania plant and a Matsushita Electric complex in Japan which serves to give a full view of the Japanese life style and attitudes toward work.

UGETSU. Daiei, 1954. 96 min. b/w. In Japanese with English subtitles. Directed by Kenji Mizoguchi; screenplay by Matsutaro Kawaguchi and Yoshikata Yoda from the stories of Akinari Veda. With Machiko Kyo, Masayuji Mori, Kinuyo Tanaka. JAN, NLC
An eerie fable about two reckless husbands with ambitions that cause misfortunes to fall upon them--one who aspires to be a samurai neglects his wife and finally he finds she has become a prostitute; the other, dreaming of riches, is seduced by a glamorous and exotic woman who turns out to be a ghost. Ugetsu means "pale and mysterious moon after the rain."

UKIGUSA. (FLOATING WEEDS.) Yasujiro Gzu, 1959. 128 min. color. In Japanese with English subtitles. Directed by Yasujiro Ozu; screenplay by Kogo Nada and Yasujiro Ozu; based on a story by Ozu; photography by Kazuo Miyagawa; music by Takanobu Saito. With Ganjiro Nakamura, Haruko Sugimura, Hiroshi Kawaguchi, Machiko Kyo, Ayako Wakao. MAC[1]
An unsuccessful troupe of actors stops at a small town, hoping for better luck. When things don't work out the leader decides to retire but a conflict develops between his past and present mistresses.

UKIYO-E. Art Institute of Chicago, 1960. 27 min. color. MAC
Presents works of twelve 17th and 18th century Japanese artists
from the collection of the Art Institute of Chicago. Narrated by
James A. Michener and made with the assistance of the Japan Society.

THE UNITED STATES AS SEEN BY JAPANESE STUDENTS. University of Utah, 1968. 25 min. color. UUT
How a group of Japanese students reacted to a tour of various
cities in the U. S.

VILLAGE LIFE IN THE NEW JAPAN. University of Michigan,
1961. (Japan: The Changing Years Series.) 29 min. b/w.
IND
About life in a contemporary Japanese village reflecting a gradual
social change.

THE VILLAGE POTTERS OF ONDA. F. Sperry, 1966. 25 min.
b/w. PEN
How Japanese folk potters in Onda, a remote village in the mountains, make their pots in the traditional manner.

VILLAGE SKIN. Yoichi Takabayashi, n. d. 14 min. b/w. MAC[1]
An expressionistic film by Yoichi Takabayashi which expresses the
loneliness and sexual and emotional frustration of a young woman.
Uses the girl's nude body and the objects in her environment in an
abstract manner.

WAR GAMES. Donald Richie, 1963. 19 min. b/w. MAC[1]
Donald Richie's film about boys who play with a goat but accidental-
ly kill it. Filmed near the seashore in Tokyo.

WE, THE JAPANESE PEOPLE. U. S. Dept. of the Army, 1952.
25 min. b/w. NAC
The U. S. government looks at the democratic changes in the Japanese way of life since 1945.

WINGS TO JAPAN. Pan-American World Airways, 1967. 29 min.
color. ASF, PAN
A travelogue designed to promote tourism in Japan.

WOMAN IN THE DUNES. (SUNO NO ONNA.) Teshigahara, 1964.
123 min. b/w. In Japanese with English subtitles. Directed
by Hiroshi Teshigahara; scenario and adaptation by Kobo Abe;
cinematography by Hiroshi Segawa; music by Toru Segawa.
With Eiji Okada and Kyoko Kishida. MGH
A much-awarded film allegory about a man who is captured by a
woman and kept at the bottom of a sandpit to help her shovel sifting
sand.

YAKUSHIJI TEMPLE. Films Inc. , 1968. 30 min. color. FI
Shows the 1,200-year-old pagoda preserved in its original state in
the ancient capital of Nara.

YOJIMBO.   Akira Kurosawa for Toho, 1961.   110 min.   b/w.
cinemascope.   In Japanese with English subtitles.   Directed by
Akira Kurosawa; screenplay by Akira Kurosawa, Ryuzo Kikushima, Hideo Oguni; photography by Kazuo Miyagawa; music
by Masaru Sato.   With Toshiro Mifune, Eijiro Tono, Seizabuto
Kawazu, Isuzu Yamada.   MAC[1]
This is director Kurosawa's first full-length comedy, a satiric adventure involving an unemployed samurai warrior who comes to a
village uprooted by two warring factors.   He sells his services to
one group, then the other.   At last he provokes confrontation in
which both sides fight and wipe each other out.

YUKATA.   Masaya Hotatsu, n. d.   10 min.   color.   UCA
How Japanese yukata cloth is made in the traditional manner for
kimonos.

ZEN IN RYOKO-IN.   Ruth Stephan, 1971.   71 min.   color.   MAC[1]
Ruth Stephan, American writer and poet, presents the Japanese
temple of Ryoko-in, located in Kyoto.   Although closed to the public, the temple and Zen Buddhism are revealed thanks to Ruth Stephan's involvement with the temple family.   Directed, written and
produced by Ruth Stephan.   Also available in 3 parts, 25 min.
each.

Korea

BUDDHIST DANCES OF KOREA.   University of Washington, 1971.
(The Washington Films Series.)   18 min.   color.   UWAP
Monks of Korea perform Buddhist dances while they chant from
sacred texts.

DIARY OF YUNBOGI BOY.   Nagisa Oshima, n. d.   24 min.   b/w.
NYF
The diary and still shots of Yunbogi, a ten-year-old deserted Korean boy, who roams the streets, a victim of Asian politics.   Directed by Japanese director Nagisa Oshima.

KOREA: THE LINE.   CBS, 1965.   26 min.   b/w.   MAC
A visit in the Demilitarized Zone of Korea.   Shows a meeting of
the Military Armistice Commission at Ranmunjom at which armistice violations in the joint security are the topic of discussion.   A
CBS-News telecast of January 17, 1965.

KOREA, THE LONG ROAD TO PEACE.   March of Time, 1953.
29 min.   b/w.   UCO
An old film, still in use, that reviews military and political events
during the Korean War from June 1950 to December 1952.

KOREA: 38TH PARALLEL.   Metromedia, 1954.   50 min.   b/w.
VEC
Richard Basehart narrates this study of the Korean War in relation
to the role of the United Nations and the removal of General Mac-
Arthur.

KOREAN COURT MUSIC. University of Washington, 1971. (The
     Washington Films Series.) 15 min. b/w. UWAP
An overview of the variety of Korean court music including religious ceremonial music and banquet music. Illustrates with actual
performances.

KOREAN FOLK DANCES. University of Washington, 1971. (The
     Washington Films Series.) 25 min. b/w. UWAP
Shows a number of folk dances, including the spectacular dance
featuring a tightrope.

THE KOREAN PEOPLE. International Film Bureau, 1961. 11
     min. color. EFD, IFB
A brief description of the Koreans' life style with emphasis on the
cultural aspects in relation to the geographical location.

THE LONG JOURNEY. United Nations, 1955. 30 min. b/w.
     UUT
The long journey of the Koreans from war back to rehabilitation of
the land. Shows the post-war life of a North Korean farmer who
made his way south in the winter of 1951.

SPRING FRAGRANCE. (SUNG CHOONKYANG.) Shin San Okk,
     1964. 90 min. color. In Korean with English subtitles.
     Directed by Shin San Okk; screenplay by Im Hi Jai, based on
     a Korean folk tale; photography by Lee Hyong Pyo; music by
     Jyung Yoon Joo. With Choi Eun Hi, Kim Jin Kyoo, Do Kum
     Bong, Hugh Jang Kang. MAC[1]
A prize-winning film based on a Korean folk tale, set in the 18th
century, about a young lord who falls in love with a girl of lower
social status. The girl repulses a local magistrate's advances and
is thrown in jail to face execution. Classical Korean music accompanies the action.

Ryukyu Islands

ASPECTS OF OKINAWA. Productions Unlimited, 1963. (Thirteen
     from Asia Series.) 15 min. color. MAC
Asians wrote and filmed this report on the present-day life and
background of Okinawa.

THE GATE OF SHUREI. Productions Unlimited, 1963. (Thirteen
     from Asia Series.) 15 min. color. MAC
Written and filmed by Asians about the present-day life and background of Okinawa.

Taiwan (Formosa)

A CHINESE FARM WIFE. Norman N. Miller, 1974. (Faces of
     Change Series.) 17 min. color. FF
A visit with Mrs. Li, a housewife who runs her family, works in
the rice fields, and is active in her community.

CHINESE ART: AN ODYSSEY. Sterling, 1974. 20 min. color.
    SEF
A report on the amassing of one-quarter million pieces of Chinese
art at the National Palace Museum, north of Taipei. Traces the
packing up of historic treasures which started back in 1931 during
the war with Japan and continued to 1949.

LIU PI-CHIA. Contemporary, 1967. 24 min. color. MGH, PEN
A former Chinese Nationalist soldier works on a land reclamation
project in Formosa to provide farms for other retired soldiers.

THE MOUNTAIN. Epigoni, 1966. 17 min. b/w. In Mandarin
    with English subtitles. UCA
Filmmaker Richard Chen interviews three art students in Formosa
and follows them on their vacation to a mountain. With Western
rock music and traditional music.

NEW FORMOSA. CCM, 1963. (Thirteen from Asia Series.) 15
    min. color. MAC
Asians wrote and filmed this study of present-day life and background of Formosa.

PEOPLE ARE MANY, FIELDS ARE FEW. Norman N. Miller,
    1974. (Faces of Change Series.) 32 min. color. FF
Members of farming families in Taiwan compare their life style
with that of industrial workers and view with concern certain conditions of farming.

THE RURAL COOPERATIVE. Norman N. Miller, 1974. (Faces
    of Change Series.) 15 min. color. FF
A report on the Tsao Tung Farmers Association, a typical Taiwan
cooperative that serves as social and economic center for the
thousands of families who own the cooperative and also use its many
agricultural services, e.g., irrigation, crop storage, marketing.

T'AI CHI CH'UAN. Tom Davenport, n.d. 8 min. b/w. DAV
Shows Zen master Nan Huai-chin performing the most important of
the Chinese martial arts. Filmed on Taiwan.

TAIWAN. Taiwan, n.d. 36 min. color. UWY
A Taiwan-produced film showing the island's educational system,
agricultural features and transportation.

TAIWAN, THE FACE OF FREE CHINA. Golden Reel, 1960. 27
    min. color. GRP
A visit in Taiwan with emphasis on industrial development and customs of the people.

THEY CALL HIM AH KING. Norman N. Miller, 1974. (Faces of
    Change Series.) 24 min. color. FF
A boy of Taiwan must choose between his inherited role as farmer
and a career in industry with its concomitant urban life style.

THE TREASURES OF TAIWAN. John Savage, 1973. 28 min.
     color. COM
A travel film that emphasizes the best features of Taiwan.

WET CULTURE RICE. Norman N. Miller, 1974. (Faces of
     Change Series.) 17 min. color. FF
Illustrates how the rice farmers of Taiwan rely more on human effort than mechanical means for agriculture. The reported result
is the highest per acre yields in the world.

Southeast Asia

     (Includes Burma, Cambodia, Indonesia, Laos, Malaysia, The
     Philippines, Singapore, Thailand, Vietnam.)

General

END OF AN EMPIRE. CBS, 1968. 26 min. b/w. AIM, UCA
Walter Cronkite, CBS news correspondent, reports on the French
seven-year war and Communist take-over in what was formerly
known as Northern Indochina. Uses some of the Soviet Union's
footage showing the build-up of Ho Chi Minh's troops.

FOOD OF SOUTHEAST ASIA. Wayne Mitchell, 1966. 18 min.
     color. BFA
How fish, rice and vegetables provide the subsistence of Southeast
Asian people.

MAINLAND SOUTHEAST ASIA. Universal Education and Visual
     Arts, 1972. 13 min. color. UEVA
Includes descriptions of life in Bangkok, Cambodia and Malaysia.

MEKONG. Shell, 1963. 25 min. color. SFL, UUT
A survey of the Mekong River project directed by the United Nations Economic Commission for Asia and the Far East. Follows
the river from its source through Southwestern China and Southeast
Asia. Considers the impact on the lower river basin.

MEKONG. Encyclopaedia Britannica Educational Corporation, 1967.
     25 min. color. Edited version. EBEC, UCO
Studies the impact of the Mekong River area's development and related problems on the Vietnam conflict and other matters. Discusses the need for coordinated development and projections for the
future.

NATURAL RESOURCES OF SOUTHEAST ASIA. Wayne Mitchell,
     1967. BFA
About the importance of Southeast Asia's natural resources to the
rest of the world.

THE OPIUM TRAIL. Independent Television Corporation, n. d.   60
   min. color. ITC
A probing survey of the opium-smuggling industry that operates from
Burma to Hong Kong. Describes the enormous profits at the expense
of the growers, the despair of addicts and the corruption in Southeast China and elsewhere.

RISE OF NATIONALISM IN SOUTHEAST ASIA. McGraw-Hill,
   1962. 15 min. b/w. MGH, UCA
Surveys the factors that contributed to nationalism in Southeast
Asia. Based on "The Challenge of Democracy" by Blaich and
Baumgartner.

SOUTHEAST ASIA FAMILY. Art Evans, 1966. 15 min. color.
   BFA, UCO
How the climate helps crop production in Southeast Asia, as seen
through the eyes of one family.

SOUTHEAST ASIA GEOGRAPHY. Art Evans, 1968. 21 min. color.
   BFA, UCO, UUT
A look at the economic realities of Burma, Laos, Thailand, Cambodia and Malaya in terms of their raw materials and related political importance.

SOUTHEAST ASIA: LANDS AND PEOPLES. Coronet, 1957. 14
   min. b/w. COR
The political and economic developments of Southeast Asia in the
twentieth century, as seen from the mid-century perspective.

SOUTHEAST ASIA STORY: THE LAND. Shaw, 1964. 15 min.
   color. UCO
A report on the resources and other important features of Southeast Asia and why it attracts China's interest.

SOUTHEAST ASIA STORY: THE PEOPLE. Shaw, 1964. 15 min.
   color. UCO
A report on the people of Southeast Asia showing the varieties of
race, religion, traditions and language to be found there.

TAMING OF THE MEKONG. CBS, 1965. 26 min. b/w. MAC
A television documentary about the United Nations plan to control
the waters of the Mekong River with cooperation of Southeast Asian
countries.

THE THIRD CHINA. CBS, 1969. 16 min. color. CAR
About the twenty million expatriate Chinese who live in Southeast
Asia, their economic, political and cultural life. With Harry
Reasoner and Mike Wallace.

                              Burma

BURMA, BUDDHISM AND NEUTRALISM. CBS, 1957. 55 min.
   b/w.

The religion, neutralism, and life style of the Burmese people.
Includes an interview with the United Nations chairman of Burma's
political party in power.

BURMA: PEOPLE OF THE RIVER. Encyclopaedia Britannica Educational Corporation, 1957. 14 min. color. EBEC, UCA,
UCO, UUT, UWY
A visit with the people who live along the rivers, in the delta and
river valleys, rice fields, in the jungles and in Rangoon.

THE GOLDEN TOWER. Productions Unlimited, 1963. (Thirteen
from Asia Series.) 15 min. color. MAC
Written and filmed by Asians about the present-day life and background of Burma. Shows city life in Rangoon.

SOUTHEAST ASIA: BURMA AND THAILAND. Coronet, 1972. 13
min. color. COR
A comparison of Burma, rich in natural resources, with the more
industrialized Thailand. Variety of Burma's distinct ethnic groups
is illustrated and compared with the greater ethnic homogeneity of
Thailand.

Cambodia

ANGKOR, THE LOST CITY. National Film Board of Canada, 1965.
13 min. b/w. MGH
A look at the six hundred monuments of Angkor, the greatest assembly of sculpture in the world, which in turn reveal the great
achievements of the Khmer civilization.

ANGKOR WAT. CCM, 1972. (Thirteen from Asia Series.) 15
min. color. MAC
Written and filmed by Asians about the present-day life and background of Cambodia. With views of the capital, Angkor Thom.

CAMBODIA: THE ANGKOR MYSTERY. Interlude, 1970. 14 min.
color. TFC
Discussion and detailed views of the Angkor ruins. With conjectures and fact about the civilization that produced these structures.

THE HILL OF QUEEN PENH. Productions Unlimited, 1963.
(Thirteen from Asia Series.) 15 min. color. MAC
Written and filmed by Asians about the present-day life and background of Cambodia. Shows the capital city, Pnom-Penh ("The Hill
of Queen Penh") and the Mekong River area.

SOUTHEAST ASIA: VIETNAM, CAMBODIA, LAOS. Coronet, 1973.
20 1/2 min. color. COR
An account of the differences in land use, despite the geographic
similarities of North and South Vietnam, and a comparison of Laos
with the fertile plains of Cambodia.

Indonesia
(Sumatra, Bali, Java, Obi, Borneo, West Irian)

BALI: THE MASK OF RANGDA. Hartley, 1975. 30 min. color.
   HARP
Explores the folk-psychology of exorcising violence in order to pre-
serve what the Balinese call the "Spirit of Cooperation."

BALI TODAY. Hartley, 1968. 17 min. color. ACI, UCA
Traces the unusual culture of Bali, including art and religion, with
commentary by ethnographer Margaret Mead.

CHILDHOOD RIVALRY IN BALI AND NEW GUINEA. New York
   University, 1952. (Character Formation in Different Cultures
   Series.) 17 min. b/w. NYU, UCA
Children and their mothers of two different cultures are compared.
The Balinese mother gives conspicuous attention to other babies,
while the New Guinea mother tries to keep her child from becom-
ing jealous.

DANI SWEET POTATOES. Karl G. Heider, 1973. 19 min. color.
   UCA
Studies the highly developed skill in sweet potato horticulture of
the Dani--a Papuan group in the province of Irian Jaya (West New
Guinea).

DISCOVERING THE ARTS OF BALI. Diana Colson, 1974. 15
   min. color. ACI
About the natural and man-made beauty of Bali with focus on arts,
carving, painting, weaving, drama and dance.

FAITH IN REVOLUTION. National Council of Churches, 1968. 28
   min. color. NACC
An artistic film presentation covering the past and present of Indonesia, its political turmoil, social unrest.

INDONESIA, A TIME OF TRANSITION. Peter Drummond, n.d. 29
   min. color. EFD, IFF
Contrasts urban and rural tradition and development. Shows problems of education and economics, as well as the religious beliefs
and culture of Sumatra, Java and Bali.

INDONESIA: AN ISLAND NATION'S PROGRESS. Universal Education and Visual Arts, 1972. 15 min. color. UEVA
Covers the rich resources and developing industry of Indonesia.

INDONESIA, NEW NATION OF ASIA. Encyclopaedia Britannica Educational Corporation, 1959. 16 min. color. EBEC
The complex story of how eighty million people of a variety of
races and religions came to be in Indonesia and how they cope with
the problems of crowded cities and below standard food production.

INDONESIA: THE LAND AND THE PEOPLE.   Coronet, 1957.   2nd
    ed. , 1966.   13 min.   color.   COR, UCO
The people's move to independence contrasted with the geographic
and cultural aspects of the rich islands of the former colonial East
Indies.

JALAN, JALAN.   National Film Board of Canada, 1974.   20 min.
    color.   FI
A description of the people of Jakarta, Indonesia, made by Canadian filmmaker Michael Rubbo.

KARBA'S FIRST YEARS.   New York University, 1950.   (Character
    Formation in Different Cultures.)   19 min.   b/w.   UCA
A few scenes in the life of a Balinese child showing his early relationships with members of his family and other children.

LETTER FROM INDONESIA.   Churchill-Wexler, 1955.   16 min.
    color.   UMN
A report on Indonesia's growth as a nation, including educational
and social reform.

MA' BUGI': TRANCE OF THE TORAJA.   Lee Rhoads and Eric
    Crystal, 1974.   21 min.   color.   UCA
A study of spirit possession ritual in the Toraja Highlands of Sula-
wesi Island in Indonesia.

THE MIDDAY SUN.   (Miracle of Bali Series.)   BBC, 1972.   PART
    1:   24 min.   color; PART 2:   27 min.   color.   XER
A report on Bali's sophisticated culture in which people will drop
their work (fishing, farming, and the like) to spend time on artistic
projects, such as playing music, painting.   Also available in shorter version, ART AND RELIGION.

NIGHT.   (Miracle of Bali Series.)   BBC, 1972.   Part 1:   28 min.
    color; Part 2:   28 min.   color.   XER
A discussion of religious beliefs in Bali.   Also available in a shorter version, TRANCE AND RITUAL.

A RECITAL OF MUSIC AND DANCING.   (Miracle of Bali Series.)
    BBC, 1972.   Part I.   20 min.   color; Part II.   14 min.
    color.   XER
Presents examples of classical Balinese dance and gamelan music
in performance.   Also available in shorter version under title A
RECITAL.

TRANCE AND DANCE IN BALI.   New York University, 1951.
    (Character Formation in Different Cultures.)   20 min.   b/w.
    NYU, UCA
A look at a Balinese ceremonial dance drama in which a witch and
a dragon struggle against comic interludes and violent trance
seizures.   With authentic Balinese music.

TROPICAL MOUNTAIN ISLAND: JAVA. Louis de Rochemont,
    1948. 20 min. b/w. UCO, UWY, UEVA
Presents a tropical country--its coastal area, mountains, urban and
rural life. Stresses the rich natural resources such as teak, rubber, oil, quinine and rich volcanic soil.

Laos

LAOS. BBC and Odyssey, 1967. (Asia Series.) 25 min. color.
    TL
While a man searches for his lost friend in Laos, views of remote
villages and their people's customs are also presented. Narrated
by Lowell Thomas.

THE PEOPLE AND THEIR GUNS. Impact, 1970. 97 min. b/w.
    IMP
A view of the Laotian people, liberated by the Laotian Patriotic
Front, in their efforts to establish a socialist life style.

SOUTHEAST ASIA: VIETNAM, CAMBODIA, LAOS. Coronet, 1973.
    20 1/2 min. color. COR
Describes differences and similarities of North and South Vietnam
along with a comparison of Laos with its rugged terrain to the
plains of Cambodia.

Malaysia
(Malaya, Borneo, Singapore)

THE DAYAK: PEOPLE OF BORNEO. Les Productions du Dragon,
    1970. 29 min. color. MGH
The truth, not the legend, about the Dayak people, "head hunters"
of Borneo. Shows rituals.

FAMILY LIFE IN MALAYSIA: WE LIVE IN A KAMPONG. Mc-
    Graw-Hill and Authentic, 1970. 13 min. color. MGH
Follows one young boy in his homeland which contains people of
various races and religions. Shows English and all-Malay schools,
crafts, trades, life style at home, including reading the Koran.
Uses no narration but actual sounds and music. An award-winning
film.

FLOATING IN THE AIR, FOLLOWED BY THE WIND. Michigan
    State University, 1975. 34 min. color. IND
Studies an annual Hindu religious festival celebrated near Kuala
Lumpur, Malaysia.

THE GOLDEN PEARL. CCM, n.d. 14 min. color. MAC
About Singapore's crafts and industries.

HOW TO FIGHT A GUERRILLA WAR. CBS, 1966. 26 min. b/w.
    MAC

About the Malaysian War after World War II in which the Malaysi-
ans fought to maintain their independence from communists.

LAND DAYAKS OF BORNEO.   William R. Geddes, 1966.   38 min.
    UCA
A look at Borneo's Land Dayaks in Mentu Tapuh going through their
customary routines of the day despite the war nearby.

LEE KUAN YEW OF SINGAPORE.   BBC, n. d.   50 min.   color.
    TL
A candid view of the controversial prime minister of Singapore who
describes the Japanese occupation of Singapore and his ever-contin-
uing fight with the Communists for control of Singapore's government.

THE LOST MEN OF MALAYA.   BBC and Odyssey, 1967.   (Asia
    Series.)   25 min.   color.   TL
An account of the Temiar people, filmed in the heart of the Malayan
jungle.   Shows their life in a cooperative community where their
only personal possession is a blowpipe.   Narrated by Lowell
Thomas.

MAGIC IN THE HILLS.   BBC, 1971.   52 min.   color.   TL
A medical man and his wife travel into the Malayan interior to
study the ritual of the Jah Huts, an obscure people who perform
magic in total darkness.   Some footage was shot on infra-red film
as needed.

MALAY PENINSULA, PEOPLE AND PRODUCTS.   Coronet, 1948.
    11 min.   b/w.   UCO, UUT
Traditions and technology meet in Malay.   Shows scenes in Singapore.

MALAYA: LAND OF TIN AND RUBBER.   Encyclopaedia Britannica
    Educational Corporation, 1957.   14 min.   color.   EBEC,
    UCO, UUT, UWY
A visit with the people of the Malaya Peninsula on their rubber
plantations, in their mines and colorful rain forests.

MALAYA: NOMADS OF THE JUNGLE.   United World, n. d.   18
    min.   b/w.   UCA
A view of what it feels like to be in a Malayan jungle and how a
Malayan boy prepares for adulthood.

THE NEW STAR.   Productions Unlimited, 1963.   (Thirteen from
    Asia Series.)   15 min.   color.   MAC
Written and filmed by Asians about the present-day life and background of the Federation of Malaya.   Studies urban and village life,
economy, transportation, government.

NOMADS OF THE JUNGLE: MALAYA.   Louis de Rochemont, 1948.
    20 min.   b/w.   UCO, UEVA
How the nomads live in the rain forests of Malaya.

SINGAPORE.   Productions Unlimited, 1963.   (Thirteen from Asia
     Series.)   15 min.   color.   MAC
Written and filmed by Asians about the present-day life and background of Singapore.

SINGAPORE, MALAYA: NEW STATES IN SOUTHEAST ASIA.
     Dudley, 1963.   17 min.   color.   UEVA
A brief look at the busy, modern city of Singapore.

SOUTHEAST ASIA: MALAYSIA AND SINGAPORE.   Coronet, 1973.
     12 1/2 min.   color.   COR
The economic differences that exist despite ethnic similarities of
Malaysia and Singapore.

SPIRIT MEDIUMS AND MEDICO MAGIC.   BBC and Odyssey, 1967.
     (Asia Series.)   25 min.   color.   TL
Shows a Buddhist fisherman who is also a spirit medium in celebrations, rituals.   Also shows scenes of Singapore where firewalk-
ers move over hot coal beds.   Narrated by Lowell Thomas.

THREE FAMILIES OF MALAYSIA.   Gateway, 1973.   16 min.
     color.   COR
A survey of Malaysia's three main racial groups as seen on a trip
by river boat from the cities, where Chinese and Malay families
reside, to visit an Iban family.

THREE TRIBES OF BORNEO.   CCM, n. d.   13 min.   color.   MAC
A view of the life and work of Dyak people, the Kyans and the
Punans of Borneo.

TROPICAL JUNGLE.   International Film Bureau, 1966.   15 min.
     color.   EFD, UCA, UUT
Presents the sounds and sights of a Malayan jungle and what accounts for a tropical jungle's existence.

VOICES OF MALAYA.   British Information Service, 1947.   35
     min.   b/w.   UWY
What Malaya was like after World War II for the five million Mala-
yans, Chinese, Indians and Europeans who lived and worked there.

The Philippines

ANG BAYAN KONG PHILIPINAS.   Alfred T. Palmer, n. d.   23
     min.   color.   UCA
A Filipino man tells the background story of his country and its
culture.

BAYANIHAN.   Robert Snyder, 1962.   58 min.   color.   SNY
A dance company from the Philippines performs dances which reflect the ritual, work and customs of their country.

THE CAVE PEOPLE OF THE PHILIPPINES. NBC, 1972. 38
min. color. FI
Perhaps a last look at the Tasaday people of Mindanao, The Philippines, who lived undisturbed in the rain forest until 1971, when they were discovered.

HANUNOO. H. C. Conklin, 1958. 17 min. color. PEN
The Hanunoo mountain farmers of the jungle on Mindoro Island, The Philippines, perform their daily routines in the house, at work, and at leisure. Sound track uses Hanunoo music. No English narration.

LAND OF THE MORNING. Pan-American World Airways, n. d.
13 min. color. ASF, PAN
A travelogue designed to promote tourism in The Philippines.

LAST TRIBES OF MINDANAO. National Geographical Society,
1971. 51 min. color. FI, VEC
About the last of the pre-industrial tribes and the effort of one man to help them protect their customs and heritage.

MABUHAY. Douglas Aircraft, 1965. 28 min. color. MAC
A travel film with emphasis on scenic and cultural attractions of The Philippines.

MAGUINDANAO KULINTANG ENSEMBLES FROM MINDANAO, THE
PHILIPPINES. University of Washington, 1971. 16 min.
b/w. UWAP
About the complex gong music of the Maguindanao people. Shows the kulintang, the main instrument, and other types of gongs and drums.

MUSIC AND DANCE FROM MINDANAO, THE PHILIPPINES. University of Washington, 1971. 23 min. b/w. UWAP
Music and dancing by the Tirurai, the Maguindanao and the Maranao people--the latter two groups an example of Muslims in The Philippines.

MUSIC AND DANCE OF THE BAGOBO AND MANOBO PEOPLES
OF MINDANAO, THE PHILIPPINES. University of Washington,
1971. 12 min. color. UWAP
Manobo dancers and a gong group of the Bagobo people in actual performance.

MUSIC AND DANCE OF THE HILL PEOPLE OF THE NORTHERN
PHILIPPINES. PART 1. University of Washington, 1971. 29
min. color. UWAP
In this first part of a two-part film, examples of gong playing, singing and dancing are presented.

MUSIC AND DANCE OF THE HILL PEOPLE OF THE NORTHERN
PHILIPPINES. PART 2. University of Washington, 1971.
12 min. color. UWAP

Examines traditional styles in music and dance. Shows a pakkong instrument made of bamboo being played.

MUSIC AND DANCE OF THE IBALOY GROUP OF THE NORTHERN
    PHILIPPINES. University of Washington, 1971. 12 min.
    b/w. UWAP
Examples of a healing dance, plus music performances of the Ibaloy people.

MUSIC AND DANCE OF THE MARANAO PEOPLE OF MINDANAO,
    THE PHILIPPINES. University of Washington, 1971. 21 min.
    color. UWAP
How the Maranao people make music and dance. With examples of their gong orchestra.

MUSIC AND DANCES OF THE YAKAN PEOPLES OF BASILAN
    ISLAND, THE PHILIPPINES. University of Washington, 1971.
    12 min. color. UWAP
About the Yakans of Basilan Island, their music and dances. Includes war dances, a performance by their tuned gong group and other performances, such as on the end-blown flute and the bamboo xylophone.

PEASANT ECOLOGY IN THE RURAL PHILIPPINES. G. M. Guthrie, 1971. 30 min. color. COR, PEN
Shows the relationship of crop cultivation and environment to health and growth of the residents.

PHILIPPINES, GATEWAY TO THE FAR EAST. Coronet, 1957.
    11 min. b/w. COR
An account of the past as well as the present (from the perspective of the 1950s) and the future of The Philippines. Contrasts rural and urban life, scenes of farms and city activities.

THE PHILIPPINES: ISLAND REPUBLIC. McGraw-Hill, 1968.
    16 min. color. MGH
Explores the physical details of the Philippine Islands, and the role of this new country in Southeast Asia and the world.

THE PHILIPPINES: LAND AND PEOPLE. Encyclopaedia Britannica Educational Corporation, 1960. 14 min. color. EBEC,
    UUT, UWY
Traces the history of Spanish and American rule as heritage for the present. Includes village life and scenes in Manila.

THE PHILIPPINES: NATION OF ISLANDS. United World, n. d.
    17 min. color. UEVA
About post-World War II developments in education, transportation and industry in Manila, Cebu, Mactan and Mindanao.

PHILIPPINES: SOCIAL PROGRESS. United Nations, 1953. 10
    min. b/w. MGH
How the United Nations Technical Assistance Program worked to

help improve the health and educational system in the Philippine
Islands.

THE REPUBLIC OF THE PHILIPPINES. United World, 1959.   18
min.   color.   UEVA
Describes the Filipinos' transition to independence from Japanese
control.

SIGABOY.   Maryknoll Fathers, 1971.   52 min.   color.   WHF
A report on a small village on Minanao Island in The Philippines.
Discusses the people and the problem of change they now face in
their society and political life.   Also available in two parts: 29
and 24 min. respectively.

TRIBAL PEOPLE OF MINDANAO.   National Geographic Society,
n. d.   20 min.   color.   VEC
About the current problems of the Tasadays, who, when contacted
in 1966, knew nothing about their country called The Philippines.

WHO INVITED US?   NET, 1970.   60 min.   b/w.   IMP
A review of the U. S. involvement in The Philippines up through
the Vietnam War.

Thailand

BANGKOK.   Films Inc. , 1969.   18 min.   color.   FI, UMN, VEC
Life in the capital of Thailand.   Includes scenes alone the canals.

BANGKOK BY BULBLIGHT.   CCM, n. d.   13 min.   color.   MAC
A view of the canals and tributaries of the Nenam Chao Phya River
and the market activities of the Bangkok people.

CHILDREN OF BANGKOK.   John Morris and Thanom Soongnarata,
1973.   FAU
Follows three boys from a variety of social levels and cultures in
Bangkok.

CHILDREN OF THE WORLD: THAILAND.   NET, 1968.   29 min.
color.   IND
A twelve-year old boy from Thailand demonstrates his daily life
and the impact of Buddhism on almost everyone.

THE FABULOUS TEMPLES OF THAILAND.   Diana Colson, 1974.
10 min.   color.   ACI
An introduction to Thailand's history and a look at the architecture
and sculpture of its temples and palaces.

FAMILY OF THE RIVER: THE RIVER, MY HOME.   McGraw-Hill
and Pan-American World Airways with Vision Associates, 1970.
12 min.   color.   MGH
A nine-year old girl narrates her story about her family and environment on a houseboat.   Shows how they travel up the river to
sell a cargo of salt.   Winner of an award.

FLOATING MARKET, BANGKOK.   ACI, 1970.   11 min.   color.
  ACI
Traces the daily routines of a young woman who travels up and
down the river in Bangkok's famous floating market.

MIAO YEAR.   William R. Geddes, 1968.   61 min.   color.   MGH
About the daily life style of the Blue Miao people, so-named because of their traditional clothes.   Indicates the changes felt since
new legislation has curtailed their cultivation of a staple crop,
opium.   Also available in two parts: 30 and 31 min.   respectively.

NEW HORIZONS: THAILAND.   Pan-American World Airways, n. d.
  13 min.   color.   ASF, PAN
A travelogue designed to promote tourism in Thailand.   Focuses
on major highlights.

ON THE MENAM RIVER.   Productions Unlimited, 1963.   (Thirteen
  from Asia Series.)   15 min.   color.   MAC
Written and filmed by Asians about the present-day life and background of Thailand.   Examines the life of the people who live near
the Menam River.

RICE FARMERS IN THAILAND.   Films Inc., 1969.   19 min.   color.
  FI, VEC
Shows a rice farmer who irrigates his land in contrast to those who
wait for the rainy season; the king gives the traditional blessing of
the rice; Buddhist priests bless the crop.

SIAM: THE PEOPLE OF THAILAND.   Walt Disney, 1958.   (People
  and Places Series.)   31 min.   color.   ASF, UUT
A look at the people who live in Thailand, their customs, their life,
work and play.

SOUTHEAST ASIA: BURMA AND THAILAND.   Coronet, 1972.   13
  min.   color.   COR
A comparison of Burma, rich in natural resources with the more
industrialized Thailand.   Describes the variety of Burma's distinct
ethnic groups and the greater ethnic homogeneity of Thailand.

THAI IMAGES OF THE BUDDHA.   Indiana University, 1963.   (Arts
  of the Orient Series.)   14 min.   color.   IND
How the Buddha image in the arts of Thailand was transformed
from a revered teacher to a supreme deity.

THAILAND.   U. S. Department of the Army, 1963.   29 min.   color.
  NAC
A visit to the "Kingdom of Thailand" and a report on help offered
by members of the U. S. Army.

THAILAND, LAND OF RICE.   Encyclopaedia Britannica Educational
  Corporation, 1957.   14 min.   color.   EBEC, UCA, UCO, UUT,
  UWY
Shows Bangkok, rice farming, the floating market on canals, and
other scenes as setting for the way people live.

THAILAND: PAST AND PRESENT. Unicorn, 1973. 15 min.
   color. COR
Surveys the many people of Thailand, farmers, boatmen, mer-
chants, in their attempt to preserve their traditions in the contemporary world.

TOWER OF DAWN. Productions Unlimited, 1963. (Thirteen from
   Asia Series.) 15 min. color. MAC
Written and filmed by Asians about the present-day life and background of Bangkok. Illustrates Thai art, dance and music and discusses the oldest temple in Bangkok.

TOWN ON THE WATER. Productions Unlimited, 1963. (Thirteen
   from Asia Series.) 15 min. color. MAC
Written and filmed by Asians about the present-day life and background of Bangkok. Describes Buddhism, the caste system, architecture, Western influences.

Vietnam

END OF AN EMPIRE. CBS, 1968. 26 min. b/w. MAC
A television documentary about France's Indo-Chinese War and the
roots of the United States' involvement in Vietnam.

EYE WITNESS: NORTH VIET NAM. James Cameron, 1967. 100
   min. b/w. IMP
A documentary compilation of the first newsreel footage of North
Vietnam, made by James Cameron, British journalist, who is seen
in an interview with North Vietnam premier, Pham Van Dong.

FAR FROM VIETNAM. (LOIN DU VIETNAM.) Chris Marker, et
   al., 1967. 90 min. color. NYF
A number of filmmakers, including Alain Resnais, Jean-Luc Godard,
Chris Marker, and Agnes Varda, contributed to this French film
collage dedicated to the support of the National Liberation Front in
Vietnam.

FOR A VIETNAMESE VIETNAM. Roger Pic, 1972. 28 min.
   color. TRI
A documentary made by a French journalist/filmmaker, on life inside North Vietnam during the spring of 1972 just before the escala-
tion of the air war by U.S. forces. Presents interviews with captured U.S. pilots. Narrated by Wilfred Burchett.

HANOI, TUESDAY THE 13TH. Santiago Alvarez, 1967. 42 min.
   color/b/w. TWN
Cuban filmmaker Santiago Alvarez made this film as tribute to the
Vietnamese people who continued working productively despite the
effects of war. With English soundtrack.

HO CHI MINH. CBS, 1968. 26 min. b/w. MAC, UCA
A television documentary on the late "Mystery Man of Asia."

INSIDE NORTH VIETNAM.   Felix Greene, 1967.   91 min.   color.
    IMP, GRO
Felix Greene's unique coverage of the people of North Vietnam.
Shows war-devastation, interviews with leaders.

INTERVIEW WITH HO CHI MINH.   Impact, 1970.   8 1/2 min.
    color.   IMP
An interview with Ho Chi Minh several months before his death,
during a conversation with Prime Minister Pham Van Dong and
soldiers of the regular army.

PEOPLE'S WAR.   Third World Newsreel, 1969.   40 min.   b/w.
    TWN
A view of North Vietnam by an American camera crew.   Shows
commitment to National Liberation and also the effort to overcome
economic underdevelopment left from colonial days.

SAD SONG OF YELLOW SKIN: PARTS I AND II.   National Film
    Board of Canada, 1970.   58 min.   color.   FI, PEN
A documentary on three Americans residing in Saigon--one who
lives with Vietnamese; the second, a journalist, tours a run down
Saigon neighborhood known as "The Graveyard"; and the third,
John Steinbeck, Jr., who lives on the Island of Peace in the Mekong
Delta.

17TH PARALLEL.   Joris Ivens, 1968.   110 min.   b/w.   IMP
About the life of North Vietnamese who live around Vinh Linh,
north of the 17th parallel.   Studies the life style and commitment
of people at war.

79 SPRINGS OF HO CHI MINH.   (LAS 79 PRIMAVERAS DE HO
    CHI MINH.)   Santiago Alvarez, n.d.   25 min.   b/w.   TWN
Tells the story of the life of Ho Chi Minh, using photographs and
newsreel footage.   A eulogy by Cuban filmmaker Santiago Alvarez.
Has musical soundtrack and Spanish titles.

SOUTHEAST ASIA: VIETNAM, CAMBODIA, LAOS.   Coronet, 1973.
    20 1/2 min.   color.   COR
An account of the differences in land use, despite the geographic
similarities of North and South Vietnam.   A comparison of rugged
Laos with the fertile plains of Cambodia.

VIETNAM: JOURNAL OF A WAR.   BBC, 1967.   52 min.   b/w.
    TL
What the Vietnam War has done to the Vietnamese people.

YOUNG PUPPETEERS OF SOUTH VIETNAM.   National Liberation
    Front, South Vietnam, n.d.   25 min.   b/w.   TWN
Shows teenagers in the South Vietnam areas occupied by the National Liberation Front (before the close of the War) making puppets
from scraps of U.S. war materials for use for children's puppet
shows.

THE PACIFIC

Includes: Hawaii; Oceania (Islands of Central and South Pacific); Australasia (Australia, New Zealand, New Guinea and neighboring islands); Melanesia (Northeast of Australia); Micronesia (Mariana Islands, Caroline and Marshall Islands); Polynesia (area between Hawaii and New Zealand).

ACROSS THE SOUTH PACIFIC. United World, 1964. 17 min. color. UEVA
Description of Hawaii, Fiji, New Zealand and Australia.

AKU-AKU. Thor Heyerdahl, 1951. 84 min. color. MGH
A Swedish film which describes the archeological findings on Easter Island and its neighboring islands, including 60-ton stone heads, cave carvings, relics.

AMERICAN SAMOA: PARADISE LOST? NET, 1968. 55 min. color. IND
Compares the American educational system, which stresses independent thinking, with Samoan values which emphasize obedience to family and authority.

ARTIFACTS OF OLD HAWAII. Ciné-Pic Hawaii, n. d. 11 min. color. IFP
A report on the life of Hawaiians before the Europeans arrived. Uses artifacts to illustrate the story. Based on the book "Ancient Hawaiian Life."

ARTS OF POLYNESIA. Ciné-Pic Hawaii, n. d. 11 min. color. IFP
A survey of the arts of Polynesia with special attention to New Zealand, Hawaii, Tahiti and Easter Island. Uses the Bishop Museum in Honolulu.

AUSTRALIA. Encyclopaedia Britannica Educational Corporation, 1959. 22 min. color. EBEC
A survey of the wide variety of cultural and geographic aspects of Australia.

AUSTRALIA: DOWN UNDER AND OUTBACK. National Geographic Society, 1973. 26 min. color. NGS

117

Shows the desert interior of Australia with its sheep ranches, opal mines, cattle ranches, plus the life style of the aborigines.

AUSTRALIA, ISLAND CONTINENT. Dudley, 1964. 17 min. color. UEVA
Describes the modern, developing cities of Australia: Melbourne, Hobart, Adelaide and Perth.

AUSTRALIA NOW. Australian News and Information Bureau, 1969. 18 min. color. ACI
An analysis of Australia and the life patterns of its people. With a script by documentarist Stuart Legg.

AUSTRALIA: THE TIMELESS LAND. National Geographic Society, 1969. 53 min. color. MGH
A comprehensive view of Australia, where diverse peoples live side by side.

AUSTRALIA TODAY. International Film Bureau, 1966. 22 min. color. EFD
Survey of the bush country and Australia's yet undeveloped wealth.

THE BIKINIANS. Hill Bermont, 1974. 29 min. color. WGTV
Concerns the population of Bikini Island who were evacuated and discusses the Bikinians' controversy with U. S. officials.

BOYHOOD OF KAMEHAMEHA. George Tahara, 1973. 27 min. color. CIPI
The early years of Hawaii's King Kamehameha.

CANE CAMP. Solfilm International, n. d. 20 min. color. SOL
An account of the Japanese who emigrated to Hawaii--how they successfully overcame obstacles of prejudice and language. Narrated by a Buddhist who reflects on the circumstances which brought his people to Hawaii. Uses some archival footage.

CARNARVON. Australian Museum, 1969. UCA
Shows the prehistoric art of the Australian aborigines found in the Carnarvon Ranges.

CARNIVAL UNDER THE SEA. R. L. A. Catala, n. d. 70 min. color. UCA
An entertaining look at the organisms under the sea among the coral reefs of New Caledonia and in the aquarium of Nouméa. Winner of several international film festival awards.

CHANGING MATILDA: THE NEW AUSTRALIA. NBC, 1965. 24 min. color. EBEC
About contemporary Australia's problems of growth and survival as a neighbor to Asiatic countries. Narrated by Chet Huntley.

CHILDHOOD RIVALRY IN BALI AND NEW GUINEA. New York University, 1952. (Character Formation in Different Cultures

Series.) 17 min. b/w. NYU, UCA
Children and their mothers of two different cultures are compared.
The Balinese mother gives conspicuous attention to other babies,
while the New Guinea mother tries to keep her child from becoming
jealous.

CLICK GO THE SHEARS AND THE OLD BULLOCK DRAY. Peter
    Hamilton, 1961. (Australian Folk Song Series.) 6 min.
    b/w. MAC1
Animation treatment of two humorous folk songs, one a sheep
shearing song, and the other, an account of an oxcart driver who
seeks a wife.

CORAL WONDERLAND. Australian News and Information Bureau,
    1950. 30 min. color. UCA
Shows the coral growths of Australia's Great Barrier Reef and the
underwater creatures also to be found there.

DANCE TRIP. Solfilm International, 1974. 27 min. color. SOL
How the descendants of Filipino laborers, imported to work in
Hawaii's cane fields, still perform to perfection the native dances
of the Philippines in their new environment. Also shows the religious, social and economic activities of the Filipino people living
in Hawaii.

DEAD BIRDS. Peabody Museum, 1963. 83 min. color. PHO
Studies the resemblances of neolithic culture of the Dani people,
who live in the Grand Valley of the Balicm in Western New Guinea,
to our own culture. Dead birds are persons killed by the enemy.

DESERT PEOPLE. Australian Institute of Aboriginal Studies, 1966.
    51 min. b/w. MGH, UCA, VEC
A look at the traditional way of life of Australia's aborigines of the
Western Desert area, most of whom have left for federal camp-
grounds, thus gradually becoming assimilated into the mainstream
of Australian society.

DOWN UNDER. Pan-American World Airways, n.d. 28 min.
    color. ASF, PAN
A travelogue designed to promote tourism in Australia. Shows
scenic highlights.

EASTER ISLAND: PUZZLE OF THE PACIFIC. Arnold Eagle,
    1970. 28 min. color. MAC
Two archeologists theorize about the astounding culture produced by
the remote people of Easter Island. Narrated by Peter Jennings,
ABC News; written by James Giggans.

EMU RITUAL AT RUGURI. University of Calif. Extension Media
    Center, 1967. 33 min. color. UCA
A look at a Walbiri tribal ceremony to promote the fertility of
emus, formerly a staple in the Walbiri diet.

ENIGMAS OF EASTER ISLAND. (LES ENIGMES DE L'ILE DE
PAQUES.) Explo-Mundo, n. d. 52 min. color. RAY, RIT
Francis Mazière, archeologist, explores the island to attempt an-
swers to puzzling questions about its people and their origins. A
television production. French language version available.

FAMILY OF THE ISLAND: HER NAME IS WASAMANTHA. Mc-
Graw-Hill, Pan-American World Airways with Vision Associates, 1970. MGH
About a day's adventure in the life of a ten-year-old girl who lives
in the Fiji Islands. An award-winning film.

FIJI: A SOUTH PACIFIC ISLAND. United World, 1964. 17 min.
color. UEVA, UUT
How the variety of people in Fiji--Fijians, Europeans, Indians and
Chinese--live and work side by side.

FIJI: THE THREE-LEGGED STOOL. R. Barrington Scott, 1969.
20 min. color. ACI
Presents the geography of Fiji through comparisons of three cultures: the Fijian, the Indian and the European.

THE GOLD DIGGERS. Peter Hamilton, 1961. (Australian Folk
Song Series.) 3 min. b/w. MAC[1]
An authentic rendition of a song by two prospectors who are frus-
trated by bad weather, costly water, hard rocks, the lure of grog,
and the lack of gold.

THE GOLD DIGGERS BALLAD. Educational Media, Australia,
n. d. 7 min. color. EFD
The watercolors of artist S. T. Gill, painted in the 1800s, give a
feeling of the Australian gold rushes and the hunger for gold. Accompanied by Australian ballads.

THE GREAT BARRIER REEF. NBC, 1970. 54 min. color. FI
How a variety of starfish that eats live coral is threatening the
Great Barrier Reef which serves as a shelter for unusual sea crea-
tures.

THE GREAT FISH OF MAUI. International Film Foundation, 1973.
7 min. color. EFD, IFF
Clay animation is used to tell the folk legend from New Zealand
about a youth who joins his fisherman brothers as a stowaway on a
fishing expedition, where he uses his powers to bring in a large
catch.

THE GREAT UNFENCED. Contemporary, 1964. 33 min. color.
MGH
Aborigines of Western Australia are studied in the rugged atmos-
phere of a million-acre cattle station.

GUAM, U. S. A. Avis, 1969. 13 min. color. MAC
Traces paths of early settlers from Malaysia. Shows artifacts of
early peoples and describes life today.

HAWAII: POLYNESIA IN THE U.S.A.   CCM, 1972.   (Our Land,
   Our People, U.S.A. Series.)   17 min.   color.   MAC
Life of Hawaii today as contrasted with the period of its discovery
by Captain Cook, the reign of Kamehameha and the role of early
missionaries.

HAWAII: THE 50TH STATE.   Encyclopaedia Britannica Educational
   Corporation, 1959.   17 min.   color.   EBEC
The history of Polynesian settlement and the influence of varied
cultures on present-day Hawaii.

HAWAIIAN NATIVE LIFE.   Encyclopaedia Britannica Educational
   Corporation, 1940.   11 min.   b/w.   EBEC, UWY
An old film that gives a view of multi-racial Hawaii and the cir-
cumstances that stimulated immigration from the Orient.

HILA.   Ciné-Pic Hawaii, n.d.   11 min.   color.   IFP
A legend about a Hawaiian chief who abuses his power and is turned
into a Hila (a weed).

ISLANDS OF THE SOUTH PACIFIC.   Barr, 1959.   15 min.   color.
   UWY
Covers general geographical background and also discusses types of
islands, origin of natural life, and the various peoples who have
migrated to this area.

KEREPE'S HOUSE: A HOUSE BUILDING IN NEW GUINEA.   M.
   Jablonko, 1966.   50 min.   color.   PEN
How the Fungai people of New Guinea build a house from vines,
leaves, and trees of the forest.   Discusses construction in relation
to the history and customs of the Fungai.

KRAKATOA.   Educational Films, 1932.   30 min.   b/w.   PAR
An Academy Award-winning documentary about the rebirth of Kra-
katoa, the volcanic island in the Sunda Strait that exploded in 1883.
Narrated by Graham McNamme.

KRAKATOA.   Joe Rock, 1966.   28 min.   b/w.   MAC
Provides historical background of the volcanic island's destruction
in 1883.   Examines volcanoes and the factors involved in eruptions.

KUMARA.   Ciné-Pic Hawaii, 1964.   11 min.   color.   IFP
Kumara, which means "sweet potato" in Hawaii, is the story about
how this food staple was introduced to the Hawaiian Islands by a
foreigner many years ago.

LAND DIVERS OF MELANESIA.   Karl Muller and Robert Gardner,
   1974.   30 min.   color.   PHO
An award-winning film about the practice of some men of Pentecost
Island who dive headfirst from a tower one hundred feet high in order to insure a good yam crop.   Shows the place of such ritual
among the other rites, such as blessing the taro crop, circumci-
sion, feasts.

LEE SUZUKI: HOME IN HAWAII. Learning Corporation, 1973.
    (The Many Americans Series.) 19 min.   color.   LEC
A young boy, part Hawaiian, Japanese, Filipino, plus Irish and
Swedish, is typical of the racial mixtures found among Hawaii's
population. Using a simple story line, the film follows the multi-
ethnic life style of the Hawaiian people. Written and directed by
Bert Salzman.

LEGEND OF THE NIU. Ciné-Pic Hawaii, 1965. 11 min. color.
    IFP
The legend of a Hawaiian boy who moves into manhood, according
to custom carrying only a few provisions which are supposed to
remain intact. Instead he gives his food to a hungry stranger.
This act, in turn, brings the coconut (niu) to all the Islanders.

LIFE ON A CORAL ATOLL. Authentic, 1969. 20 min. color.
    MGH
How the inhabitants of small coral islands in the Pacific Ocean
adapt to their environment.

MARGARET MEAD'S NEW GUINEA JOURNAL. NET, 1969. 90
    min. color. IND
How Margaret Mead studied the differences in the life style of the
village of Peri on Manus Island between her visits of 1928 and 1953
and filmed in her 1967 visit.

MASTER AND SLAVE. Ciné-Pic Hawaii, n. d. 11 min. color.
    IFP
About a much-abused slave who saves his prince from a volcano
eruption, an event that leads to the abolishment of slavery in the
country. A Hawaiian legend.

MATJEMOSH. Stichting Film en Wettenschap, Universitaire Film,
    Utrecht, Netherlands, 1964. 27 min. color. UCA
Shows a wood carver of the Asmet tribe in New Guinea talking
about his life and working on wood he has cut from a tree to make
a drum.

MEN OF THE DREAM TIME. BBC and Odyssey, n. d. (Australian
    Aborigines Series.) 25 min. color. TL
About the aborigines of Australia's Outback region, their hunting,
ritual and legend which go back to pre-historic days.

MICRONESIA. Dcena, 1959. 13 min. color. UUT
Describes the life of people and the natural features of one of the
Micronesian islands.

MICRONESIA. Avis, 1969. 25 min. color. MAC
Background about the high islands and atolls in Micronesia and the
life of the people there. Includes Yap, the land of stone money.

MOANA. Robert J. Flaherty and Frances H. Flaherty, 1926. 66
    min. b/w. silent. PFS

Robert Flaherty's first film made with the improved panchromatic film of his day--a picture of life on the South Sea Island Samoa. Titles by Julian Johnston.

MULGA SEED CEREMONY. University of California, 1967. (Australian Institute of Aboriginal Studies Series.) 25 min. color. UCA
A report on a ceremony intended to encourage the fertility of mulga, a desert tree valued for food and fuel. The setting is near the Petermann Range in Australia.

NEW GUINEA. McGraw-Hill, 1967. 16 min. color. MGH, UCO
One of the last examples of a stone age culture. Explains that this country is divided politically into two parts--one under Indonesian administration, the other under Australian administration.

NEW LIVES FOR OLD. Margaret Mead, 1959. 20 min. color. ETS, PEN
Dr. Margaret Mead discusses the social and cultural transformation of the Manus people of Admiralty Island over a twenty-five-year period.

NEW ZEALAND, NATION OF CONTRASTS. Universal Education and Visual Arts, 1964. 17 min. b/w. UEVA
Describes the physical and economic attributes of contemporary New Zealand.

NUKUMANU, AN ATOLL IN THE PACIFIC. Denmark, 1967. 28 min. color. STA
A rare look at a people who live on an island in a coral reef removed from the world of white men.

OLD BLACK BILLY. Peter Hamilton, 1961. (Australian Folk Song Series.) 5 min. b/w. MAC[1]
A dramatic setting for an Australian folk song. Shows a swagman who hikes, sings and cooks with his "old black billy" (cooking utensil).

THE OLD WARRIOR. Ciné-Pic Hawaii, 1963. 11 min. color. IFP
A legend to explain why the morning glory grows wild on some Hawaiian shores. Tells of the good deeds performed by an old warrior who was left to die on a barren island.

THE OVERLANDERS. Michael Balcon, 1946. 107 min. b/w.
Directed by Harry Watt; scenario by Harry Watt; photography by Osmond Borrowdaile; music by John Ireland. With Chips Rafferty, John Nugent Hayward, Daphne Campbell, Jeanne Blue. MGH, UCA
Australia's first epic and first film to win international attention. A true story about a man who drove a herd of 1,000 cattle many miles across the country to save them from the Japanese.

PACIFIC.   Thames Television, 1973.   (The World at War.)   60
    min.   b/w.   RAY, RIT
The step-by-step story of the fighting in the Pacific during World
War II.   Narrated by Lord Laurence Olivier.

PACIFIC ISLAND.   International Film Foundation, 1949.   18 min.
    b/w.   EFD, IFF, PEN
Life on a South Pacific atoll, Likiep Island.   Shows the people at
work and at play.   Includes an undersea diver catching a giant
clam, the capture of a large turtle, and a typical birthday feast.

PAN AM'S WORLD: THE SOUTH PACIFIC.   Pan-American World
    Airways, n. d.   20 min.   color.   ASF, PAN
A travelogue designed to promote tourism in the South Pacific.
Gives scenic sights of the various islands.

PAPUA AND NEW GUINEA.   Australian News and Information
    Bureau, 1970.   17 min.   color.   FI, VEC
Discusses signs of change in New Guinea, local political development, social and economic expansion as well as education, medicine, use of resources.

PEOPLE OUT OF TIME.   BBC, 1970.   30 min.   color.   TL
A look at the Bindibu people of the Great Sandy Desert of Australia
once thought to have perished.   Shows their successful adaptation
and mastery of environment under stone age conditions.

PEOPLES OF THE ISLAND WORLD.   Bailey, 1964.   17 min.
    color.   UCO
The life and work of the Melanesians, Micronesians and Polynesi-
ans.

POLYNESIAN ADVENTURE.   National Geographic Society, 1969.
    51 min.   color.   MGH, NGS
A leisurely trip with a marine biologist and his family through
Polynesia, the islands scattered over 15 million square miles of
the Pacific Ocean.

REEDY RIVER.   Peter Hamilton, 1961.   (Australian Folk Series.)
    5 min.   b/w.   MAC1
A folk song about an old settler who comments on the bad and the
good of settling in frontier territory and the loss of his wife.

RETURN TO THE DREAMING.   Cecil Holmes, n. d.   47 min.
    color.   IMP
A look at the great aboriginal painter, Yirriwalla and the effect of
white Europeans on the culture and economic status of the Australian aborigine.

THE ROARING SERPENT OF ARNHEM LAND.   BBC and Odyssey,
    1967.   (Australian Aborigines Series.)   25 min.   color.   TL
A visit with the people of Australia's coastal area and with the
aborigines during a secret ceremony.   Narrated by Lowell Thomas.

ROCK ENGRAVINGS. Australian Museum, 1969. 7 min. color.
UCA
A study of aboriginal rock art created thousands of years before
settlement by whites.

SAMOA. Walt Disney, 1961. (People and Places Series.) 30
min. color. ASF, DIS
Describes the beauty, heritage and daily life of the Samoan people.

SATIN SLIPPERS. Hyperion, 1949. 32 min. b/w. MAC[1]
All the factors involved in the rise of ballet in Australia. Includes
sections of the Australian ballet "Corroboree" based on the rhythm
and tribal dances of Australian aborigines.

THE SKY ABOVE, THE MUD BELOW. Ardennes, 1962. 90 min.
color. MAC[1]
A French documentary made in Dutch New Guinea that describes
an expedition into unexplored areas of Dutch New Guinea by a
French and Dutch group of explorers under the leadership of
Pierre-Dominique Gaisseau. Includes views of pygmies who've
never seen white men before, a mock-birth ritual, and head-hunt-
ers who wear human skulls as adornments. With English narration.

SOUTH SEA ISLAND LIFE: THE DOLPHIN HUNTERS. John
Crew, 1970. 18 1/2 min. color. COR
The centuries-old life on Solomon Island, including making shell
money, hot stone cookery, market barter, religious ceremonies.

SPORTS OF OLD HAWAII. Ciné-Pic Hawaii, 1966. 11 min.
color. IFP
Shows traditional sports of Hawaii's early history as performed by
students of the Kamehameha School in Honolulu.

THE STONE AGE SURVIVORS. Explo-Munod, n.d. 52 min.
color. RIT
A documentary on the last of the aboriginal people in the Central
Australian desert, the Pitjanjaras. Shows initiation ceremonies,
kangaroo hunts, medical practices, religious rites.

TAHITI CALLS. Ciné-Pic Hawaii, 1955. 11 min. color. IFP
Presents scenes of attractive locales, rural and market life in
Papeete and on Moorea Island. Includes Tahiti's big Bastille Day
festivities.

TAUU, AN ATOLL IN THE PACIFIC. Denmark, 1967. 32 min.
color. STA
A study of the people who live on an atoll in the Pacific. Emphasis is on local items made for local use.

A VILLAGE IN SAMOA. Hayward, n.d. 21 min. color. IFP
A view of western Samoa, the only part where Samoans still live
in the traditional manner. Shows dances, music and entertainment.

VILLAGE LIFE IN TONGA.   Harvard University, 1971.   20 min.
    color.   ACI
A documentary about Polynesian culture filmed in Hoi, a village in
the Tonga Islands of the South Pacific.

WALBIRI RITUAL AT GUNADJARI.   University of California, 1969.
    (Australian Institute of Aboriginal Studies Series.)   28 min.
    color.   UCA
Describes a three-day ceremony at a spot where the Walbiri and
Pintubi tribal lands join.

WALBIRI RITUAL AT NGAMA.   University of California, 1966.
    (Australian Institute of Aboriginal Studies Series.)   23 min.
    color.   UCA
Presents an "increase ceremony" of the Walbiri people of Australia
--a ritual devoted to fertility and initiation.   Includes some rare
ceremonial scenes.

WALKABOUT.   Australian News and Information Bureau, 1946.
    17 min.   color.   PEN
Shows a camel expedition southwest of Alice Springs, Australia,
the cooking of kangaroo meat ceremony devoted to the kangaroo as
myth; with examples of aboriginal cave paintings and language.

WALKABOUT.   Twentieth Century-Fox, 1972.   95 min.   color.
    Directed by Nicholas Roeg; screenplay by Edward Bond from
    the novel by James Vance Marshall.   With Jenny Agutter,
    Lucian John, David Gumpilil, John Meillon.   FI
A white girl and her brother are left in the Australian wilderness
by their father, and wander until they encounter an aborigine boy
on a walkabout, i. e. , a six-month survival test.   The latter shares
his ease with, and love of, nature with them.

WHAT HAVE YOU DONE WITH MY COUNTRY?   Frank Heimans,
    D. Baglin, 1975.   20 min.   color.   ACI
How the life of the Australian aborigines has been changed; how they
have been moved out of their home environment, hurt by pollution
and deprived of their animals.

WHITE CLAY AND OCHRE.   Australian Museum, 1969.   15 min.
    color.   UCA
Studies the aborigines of Western New South Wales, their hunting,
their art works.

General

AIN'T GONNA EAT MY MIND. WNET, 1972. 34 min. color.
    IMP
Explores the reasons behind death and violence in poor neighborhoods. After the funeral of Black Benjy, black and Puerto Rican gangs meet to end conflict and act to help their neighborhood in the South Bronx, N. Y. An Emmy Award winner.

CONFRONTATION IN WASHINGTON: RESURRECTION CITY. Koplin and Grinker, 1970. 15 min. color. PIC
The gathering in Washington in May 1968 of the Nation's poor, including Afro-Americans, Native Americans, Mexican-Americans as well as Appalachian whites. Their arrival by mule train, truck, bus, rail and on foot is shown as well as their erection of Resurrection City.

THE GAME. Roberta Hodes in cooperation with Mobilization for Youth, 1967. 17 min. b/w. GRO
Black and Puerto Rican youth in New York City experience violence and prejudice in a story told by one black teenager who is beaten by a gang. Told in a chanted and pantomimed story. Based on a play by George Houston Bass.

HIGH SCHOOL RISING. Third World Newsreel, 1969. 15 min. b/w. TWN
A discussion of how education perpetuates social class differences: IQ tests, tracking system, vocational shops, omission of Black, Brown, Asian, and poor white struggles from history texts.

HUNGER IN AMERICA. CBS, 1968. 45 min. b/w. CAR, IMP, UCA
Shows the poor conditions of segments of various ethnic groups: black sharecroppers in Alabama, Navajo Indians in Arizona, and Mexican-Americans in San Antonio, plus starving tenant farmers near Washington, D. C. An award-winning film.

MINORITIES: FROM AFRICA, ASIA AND THE AMERICAS. Coronet, 1972. 15 min. color. COR
An account of the cultural diversity and contributions to American society of people from various ethnic minorities.

THE OTHER AMERICANS. WJZ-TV, 1969. 52 min. color.
    WJZ
Shows the effect of extreme poverty on health--especially that of
children. Individuals who achieved success despite their roots in
poverty, which affects minority groups particularly, talk about their
struggle.

RANK AND FILE. NET, 1970. (Black Journal Series.) 15 min.
    b/w. IND
Shows blacks and Puerto Ricans fighting to form their own union to
counter present discrimination.

ROMPIENDO PUERTAS. (BREAKING DOWN DOORS/BREAK AND
    ENTER.) Third World Newsreel, 1971. 42 min. b/w. In
    Spanish and English. TWN
Describes a protest movement of March 1970 in New York which
developed into Operation Move-In and a plan for urban renewal
within the city.

SOME ARE MORE EQUAL THAN OTHERS. CBS, 1971. 40 min.
    b/w. IMP
The legal treatment of various ethnic minorities: inequities in the
bail system, jury selection practices and civil actions involving
debts, property.

Afro-Americans

A. PHILIP RANDOLPH. Rediscovery Productions, 1972. (Por-
    trait in Black Series.) 10 min. color. NACC, SEF
Randolph reminisces about his confrontations with Roosevelt and
Kennedy and the continuing struggle of black Americans.

ADAM CLAYTON POWELL. Mert Koplin and Charles Grinker,
    1970. (Black Views on Race Series.) 4 min. color. TL
Powell's actual public remarks, as example of black opinion in the
U. S.

AFRO-AMERICAN DANCE: ESTABLISHING A CULTURAL HERI-
    TAGE. Raymond Fischer and Stanley Woodward, 1971. 20
    min. color. TL
A group of black students establish an African dance organization
on campus in order to preserve and understand aspects of African
culture.

AFRO-AMERICAN WORKSONGS IN A TEXAS PRISON. Peter and
    Toshi Seeger, 1975. 29 min. b/w. RAD
Black prisoners in Texas are viewed singing five tree-chopping
songs plus a short hoeing song and "Down by the Riverside. "

AN AFRO-AMERICAN THING. Royce Vaughn, 1969. 25 min.
    b/w. PAR
Uses soul music and African dances to compare African and Black-
American cultures.

AKKI: A BLACK POET. WKYC, 1972. 25 min. color. FI
A young black poet, Akki Jomo Onyango, talks about his background, his inner thoughts and his writing. An award-winning film.

AL STACEY HAYES. Camiel, 1970. 28 min. color. JAS
About a black teenager who works to canvass black people of a
Mississippi town before an election.

ALL MY BABIES. Center for Mass Communications, Columbia
    University, 1952. 55 min. b/w. UCA
Follows Miss Mary, a licensed midwife, who demonstrates the
method by which black babies in Georgia were being delivered at
the time the film was made by George Stoney. Includes actual
delivery sequences.

ALL THE PEOPLE AGAINST SOME OF THE PEOPLE. Koplin
    and Grinker, 1970. (The Turning Points: America in the
    20th Century.) 15 min. color. PIC
Concerns the events of 1963 when Governor Wallace of Alabama
tried to prevent black students from registering at the University
of Alabama, a federal judge ruled in favor of the students, and
President Kennedy sent out the National Guard to enforce the court
order.

ALL THE WAY HOME. Dynamic, 1957. 30 min. b/w. MAC1
What happens when a black family pauses in front of a "For Sale"
sign. Shows the anxiety and irrationality that contribute to the integration problem in housing.

THE AMERICAN NEGRO SINGS. Futura, 1968. 24 min. color.
    MLA
With music and song black roots and aspirations are explored.

ANACOSTIA: MUSEUM IN THE GHETTO. NET, 1968. 17 min.
    b/w. IND, UCA
About a branch of the Smithsonian Institution founded to bring a
ghetto's residents into cultural and community activities.

ANGELA DAVIS: PORTRAIT OF A REVOLUTIONARY. Yolande de
    Luart, 1971. 60 min. and 35 min. versions. b/w. NYF
A profile of Angela Davis done by UCLA students while she was
philosophy instructor. Contains unique coverage not found elsewhere.

ANGRY NEGRO. NET, 1966. (Radical Americans Series.) 30
    min. b/w. IND, UCA
The wide range of opinions among black people on peaceful life between blacks and whites in the U.S., how to attain rights, freedom, education and power.

THE ANGRY PROPHET: FREDERICK DOUGLASS. WRC-TV, 1970.
    24 min. color. FI
An Emmy Award-winning film on the black leader of the pre- and
post-Civil War periods, using his actual words throughout.

ANGRY VOICES OF WATTS.   NBC, 1966.   (Civil Rights Movement
    Series.) 56 min. b/w.   FI, UCA
About the Watts Riot of 1965 and the expressions of black writers
at Budd Schulberg's writers' workshop after the event.   Includes
footage showing the streets and faces of Watts.

ARETHA FRANKLIN, SOUL SINGER.   ABC, 1969.   25 min.   color.
    MGH
Follows Aretha Franklin, leading exponent of soul music, through
her daily work and as she comments on her early years.

THE AUTOBIOGRAPHY OF MISS JANE PITTMAN.   Tomorrow
    Entertainment, 1974. 109 min.   color.   Directed by John
    Korty.   With Cicely Tyson, Richard A. Dysart, Katherine
    Helmond, Michael Murphy, Roy Poole, Josephine Premice.
    LEC
Based on stories by Ernest Gaines set in his native Louisiana.
The story of a courageous black woman from her childhood as a
slave to her present age of 110 years.   Winner of four Emmy
Awards.

THE BADDEST DADDY IN THE WHOLE WORLD.   Fred Haines,
    1972. 52 min.   color.   NYF
A documentary about Muhammad Ali in 1971 before the Juergen
Blin fight.   Shows Ali as family man, out-spoken, concerned black
man, and as boxer.

THE BATTLE OF EAST ST. LOUIS.   CBS, 1970.   46 min.   b/w.
    CAR
In spring of 1969 fear of violence in East St. Louis brought white
policemen and black militants together in a sensitivity training program.   The results are examined in terms of their possible use-
fulness in other cities.

BAYARD RUSTIN.   Mert Koplin and Charles Grinker, 1970.   (Black
    Views on Race Series.) 4 min.   color.   TL
Rustin's actual public remarks, as example of black opinion in the
U.S.

BEGINNINGS ... THE STORY OF BOGGS ACADEMY.   Rediscovery,
    n.d. 12 min.   color.   NACC
About the roots of Oscar McCloud of the Presbyterian Church in
Georgia's Boggs Academy, the only predominantly black prep school
that is accredited.

BENJAMIN BANNEKER: MAN OF SCIENCE.   Encyclopaedia Brit-
    annica Educational Corporation, 1971. 9 min.   color.   EBEC
How equal opportunity helped a free black man, Benjamin Banneker,
make great achievements in science.

BERNIE CASEY: BLACK ARTIST.   Multi-Cul, 1971.   21 min.
    color.   ACI
A visit with the former football player who became a successful
painter.

BESSIE SMITH.   Paradigm, n. d.   13 1/2 min.   b/w.   PARD
Old Bessie Smith recordings accompany the film images of Charles
Levine that are adroitly pulled together from stock footage of black
people marching and fires plus Bessie Smith's only film, ST.
LOUIS BLUES.

BILL COSBY ON PREJUDICE.   Pyramind, 1971.   25 min.   color.
   PYR
A Bill Cosby monologue in which he utters almost every thought
ever dreamt of by bigots through the ages in reference to almost
every ethnic minority group.

THE BILL OF RIGHTS IN ACTION: EQUAL OPPORTUNITY.
   Bernard Wilets, 1970.   22 min.   color.   BFA
A black worker is promoted over a white worker and the white worker protests.   An open-ended film in which the case is argued before an arbitrator.

BIOGRAPHY OF A ROOKIE.   David Wolper, 1961.   60 min.   b/w.
   SEF
The carcor of Willie Davis from the day he was discovered by a
Dodger scout to his tryout with the team.

BISHOP TURNER: BLACK NATIONALIST.   Encyclopaedia Britannica Educational Corporation, 1970.   9 min.   color.   EBEC
How Bishop Henry McNeal Turner, the first black chaplain in the
Union Army during the Civil War, organized a back-to-Africa
movement.

THE BLACK AMERICAN DREAM.   BBC, 1973.   65 min.   color.
   TL
A view of today's cooler atmosphere in the Black Power movement
through exclusive meetings with black leaders, such as Stokely
Carmichael and Jesse Jackson.

BLACK AND WHITE TOGETHER?   NET, 1969.   58 min.   b/w.
   IND
A report on a not-too-successful project promoting inter-racial harmony and involving high school students in Atlantic City, New Jersey.

BLACK AND WHITE: UNLESS WE LEARN TO LIVE TOGETHER.
   Jesse Sandler, n d.   16 min.   color.   AEF
Leonard Nimoy is narrator for this study of two men--one, a black
man who must contend with the loss of a great leader and friend,
and a white man who must reckon with the hatred of his black
neighbors.

BLACK AND WHITE: UPTIGHT.   Avanti, 1969.   35 min.   color.
   BFA, PEN
A documentary on racial prejudice, socio-economic differences be-
tween blacks and whites, riots, efforts to work together.

BLACK ARTISTS. Paul Highman, 1969. 28 min. color. AFGR
The work and motivation of three black artists is examined: Sam-
ella Lewis (oil painting), William Pajaud (watercolor), John Riddle
(sculpture).

BLACK COP. NET, 1969. 16 min. b/w. IND, PEN
How the black policeman relates to other blacks. Studies repre-
sentatives of both sides in New York City and Los Angeles.

BLACK FANTASY. Lionel Rogosin, 1972. 78 min. color. IMP
A combination of poetic fantasy and factual reality to tell what it's
like to be black and married to a white woman. The protagonist
is Jim Collier, a young musician. A much-awarded film. Directed
by Lionel Rogosin.

THE BLACK G. I. NET, 1970. 55 min. b/w. IND, UCA
About the black soldier's experience with discrimination on and off
military bases.

BLACK HAS ALWAYS BEEN BEAUTIFUL. NET, 1971. 17 min.
    b/w. IND
Master black photographer James Van DerZee photographs a young
woman while he discusses the art of photography, which he has been
practicing in Harlem for many decades.

BLACK HISTORY: LOST, STOLEN OR STRAYED. CBS, 1968.
    (Of Black America Series.) 55 min. b/w. BFA, PAR, UCA
A CBS television program (July 2, 1968) which brought attention "to
the misrepresentation of Negroes by the motion picture medium."
Narrated by Bill Cosby. Also available in two parts: Part I, 26
min.; Part II, 27 min.

BLACK JEWS. Avraham Goren, 1973. 25 min. color. NLC
About black Jews who live in a community in New Jersey.

THE BLACK KING. (HARLEM HOT SHOT.) Southland, 1932. 70
    min. b/w. Directed by Bud Pollard; from the story by Donald
    Heywood. With Vivianne Baker, Harry Gray, Knolly Mitchell,
    Mary Jane Watkins, A. B. Comethiere. PAR
White director Bud Pollard's first black film. An all-black production about a crooked minister who takes over a parish, sponsors
a Back to Africa movement, and proclaims himself King of the
United States of Africa. (Note: available prints have defects.)

BLACK LIKE ME. Continental, 1964. 110 min. b/w. Directed
    by Carl Lerner. Rest of credits unlisted. With James Whit-
    more, Will Geer, Raymond St. Jacques, Thelma Oliver, Ros-
    coe Lee Browne, Al Freeman, Jr. BUDG, READ
This is John Howard Griffin's written account of his masquerade
as a black in the South transferred to film. An attempt to expose
racism in the U. S.

BLACK MEN AND IRON HORSES. 18 min. color. Sterling,
     1970. SEF
How black Americans built and improved our railroads.

BLACK MUSIC IN AMERICA: FROM THEN TILL NOW. Screen
     Gems, 1970. 28 min. color. LEC
The history of the black contribution to American music, featuring
Louis Armstrong, Mahalia Jackson, B. B. King, "Leadbelly,"
Count Basie, Nina Simone, and Bessie Smith.

BLACK MUSLIMS SPEAK FROM AMERICA. BBC, n. d. 33 min.
     b/w. TL
Seven young Black Muslims talk with Malcolm Muggeridge about
their beliefs, which include the eventual perishing of America and
of all white people, good and bad, establishment of a separate black
state, and Elijah Muhammed as leader.

BLACK PANTHER. S. F. Nowsreel, 1968. 20 min. b/w. TWN
An authorized film about the history and position of the Black Pan-
ther Party. With interviews with Eldridge Cleaver and Huey P.
Newton.

BLACK PEOPLE IN THE SLAVE SOUTH, 1850. Encyclopaedia
     Britannica Educational Corporation, 1971. 11 min. color.
     EBEC
About the slave trade in 1850 which brought black people to the
Southern United States.

BLACK POLICEMAN: THE WRITING ON THE WALL. Jesse
     Sandler, n. d. 16 min. color. AEF
Dennis Weaver narrates during this film about a black police officer
who experiences racism at his own station house. A discussion
film.

BLACK POWER IN DIXIE. WCBS, 1969. 60 min. b/w. 2 parts.
     BFA
In part 1 narrator Lerone Bennett talks about the period 1867-1877
when many blacks became influential in Southern legislation. In
part 2 discussion centers on black consciousness in the Reconstruction Period.

BLACK POWER: THE SPOKESMEN. Koplin and Grinker, 1969.
     (The Turning Points: America in the 20th Century.) 15 min.
     color. PIC
Black leaders discuss their thoughts on black power--Martin Luther
King, Jr. , Stokely Carmichael, Muhammad Ali, Malcolm X, Adam
Clayton Powell, Floyd McKissick, H. Rap Brown, Alexander Allen,
Whitney Young, Dick Gregory and Eldridge Cleaver.

BLACK POWER: WE'RE GOIN' TO SURVIVE AMERICA! Leonard
     M. Henry, n. d. 15 min. b/w. /color. TWN
Presents Stokely Carmichael's address to the Black Panthers after
his trip around the world. Includes dancing by the Uzozi Aro'ho
Dancers.

BLACK POWER, WHITE BACKLASH. CBS, 1966. 50 min. b/w.
  CBS
A telecast of Sept. 27, 1966 in which Mike Wallace interviews lead-
ers of the black movement: Stokely Carmichael, Martin Luther
King, Jr., and Daniel H. Watts; also with individuals of Cicero,
Illinois who typify the "white backlash."

BLACK PROTEST: THE QUEST FOR CIVIL LIBERTIES. Koplin
  and Grinker, 1969. (The Turning Points: America in the 20th
  Century.) 15 min. color. PIC
Traces the modern-day fight for full emancipation, from Harry
Truman's 1947 speech to the NAACP to recent events.

BLACK RODEO. Cinerama, 1972. 87 min. color. Directed by
  Jeff Kenew. With Woody Strode, Muhammad Ali. SWA
A documentary on a rodeo with black participants viewed by black
audiences in New York. Captures the comments and actions of performers and viewers.

BLACK ROOTS. Lionel Rogosin, 1970. 61 min. color. IMP
The history and culture of the black American as seen through five
autobiographical sketches. With Flo Kennedy, Rev. Frederick
Douglass Kirkpatrick, Rev. Gary Davis, Jim Collier, Larry
Johnson. Directed by Lionel Rogosin. Winner of several
awards.

THE BLACK SOLDIER. CBS, 1968. (Of Black America Series.)
  30 min. b/w. BFA, UCA
Bill Cosby narrates the story of black participation in U.S. armed
forces from the Revolutionary War to the Vietnam War.

BLACK THUMB. King Screen, 1970. 6 1/2 min. color. BFA
Follows the activities of a black man tending the garden of a suburban home and a white salesman beginning his working day. When
the two meet eventually, the salesman at first assumes the black
man is the gardener, not the owner. A film for discussion.

THE BLACK WOMAN. NET, 1970. 52 min. b/w. IND
Black women discuss their role and problems in contemporary society. With Lena Horne, Bibi Amina Baraka, and others. Shows
Roberta Flack singing, dancing by Loretta Abbott, and poetry reading by Nikki Giovanni.

BLACK WORLD. CBS, 1968. (Of Black America Series.) 55
  min. b/w. BFA
Black American and African leaders confer on the struggle for freedom in both societies. Mike Wallace serves as narrator.

THE BLACKS TODAY. BBC, 1967. (The Blacks Series.) 40
  min. b/w. TL
A description of black life in Los Angeles, Britain, Harlem, Rio
de Janeiro, Johannesburg and South London.

BLIND GARY DAVIS. Harold Becker, 1964. 12 min. b/w. MGH
A profile of Rev. Gary Davis, a black man, blind since birth, who
demonstrates his virtuosity on the guitar.

A BLOCK IN HARLEM. WNBC-TV, 1969. 26 min. color. FI
About a rehabilitation project attempted on one block in Harlem between 7th and 8th Avenues at 114th Street. Shows why projects fail.

BLOOD OF JESUS. Spencer Williams, 1941. 68 min. b/w.
Directed by Spencer Williams. Cast unlisted. PAR
A low-budget film produced by amateurs for all-black audiences.
The story concerns the shooting of a man's wife and the religious
faith that helps her revive. An example of the movies made for
black theater circuits in the 1940s and earlier.

THE BLUES. Samuel Charters, 1963. 21 min. color. MAC[1]
About the music and environment of surviving blues singers of the
South. Comments and music trace the poverty and discrimination
that influenced the development of the blues. Directed and photographed by Samuel Charters.

BLUES LIKE SHOWERS OF RAIN. John Jeremy, 1971. 31 min.
   b/w. IMP
The story of the conditions in the South that produced the blues.
With the voices of Blind Arvella Gray, J. B. Lenoir, St. Louis
Jimmy and many others.

BOBBY SEALE. Koplin and Grinker, 1970. (Black Views on Race
   Series.) 4 min. color. TL
Seale's actual public remarks as example of black opinion in the
U. S.

BODY AND SOUL: BODY, PART 1. CBS, 1968. (Of Black
   America Series.) 30 min. b/w. BFA, UCA
Harry Reasoner traces the black American's contributions to sports.

BODY AND SOUL: SOUL, PART 2. CBS, 1968. (Of Black Amer-
   ica Series.) 30 min. b/w. BFA, UCA
Ray Charles narrates the history of soul music in America. With
Mahalia Jackson, Billie Holliday and Aretha Franklin.

BOOKER T. WASHINGTON. Vignette, 1966. 11 min. color.
   BFA
The early career of the slave-become-scholar who founded Tuskegee
Institute.

BRIGHT ROAD. MGM, 1953. 69 min. b/w. Directed by Gerald
   Mayer; screenplay by Emmet Lavery, from a magazine story
   by Mary Elizabeth Vroman. With Dorothy Dandridge, Philip
   Hepburn, Harry Belafonte. FI
Considered the first "serious" black film of the 1950s. The story
focuses on a disturbed, anxious black boy and his school life.
Dorothy Dandridge is the grade-school teacher and Philip Hepburn
the youth.

BROTHER.   U. S.   Federal Aviation Administration, 1970.   14 min.
    color.   NAC
Covers problems of minorities in getting jobs and what the FAA is
doing to improve the situation.   Features two black men who "made
it" in the aviation field.

BROTHER JOHN.   Columbia, 1971.   94 min.   color.   Directed by
    James Goldstone; produced by Joel Glickman; photography by
    Gerald Perry Finnerman; music by Quincy Jones; edited by
    Edward A. Biery.   With Sidney Poitier, Will Geer, Bradford
    Dillman, Beverly Todd, Ramon Bieri.   MAC[1], CPC
Sidney Poitier plays a well-dressed angel who returns to his home
town in Alabama to check up on things before Judgment Day.

BUCK AND THE PREACHER.   E & R and Belafonte Enterprises,
    1971.   102 min.   color.   Directed by Sidney Poitier; produced
    by Joel Glickman; screenplay by Ernest Konoy; music by Benny
    Carter; photography by Alex Phillips, Jr. ,; edited by Pembroke
    J. Herring.   With Ruby Dee, Harry Belafonte, Sidney Poitier,
    Cameron Mitchell, Denny Miller.   AST
A popularization of black history, in this case a black western
which covers the post-Civil War period when freed slaves were
tracked down by sadistic bounty hunters and forced to return to
unofficial slavery in the South.

BUCK DANCER.   Edmund Carpenter, Bea Lomax Hawes, and Alan
    Lomax, 1974.   6 min.   b/w.   RAD
Ed Young, a Mississippi fife player, plays Southern black music as
it sounded during its heyday years ago.

THE BURNING CROSS.   Somerset-Screen Guild, 1947.   79 min.
    b/w.   Directed by Walter Colmes; screenplay by Aubrey Wis-
    berg.   With Hank Daniels, Virginia Patton, Joel Fluellyn,
    Dick Rich, Raymond Bond and Matt Willis.   IVY
An exposé of the Ku Klux Klan that stresses physical violence, tar-
ring and feathering of victims, and vandalism.   Tells how a young
veteran is maneuvered into joining the Klan.

THE BUS.   Haskell Wexler, 1965.   62 min.   b/w.   MAC[1]
Film director Haskell Wexler, director of MEDIUM COOL, joined
the San Francisco delegation to the August 1963 Civil Rights demonstration.   This is his candid account of the trip.

CABIN IN THE SKY.   MGM, 1943.   100 min.   b/w.   Directed by
    Vincente Minnelli; screenplay by Joseph Schrank, based on the
    musical play with book by Lynn Root, lyrics by John Latouche
    and music by Vernon Duke.   With Ethel Waters, Eddie
    "Rochester" Anderson, Lena Horne.   FI
Despite the stereotyped characterizations, this film offers a look at
the great black entertainers of the 1940s in a story about the soldiers of heaven and the devil's men fighting over the soul of Little
Joe Jackson.

CARL STOKES.   Mert Koplin-Charles Grinker, 1970.   4 min.
    color.   TL
Stokes' actual public remarks, as example of black opinion in the
U. S.

CARMEN JONES.   Otto Preminger, 1954.   107 min.   color.
    cinemascope.   Directed by Otto Preminger; screen play by
    Harry Kleiner from book and lyrics by Oscar Hammerstein 2d;
    music by Georges Bizet.   With Harry Belafonte, Dorothy
    Dandridge.   FI
The film version of the black stage version of Bizet's opera "Carmen" which played on Broadway in 1943.   The opera's story, based
on a work by Prosper Merimée, was transformed into an American
locale--in this case, Carmen is a parachute factory worker in the
South, and a G. I. named Joe is about to go to flying school.   The
toreador has become a prize fighter.   The most lavish of all black
spectacles of the 1950s.

CASSIUS CLAY (MUHAMMAD ALI).   Merton Koplin-Charles Grink-
    er, 1970.   4 min.   color.   TL
Muhammad Ali's actual public remarks, an example of black opinion
in the U. S.

CHARLES DARDEN: CONDUCTOR.   Sue Lederer, 1972.   13 1/2
    min.   color.   BFA
A visit with a young music teacher and conductor of the Berkeley
Free Orchestra as he discusses his career and the role of music
in today's society.

CHARLES LLOYD: JOURNEY WITHIN.   Eric Sherman, 1968.   60
    min.   b/w.   MAC[1]
A film portrait of the famous jazz artist's life struggle, his back-
ground in Memphis and his U. S. and international concert triumphs.
Directed, written and photographed by Eric Sherman.

THE CHILDREN WERE WATCHING: INTEGRATION IN NEW OR-
    LEANS.   Drew Associates and Time-Life, 1967.   30 min.
    b/w.   TL
A disturbing view of how a black child feels as she enters the first
integrated school in New Orleans.

CHISHOLM: PURSUING THE DREAM.   Freedonia, 1973.   42 min.
    color.   NLC
A study of Congresswoman Shirley Chisholm in her bid for the
1972 Democratic presidential nomination.

CICERO MARCH.   The Film Group, 1968.   (New Militants and the
    Urban Crisis Series.)   8 min.   b/w.   UCA, UCO
About the march in Sept. 1966 of black and white people through the
streets of a community devoted to white supremacy.

THE CITIES: DILEMMA IN BLACK AND WHITE.   CBS, 1968.
    54 min.   color.   BFA

A study of the fast growth of the black population trapped by circumstances in the city's inner core. Shows a restoration project in New York's Bedford-Stuyvesant section. Narrated by Walter Cronkite.

CIVIL DISORDER: THE KERNER REPORT. NET, 1967. 80 min. b/w. IND, UIL
Three eminent black men, Charles V. Hamilton, Bayard Rustin, and Kenneth Clark discuss the Kerner Report and their doubts about its impact.

CIVIL RIGHTS MOVEMENT: PART 1, HISTORIC ROOTS. NBC, 1961. (Civil Rights Movement Series.) 16 min. b/w. UCA
Part of an NBC News special which traces the origins of the civil rights movement, beginning with the slave trade and the abolitionist movement of the nineteenth century.

CIVIL RIGHTS MOVEMENT: PART 2, PERSONAL VIEW. NBC, 1966. (Civil Rights Movement Series.) 25 min. b/w. UCA
Discusses community race relations and reviews the stereotyping in fiction and films that has distorted the image of black people.

CIVIL RIGHTS MOVEMENT: PART 3, SOUTH. NBC, 1966. (Civil Rights Movement Series.) 28 min. b/w. UCA
Covers the civil rights movement in the Southern U.S. after the Supreme Court's desegregation decision.

CIVIL RIGHTS MOVEMENT: PART 4, NORTH. NBC, 1966. (Civil Rights Movement Series.) 28 min. b/w. UCA
What happened when blacks moved into a white area and other characterizations of race relations in the U.S. North.

CIVIL RIGHTS MOVEMENT: PART 5, MISSISSIPPI SUMMER PROJECT. NBC, 1966. (Civil Rights Movement Series.) 17 min. b/w. UCA
Edited from an NBC News Special, an account of black people operating freedom schools, facing police brutality and trying to achieve racial harmony in the U.S.

THE COLOR OF JUSTICE. Sterling, 1971. 26 min. color. SEF
The black American's search for equality in justice, from the Dred Scott case to the school busing controversy.

COLOR US BLACK! NET, 1968. 60 min. b/w. IND, UCA
How students took over the administration building of the black campus of Howard University in Washington, D.C. in a demand for a significant curriculum that would not reflect white guidelines.

COME BACK CHARLESTON BLUE. Warners, 1972. 101 min. color. Directed by Mark Warren; screenplay by Bontche Schweig and Peggy Elliott, based on the novel "The Heat's On" by Chester Himes; photography by Dick Kratina; edited by Gerald Greenberg; music by Donny Hathaway. With Raymond St.

Jacques, Godfrey Cambridge, Peter De Anda, Jonelle Allen. MAC[1]
A sequel to COTTON COMES TO HARLEM. A fashion photographer is out to take Harlem's dope business away from a gang. Full of gun fights, auto chases.

CONFRONTATION: DIALOGUE IN BLACK AND WHITE. NET, 1967. 35 min. b/w. IND
A report on how one hundred citizens faced each other at station WTTW in Chicago after a tense summer.

CONFRONTATION IN COLOR. Greater Philadelphia Movement, 1968. 40 min. color. AFR
A group of blacks and whites discuss "who is human." A provocative film for group discussion.

CONFRONTED. NET, 1964. 59 min. b/w. IND, UCA
A behind-the-scenes look at the issue of black integration in schools, housing and employment in northern cities of the U.S.

THE CONSTITUTION AND THE RIGHT TO VOTE. Center for Mass Communications, Columbia University, 1959. (Decision: The Constitution in Action Series.) 29 min. b/w. IMP
The struggles of black people for voting rights as seen in two law suits attacking the constitutionality of the "white primary."

COOL BREEZE. MGM, 1972. 101 min. color. Directed by Barry Pollack; screenplay by Barry Pollack; from a novel by W. R. Burnett; music by Solomon Burke; photography by Andrew Davis; edited by Morton Tubor. With Raymond St. Jacques, Thalmus Rasulala, Jim Watkins, Judy Pace, Lincoln Kilpatrick, Sam Laws. FI
A black remake of ASPHALT JUNGLE, about a carefully planned jewel theft that falls apart because of the weaknesses of the characters involved.

THE COOL WORLD. Frederick Wiseman, 1964. 104 min. b/w. Directed by Shirley Clarke; screenplay by Shirley Clarke and Carl Lee, based on Warren Miller's novel and the play by Warren Miller and Robert Rossen. With Hampton Clanton, Yolanda Rodriguez, Joe Oliver, Carl Lee. ZIP
Attempts to expose the seamier side of black ghetto life--in this case, crime among black youths in Harlem.

CORETTA KING. Mert Koplin-Charles Grinker, 1970. (Black Views on Race Series.) 4 min. color. TL
Coretta King's actual public remarks, an example of black opinion in the U.S.

THE CORNER. Robert Ford, 1963. 26 min. b/w. MAC
The members of a black gang, "The Vice Lords," in Chicago describe their way of life, their code of behavior.

COTTON COMES TO HARLEM.   United Artists, 1970.   90 min.
   color.   Directed by Ossie Davis; screenplay by Ossie Davis,
   based on the novel "Cotton Comes to Harlem" by Chester
   Himes; photography by Gerald Hirschfeld; music by Galt Mac-
   Dermot.   With Calvin Lockhart, Raymond St. Jacques, Godfrey
   Cambridge, Judy Pace, Redd Foxx.   UNAR
Written, directed and acted by blacks.   About two black detectives
who search for stolen money to solve a case in Harlem.   An updated version of Chester Himes' novel.

CRISIS IN LEVITTOWN.   Dynamic, 1957.   (When a Neighborhood
   Changes Series.)   30 min.   b/w.   MAC[1]
An analysis of what happened when a black family moved into all-
white Levittown, Pennsylvania.   Directed by Lee R. Bobker and
Lester Becker.   Commentary and analysis by Dr. Dan W. Dodson.

CRISIS IN MEDICINE.   NET, 1969.   50 min.   b/w.   IND
Covers efforts to train more black doctors and improve medical
and dental care for black communities.

DANIEL WATTS.   NETC, 1967.   (Dissenters Series.)   30 min.
   b/w.   IND, UCA
The editor of "Liberator" is interviewed by Donald Fouser on urban
riots, an anticipated racist revolution, and Black Power.

DEAD ENDS AND NEW DREAMS.   Robert Ornstein, n.d.   25 min.
   color.   MGH
Young black poet Norman Jordan shows how his poetry tries to
deal with contemporary realities.

DIARY OF A HARLEM FAMILY.   NET, 1968.   20 min.   b/w.
   UCA
Black photographer and novelist Gordon Parks studies the predicament of a Harlem family with little education, job opportunities,
and ineffectual poverty agencies from which to seek help.

DICK GREGORY.   Merton Koplin-Charles Grinker, 1970.   (Black
   Views on Race Series.)   4 min.   color.   TL
Gregory's actual public remarks, as example of black opinion in
the U.S.

DRY WOOD AND HOT PEPPER.   Les Blank, 1973.   91 min.
   color.   FLOF
Examines the culture, including the music, of the black French-
speaking people of Southwest Louisiana.   Dry Wood refers to rural
people and Hot Pepper is concerned with Clifton Chenier, known
as "Zydeco Blues King."

DUKE ELLINGTON SWINGS THROUGH JAPAN.   CBS, 1964.   26
   min.   b/w.   MAC
About jazz musician Ellington and his side-men on their tour of
Japan.

DUTCHMAN. Gene Persson, 1967. 55 min. b/w. Directed by
    Anthony Harvey; screenplay and play by LeRoi Jones. With
    Shirley Knight and Al Freeman, Jr. READ
A dialogue between a black man and a provocative white woman on
a New York subway during which she goads him, then stabs him.
Jones introduces the idea that there is "a concealed black within
every Negro. "

EDDIE KENDRICKS. Chiaramonte, 1975. 7 min. color. PHO
About the black popular musician-singer who performs "You gotta
keep on truckin," which also represents his philosophy of life.

EDGE OF THE ARENA: PORTRAIT OF A BLACK CANDIDATE.
    Rediscovery, 1972. 28 min. color. NACC, SEF
About Andrew Young, Georgia's first black candidate for a national
office since the Reconstruction, and the role of black politicians.

EDWARD BROOKE. Mert Koplin-Charles Grinker, 1970. (Black
    Views on Race Series.) 4 min. color. TL
Brooke's actual public remarks, an example of black opinion in the
U. S.

1861-1877: CIVIL WAR AND RECONSTRUCTION. McGraw-Hill,
    1967. (A History of the Negro in America Series.) 20 min.
    b/w. MGH
Studies the factors that brought about the Civil War and the intent
of the Thirteenth, Fourteenth and Fifteenth Amendments to protect
black Americans.

1877-TODAY: FREEDOM MOVEMENT. McGraw-Hill, 1967. (A His-
    tory of the Negro in America Series.) 10 min. b/w. UCO, MGH
A history of the struggle for civil rights from the post-Civil War
period to the 1950s.

EMPEROR JONES. United Artists, 1933. 80 min. b/w. Di-
    rected by Dudley Murphy; adaptation of the play by Eugene
    O'Neill with added scenes by DuBose Hayward. With Paul
    Robeson, Fredi Washington, Dudley Digges, Frank Wilson.
    RAD, PAR, BUDG
Considered "a landmark for the Negro in films" in that for the
first time a black man plays the leading role in a film containing
white actors. A railway porter in the U. S. rises to become King
Brutus on a fictitious Caribbean island.

EPHESUS. Fred Padula, 1965. 25 min. b/w. MAC, UCA
The Sunday evening service at a black "Holiness" church where the
people follow the Bible's dictum, "Be not drunk with wine, but be
filled with the Spirit. "

EXPRESS YOURSELF: REVENGE. Afram, n. d. 50 min. color.
    AFR
The black view of the oppression of black prisoners in Trenton State
Prison, New Jersey, controlled by whites.

FANNIE LOU HAMER.   Rediscovery, 1972.   (Portrait in Black
    Series.)   10 min.   color.   SEF
The woman who is a heroine in the struggle for justice in Mississippi.

FINALLY GOT THE NEWS.   Black Star, 1970.   55 min.   color
    and b/w.   IMP, TRI
How the League of Revolutionary Black Workers in Detroit works
to combat racism, dangerous working conditions, and other problems faced by black and white employees.

FOR ALL MY STUDENTS.   Bonnie Sherr, 1968.   36 min.   b/w.
    UCA
A study of why many black students have failed in school.   A discussion film.

FRAME-UP!   THE IMPRISONMENT OF MARTIN SOSTRE.   Pacific
    Street Film Collective, 1974.   30 min.   color.   PSFC
About the black bookstore proprietor who claims he was framed on
a drug charge and is serving time in prison because he was out-
spoken in expressing his political beliefs.

FREDERICK DOUGLASS.   Encyclopaedia Britannica Educational
    Corporation, 1972.   9 min.   color.   EBEC
How Frederick Douglass, a runaway black slave, initiated the black
protest movement and served as advisor to Presidents.

FREDERICK DOUGLASS.   I. W. , 1964.   (Profiles in Courage
    Series.)   59 min.   b/w.   UCA
Based on a chapter in John F. Kennedy's book "Profiles in Courage"--a biography of one of the first black men to speak out against
slavery and abuse of blacks in the North.

FREDERICK DOUGLASS: THE HOUSE ON CEDAR HILL.   Carlton
    Moss, 1953.   17 min.   b/w.   MGH, UCO, UCA
A biography of Frederick Douglass using Douglass's writings for
the narration.   The musical score is based on black folk songs.
An award-winning film.

FREE AT LAST.   NET, 1965.   (History of the Negro People
    Series.)   30 min.   b/w.   IND, UCA, UCO, IMP
The history of the black Americans from emancipation to the end
of World War II.   Includes dramatic readings of words by Frederick Douglass, Booker T. Washington, W. E. B. DuBois and Marcus Garvey.

FROM THE INSIDE OUT.   Contemporary, 1967.   24 min.   b/w.
    MGH, UCA
Black teen-agers of a Northern California community wrote and
directed this filmed attempt to communicate their concerns about
ghetto life to white people.

FROM THESE ROOTS.   William Greaves, 1974.   29 min.   b/w.
    GRE
Focuses on the cultural, political and social life of black people
who participated in "the Harlem renaissance" of the 1920s in the
U. S.

THE FUTURE AND THE NEGRO.   NET, 1965.   (History of the
    Negro People Series.)   IND, UCA
An international view of the black people's future by a panel of
British, Nigerian, Brazilian and American commentators.   Moder-
ated by Ossie Davis at the Carnegie International Center in New
York City.

GEORGE WASHINGTON CARVER.   Vignette, 1966.   11 min.   b/w.
    BFA
Describes the achievements of the scientist who was born a slave,
using some historic footage of Dr. Carver at work in his labora-
tory.

GEORGIA, GEORGIA.   Cinerama, 1972.   91 min.   color.   Directed
    by Stig Bjorkman; screenplay by Maya Angelou; songs by Maya
    Angelou; background music by Sven Olaf Waldorf; photography
    by Andreas Bellis; edited by Sten-Goran Camitz.   With Diana
    Sands, Mini Gentry, Dirk Benedict, Roger Furman, Terry
    Whitmore.   SWA
An American pop star on tour in Stockholm becomes involved in a
love affair with a white American photographer.   She is also surrounded by various troubled and militant figures who complicate
her struggle for identity.

THE GIFT OF THE BLACK FOLK.   Carlton Moss, 1974.   12 min.
    color.   PYR
Filmmaker Carlton Moss presents stories which demonstrate the
humanistic contributions of black people: the slave revolt of Denmark Vesey in 1822, Harriet Tubman's leadership in the Underground Railroad, and Frederick Douglass's refutation of the view
that the Union had to be destroyed.   The Fisk University Orchestra
provides the background for narrative and is, in turn, viewed between stories as a further example of black gifts to American culture.

GO, MAN, GO!   Sirod, 1954.   82 min.   b/w.   With the Harlem
    Globetrotters, Dane Clark, Sidney Poitier.   CHAR, CCRC,
    CPC
The story of the promoter and coach who developed the famous
basketball team.

GONE ARE THE DAYS.   Trans Lux, 1964.   97 min.   b/w.   Di-
    rected by Nicholas Webster.   With Ossie Davis, Ruby Dee,
    Beah Richard.   MAC1
Based on Ossie Davis's play "Purlie Victorious," a satire on the
"racial mores of the South."   The first statement of the black is
beautiful credo.

GOODBYE AND GOOD LUCK. NET, 1967. 30 min. b/w. IND,
    UCA
A black veteran soldier from Vietnam who became used to living
with whites must face rejection and alienation upon his return
home to the U. S.

GOT TO TELL IT: A TRIBUTE TO MAHALIA JACKSON. CBS,
    1974. 33 min. color. PHO
The music and comments of the great gospel singer are heard while
old photographs and movie footage reveal her life story and impact
on people.

GRAVEL SPRINGS FIFE AND DRUM. Bill Ferris, David Evans
    and Judy Peiser, 1971. 10 min. color. IND
A view of a northern Mississippi community where fife and drum
music resembling West African traditional music has somehow survived.

THE GREAT AMERICAN DREAM: THREE VIEWS. NET, 1971.
    36 min. b/w. IND
Three black Americans from different walks of life discuss their
lives.

THE GREAT WHITE HOPE. Twentieth Century-Fox, 1970. 103
    min. color. Directed by Martin Ritt; screenplay by Howard
    Sackler, based on his play; photography by Burnett Griffey.
    With James Earl Jones, June Alexander, Beah Richards,
    Chester Morris, Hal Holbrook. FI
James Earl Jones repeats his stage characterization of the black
heavyweight champion, Jack Johnson.

GWENDOLYN BROOKS. NET, 1966. 30 min. b/w. IND, UCA
A portrait of Gwendolyn Brooks, black poet and Pulitzer Prize
winner, including readings from her work, and a view of her work
environment in Chicago.

H. RAP BROWN. Mert Koplin-Charles Grinker, 1970. (Black
    Views on Race Series.) 4 min. color. TL
H. Rap Brown's actual public remarks, an example of black opinion
in the U. S.

THE HARLEM GLOBETROTTERS. Columbia, 1951. 80 min.
    b/w. Credits unlisted. With Thomas Gomez, Dorothy Dan-
    dridge and the Harlem Globetrotters. BUDG, MAC[1]
A follow-up to GO, MAN, GO with a story about a college student
who leaves his studies to tour with the famous basketball team.

HARLEM HOTSHOTS. 1940. 20 min. b/w. No credits listed.
    BUDG, PAR
A short musical film with Lena Horne, Leon Gross and the Core
Harriss Orchestra and the Red Lilly Chorus with Teddy Wilson.

HARLEM IN THE TWENTIES. Encyclopaedia Britannica Educational
   Corporation, 1970. 10 min. color. EBEC
About the development of Harlem as black ghetto in the 1920s, an
atmosphere which produced stars such as Bill Robinson, Ethel
Waters, Josephine Baker, Paul Robeson, Duke Ellington.

HARLEM RENAISSANCE: THE BLACK POETS. CBS, 1970. 20
   min. color. IMP
The literary history of black Americans from the 1920s and '30s
to the 1960s. Includes poetry of Countee Cullen, Waring Cuney,
Georgia Douglas Johnson, Fenton Johnson, W. E. B. DuBois and
Langston Hughes.

HARLEM WEDNESDAY. John Hubley, 1959. 10 min. color.
   MAC[1]
An ordinary Wednesday in Harlem, featuring scenes by painter
Gregorio Prestopino and jazz by Benny Carter.

HARRIET TUBMAN AND THE UNDERGROUND RAILROAD. CBS,
   1964. 54 min. b/w. MGH
The story of the ex-slave who helped other slaves escape to freedom. With a distinguished cast that includes Ethel Waters, Ruby
Dee, and Ossie Davis.

HARRY BELAFONTE. Mert Koplin-Charles Grinker, 1970. (Black
   Views on Race Series.) 4 min. color. TL
Belafonte's actual public remarks, an example of black opinion in
the U. S.

HEAD START IN MISSISSIPPI. NET, 1966. 60 min. b/w.
   IND, UCA
The plight of the Head Start program in Mississippi in 1966, its
first year. Shows the opposition, diversion of funds, poor stand-
ards, which brought forth the black community's resolve to continue
with its own staff.

THE HEART IS A LONELY HUNTER. Warners, 1968. 124 min.
   color. Directed by Robert Ellis Miller; screenplay by Thomas
   C. Ryan, from the novel by Carson McCullers. With Alan
   Arkin, Sondra Locke, Percy Rodriguez. WARB
Percy Rodriguez plays a small-town General Practitioner in the
South who has a conflict with his militant daughter, Cicely Tyson.

HENRY O. TANNER: PIONEER BLACK AMERICAN ARTIST.
   Corsair, 1971. 12 min. color. DIS
The story of the first important black American painter, his early
life and his travels abroad.

HERITAGE IN BLACK. Shana, 1969. 29 min. color. EBEC,
   UCO
A study of the black people's heritage of participation in American
life. A sweeping panorama of contributions.

HERITAGE OF SLAVERY. CBS, 1968. (Of Black America Series.)
    55 min. b/w. BFA, UCA, UCO
The history of slavery from the 17th century to the emancipation,
using first-hand accounts of slaves and masters. Also available
in two parts: Part I, 26 min.; Part II, 27 min.

HERITAGE OF THE NEGRO. NET, 1965. (History of the Negro
    People Series.) 30 min. b/w. IMP, IND, UCA, UCO
About the civilization of ancient Africa and its meaning for the
black American today. Examines arts which reflect the old cultures.

HEY, CAB! King Screen, 1970. 10 1/2 min. color. BFA,
    UUT
Drawn from "Letters to a Black Boy" by Bob Teague, black journalist, this film describes his actual experience in trying to hail a
cab at night in the ghetto.

HEY, MAMA. Vaughn Obern, 1968. 18 min. color. OBE, UNE
A documentary of the black experience in Venice, California.
Scenes from various parts of the black community, in private
homes, on streets, in playgrounds, barbershops.

HISTORY OF THE BLACKS. BBC, 1971. (The Blacks Series.)
    40 min. b/w. TL
Over three hundred years of black history up to the present.

HOLIDAYS ... HOLLOW DAYS. Indiana University, 1974. 59
    min. b/w. IND
Black prison inmates perform in a drama written by another in-
mate--a convicted murderer, Rhozier T. "Roach" Brown. The
drama reflects on America's penal system from the prisoners'
point of view.

HOME OF THE BRAVE. Stanley Kramer, 1949. 88 min. b/w.
    Directed by Mark Robson; screenplay by Carl Foreman, from
    the play by Arthur Laurents; music by Dimitri Tiomkin; photog-
    raphy by Robert De Grasse. With Douglas Dick, Steve Brodie,
    Jeff Corey, Lloyd Bridges, Frank Lovejoy, James Edwards.
    MGH, BUDG
One black soldier and four white soldiers patrol behind enemy lines
and learns to understand each other despite the tensions of battle.
One of the first honest treatments of race conflict by a Hollywood
production.

HOW COME IT'S THUNDERIN'? ... YOU DON'T SEE THE MOON.
    Steve Gordon, 1967. 13 min. b/w. MAC[1]
Junior high school youth are viewed through the perspective of one
of their teachers who tried to use art to help the students sense
their potential worth. Produced, written, directed and photographed
by Steve Gordon with the cooperation of Junior High School 43,
Harlem, and the advice of Dr. Edwin Ziegfeld of Teachers College,
Columbia University, Chairman of the Department of Art and Education.

THE HURDLER. Sterling, 1970. 16 min. color. SEF
A biography of the late Dr. Charles Drew whose research led to
the development of the first blood bank system.

I AIN'T PLAYIN' NO MORE. Morgan Community School, 1970.
    61 min. b/w. AFR
Shows healthy interaction among parents, teachers and students in
a community-controlled situation at Morgan Community School in
Washington, D. C.

I AM SOMEBODY. American Foundation of Non-Violence, 1970.
    28 min. color. MGH
Describes the Charleston, South Carolina black hospital workers'
strike in which they changed the social fabric of a southern community.

"I HAVE A DREAM...": THE LIFE OF MARTIN LUTHER KING.
    CBS, 1968. 35 min. b/w. BFA
The story of Dr. King's work in the civil rights movement of the
1950s and 1960s.

I WISH I KNEW HOW IT WOULD FEEL TO BE FREE. Yale Uni-
    versity, 1968. 20 min. b/w. UCA
Using the Billy Taylor song, "I Wish I Knew How It Would Feel to
Be Free," as sung by Nina Simone, filmmaker Peter Rosen shows
a close-up view of a typical American ghetto.

I WONDER WHY. Robert M. Rosenthal, 1965. 6 min. b/w.
    MGH
A black girl wonders why people don't like her. Narrated by Alexander Scourby. Music by Don Elliot.

I'M A MAN. Peter Rosen, 1969. 20 min. b/w. MGH, UNE
About black militant John Barber and his struggle for freedom and
identity.

I'M SORRY. Communication Arts, 1966. 30 min. b/w. UCA
In a dramatic film, a young black man shows the factors in contemporary society that influence him to take up radical politics.

IMITATION OF LIFE. Universal, 1934. 109 min. b/w. Directed
    by John Stahl; based on Fannie Hurst's novel. With Louise
    Beavers, Fredi Washington, Claudette Colbert, Rochelle Hud-
    son, Neil Sparks, Warren William. TMOC
Considered the first important black film of the 1930s. Traces the
lives of two widows, one white, the other black, who meet by
chance and decide to throw their lots together. A harsh statement
on race relations in the U. S. during the 1930s.

THE IMPACT OF ABE LINCOLN AND MARTIN LUTHER KING.
    Koplin and Grinker, n. d. (A Better World Series.) 26 min.
    color. PIC
A comparison of Lincoln and King as workers for unity against
great opposition.

THE IMPACT OF JACKIE ROBINSON.   Koplin and Grinker, n. d.
(A Better World Series.) 26 min.   color.   PIC
A view of Jackie Robinson, the baseball star, as one who fought
for a better world.

THE IMPACT OF JERSEY JOE WALCOTT/SHERIFF ARNOLD
CREAM. Koplin and Grinker, n. d.   (A Better World Series.)
26 min.   color.   PIC
How Joe Walcott dreamed of becoming heavyweight champion of the
world and did so.   Also a look at his newer career as first black
sheriff of Camden, New Jersey.

IN SEARCH OF A PAST.   CBS, 1968.   (Of Black America Series.)
55 min.   b/w.   BFA, UCA, UCO
How three black American students searched for their identity in
Ghana during a one-month trip.

INTERVIEW WITH BOBBY SEALE.   Third World Newsreel, 1969.
15 min.   b/w.   TWN
The interview portrait of Bobby Seale, Chairman of the Black Panther Party, filmed in the San Francisco jail.

INTERVIEW WITH BRUCE GORDON.   Harold Becker, 1964.   17
min.   b/w.   MGH
A young SNCC organizer discusses the reasons he became active
in the civil rights movement in Alabama.

IT'S NATION TIME.   NET, 1970.   21 min.   b/w.   IND
Prominent blacks speak about nationalism and Pan-Africanism at the
Congress of African people in Atlanta, Georgia.   Includes Imamu
Amiri Baraku (LeRoi Jones), Julian Bond, Richard Hatcher, Rev.
Jesse Jackson and Minister Louis Farrakhan.

IVANHOE DONALDSON.   Harold Becker and Warren Forma, 1964.
57 min.   b/w.   MAC
The first documentary feature film on civil rights work in the
South.   Shows CORE and SNCC projects, hunger vigils, Freedom
Walks, along with the actual experiences of a SNCC field secretary.

JACK JOHNSON.   Jim Jacobs, 1970.   90 min.   b/w.   ASF, MAC[1]
The career of Jack Johnson, the famous black heavyweight champion
of the world.   An award-winning documentary.   Directed by William
Cayton; music by Miles Davis; narrated by Brock Peters.

JACKIE ROBINSON.   Sterling, 1965.   27 min.   b/w.   SEF
A study of the great baseball star who was the first black player
in a major league.

JACKIE ROBINSON.   Mert Koplin-Charles Grinker, 1970.   (Black
Views on Race Series.)   4 min.   color.   TL
Robinson's actual public remarks, as example of black opinion in
the U. S.

THE JACKIE ROBINSON STORY.   Eagle-Lion, 1950.   76 min.
   b/w.   Directed Alfred E.   Green; screenplay by Lawrence Taylor and Arthur Mann.   With Jackie Robinson, Ruby Dee, Lou-
   ise Beavers, Bernie Hamilton, Joel Fluellen.   FI
A faithful biography of the famous baseball player and first black
man to play in the major leagues.

JAMES BALDWIN, FROM ANOTHER PLACE.   Sedat Pakay, 1975.
   11 1/2 min.   b/w.   RAD
James Baldwin is shown living as an exile in Istanbul.   He discusses his past and present life.

JAMES BALDWIN'S HARLEM.   Metromedia, 1967.   (Part II: My
   Childhood Series.)   25 min.   b/w.   BEF
An award-winning film about James Baldwin in which he speaks of
the despairing parts of his childhood.   A 51 min. version of this
film is available in which the childhoods of Hubert Humphrey and
James Baldwin are contrasted.

JAMES BROWN.   Mert Koplin-Charles Grinker, 1970.   (Black
   Views on Race Series.)   4 min.   color.   TL
James Brown's actual public remarks, an example of black opinion
in the U.S.

JAMES BROWN, THE MAN.   NBC, 1974.   13 min.   color.   SEF
The story of the famous singer-entertainer from Georgia who as a
child used to sing and dance for coins.

JAMES WELDON JOHNSON.   Oxford, 1972.   (Poetry by Americans
   Series.)   12 min.   color.   OXF
A portrait of the black poet, musician and teacher, as well as dip-
lomat, who also served as Executive Secretary of the NAACP.   In-
cludes a reading by Raymond St. Jacques of Johnson's poem "The
Creation."

JAZZ IS MY RELIGION.   John Jeremy, 1972.   50 min.   b/w.
   IMP
Explores the roots of jazz from the Blues to the new sounds.   Fea-
tured artists are John Hendricks, Johnny Griffin, Dizzy Reece,
Lol Coxhill, Raschied Ali, Dizzy Gillespie.   Winner of London Film
Festival Award.

JERICHO.   (DARK SANDS.)   Walter Futter, 1937.   75 min.   b/w.
   Directed by Thornton Freeland; from a story by Walter Futter;
   adaptation by Robert N. Lee and Peter Rurie; scenario by
   George Barraud.   With Paul Robeson, Henry Wilcoxon, Wallace
   Ford.   PAR
About a convicted soldier who lives as a sheik in Africa after fleeing war-time France (World War I).   A rare type of film for its
date because, for a change, the hero is black, intelligent and attractive.   A British production.

JESSIE OWENS RETURNS TO BERLIN.   Cappy, 1965.   54 min.
   b/w.   MGH
Shows what Jessie Owens feels about his part in the 1936 Olympic
Games.   Uses old footage to show highlights of his Olympic performance.   Also available in two 27 min. films.

JIM BROWN.   Mert Koplin-Charles Grinker, 1970.   (Black Views
   on Race Series.)   TL
Jim Brown's actual public remarks, an example of black opinion in
the U. S.

JITTERING JITTERBUGS.   1938.   No credits listed.   With Ham-
   tree Harrington, Lee Norman's Orchestra and Arthur White's
   Lindy Hoppers.   PAR
A short comedy set in Harlem.   An example of early films made
by black performers for black theater circuits.

JIVIN' IN BE BOP.   Leonard Anderson, 1947.   60 min.   b/w.
   Directed by Leonard Anderson.   With Dizzy Gillespie, Helen
   Humes, Ray Sneed, Sahji, Freddie Carter, Ralph Brown, Dan
   Curley, Johnny Taylor, Phil and Audrey, Johnny and Henry,
   Daisy Richardson and Pancho and Dolores.   PAR
A musical variety show produced for all-black theaters.

THE JOE LOUIS STORY.   United Artists, 1953.   87 min.   b/w.
   Directed by Robert Gordon; screenplay by Robert Sylvester;
   produced by Sterling Silliphant.   With Coley Wallace, Hilda
   Sims, James Edwards, Paul Stewart.   ASF, BUDG, MAC[1]
The life story of the world champion boxer, starring Coley Wallace
as the champ.   Includes actual scenes of Louis's great fights.

JOHN OUTERBRIDGE: BLACK ARTIST.   Lewis-Wong, 1971.   21
   min.   color.   ACI
A metal sculptor is shown at work on a major piece of work.
Stresses the role of ideas in art.

JOSHUA.   Bert Salzman, 1968.   15 min.   b/w.   ACI
A young black man about to enter college feels his black identity
is threatened, and so he goes on a running spree through the park,
where he is confronted by several situations that lead to increased
awareness.

JULIAN BOND.   Mert Koplin-Charles Grinker, 1970.   (Black Views
   on Race Series.)   4 min.   color.   TL
Bond's actual public remarks, as example of black opinion in the
U. S.

THE JUNGLE.   Churchill, 1968.   22 min.   b/w.   UCA
A film made by black ghetto youths with borrowed equipment and little technical assistance, to present a gripping study of gang war
and the life of the streets in Philadelphia.

KEITH TURNS 18.   John Friedman, 1974.   18 min.   color.   EDC
Follows Keith, a young black man pursuing his interest in classic
ballet.   Also shows his participation in a jazz dance group he has
helped to form.

KU KLUX KLAN: THE INVISIBLE EMPIRE.   CBS, 1965.   47 min.
   b/w.   CAR
An award-winning documentary that reveals the inner workings of
the Ku Klux Klan, including one case of mob violence.

THE LADY FROM PHILADELPHIA.   CBS, 1958.   55 min.   b/w.
   MGH
Follows Marian Anderson on a tour of twelve Asian countries.

LADY IN THE LINCOLN MEMORIAL.   Sterling, 1971.   18 min.
   color.   NACC, SEF
A portrait of Marian Anderson, from her early career to her international concert tours.

LADY SINGS THE BLUES.   Motown/Paramount, 1972.   144 min.
   color.   cinemascope.   Directed by Sidney J. Furie; screenplay
   by Terence McCloy, Chris Clark and Suzanne de Passe, based
   on the book by Billie Holliday and William Duffy; music by
   Michel Legrand; photography by John Alonso.   With Diana
   Ross, Richard Pryor, Billy Dee Williams.   PFS, FI
A biography of the famous blues singer whose life ended in tragedy.

LANDMARK SPIRITUAL TEMPLE.   Ethnographic, 1968.   25 min.
   b/w.   UCA
About a black church service in San Francisco, showing emotionally
intimate views of various congregation members.

LANGSTON HUGHES.   CBS, 1970.   24 min.   color.   IMP
A comprehensive biography on the poet laureate of Harlem.   Selec-
tions of Hughes' poetry are presented by various black artists.

LAY MY BURDEN DOWN.   NET, 1966.   60 min.   b/w.   IND,
   UCA
An award-winning production on the harsh realities of rural life
for blacks in the South one year after the Selma-Montgomery
march and the Voting Rights Act.

THE LEARNING TREE.   Warner Bros., 1969.   107 min.   color.
   Directed and written by Gordon Parks; music by Gordon Parks.
   With Kyle Johnson, Alex Clarke, Estelle Evans.   MOSP,
   MAC[1], TWY
The first film since RAISIN IN THE SUN to treat the black family
sensitively and the first example of a major Hollywood production
directed by a black man.   The story is based on Parks's autobiographical novel about two boys--one who turns out well and another
who turns out badly.

LEGACY OF A DREAM.   Richard Kaplan, 1974.   29 min.   color.
   KING
Covers Martin Luther King, Jr. 's campaigns and how his work is
continued today by his wife, Coretta Scott King and Rep. Andrew
Young.   James Earl Jones is narrator.

THE LEGEND OF JIMMY BLUE EYES.   Robert Clouse, 1964.   22
   min.   color.   MAC
An adaptation of the Faust legend in which a young black musician
sells his soul so he can perform well on the trumpet.   Told en-
tirely in rhyme.

THE LEGEND OF NIGGER CHARLEY.   Paramount, 1972.   115
   min.   color.   Directed by Martin Goldman; screenplay by Lar-
   ry Spangler and Martin Goldman; music by Lloyd Price.
   With Fred Williamson, Don Urville, Pedro Calley, Maria Mc-
   Broom, Joe Santos.   FI
A black slave and two friends escape from a plantation and head
West to find freedom.

LET THE CHURCH SAY AMEN!   Chamba, 1973.   75 min.   color.
   NACC
Follows the travels of a young black man who is a minister trying
to find his role in the ministry.   An award-winning film.

LIKE A BEAUTIFUL CHILD.   John Schultz, 1967.   27 min.   b/w.
   MAC
An account of black union workers in their struggle for dignity and
adequate wages.   Directed by John Schultz and presented by Local
1199, Drug and Hospital Employees Union, AFL-CIO.

LISTEN WHITEY.   Granada, n. d.   30 min.   b/w.   IMP
Filmed in Washington D. C. 's black ghetto following the assassination
of Martin Luther King, Jr. in 1968.   Includes homages from blacks
and whites.

LOOK OUT SISTER.   1948.   67 min.   b/w.   No credits listed.
   With Louis Jordon and His Tympany Five, Suzette Harbin.
   BUDG
A musical made for black audiences, featuring an all-black cast.

LORRAINE HANSBERRY: THE BLACK EXPERIENCE IN THE
   CREATION OF DRAMA.   Films for the Humanities, n. d.   35
   min.   color.   FFTH
Studies the life of black playwright Lorraine Hansberry.   Includes
excerpts from various plays: "A Raisin in the Sun," "The Sign in
Sidney Brustein's Window" and "Les Blancs."   Play excerpts performed by Sidney Poitier, Ruby Dee, Diana Sands, Al Freeman,
Jr. , Roy Scheider and Claudia McNeil, who also serves as narrator.

LOSING JUST THE SAME.   NET, 1966.   59 min.   b/w.   UCA
An analysis in psychological terms of the Negro ghetto world, using
one family as example.

LOST BOUNDARIES. Louis de Rochemont, 1949. 97 min. b/w.
   Directed by Alfred L. Werder; screenplay by Virginia Shaler
   and Eugene Ling with additional dialogue by Furland de Kay
   from a Charles A. Palmer adaptation of the W. L. White
   story. With Mel Ferrer, Beatrice Pearson, Richard Hylton,
   Canada Lee. WARB
A semi-documentary about a black physician and his family and
what happened to them as a result of their attempt "to pass."

THE LOST MAN. Universal, 1969. 110 min. color. Directed
   by Robert Alan Aurther; screenplay by Robert Alan Aurther.
   With Sidney Poitier, Joan Shimkus, Al Freeman, Jr., Richard
   Dysart. UNIV, TWY
In a story based on "Odd Man Out" a veteran becomes involved in
a robbery to pay for families of imprisoned black brothers. He is
wounded and sought by the police. An attempt to portray the black
revolution, it was criticized for the romance between the black hero
and a white society girl.

LOUIS ARMSTRONG. United Artists, 1962. 28 min. color.
   PAR
Features Louis Armstrong, vocalist Jewel Brown and musicians
Trummy Young, Billy Kyle, Joe Darensbourg, Danny Barcelona
and Billy Cronk.

LOUISIANA DIARY. NET, 1963. 59 min. b/w. IND, UCA
How the Congress of Racial Equality (CORE) helped encourage voter
registration of black people in one Louisiana Congressional District.

MALCOLM X. Mert Koplin-Charles Grinker, 1970. (Black Views
   on Race Series.) 4 min. color. TL
Actual public remarks of Malcolm X, as example of black opinion
in the U.S.

MALCOLM X SPEAKS. ABC, 1970. 44 min. b/w. GRO
A report on the life and philosophy of black leader, Malcolm X.

MALCOLM X: STRUGGLE FOR FREEDOM. Grove, 1964. 22
   min. b/w. UCA
Follows the black leader during a trip to Europe and Africa shortly
before his death.

A MAN CALLED ADAM. Embassy, 1966. 99 min. b/w. Di-
   rected by Leo Penn; screenplay by Les Pine and Tina Rome.
   With Sammy Davis, Jr., Cicely Tyson, Ossie Davis, Louis
   "Satchmo" Armstrong, Frank Sinatra, Jr., Lola Falana.
   MAC[1], MOSP
Ike Jones, a black man, co-produced this film for Sammy Davis,
Jr.'s Trace-Mark Productions. About a drunken trumpet player
whose intoxication has caused the accidental death of his wife and
child as well as the blindness of a fellow musician. The music of
the leading character is actually played by "Cannonball" Adderley.

A MAN NAMED CHARLIE SMITH.   N. H. Cominos, n. d.   26 min.
    b/w.   MAC
An aged man, approximately 120 years old, recalls his capture into
slavery in Liberia at the age of 12 and his subsequent adventures
and experiences in the U. S.   Uses old newsreels and photographs
to cover periods described.   Narrated by James Whitmore.

MARIAN ANDERSON.   World Artists, 1952.   26 min.   b/w.   LES
An old film with scenes of Marian Anderson's early life as a young
singer and as she performed in a Town Hall concert singing old
favorites, such as Schubert's "Ave Maria," and spirituals.

MARTIN LUTHER KING.   BBC, 1970.   30 min.   b/w.   TL
A filmed interview with the Nobel Peace Prize winner in which he
describes the 381-day bus boycott and his own inner convictions.

MARTIN LUTHER KING.   Mert Koplin-Charles Grinker, 1970.
    (Black Views on Race Series.)   4 min.   color.   TL
Martin Luther King's actual public remarks, an example of black
opinion in the U. S.

MARTIN LUTHER KING, JR.   Encyclopaedia Britannica Educational
    Corporation, 1972.   10 min.   color.   EBEC
About the role of Martin Luther King, Jr. as civil rights leader.

MARTIN LUTHER KING, JR. :   FROM MONTGOMERY TO
    MEMPHIS.   Film Associates, 1969.   26 1/2 min.   b/w.
    BFA
The role of Martin Luther King, Jr. in opposing segregation in the
southern U. S.

MARTIN LUTHER KING: THE MAN AND THE MARCH.   NET,
    1968.   83 min.   b/w.   IND, UCA
An account of the Poor People's March planned by Martin Luther
King before his assassination.

MAYBE NEXT WEEK SOMETIME.   David Boatwright, 1974.   30
    min.   color.   RAD
A film about black music as a way of life with jazz, blues, gospel
and other varieties of music performed by non-commercial artists.

MEETING THE MAN.   Terence Dixon, 1971.   27 min.   color.
    IMP
A portrait of Baldwin the man, and the conflict between his identity
as black revolutionary and as exotic writer.

MINGUS.   Thomas Reichman, 1966.   60 min.   color.   IMP
About the night that Charles Mingus, bassist and composer, was
evicted from his Bowery loft for non-payment of rent.

MINORITY YOUTH: FELICIA.   Stuart Roe, 1971.   11 1/2 min.
    b/w.   BFA
A young black woman describes her concern about her people and
the apathy that stems from discrimination and lack of opportunity.

THE MURDER OF FRED HAMPTON.   Mike Gray Associates, 1971.
    90 min.   b/w.   TWN
Describes the death of Fred Hampton and Mark Clark in 1969 at
the Illinois Branch of the Black Panther Party during a police raid.
An attempt to refute the "official" version of the incident.

MURDER ON LENOX AVENUE.   Goldberg, 1941.   60 min.   b/w.
    Directed by Arthur Dreifuss; from a story by Frank Wilson;
    lyrics and music by Donald Heywood.   With Mamie Smith,
    Alex Lovejoy, Dene Larry, Norman Astwood, Gus Smith, Edna
    Mae Harris, Alberta Perkins and George Williams.   BUDG
An all-black film produced in Florida.   The story has a racketeer
exposé theme with murder and mystery.   Typical of films made in
the 1940s for black theaters.

THE NEGRO AND THE AMERICAN PROMISE.   NET, 1963.   60
    min.   b/w.   IND, UCA
James Baldwin, Martin Luther King, Jr. and Malcolm X are inter-
viewed by Dr. Kenneth Clark, psychology professor at New York
City College.

THE NEGRO AND THE SOUTH.   NET, 1965.   (History of the
    Negro People Series.)   30 min.   b/w.   IND, UCA, UCO
Interviews and observations are used to describe the "Southern way
of life," its meaning and impact on blacks and whites.

NEGRO HEROES FROM AMERICAN HISTORY.   Atlantis, 1966.
    11 min.   color.   ATL, NYU, USC
Illustrates the lives of relatively unknown black heroes from the
Revolutionary War to the present.

THE NEGRO IN ENTERTAINMENT.   1949.   10 min.   b/w.   No
    credits listed.   BUDG
A short film on black performers, such as W. C. Handy, Ethel
Waters, Louis Armstrong, Bill Robinson, Duke Ellington, and
Fats Waller.

NEGRO SOLDIER.   U. S. War Department, 1944.   40 min.   b/w.
    MAC[1], UCO
The history of black people in the U. S. and black participation in
World War II.   Langston Hughes hailed this as "the most remark-
able Negro film ever flashed on the screen."   Supervised by Frank
Capra.

NEW MOOD.   NET, 1965.   (History of the Negro People Series.)
    30 min.   b/w.   IND, UCA, UCO
Covers important moments in the history of the civil rights efforts
after the Supreme Court school decision of 1954.

NEW SOUTH.   NET, 1970.   58 min.   b/w.   IND
Black and white citizens of Georgia give their opinions about South-
ern social and economic conditions to author Pat Watters ("Climbing
Jacob's Ladder" and "The South and the Nation").

NI SIKU MPYA. (IT'S A NEW DAY.) Council of Black Institutions,
    n. d.   30 min.   b/w.   AFR
Recommendations for black education and a report on black educational institutions.

NO HIDING PLACE. NET, 1968. 59 min. b/w. IND
Interviews with white people to reveal their thoughts on racial problems in a typical American suburban town.

NO HIDING PLACE. Talent Associates-Paramount, 1963. (East
Side/West Side Series.) 51 min. b/w. CAR, IND, UCA
An award-winning dramatization from the television series "East
Side/West Side," in which a black family moves into a white sub-
urban community in the North.   Shows issues involved, including
real estate "block-busters."

NO JAIL CAN CHANGE ME. School of Social Welfare, University
of California, 1968.   30 min.   b/w.   UCA
A counselor talks to a young black man who has spent most of his
life in correctional institutions.

NO MAN IS AN ISLAND. CBS, 1961. 29 min. b/w. CAR
About two young men, one white, the other black, who become good
friends in the army, but return home to be confronted by the anxi-
eties and prejudices of their families and friends.

NO VIETNAMESE EVER CALLED ME NIGGER. Paradigm, 1969.
68 min.   b/w.   TRI
A group of blacks is seen marching through Harlem in New York
City to protest the United States' involvement in Vietnam.   Also
presents interviews with three black veterans of the Vietnam conflict.

NO WAY OUT. Twentieth Century-Fox, 1950. 106 min. b/w.
Directed by Joseph L. Mankiewicz; screenplay by Joseph L.
Mankiewicz and Lesser Samuels.   With Sidney Poitier, Richard
Widmark, Linda Darnell, Ruby Dee, Ossie Davis, Bill Walker,
Ray Biddle.   FI
Sidney Poitier's first film.   Shows black people trying to live de-
cently under difficult conditions in an atmosphere of bigotry.   The
story centers on a black doctor, the only black on an otherwise all-
white staff of a hospital.

NON-VIOLENCE: MAHATMA GANDHI AND MARTIN LUTHER
KING, THE TEACHER AND THE PUPIL.   Intext, n. d.   15
min.   color.   RFSV
Contains interview with Gandhi in which he explains why he was
imprisoned for his cause, and contrasts Gandhi's philosophy with
that of Martin Luther King to show the interrelationship between the
two.

NOTHING BUT A MAN. Cinema V, 1963. 92 min. b/w. Directed
by Michael Roemer; screenplay by Michael Roemer and Robert

Young. With Ivan Dixon, Abbey Lincoln, Stanley Greene, Julius Harris, Gloria Foster. ASF, MAC[1]
A low-budget film with characterizations that ring true. About the struggle of a Southern black man and his wife in a hostile society.

NOVEL: RALPH ELLISON ON WORK IN PROGRESS. NET, 1968. 29 min. b/w. IND, UCA
A rare look at the author of "The Invisible Man" and how he feels about his second novel in progress.

NOW. Santiago Alvarez, 1964. 5 min. b/w. TWN
Lena Horne sings "Now," a song which recalls the civil rights struggle of the 1950s and '60s. A dramatic film which captures the spirit of the black power movement in America. Composed and edited by Cuban filmmaker Santiago Alvarez.

NOW IS THE TIME. WCAU-TV, 1968. 36 min. b/w. CAR, UCA
A production designed for television that includes black literary readings by Ossie Davis and Ruby Dee, fragments of speeches by black political leaders, music and film footage describing civil rights demonstrations.

ODDS AGAINST TOMORROW. Harbel, 1959. 95 min. b/w. Directed by Robert Wise; screenplay by John O. Killens from the book by William P. McGivern. With Harry Belafonte, Shelley Winters, Robert Ryan, Ed Begley. UNAR
Filmed by Harry Belafonte's own company with a script by black novelist John O. Killens. About a black man, ensnared by gambling debts and a marriage that has failed, who turns to crime but is distrusted by his bigoted, white partner-in-crime.

OH, FREEDOM! Sterling, 1971. 28 min. color. NACC, SEF
The movement for black equality in America today from 1955 to the beginnings of the Black Power movement. An award-winning film.

OLD, BLACK AND ALIVE! New Film, 1974. 28 min. color. NACC, NEF
A report on the lives and thoughts of several aged black people of various backgrounds, some in nursing homes, some in their own homes, some still at work. Produced for the National Center on Black Aged.

OMOWALE; THE CHILD RETURNS HOME. NET, 1965. (History of the Negro People Series.) 30 min. b/w. IND, UCA, UCO
A visit by black American novelist John Williams to Badagary, Nigeria, the port from which his ancestors left for America as slaves.

ON THE BATTLEFIELD. Peter Biskind, 1972. 85 min. b/w. TRI
Describes how the black community of Cairo, Illinois withstood

white harrassment since 1969 with the help of the United Front.
Shows the trend toward developing an alternative black economy.

ONE POTATO, TWO POTATO. Cinema V, 1965. 92 min. b/w.
    Directed by Larry Peerce; screenplay by Raphael Hayes and
    Orville H. Hampton. With Barbara Barrie, Bernie Hamilton,
    Robert Earle Jones, Vinnette Carroll. MGH, TWF, UCA,
    CPC
Julie, who has divorced Joe, meets a black man in a factory. The
first American film to deal with interracial marriage between a
black man and a white woman.

OPERATION BOOTSTRAP. Educational Communications and Opera-
    tion Bootstrap, 1968. 58 min. b/w. EBEC
Discussions with blacks and whites show how and why Watts, California had successfully pulled itself together by the late 1960s.

THE OTHER FACE OF DIXIE. CBS, 1962. 54 min. b/w. CAR
Contrasts the segregation wars of only a few years ago with today's
more cooperative spirit in the South. Shows schools, business relationships, and new attitudes toward civil rights generally.

OUR COUNTRY, TOO. NET, 1965. (History of the Negro People
    Series.) IND, UCA, UCO
A description of the black American's world, including social
events, newspapers, radio stations, sports, and other activities
and enterprises.

PALMOUR STREET. Department of Public Health, Georgia, 1956.
    27 min. b/w. UCA
About a small rural Georgia town and the problems of black people
who live on a typical street. A documentary by George Stoney.

THE PANTHERS. ABC, 1971. 25 min. color. XER
A documentary that reveals what black and white Americans think
about the Panthers, and examines the Panthers' impact on U.S.
society. Scenes show the Panthers at work in their headquarters
and in the community, and conversations with Julian Bond, Rev.
Andrew Young, Cecil Poole and David Hilliard.

PARADISE IN HARLEM. Joseph Seiden, 1939. 85 min. b/w.
    Directed by Joseph Seiden. With Mamie Smith, Frank Wilson,
    Edna Mae Harris, Lucky Milliner and His Orchestra, Juanita
    Hall Singers, Joe Thomas, Perry Bradford, Vincent Valentini,
    The Alphabetical Four. BUDG, PAR
A musical produced for all-black audiences. The story concerns
racketeers and features many black entertainers of the 1930s.

PAUL LAURENCE DUNBAR: AMERICAN POET. Vignette, 1966.
    14 min. color. BFA
A portrait of the son of an escaped slave who became the author of
poems, songs, plays and novels.

PAUL LAURENCE DUNBAR: AMERICA'S FIRST BLACK POET.
Carlton Moss, 1972.   23 min.   color.   PYR
A collage of still pictures, paintings, art, dramatizations, poetry
and biography provide the story of the first American black man
recognized as a poet.

PHYLLIS AND TERRY.   Center for Mass Communications, 1965.
36 min.   b/w.   CEMC, UCA
Concerns two black girls who face ghetto life in the New York
slums.

PORTRAIT IN BLACK AND WHITE.   CBS, 1968.   (Of Black America Series.)   54 min.   b/w.   BFA, UCA, UCO
A film survey of the opinions blacks and whites have about each
other.

PORTRAIT OF A DEAF CITY.   Sterling, 1972.   15 min.   color.
SEF
How those in power and the powerless view their city.   The focus
is on people from various walks of life: deputy mayor, the black
militant, the businessman and others.

PORTRAIT OF JASON.   Shirley Clarke, 1967.   105 min.   b/w.
NYF
A portrait of Jason Holliday, black performer and male prostitute,
including his female impersonations, stories of his earlier days,
his traumas.   The camera crew and friends nearby during the
filming are also part of the psychodrama.

PRELUDE TO REVOLUTION.   John Evans, Stephen Lighthill, Jerry
Stoll, 1967.   36 min.   color.   IMP
An interview with Black Panther, Huey P. Newton, prior to his
arraignment in 1968 for a murder charge.   Gives Newton's view
of the black liberation movement and the role of the Black Panther
Party.

PUTNEY SWOPE.   Cinema V, 1969.   84 min.   b/w./color.   Directed by Robert Downey; written by Robert Downey; music by
Charley Cuva.   With Arnold Johnson, Laura Greene.   CF
A comedy about a group of blacks who take over an advertising
agency.   They are "committed to the overthrow of the establishment."   Contains reversals of the standard black and white stereotypes, e.g., a black couple have a lazy white maid.

THE QUIET ONE.   Mayer-Burstyn, 1948.   67 min.   b/w.   MGH,
PAR, UCA
One of the first intelligent treatments of the black child in American
movies.   About a rejected child who withdraws into loneliness be-
fore he is sent to the Wiltwyck School for treatment.   Narrated by
Gary Merrill with commentary and dialogue written by James Agee.
Directed by Sidney Meyers.   An award-winning film.

THE RAFER JOHNSON STORY. Sterling, 1961. 55 min. b/w.
    SEF
A report on one of the most honored black athletes of all time--
Rafer Johnson.

A RAISIN IN THE SUN. Columbia, 1961. 128 min. b/w. Di-
    rected by Daniel Petrie; screenplay and original play by Lor-
    raine Hansberry; music by Laurence Rosenthal; photography by
    Charles Lawton, Jr. With Sidney Poitier, Claudia McNeil,
    Ruby Dee, Diana Sands, Ivan Dixon. MAC[1], MGH, CPC
The film version of Lorraine Hansberry's Pulitzer Prize-winning
play about the intra-relationships of the Younger family--"a glimpse
of real life black people, not mere stereotypes."

RALPH ABERNATHY. Mert Koplin-Charles Grinker, 1970. (Black
    Views on Race Series.) 4 min. color. TL
Abernathy's actual public remarks, an example of black opinion in
the U. S.

RAPPING. Frith, 1969. 14 min. b/w. PAR, UCA
A revealing visit with the leader of San Francisco's Mission Rebels
who became an accepted counselor and leader for young people because of his own early experiences with drugs and a correctional
institution.

REET, PETITE AND GONE. Astor, 1947. 75 min. b/w.
    Credits unlisted. With Louis Jordan and His Tympany Five,
    June Richmond. BUDG
A musical with an all-black cast. An example of films made especially for black theaters in the 1940s.

REGGIE. 3J, 1971. 10 min. color. ACI
A young black artist paints in personal themes of frustration and
alienation. A look at the work of Reginald Gammon.

REMEDY FOR RIOT. CBS, 1968. 37 min. b/w. CAR
A film study of the elements of "civil disorders," with suggestions
for remedial action.

RHYTHM RODEO. 1938. 20 min. b/w. Directed and written by
    George Randol. With Troy Brown, Jackson Brothers, Rosalie
    Lincoln, Jim Davis. PAR
A musical western made for all-black audiences.

RHYTHMETRON: THE DANCE THEATRE OF HARLEM WITH
    ARTHUR MITCHELL. Milton Fruchtman, 1973. 40 min.
    color. MGH
Arthur Mitchell explains why the dancers of the dance theatre of
Harlem do certain exercises. Also he discusses dance styles and
the relationship of classical ballet to daily life.

RIGHT ON! New Line, 1972. 85 min. color. NLC
An entertaining documentary presenting three young black men speaking
revolutionary poetry on a Harlem rooftop. "A spoken blues concert."

ROBERTA FLACK. WGBH-TV, 1971. (Artists in America Series.)
     30 min. color. IND, IMP
Roberta Flack, the black singer and pianist, as she performs at the
Newport Jazz Festival, at Mr. Henry's in Washington, D. C. and
as she discusses problems of mixed marriage and dual careers.

ROMANCE ON THE BEAT. All American, 1945. 30 min. b/w.
     Directed by Bud Pollard. With Lord Randall, Lionel Monagas,
     Tiny Dickerson, Hughie Walker, The Four Master Keys, Doc
     Rhythm. PAR
A musical produced for all-black audiences. An example of films
made for black theaters in the 1940s.

ROOSEVELT CITY. NET, 1968. 9 min. b/w. IND
About a new, all-black city in Alabama; how it functions with little
money. Produced by black filmmakers.

THE ROXBURY EXPERIMENT. Afram, n. d. 30 min. b/w. AFR
How the Highland Park Free School in Roxbury, Mass. became a
parent-controlled school.

RUN FROM RACE. George Stoney, 1964. (Metropolis: Creator
     or Destroyer? Series.) 30 min. b/w. IND, UCA
Black people in Philadelphia analyze their concerns with community
life.

ST. LOUIS BLUES. Dudley Murphy, 1929. 17 min. b/w. MAC[1]
This is the great jazz singer Bessie Smith's only movie; a short
film but a good look at the singer at work.

ST. LOUIS BLUES. Paramount, 1958. 93 min. b/w. Directed
     by Allen Reisner; written by Robert Smith and Ted Sherdeman.
     With Nat "King" Cole, Eartha Kitt, Pearl Bailey, Cab Callo-
     way, Ella Fitzgerald, Mahalia Jackson, Ruby Dee, Juano
     Hernandez, Billy Preston. FI, PFS
A biography of the black composer, W. C. Handy. Stresses the
impact of his fundamentalist father who believed jazz and popular
music were the Devil's work.

SAM "LIGHTNIN'" HOPKINS. NET, 1971. (Artists in America
     Series.) 30 min. color. IND
The blues musician tells of his life and sings more than ten songs.

SCAR OF SHAME. Colored Players of Philadelphia, 1929. 69
     min. b/w. silent. With Harry Henderson, Lucia Moses.
     STD
The story of the troubled marriage of a black concert pianist and
a "poor lower-class black girl." Their different worlds pull them
apart and lead to the wife's accidental disfigurement and subsequent
suicide. Considered to be the finest of the independently produced
black films of this early period.

SEGREGATION: NORTHERN STYLE. CBS, 1964. 33 min. b/w.
    CAR
A black couple tries to buy a home in a suburban part of New Jersey while hidden tape recorders and telephoto equipment reveal the antics of real estate brokers. By contrast, a successful integration effort is shown in New Rochelle, N. Y.

"SEPARATE BUT EQUAL." Encyclopaedia Britannica Educational
    Corporation, 1971. 8 min. color. EBEC
Explores the events after the Civil War which perpetuated segregation and inequality in the U. S.

SHADOWS. Lion International, 1960. 81 min. b/w. Directed
    by John Cassavetes. With Leila Goldoni, Ben Carruthers,
    Hugh Hurd. MAC[1], ROAF, TWY
The problems of an interracial romance involving a black girl, who looks white and is "passing," and a white man, who is driven away when he meets her relatives. Shot without a screenplay--an improvised cinema drama.

SHAFT. MGM, 1971. 98 min. color. Directed by Gordon Parks.
    With Richard Roundtree, Moses Gunn. FI
This is the second film directed by Gordon Parks. A black detective is hired by a Harlem mobster and finds himself in the midst of a war between the Mafia and a group of black revolutionaries.

SHAFT'S BIG SCORE. MGM, 1972. 105 min. color. Directed
    by Gordon Parks; screenplay by Ernest Tidyman; photography
    by Urs Furrer. With Richard Roundtree and Moses Gunn. FI
A quarter of a million dollars is hidden in a coffin and everyone is searching for the money. A sequel to SHAFT.

SHIRLEY CHISHOLM. Mert Koplin-Charles Grinker, 1970. (Black
    Views on Race Series.) 4 min. color. TL
Chisholm's actual public remarks, an example of black opinion in the U. S.

SIDNEY POITIER. Mert Koplin-Charles Grinker, 1970. (Black
    Views on Race Series.) 4 min. color. TL
Poitier's actual public remarks, an example of black opinion in the U. S.

SIT-IN. NBC, 1961. 54 min. b/w. UCA
An account of the first "sit in" at lunch counters in Nashville on May 10, 1960.

1619-1860: OUT OF SLAVERY. McGraw-Hill, 1965. (History of
    the Negro in America Series.) 20 min. b/w. MGH, UCO
Traces the roots of slavery in ancient times as background to a discussion of slavery in America.

SKEZAG. Joel L. Freedman and Philip F. Messina, 1970. 73
    min. color. SOH

A disturbing film made from a chance encounter of the filmmakers with a black hustler, Vietnam veteran and dope pusher who brags of his ability to shoot dope without being hooked. Ultimately he becomes an addict as the footage shot months later shows. Coverage also includes race relations and the ghetto. An award-winning film.

SLAVERY. NET, 1965. (History of the Negro People Series.)
    30 min. b/w. UCA, UCO, IMP, IND
From the words of actual former slaves, the story of what life was like under slavery in the U.S. Includes choral singing of old spirituals. With Ossie Davis and Ruby Dee.

SLAVERY AND SLAVE RESISTANCE. New York Times, 1969.
    23 1/2 min. color. COR
A documentary on black Americans' endurance and resistance to slavery, including the achievements of famous runaway slaves.

SLAVERY, THE BLACK MAN AND THE MAN. Silvermine, 1972.
    22 min. color. MAC
Scenes of youth in the modern drug and poverty-ridden ghetto are contrasted with graphics picturing the days of slavery, to show the relation of today's unofficial bondage with "official" slavery. Damon Braswell of the Negro Ensemble Company is narrator. Directed by John Chandler; music by Frank Leadley Moore.

SLAVES. Continental, 1969. 102 min. color. Directed by Herbert Biberman; screenplay by Herbert J. Biberman, John O. Killens and Alida Sherman. With Ossie Davis, Barbara Ann Teer, Robert Kya-Hill, Julius Harris, Eva Jessye, Dionne Warwick, Stephen Boyd. READ
Shows the plight of black people prior to the Civil War, in what has been called an "undercover remake" of "Uncle Tom's Cabin." Filmed in Shreveport, Louisiana and written in collaboration with black novelist John O. Killens.

A SLAVE'S STORY: RUNNING A THOUSAND MILES TO FREE-
    DOM. Learning Corporation, 1972. 29 min. color. LEC
A dramatization of the actual escape of two slaves, William and Ellen Croft, from the South to Philadelphia in 1848. With an introduction by their great-granddaughter.

SOME OF MY BEST FRIENDS ARE WHITE. BBC, 1968. 30 min.
    b/w. TL
Interviews with successful middle-class black people, including Gordon Parks, celebrated photographer-author-filmmaker and a look at the middle class black American's values and attitudes.

SOME TALK ABOUT POOL ROOMS AND GIN MILLS. Paulist Pro-
    ductions, 1967. 28 min. b/w. AIM, IFP
A white gunman seeks shelter by force in the tenement of a black family. The conversation reveals the philosophy of life of the various family members.

SONG OF FREEDOM.   British Lion-Hammer, 1937.   70 min.   b/
    w.   Directed by J. Elder Wills; from a story by Dorothy Hol-
    loway and Claude Wallace.   With Paul Robeson, Elizabeth
    Welch, George Mozart.   PAR, RAD
Based on an African legend about a black stevedore who learns he
is a descendent of an important line of African kings and that his
tribe is in need of a leader.

SOUL CITY.   NET, 1970.   13 min.   b/w.   IND
In North Carolina black people are planning and developing a community under the lead of Floyd McKissick.

SOUNDER.   Twentieth Century-Fox, 1972.   105 min.   color.   Di-
    rected by Martin Ritt; screenplay by Lonne Elder III, based on
    the novel by William H. Armstrong; photography by John Alon-
    zo; music by Taj Mahal.   With Paul Winfield, Cicely Tyson,
    Janet MacLachlan, Kevin Hooks.   FI
The story of a strong, unyielding black family in the rural, southern U. S. in the early part of the 20th century.   The portrayals of
the children are very effective, as are those of the mother and
father, played by Cicely Tyson and Paul Winfield respectively.

SPIRIT OF YOUTH.   Grand National, 1937.   70 min.   b/w.   Di-
    rected by Harry Fraser; screenplay by Arthur Hoerle.   With
    Joe Louis, Clarence Muse, Edna Mae Harris, Mantan More-
    land, Mae Turner.   BUDG
Heavy-weight champion Joe Louis plays Joe Thomas, a boxer on
his way to success, who is saved from a knockout by the arrival
of his girl friend at the ring.

STILL A BROTHER: INSIDE THE NEGRO MIDDLE CLASS.   Wil-
    liam Greaves and William Branch for NET, 1967.   MGH, UCA,
    UCO
Black people who have joined the American middle class talk about
their conflicts, attitudes, how they feel about recent developments,
social and political, in the U. S.

STOKELY CARMICHAEL.   Mert Koplin-Charles Grinker, 1970.
    (Black Views on Race Series.)   4 min.   color.   TL
Carmichael's actual public remarks, an example of black opinion in
the U. S.

STORMY WEATHER.   Twentieth Century-Fox, 1943.   77 min.
    b/w.   Directed by Andrew Stone; screenplay by Frederick
    Jackson and Ted Koehler; adapted by H. S. Kraft from an
    original story by Jerry Horwin and Seymour B. Robinson.
    With Lena Horne, Bill Robinson, Fats Waller, Cab Calloway,
    Dooley Wilson, the Katherine Dunham dancers.   FI
Often cited as a "cavalcade of Negro entertainment."   The story
is a slightly disguised dramatization of the life of Bill Robinson.

THE STORY OF A THREE-DAY PASS.   Melvin Van Peebles, 1968.
    87 min.   b/w.   In French with English subtitles.   Directed by

Melvin Van Peebles; screenplay by Melvin Van Peebles. With
Harry Baird, Nicole Berger. MAC[1]
Melvin Van Peebles' first effort as director. The story is based
on his novel about an interracial love affair and was made in France.

STRANGERS IN THEIR OWN LAND: THE BLACKS. ABC, 1971.
12 min. color. XER
A cinematic collage of black creativity in the ghettos today. Visits
Concept East, a cultural center in the Detroit slums directed by
Frank Ditto, who comments on the center's goals.

THE STREETS OF GREENWOOD. Willis, Reavis, and Wardenburg,
1964. 20 min. b/w. MAC[1]
The black freedom drive contrasted with the Greenwood, Mississippi
white community's effort to keep the status quo. Freedom songs
performed by Pete Seeger.

THE SUN'S GONNA SHINE. Les Blank and Skip Gerson, 1972.
10 min. color. PYR
A sensitive treatment of Lightnin' Hopkins, his life and his blues
music, as filmed in his home town, Centerville, Texas.

SWEET LOVE, BITTER. (IT WON'T RUB OFF, BABY.) Film 2
Associates, 1965. 92 min. b/w. Directed by Herbert Danska; screenplay by Lewis Jacobs and Herbert Danska, based
on a novel, "Night Song," by John A. Williams. With Dick
Gregory, Robert Hooks, Don Murray. MAC[1]
Based on the novel by black author John A. Williams, a story in-
spired by the life of jazz musician Charlie "Bird" Parker, a man
with many problems.

TAKE A GIANT STEP. Roundtable, 1967. 25 min. b/w. UCA
How the Watts Manufacturing Company was formed as an experiment in employing the "unemployable" of the ghetto.

TAKE THIS HAMMER. KQED, 1963. 45 min. b/w. UCA
James Baldwin tours San Francisco and finds it lacking in liberal
qualities despite its far-flung advertising as a cosmopolitan center.

THEY BEAT THE ODDS. Dibie-Dash, 1965. 22 min. color.
DIBD
Illustrates the achievement of success by black people in a variety
of fields: science, politics, dentistry, and others. Ponders the
situation of one black youth who might drop out of school because
of limited career opportunities.

THINKING SEVENTEEN. Richard Zarlow, 1969. 16 min. b/w.
UCA
A visit with a black teen-ager in Oakland, California who describes
his inner conflict, his observations, his goals in life.

THIS IS THE HOME OF MRS. LEVANT GRAHAM. Topper Carew,
Eliot Noyes, Jr. and Claudia McNeil, 1970. 15 min. b/w.
PYR

A probing study of urban black life and of the daily life of one
woman. Prize-winner at numerous film festivals.

THREE SONGS BY LEADBELLY.   Blanding Sloan and Wah Mong
    Chang, 1945.   8 min.   color.   RAD
Old film footage reissued to show Huddie Ledbetter, known as
Leadbelly, as he sang folk songs with his 12-string guitar in 1945.

A TIME FOR BUILDING.   CBS, 1967.   60 min.   b/w.   LUTH
Various people discuss A TIME FOR BURNING and Charles Kuralt
and others in turn discuss the reactions of the other people.

A TIME FOR BURNING.   Lutheran Film Associates, 1966.   58
    min.   b/w.   MGH, UCA, UNE
A study in indifference, racial bigotry among white and black
groups in Omaha, Nebraska shortly before a race riot.   Nominated
for an Academy Award.

TO BE BLACK.   ABC, 1970.   54 min.   b/w.   MGH
Reveals the resentments and plight of black Americans as expressed
by several black people who struggle daily to find a life for themselves.

TO BE YOUNG, GIFTED AND BLACK.   NET, 1972.   90 min.
    color.   Directed by Michael A. Schultz; photography by Paul
    Goldsmith; edited by Victoria Hochberg.   With Barbara Barrie,
    Blythe Danner, Ruby Dee, Al Freeman, Jr. , Lauren Jones.
    IND
Tells the life story and struggle of writer Lorraine Hansberry, using her letters, diaries and plays.

TO FIND A HOME.   University of Wisconsin, 1963.   28 min.   b/
    w.   UCA
A comparison of two actual house-hunting experiences of black families, one a disappointing venture, the other successful.

TOUCHING GROUND.   Douglas Collins, n. d.   18 min.   color.
    NLC
Episodes in the life of Jim, black jazz musician, who seeks to follow his interest in music despite pressures to be militant and politically active.

TRIAL: THE CITY AND COUNTY OF DENVER VERSUS LAUREN
    R. WATSON.   NET, 1970.   4 parts, 90 min. ea.   b/w.   IND
Concerning the actual trial of Black Panther Lauren Watson as he
is tried by a white middle-class jury.   Discussion by James Voren-
berg, professor of law at Harvard University.
TRIAL: THE FIRST DAY.   Covers selection of the jury.
TRIAL: THE SECOND DAY.   The prosecution presents its case.
TRIAL: THE THIRD DAY.   The defense presents its case.
TRIAL: THE FOURTH AND FINAL DAY.   Instructions to the jury
and interviews with the judge, attorneys and defendant, as well as
the jurors later after the trial.

A TRIBUTE TO MALCOLM X.   NET, 1969.   (Black Journal
    Series.)   15 min.   b/w.   IND, IMP
An interview with Malcolm X's widow, Betty Shabazz, who traces
his life from childhood to his ministry and the conflict within the
Nation of Islam.

TROUBLEMAKERS.   Cinema 16, 1966.   54 min.   b/w.   GRO,
    UCA
How white organizers tried to bring about improvements in the
black ghetto of Newark, New Jersey.   The frustrations and failures
of the Newark Community Union Project in its effort to get housing
code enforcement, to get a traffic signal at a dangerous corner,
and to elect a candidate to the city council.

A TRUMPET FOR THE COMBO.   National Film Board of Canada,
    1966.   8 min.   b/w.   SEF
About two students--one white and one black--who try out for a
school combo in need of a trumpet player.   The teacher tries to
influence the group to select the black player.   An open-ended film
for discussion.

220 BLUES.   King Screen, 1970.   18 min.   color.   BFA
Sonny, a black youth and a much admired high school track star
slated for a promising career, meets a new black student, a militant who makes Sonny suddenly aware of his need to choose a side.

UMOJA: TIGER AND THE BIG WIND.   Carol Monday Lawrence,
    n. d.   8 min.   color.   AFR
Umoja ("unity" in Swahili) is an animated film which tells a folk
story narrated by an 80-year-old black American man who heard it
told by a former slave.

UP TIGHT.   Paramount, 1969.   104 min.   color.   Directed and
    produced by Jules Dassin; screenplay by Jules Dassin, Ruby
    Dee and Julian Mayfield, based on the novel "The Informer"
    by Liam O'Flaherty.   With Ruby Dee, Julian Mayfield, Roscoe
    Lee Browne, Raymond St. Jacques.   FI, PFS
O'Flaherty's "The Informer" is transposed to the black revolution
in the U. S.   The setting is Cleveland's ghetto immediately following
Martin Luther King's assassination.   The story is about a robbery
attempt by black militants, the betrayal of their leader, and the
traitor's penance.

VERONICA.   Jason, 1969.   27 min.   color.   JAS
A young middle-class black girl attends a predominantly white
school in Connecticut and comments on what her expectations are
for her future in America.

W. C. HANDY.   Vignette, 1967.   14 min.   color.   BFA
About the career of the "Father of the Blues" and the concurrent
life in the 1890-1950 period in the U. S.

WALK IN MY SHOES. ABC, 1963. 54 min. b/w. MGH, UCA,
    UCO, UUT
Black Americans speak pro and con the Black Muslim movement,
Martin Luther King, the Freedom Riders, rapid integration, and
the NAACP.

WASHINGTON: THE MAYOR AND THE CITY. Jesse Sandler, n. d.
    15 min. color. AEF
How Mayor Walter Washington of Washington, D. C. had to work
for unity and hope after the riots which crippled his city.

WATERMELON MAN. Columbia, 1970. 97 min. color. Directed
    by Melvin Van Peebles; screenplay by Herman Raucher; music
    by Melvin Van Peebles. With Godfrey Cambridge, Estelle
    Parsons, Howard Caine, Mantan Moreland. CPC
This is Melvin Van Peebles' directorial debut with a story about a
white man who awakens to discover he has turned black.

WATTS LIBRARY REACHES OUT. ACI, 1973. 19 min. color.
    ACI
How the Watts Branch of the Los Angeles Public Library tried to
reach its community with unusual, attractive activities and services.

WATTS TOWERS THEATRE WORKSHOP. KCET-TV, 1969. 27
    min. color. IND
Presents three short acts of a theatrical group of black teen-agers
from the Los Angeles Watts ghetto.

THE WAY IT IS. NET, 1967. 60 min. b/w. IND
A documentary concerning the problems and possible remedies at
one junior high school in the Bedford-Stuyvesant section of Brook-
lyn.

WE GOT TO LIVE HERE. Robert Machover and Norm Fruchter,
    1966. 20 min. b/w. UCA
A documentary about a slum of Newark, New Jersey, its history
from fashionable white neighborhood to present blight with black
people living in bitterness and despair.

WE SHALL OVERCOME. Jack Summerfield, 1965. 10 min. color.
    MAC[1]
A disturbing documentary on the civil rights movement. Uses recordings of Ku Klux Klan Meetings, interviews with white and black
leaders, views of rallies and demonstrations--the result of a hang-
ing--with the title song used as background for continuity.

THE WEAPONS OF GORDON PARKS. Warren Forma, 1966.
    (Artists at Work Series.) 28 min. color. MGH, UCA
Artist-photographer-writer Gordon Parks shares his early life,
jobs, struggles and achievements. Uses photos made by Parks
himself.

WE'LL NEVER TURN BACK. Harvey Richards for the Student Non-
Violent Coordinating Committee, 1963. 30 min. b/w. MAC,
UCA
A documentary on the effort to register potential black voters in
Mississippi.

WHAT DO YOU PEOPLE WANT? John Evans, 1968. 30 min.
color. IMP
Scenes from Black Panther Party meetings. Includes an Oakland,
California rally with appearances by James Forman, Eldridge and
Kathleen Cleaver, Bobby Seale, Stokely Carmichael and Rap Brown.

WHAT HARVEST FOR THE REAPER? NET, 1968. 59 min. b/w.
IMP
The migrant labor system along the eastern seaboard is shown to
keep black people in poverty.

WHERE IS JIM CROW? A CONVERSATION WITH BROCK PETERS.
KQED, 1964. (Where Is Jim Crow? Series.) 30 min. b/w.
UCA
Harlem-born actor Brock Peters discusses the life of a black actor
in Hollywood and the impact of the civil rights movement on avail-
able roles.

WHERE IS JIM CROW? A CONVERSATION WITH GODFREY CAM-
BRIDGE. KQED, 1964. (Where Is Jim Crow? Series.) 30
min. b/w. UCA
A lively account of little-known facts about the black American's
contribution to the growth of America and the problems of the black
entertainer.

WHERE IS JIM CROW? A CONVERSATION WITH LENA HORNE.
KQED, 1964. (Where Is Jim Crow? Series.) 30 min. b/w.
UCA
Lena Horne, the black singer, discusses the role of black women
and the potential for blacks in television.

WHERE IS JIM CROW? A CONVERSATION WITH NANCY WILSON.
KQED, 1964. (Where Is Jim Crow? Series.) 30 min. b/w.
UCA
Nancy Wilson, black singer, describes her feelings about the Watts
riots, the class implications in such violence, and her own good
fortune at avoiding discrimination.

WHERE IS JIM CROW? A CONVERSATION WITH STOKELY CAR-
MICHAEL. KQED, 1964. (Where Is Jim Crow? Series.) 30
min. b/w. UCA
The "Black Power" spokesman describes the U. S. way of condoning
violence in the southern U. S. as well as in Japan and elsewhere.
Discusses his faith in the strength of southern black people, in contrast to the northern blacks who have assumed white values.

WHO DO YOU KILL? CBS, 1967. (East Side/West Side Series.)
    51 min. b/w. CAR, UCA
A theatrical presentation about a black couple in Harlem whose
child is bitten by rats and dies on the way to the hospital because
white cab drivers will not stop to help.

WILLIAM: FROM GEORGIA TO HARLEM. Universal Creative
    Personal and Arts Guild, 1969. (The Many Americans Series.)
    15 min. color. LEC
A black youth must make a major adjustment in his move from
Georgia to New York's Harlem.

WILMINGTON. San Francisco Newsreel, 1968. 15 min. b/w.
    TWN
A report on conditions in the state of Delaware where the National
Guard maintained troops on duty in black communities of Wilming-
ton for ten months after the assassination of Martin Luther King,
Jr.

WOODCUTTERS OF THE DEEP SOUTH. Lionel Rogosin, 1973.
    90 min. color. IMP
Poor black and white workers are trying to overcome racism in
order to fight in a united front the paper and pulpwood companies
in Mississippi and Alabama.

THE WOODPILE. Paulist Productions, 1965. 29 min. b/w.
    AIM, PAUL
A large electronic firm's board of directors is faced with the decision of whether or not to hire their first black executive.

THE WORLD OF JULIAN BOND. NET, 1968. 11 min. b/w.
    IND
Julian Bond, black legislator in Georgia, states his views on contemporary events, and the progress of black people; made by black
filmmakers.

YONDER COME DAY. Milton Fruchtman, 1974. 51 min. color.
    CAPC
Bessie Jones presents the heritage of slave songs and games to
Yale University students who also share their new knowledge with
children in New Haven Schools.

YOU CAN'T CATCH IT. Education Development Center, 1973.
    40 min. color. AFR
A documentary on sickle cell anemia, the disease limited to black
people.

YOU DIG IT. Frith, 1969. 28 min. b/w. PAR, UCA
A production by young ghetto blacks of New York City in which a
young man (played by the author of the script), a member of a
good gang, becomes involved in various situations within the ghetto
which lead to his being shot.

Asian Americans

BAGGAGE. Alexander Neel, 1969. 22 min. b/w. ACI
Japanese mime Mamako Yoneyama performs a lyrical and tragic allegory against the architectural setting of San Francisco. A girl struggles with her "baggage," symbolic of psychological restrictions, in various street locales. But when she finally gets rid of it she feels lost. At last she is reunited with her burden only to give it up in death.

BUDDHISM. Films Inc., n. d. (World Religions Series.) 28 min.
   color. FI
Examines Buddhist beliefs that one is free of suffering by letting go of the ego and that people become what they have done. Focuses on young Buddhists in North America.

THE CHINESE-AMERICAN: THE EARLY IMMIGRANTS. Handel,
   1973. 20 min. color. HFC
A history of the Chinese people in the United States. Stresses their achievements, contributions and problems. Narrated by Sam Chu Lin.

THE CHINESE-AMERICAN: THE TWENTIETH CENTURY. Handel,
   1973. 20 min. color. HFC
A report on the activities and achievements of the Chinese-Americans in the U. S. Narrated by Sam Chu Lin.

CITIZEN CHANG. Stuart Reynolds, n. d. 25 min. b/w. UCA
A human relations training film that focuses on a Chinese-American boy and his communication problems with the adult world.

THE CONSTITUTION AND MILITARY POWER. NET, 1959. 29
   min. b/w. IMP, IND
Discusses military-civilian relations during war time, including the World War II case of Korematsu versus the U. S. Uses historic film of Japanese relocation.

DONG KINGMAN. Living Artists, 1954. 15 min. color. MGH
The distinguished Chinese-American water-colorist is seen working on a painting. Also, Dong Kingman's approach to art, his home and family life are described.

FACES OF CHINATOWN. KPIX-TV, n. d. 27 min. b/w. UCA
Covers the history of Chinese immigrants in San Francisco during the period 1870-1911. With music by Harry Partch.

THE GOLDEN MOUNTAIN ON MOTT STREET. WCBS-TV, 1968.
   34 min. color. CAR
Describes the fast changing life of today's Chinese-Americans who for decades past maintained many of their traditions in the face of urban life. Comments on the new "identity crisis" and how it is being met.

GUILTY BY REASON OF RACE.   NBC, 1972.   51 min.   color.
   FI
An award-winning documentary on the U. S. government's relocation
of Japanese-American citizens during World War II under Executive
Order 9066.

HIRAM FONG.   McGraw-Hill, 1970.   15 min.   color.   MGH
The life of the first Asian American to serve in the U. S. Senate--
a Chinese-American, who started as a shoe shine boy but later at-
tended Harvard Law School.

THE JAPANESE-AMERICAN.   Handel, 1974.   30 min.   color.   HFC
Traces the involvement of the U. S. in Japan and the subsequent
emigration from that country to the U. S. Describes the problems
of Japanese-Americans, including internment during World War II,
and their many achievements in the twentieth century.   Narrated by
Ken Kashiwahara.

MASUO IKEDA: PRINTMAKER.   Ellis Edmonds, 1973.   14 min.
   color.   ACI
A Japanese artist living in New York creates a color print from
copper plates as he describes his art and work.

MINORITY YOUTH: AKIRA.   Stuart Roe, 1971.   14 1/2 min.
   color.   BFA
A Japanese-American youth discusses his feelings about the two
cultures that influence his life.

THE NISEI: THE PRIDE AND THE SHAME.   CBS, 1965.   26 min.
   b/w.   AIM
About the internment of Japanese-Americans in the U. S. detention
camps during World War II.

REFLECTIONS.   ABC, 1967.   15 min.   color.   MGH
A sensitive study of a lonely Chinese boy who lives in the Lower
East Side of New York City and who strikes up a friendship with a
Puerto Rican girl.

SIU MEI WONG: WHO SHALL I BE?   Learning Corporation, 1971.
   (The Many Americans Series.)   18 min.   color.   LEC
About a young Chinese-American girl who experiences conflicts between the two cultures that influence her life.   In Chinese with English subtitles.

SUMI ARTIST.   University of California, 1954.   11 min.   color.
   UCA
Chiura Obata of the University of California at Berkeley demonstrates Japanese brush painting with sumi paint made from lamp
black.

THE TROUBLE WITH CHINATOWN.   WNBC-TV, 1970.   26 min.
   color.   FI
About the concerns of Chinese-Americans caught between a wave of
immigration and a westernized younger generation.

Latinos

AMERICA TROPICAL. KCET-TV, 1971. 30 min. color. IND
Following Mexican artist David Alfaro Siqueiros's completion of a
mural "America Tropical" in Los Angeles in 1932, which described
the poor situation of Mexican-Americans, his visa was not renewed
and the entire wall was covered with whitewash soon after. Now
many years later the mural has been restored.

AND NOW MIGUEL. U. S. Information Agency, 1953. 60 min.
   b/w. MGH, NAC
Manuel, a young boy, wants to be accepted by his father and older
brothers in this story of a sheep-raising family in the U. S. Southwest. Based on the book by Joseph Krumgold. Directed by Joseph
Krumgold.

BELLOTA. University of Arizona, 1969. 34 min. color. IFB
Five Mexican vaquero-cowboys describe their work in a cattle
roundup in the Southwestern U. S. An award-winning film.

BIRTH OF A UNION. NET, 1966. 30 min. b/w. IMP, UCA
How the National Farm Workers Association, largely made up of
Latinos, came into being. Discusses problems, strikes, recruit-
ment.

BITTER HARVEST. Maurice Hatton and Charles Stewart, n. d. 60
   min. color. ITC
About the efforts of Cesar Chavez to organize the migrant workers
of California for a struggle against grape growers and now the
Teamsters Union.

THE CASE AGAINST LINCOLN CENTER. (EL CASO CONTRA
   LINCOLN CENTER.) San Francisco Newsreel, 1968. 12 min.
   b/w. TWN
Tells how urban renewal efforts ousted 35,000 Puerto Rican families
from New York's West Side to build Lincoln Center. Probes the
problem of community destruction.

CHICANO. Gary Mitchell, 1971. 22 1/2 min. color. BFA
Explores the background of the Chicano movement and the Mexican-
American community in Los Angeles.

CHICANO. San Diego State College, 1971. 27 min. color. MGH,
   UUT
Four Mexican-Americans from San Diego, California express their
feelings about their heritage.

CHICANO FROM THE SOUTHWEST. Encyclopaedia Britannica Educational Corporation, 1970. 15 min. color. EBEC
Follows a ten-year-old Mexican-American boy with his family when
they move from a rural setting to Los Angeles for financial security.

CHICANO MORATORIUM, A QUESTION OF FREEDOM.   Cintec,
     1971.   13 min.   color.   In Spanish.   CIN
Describes what happened when a Mexican-American fiesta developed
into a confrontation between Chicanos and the Los Angeles police.
Includes the death of Rubin Salazar.

LOS COMPADRES.   St. Francis, 1971.   28 min.   color.   UUT
The roots and present life style of the Spanish Americans who live
in New Mexico and Colorado, as traced from 1598 to today.

DECISION AT DELANO.   Cathedral, 1967.   28 min.   color.   UCA
About the continuing "grape strike" of Cesar Chavez' National Farm
Workers of America that began in 1966.   Presents all points of
view.

DROP OUT NOW, PAY LATER.   Handel, 1972.   24 min.   color.
     HFC
Young people discuss why students of Spanish-speaking background
drop out from schools and why they need to complete their education.   Narrated by Ned Romero.

EDUCATION AND THE MEXICAN-AMERICAN.   University of Cali-
     fornia, 1969.   57 min.   b/w.   UCA
Covers the student walk-outs in Los Angeles during March 1968 to
protest inferior education and the subsequent arrests of the "Chicano 13. "

FELIPA: NORTH OF THE BORDER.   Learning Corporation, 1971.
     17 min.   color.   LEC
A young Chicano girl discovers much about herself and her world
as she helps her uncle get a new job.   An award-winning film.
Directed by Bert Salzman.

LOS FOUR.   Jim Tartan, 1974.   22 min.   color.   HFE
A documentary about the first Chicano art exhibit held at the Los
Angeles County Museum of Art and the aspirations of the artists
represented therein.

HARLEM CRUSADER.   NBC, 1965.   29 min.   b/w.   FI, UCA
About the contribution of a social worker who spent five years
helping people in New York's Spanish Harlem.

HENRY: BOY OF THE BARRIO.   Atlantis, 1968.   30 min.   b/w.
     UCA, UUT
Studies the "barrio" through the life of a Chicano boy covered during a two-year period: his friends, home life, prospects for the
future, his arrest for auto theft.

HOW'S SCHOOL, ENRIQUE?   Stanley R. Frager, 1971.   18 min.
     color.   UNE, UUT
How Mexican-American youth must cope with the daily problems of
alienation, English as a second language and prejudicial attitudes.

HUELGA! King Screen, 1967. 50 min. color. MGH
An award-winning documentary about the September 1965 Delano
Grape Strike (huelga) made by a group of Mexican and Filipino-
American grape pickers in their demand for union recognition, the
right to collective bargaining and a minimum wage. Directed by
Skeets McGrew.

I AM JOAQUIN. Luis Valdez, 1971. 20 min. color. UUT
About the Mexican-American heritage from the days of the Mayan
princes to today's Chicano movement, as told in Corky Gonzales'
poem about the Chicano experience.

LA RAZA, THE STORY OF MEXICAN AMERICANS. 1971. 38
   min. color. UUT
Mexican-Americans from various walks of life discuss the aspirations of Chicanos in the U. S. today.

MEXICAN AMERICAN BORDER SONGS. NET, n. d. 29 min. b/
   w. IMP
A visit to Texas and Mexico border towns as background for border
songs. With Dr. Americo Paredes, an authority on folk guitar
styles and Rio Grande border songs.

MEXICAN-AMERICAN FAMILY. Atlantis, 1970. 17 min. color.
   ATL, UAR, USC
About a Mexican-American family's customs and efforts to maintain
family solidarity despite the need to adjust to a new culture.

THE MEXICAN-AMERICAN: HERITAGE AND DESTINY. Handel,
   1971. 29 min. color. In Spanish and English versions.
   HFC
Shows the cultural achievements of the Chicanos' ancestors and current contributions to civilization. Narrated by Ricardo Montalban.

THE MEXICAN-AMERICAN SPEAKS: HERITAGE IN BRONZE. Encyclopaedia Britannica Educational Corporation, 1972. 20 min.
   color. EBEC
Traces the heritage of Spanish rule in the New World, the mixing
of races and cultures, and the new political role of Latinos in the
U. S.

MEXICAN AMERICANS: A QUEST FOR EQUALITY. Anti-Defamation League, 1971. 28 min. b/w. UUT
Dr. Ernesto Galarza talks about problems and goals of his people
in escaping the poverty of the barrios in the U. S. Southwest.

MEXICAN AMERICANS: AN HISTORIC PROFILE. Anti-Defamation
   League, 1971. 28 min. b/w. UUT
Maclovia Barraza discusses the historical roots of the Mexican-
American up to the 1970s.

MEXICAN AMERICANS: THE INVISIBLE MINORITY. Joseph Louw,
   1968. 39 min. b/w. IND, IMP, UMI, UUT

An overview of the struggle for identity and existence by the second largest U. S. minority group.

MEXICAN-AMERICANS: VIVA LA RAZA! 54 min. b/w. UMI
Mexican-American leaders, police, religious leaders, and others discuss grievances of the Mexican-Americans--poverty, poor education, discrimination--as well as the meaning of the Chicano movement.

MEXICAN OR AMERICAN. Atlantis, 1970. 17 min. color.
ATL, USC, SYR
The stresses of cultural conflict experienced by a Mexican-American.

MIGUEL: UP FROM PUERTO RICO. Learning Corporation, 1970.
(The Many Americans.) 15 min. color. LEC
A young Puerto Rican boy reflects on the contrast between life in his former island home and his crowded apartment in New York City. Shows scenes of Puerto Rico and New York. Directed by Bert Salzman.

MINORITY YOUTH: ANGIE. Stuart Roe, 1971. 10 1/2 min.
color. BFA
A Mexican-American girl reveals her feelings about being a Mexican-American in today's world.

THE MOOR'S PAVANE. Brandon, 1950. 16 min. color. MAC[1]
Shows Jose Limon and his troupe performing dances based on Shakespeare's "Othello." Choreography by Mexican-born José Limon, who is a U. S. resident.

THE MOST HATED MAN IN NEW MEXICO. NBC, 1969. 29 min.
color. FI
About the Mexican-American leader Reis Tijerina of New Mexico who brings hope to the poor of the southwestern U. S.

NO MORE MAÑANAS. Paulist Productions, 1971. (The Insight
Series.) 27 min. b/w. AIM
The story of a Mexican-American junkie whose life and environment of despair and self-hate is described with sympathy. With Rafael Campos, Frank Ramirez.

NORTH OF THE BORDER. Frith, 1971. 19 min. color. FIF
A film about the efforts of Mexican-Americans to be assimilated into the culture of their new home in the U. S. Explores contributions and problems.

NOSOTROS VENCEREMOS! (WE SHALL OVERCOME.) United
Farm Workers, 1971. 11 min. b/w. In Spanish. TRI
Uses still photographs with songs and sounds of the United Farm Workers movement.

THE PEOPLE VS. WILLIE FARAH. Harold Mayer, 1973. 20
   min. color. ACW
How Mexican-Americans went on strike against one of the largest
manufacturers of pants in the U.S. Includes the Bishop of El Paso
urging a boycott of Farah pants.

EL PUEBLO SE LEVANTA. Third World Newsreel, 1971. 40
   min. b/w. TWN
Follows the Puerto Rican struggle in the U.S. Studies health, education, food and housing, which become the focus of the Young
Lords Party's work.

RANCHO LIFE. Barr, 1964. 2nd ed. 23 min. color. BARR
   (1st ed. , 1949, UCA)
Set in 1835 on a California rancho in which a grandfather tells his
grandson the story of the rancho, how it came to be settled, and
how the old days compare with 1835.

THE REAL STORY OF JOAQUIN MURIETA. n. d. Credits and
   cast unlisted. 26 min. b/w. BUDG
The story of the Mexican outlaw who lived a life of murderous revenge in California during the 1850s.

REQUIEM 29. David Garcia, 1971. 36 min. color. TRI
The story of the Chicano Moratorium of August 29, 1970 in Los
Angeles. Explores the death of Chicano journalist Rubin Salazar
killed by police in the mass demonstration.

SALT OF THE EARTH. Paul Jarrico, 1954. 94 min. b/w. Directed by Herbert Biberman; screenplay by Michael Wilson;
   music by Sol Kaplan. With Rosaura Revueltas, Juan Chacon,
   Will Geer, and members of Local 890 of the International
   Minc, Mill and Smelter Workers. IMP, MAC[1]
Using some of the Mexican-American zinc miners who had taken
part in a year-long strike in New Mexico, this film depicts the
role of women who helped the men achieve victory. A controversial film made with blacklisted artists. Considered the first major
film to treat a minority people with understanding.

SANTIAGO'S ARK. Albert C. Waller, 1972. 47 min. color. CAR
An ABC-TV special about a boy of New York's Spanish Harlem who
sees a picture of an old American ship and sets out to build one of
his own with scraps picked up here and there. Just as it begins
to become a symbol of hope for his neighborhood, a gang decides
to destroy the ship.

LOS SIETE DE LA RAZA. San Francisco Newsreel, 1969. 30
   min. b/w. TWN
Studies the cause and the problems of the famous seven Latino
youths who were recruiting street youth into a Brown Studies Program in San Francisco when they were charged with murder during
a police clean-up campaign. Available in Spanish and English language versions.

SPANISH INFLUENCES IN THE UNITED STATES.   Coronet, 1972.
12 1/2 min.   color.   COR, UCA
The heritage that influences American life today, traced from early
Spanish territorial claims in Florida, the Southwest and Florida.

STRANGERS IN THE CITY.   Rick Carrier, 1962.   83 min.   b/w.
Directed, written and photographed by Rick Carrier; music by
Bob Prince.   With Robert Gentile, Camilio Delgado, Rosita
De Triana, Creta Marcos.   MAC[1]
A story about a Puerto Rican family living in "El Barrio," the
ghetto of Spanish Harlem.   The film shot on location, captures the
horrors of rat-infested, crime-ridden slums and contrasts the expectations of a people who originated in a land that hardly prepared
them for their U. S. experience.

STRANGERS IN THEIR OWN LAND: THE CHICANOS.   ABC, 1971.
16 min.   color.   XER
A study of the almost four million Mexican-Americans in the U. S.
Illustrates activities of Efrain and Dora Fernandez who work with
their own people to fight for their rights.

STRANGERS IN THEIR OWN LAND: THE PUERTO RICANS.   ABC,
1971.   14 min.   color.   XER
Traces the history of Puerto Ricans in the U. S. and the reasons
why they leave their homeland to seek better conditions on the
mainland.   Focuses on one typical family who are helped by the
Puerto Rican Family Institute.

EL TEATRO CAMPESINO.   NET, 1971.   61 min.   b/w.   IMP,
IND
A history of the theater of the farmworkers, which describes its
role in morale and solidarity of Chicanos.   Illustrates with skits,
music, a puppet show, and a play excerpt.

THIS IS NOT A DEMONSTRATION.   Jaime Barrios, 1969.   8 min.
color.   FMCO
A look at Enrique Vargas' Guerrilla Theater in New York.

TIJERINA.   University of California, 1969.   30 min.   b/w.   UCA,
UUT
A speech by the Mexican-American leader and founder of La Alianza
Federal de los Pueblos Libres at a symposium at U. C. L. A. in
1968.

VOICE OF LA RAZA.   William Greaves, 1970.   54 min.   color.
GRE
A tour around the U. S. with Anthony Quinn who discusses prejudice
and job discrimination against Americans with Spanish surnames.
Includes a visit with Rita Moreno.   Made for the Equal Employment
Opportunity Commission.   An award-winning film.

WALK THE FIRST STEP.   KCET-TV, 1973.   28 min.   color.   IND
An account of a training program for unemployed Mexican-Americans

to prepare them for jobs under the direction of the Los Angeles
Mexican-American Opportunity Foundation (MAOF).

WORLD OF PIRI THOMAS.   NET, 1968.   60 min.   color.   IND
The author of "Down These Mean Streets" provides a tour of Spanish Harlem, home of at least 600,000 Puerto Ricans, the "forgotten
people. "

YO SOY CHICANO.   KCET-TV, 1972.   59 min.   color.   Directed
    by Jesus Trevino; music composed and sung by Daniel Valdez;
    narrated by Victor Millan.   In Spanish with English subtitles.
    IND, TRI
Key events of the Chicano experience from pre-Columbian days to
the present are recreated by actors and interviews with Chicano
leaders.   Discusses solutions to the oppression of Chicanos.   Includes interviews with Dolores Huerta, Reies Lopez Tijerina,
Rodolfo "Corky" Gonzales and Jose Angel Gutierrez.

Native Americans

ACORNS: THE STAPLE FOOD OF THE CALIFORNIA INDIANS.
    University of California, 1962.   (American Indian Series.)   28
    min.   color.   UCA, UNE, UUT
About the use of acorns by California Indians as a staple in their
diet.   Focuses on the Pomo group, demonstrating traditional methods of harvesting and keeping the acorns.

AGE OF THE BUFFALO.   Encyclopaedia Britannica Educational
    Corporation, 1967.   14 min.   color.   UCA, UCO
Close-ups of Frederick Remington's paintings evoke details of the
life of the buffalo in the Wild West days when they roamed the
plains in freedom and played an important role in Indian life as
food, shelter, and clothing.

AKI'NAME (ON THE WALL).   National Film Board of Canada, 1969.
    23 min.   color.   NFBC
Shows two Eskimo stone carvers, Kumukuluk Saggiak and Elijah
Pudlat, at work on a wall in Expo 67's Canadian pavilion.

THE ALASKAN ESKIMO.   Disney, 1971.   27 min.   color.   DIS,
    UUT, AIM, ASF
Shows the good and bad aspects of the Eskimo's daily lives.

ALASKAN PIPE DREAM.   BBC, 1973.   31 min.   color.   TL
Although this film examines the pros and cons of the controversial
pipeline under construction that is designed to provide the U. S.
with a large supply of crude oil, it presents an unusual look at the
Alaskan Eskimos, who, because of this project, are gradually being
absorbed into technological jobs and the American way of life.
One of the few films that shows Eskimo ghettos with high rates of
disease, alcoholism, drug abuse and suicide.

THE AMERICAN INDIAN: AFTER THE WHITE MAN CAME. Handel, 1972. 27 min. color. HFC
A study of the American Indian since the discovery of the New World. Includes a view of conditions and problems today.

THE AMERICAN INDIAN: BEFORE THE WHITE MAN. Handel, 1972. 19 min. color. HFC
A historical overview of the American Indian's life in the Western Hemisphere from early migration to the development of distinct tribal groups. Narrated by Iron Eyes Cody.

THE AMERICAN INDIAN SPEAKS. Moral Rearmament, 1967. 47 min. color. AIM
A film written and produced by Native Americans expressing their thoughts about their present status and concerns for the future. Directed by Diarmid Campbell.

AMERICAN INDIANS AS SEEN BY D. H. LAWRENCE. Walter P. Lewisohn, 1966. 14 min. color. COR
Frieda Lawrence talks about her husband's beliefs and thoughts about the Indians he had known, and Aldous Huxley presents Lawrence's insights into the religious aspects of Indian culture.

AMERICAN INDIANS BEFORE EUROPEAN SETTLEMENT. Coronet, 1959. 10 1/2 min. color. COR, UWY
An account of the roots, cultural characteristics of the various Native Americans who lived in North America before the arrival of Europeans. Describes native life in the five major regions of the U. S. : Eastern Woodlands, Great Plains, Southwest, Far West and Northwest Coast.

AMERICAN INDIANS OF TODAY. Encyclopaedia Britannica Educational Corporation, 1957. 16 min. color. EBEC, UCO, UUT, UWY
The present status of Native Americans on reservations and in urban relocation centers.

... AND THE MEEK SHALL INHERIT THE EARTH. NET, 1972. 59 min. color. IND
The story of the Menominee Indians, their governing of Menominee County, Wisconsin, and their present plight as a "terminated" tribe under the Bureau of Indian Affairs' supervision.

ANGOTEE: STORY OF AN ESKIMO BOY. National Film Board of Canada, 1953. 32 min. color. IFB
The preparation of an Eskimo boy for his adult life. Shows how hunting and practical skills are developed while his future wife is also trained for her tasks in setting up a household.

THE ANNANACKS. National Film Board of Canada, 1965. 29 min. color. MGH
How an Eskimo community formed a successful cooperative in the George River area in northern Quebec.

THE APACHE INDIAN.   Coronet, 1943.   11 min.   b/w.   COR,
     UCO, UUT, UWY
An old film describing the ceremonies of the Apache people and
their increasing self-direction in work, education, and other affairs.

ARCTIC PEOPLE.   William Claiborne, 1970.   (Places People Live
     Series.) 14 min.   color.   SEF, UCO
How the Eskimo combines the traditional with modern modes of living.   Makes a comparison with the Lapp people of the lower arctic
area.

ARCTIC SEAL HUNTERS.   Bailey, 1955.   (Beyond the Yukon
     Series.) 12 min.   color.   UCO, UUT
Tells how Eskimos hunt--the kinds of animal they pursue, the processing of meat, skin, and other parts for practical uses.

AS LONG AS THE RIVERS RUN.   Carol Burns, 1971.   60 min.
     color.   IMP
A study of broken promises and Indian struggles for fishing rights
on the Nisqually River in Washington State.   Includes songs, scenes
of village life, harassment and abuse, and the capture of Alcatraz.

AT THE AUTUMN RIVER CAMP, PART I.   Q. Brown, A. Balikci,
     1967.   (The Netsilik Eskimo Series.) 30 min.   color.   PEN,
     UEVA
The Netsilik Eskimos are shown building karmaks of snow and ice,
which they cover with skins, cooking, gathering moss.   Without
narration.

AT THE AUTUMN RIVER CAMP, PART II.   Q. Brown, A. Balikci,
     1967.   (The Netsilik Eskimo Series.) 30 min.   color.   PEN,
     UEVA
Studies Netsilik Eskimos building igloos, constructing sleds, making
caribou parkas.   Shows children at play and a family packing up
and moving down the river.   Without narration.

AT THE CARIBOU CROSSING PLACE, PART I.   Q. Brown, A.
     Balikci, 1967.   (The Netsilik Eskimo Series.) 31 min.   color.
     PEN, UEVA
Traces the migration inland of the Netsilik Eskimos, following the
caribou herds.   Shows preparation of bait for fishing and the set-
up of traps to catch gulls.   Without narration.

AT THE CARIBOU CROSSING PLACE, PART II.   Q. Brown, A.
     Balikci, 1967.   (The Netsilik Eskimo Series.) 30 min.   color.
     PEN, UEVA
The Eskimos' midsummer hunt for food and fur, including activities
after the hunt.   Without narration.

AT THE WINTER SEA-ICE CAMP, PART I.   Q. Brown, A. Balik-
     ci, 1967.   (The Netsilik Eskimos Series.) 30 min.   color.
     PEN, UEVA
Netsilik Eskimo women are shown performing daily chores, caring

for children; men are seen hunting and harpooning a seal and feasting on its liver and blubber. Without narration.

AT THE WINTER SEA-ICE CAMP, PART II. Q. Brown, A. Balikci, 1967. (The Netsilik Eskimos Series.) 37 min. color.
   PEN, UEVA
Eskimo men are seen waiting to capture seals and the women play with children, sew and repair the igloo.

AT THE WINTER SEA-ICE CAMP, PART III. Q. Brown, A. Balikci, 1967. (The Netsilik Eskimos Series.) 30 min. color.
   PEN, UEVA
The Netsilik Eskimos build an enormous ceremonial igloo--each family igloo forms an alcove in the communal one. Shows feasting, storytelling, and games. Without narration.

AT THE WINTER SEA-ICE CAMP, PART IV. Q. Brown, A. Balikci, 1967. (The Netsilik Eskimos Series.) 35 min. color.
   PEN, UEVA
Shows what it's like to be inside an Eskimo igloo during a blizzard. Without narration.

ATTIUK. National Film Board of Canada, n.d. 31 min. color.
   NFBC
Describes the Montagnais tribe of nomads who live near the Strait of Belle Isle.

THE BALLAD OF CROWFOOT. National Film Board of Canada, 1970. 10 min. b/w. MGH
A song ballad is used as background for this history of western Canada and of the Indians who live there. Filmed by Canadian Indians.

BASKETRY OF THE POMO: INTRODUCTORY FILM. University of California, 1966. (American Indian Series.) 30 min. color. UCA
Presents details of the expert basket making technique of California's Pomo people.

BASKETRY OF THE POMO: FORMS AND ORNAMENTATION. University of California, 1966. (American Indian Series.) 21 min. color. UCA
Describes the background of various basket designs used by the Pomo people in California.

BASKETRY OF THE POMO: TECHNIQUES. University of California, 1966. (American Indian Series.) 33 min. color. UCA
Gives step-by-step information on how the Pomo people of California actually execute the various weaves they use.

BEAUTIFUL TREE: CHISHKALE. University of California, 1965. (American Indian Series.) 20 min. color. UCA
A history of the way California Indians harvested acorns and leeched

the ground meal to remove tannic acid, thus providing a dietary staple for many Indian communities.

BE-TA-TA-KIN. New York University, 1955. 11 min. b/w. PEN, NYU
Examines cliff dwelling, religious gathering places and animal pens of the Anasazi Indians. Shows where they cultivated corn on the canyon floor.

THE BIRCH CANOE BUILDER. Southern Illinois University, 1971. 23 min. color. ACI
How one man in Big Fork, Minnesota has maintained the traditional method of canoe building from birch bark, cedar planks and spruce roots.

BLACK COAL, RED POWER. Indiana University. 41 min. color. IND
How recent coal strip mining on Navajo and Hopi reservations in Arizona to supply the nation's needs is destroying sheep grazing land and polluting corn fields, much to the Indians' dismay.

BLUNDEN HARBOUR. Orbit, 1951. 20 min. b/w. UCA
A documentary study of a group of Kwakiutl Indians who live in the U.S. Pacific Northwest. Includes their legend of the killer whale who became a man.

BROKEN TREATY AT BATTLE MOUNTAIN. Joelli Freedman, 1974. 60 min. color. SOH
Robert Redford narrates the story of the western Shoshone Indians of Nevada and their continuing struggle to keep the land promised to them by the Federal Government.

BRYAN BEAVERS: A MOVING PORTRAIT. KVIE-TV, 1968. 30 min. color. IND
A visit with a Maidu Indian, a man of two cultures, who lives in the log cabin he built in the wilderness of Plumas County, California. Shows him performing daily routines.

BUCKEYES: FOOD OF CALIFORNIA INDIANS. University of California, 1962. (American Indian Series.) UCA, UNE
Discusses horse chestnuts, a dietary staple of Indian groups in California.

CALUMET, PIPE OF PEACE. University of California, 1964. (American Indian Series.) 23 min. color. UCA
About the role of tobacco and the pipe of peace in the culture of the Great Plains Indians. Shows rituals involving the pipe and tobacco.

THE CANOES OF THE AINU. American Educational Films, n.d. 19 min. color. AEF
How the Ainu people employ the canoe in their life scheme in a manner similar to that in which many Native Americans use the horse as the focus of their life.

CARIBOU HUNTERS. National Film Board of Canada, 1950. 18
     min. color. NFBC
How Indian hunters trap small animals of forest and stream. An
award-winning film.

CATLIN AND THE INDIANS. NBC, 1967. 24 min. color. MGH
Although concerned mainly with artist George Catlin's efforts to
preserve the culture of the American Plains Indians for posterity,
this film reveals many aspects of Indian life long since vanished
from the American scene.

CESAR'S BARK CANOE. National Film Board of Canada, 1971.
     58 min. color. EDC, NFBC
A Cree Indian of the Manowan Reserve north of Montreal demonstrates canoe building using only materials from the forest. Without narration. Text translated via subtitles in Cree, French and
English.

CHARLEY SQUASH GOES TO TOWN. National Film Board of Can-
     ada, 1970. (The Many Americans Series.) 5 min. color.
     LEC
An amusing animated film by Duke Redbird, a young Cree Indian
from Ontario, who makes the point that Indian youth should not
necessarily have to conform to the life style imposed on them by
modern society.

CHEYENNE AUTUMN. Bernard Smith, 1965. 156 min. color.
     Directed by John Ford; screenplay by James Webb, based on
     the novel by Marie Sandoz; photography by William Clothier;
     music by Alex North. With Richard Widmark, Carroll Baker,
     Karl Malden, Sal Mineo, Dolores del Rio, Ricardo Montalban,
     Gilbert Roland, Arthur Kennedy, James Stewart, Edward G.
     Robinson, John Carradine, Elizabeth Allen. MAC[1]
Critically acclaimed as a profound study of the mistreatment of
American Indians. The story concerns the Cheyenne pilgrimage of
1878 when, disgusted with their barren life on an Oklahoma reservation, they decided to march 1,500 miles back to their fertile
homeland in Wyoming.

CHILDREN OF THE PLAINS INDIANS. Centron, 1962. (The
     Children of Pioneer Times Series.) 20 min. color. MGH,
     UCO
What Indian life was like in the Great Plains area before the arrival of white men. Focuses on an Indian youth to describe the life
style of his group.

CIRCLE OF THE SUN. National Film Board of Canada, 1960.
     30 min. color. MGH, UCA
About Canada's Blood Indians of Alberta, as they live today herding
cattle and remembering traditions and roots from the past.

CLOUDS. Lance Bird, n.d. 11 min. color. NLC
Indian cowboys filmed on location at Montana rodeos and reservations.

CREE HUNTERS OF MISTASSINI. National Film Board of Canada,
    1974. 58 min. color. NFBC
Shows the conflict between the Cree Indians' culture and the white
man's attempts to dominate the scene with a hydro-electric project.

DISCOVERING AMERICAN INDIAN MUSIC. Bernard Wilets, 1971.
    24 min. color. BFA
Presents the songs and dances of various tribal groups, showing
the appropriate setting and role of music and movement in Indian
culture.

THE DISPOSSESSED. George Ballis, Maia Sorotor, Juddy Whal-
    ley and Peter Rand, 1970. 33 min. color and sepia. TRI
Covers the occupation by Pit River Indians of ancestral land along
the Pit River in northern California controlled by the Pacific Gas
and Electric Company.

DREAM DANCES OF THE KASHIA POMO: THE BOLE-MARU RE-
    LIGION WOMEN'S DANCES. University of California, 1964.
    (American Indian Series.) 30 min. color. UCA
California's Pomo women are seen performing traditional dance
movements that reflect a variety of influences.

ENCOUNTER WITH SAUL ALINSKY, PART II: RAMA INDIAN RE-
    SERVE. National Film Board of Canada, 1967. (Challenge
    for Change Series.) 33 min. b/w. NFBC, MGH
Young Indians in a meeting with activist Saul Alinsky argue for
peaceful persuasion to revise the one hundred-year-old Indian Act.
Alinsky, on the other hand, promotes a direct development to bring
about change.

END OF THE EARTH PEOPLE. Canadian Broadcasting Corpora-
    tion, n. d. 27 min. b/w. VEC
About the life of the Hareskin Indians, who live above the Arctic
Circle, who have turned away from the white man's way of life
and back to their ancestors' life style.

END OF THE TRAIL: THE AMERICAN PLAINS INDIAN. NBC,
    1967. 53 min. b/w. MGH, UCO, UWY
An account of the westward movement in America and its effect on
the life of Native Americans.

ESKIMO ARTIST KENOJUAK. National Film Board of Canada, 1964.
    20 min. color. MGH
The internationally known sculptress and her work are viewed
against a backdrop of contemporary Eskimo life.

ESKIMO ARTS AND CRAFTS. National Film Board of Canada,
    1945. 22 min. color. IFB
Eskimo people work on skins, drums, boats, bone and ivory revealing a sophisticated system of religion and tradition.

ESKIMO FAMILY.   Encyclopaedia Britannica Educational Corporation, 1959.   17 min.   color.   EBEC, UCO, UUT, UWY
Follows an Eskimo family as they move from their winter camp to
their spring hunting grounds.   Shows their hunting, trading and
daily life.

ESKIMO HUNTERS.   Louis de Rochemont, 1949.   20 min.   b/w.
UCO, UNE
Illustrates the life of the northern Alaska Eskimos who dwell in a
cold region where fishing and hunting provide a means of existence.

THE ESKIMO IN LIFE AND LEGEND: THE LIVING STONE.   National Film Board of Canada, 1960.   22 min.   color.   EBEC
Tells the legend of a seal hunter whose wish came true when his
carved piece of stone came to life.   Studies the interrelationship of
the Eskimo's life, legend and stone craft.

ESKIMO SUMMER.   National Film Board of Canada, 1949.   16
min.   color.   IFB
About the Eskimos and their summer activities that help them survive the year.

ESKIMOS: A CHANGING CULTURE.   Wayne Mitchell, 1971.   17
min.   color.   BFA
The Eskimos of Nunivak Island in the Bering Sea are studied to
determine the influence of technology on their culture.

THE EXILES.   Kent MacKenzie, 1959-1961.   72 min.   b/w.   Di-
rected and written by Kent MacKenzie; photography by Erik
Daarstad, Robert Kaufman and John Morrill; rock-and-roll
music by Tony Hilder, Bob Hafner and The Revels; authentic
Indian songs led by Eddie Sunrise and Jacinto Valenzuela.
MGH, UCO, UUT
A probing documentary that uncovers the bewildering world of the
contemporary American Indian as seen through the lives of three
Indians, portrayed by themselves, who go to Los Angeles seeking
a better life.   Also available in three parts: Part I, 25 min.;   Part
II, 25 min.;   Part III, 25 min.

THE FIRST AMERICANS.   Contemporary, 1969.   53 min.   color.
FI
Studies excavations in Siberia and the probable path of the first
Americans, originally prehistoric central Asians, across the Bering
Land Bridge into Alaska.

THE FIRST AMERICANS AND THEIR GODS.   International Film
Foundation, 1969.   (The First Americans Series.)   11 min.
color.   EFD, IFF
Covers the earliest migrations of prehistoric hunters from Asia
and the establishment of an agriculturally based civilization in
Mexico with its religious devotion to nature gods.

FISHING AT THE STONE WEIR: PART 1.   Q. Brown, A. Balikci,
   1967. (The Netsilik Eskimos Series.)   30 min.   color.   PEN,
   UEVA
The Eskimos erect a skin tent; the weir is repaired after the summer thaw; salmon are speared and cooked.

FISHING AT THE STONE WEIR: PART 2.   Q. Brown, A. Balikci,
   1967. (The Netsilik Eskimos Series.)   27 min.   color.   PEN,
   UEVA
Eskimo men are seen fishing at a stone weir while children imitate
them. Shows the men cooking the fish.

THE FORGOTTEN AMERICAN.   CBS, 1968.   25 min.   color.
   CAR, IMP, UUT, UCA
About the Indians who have become aliens in their native land.
Studies urban and rural life, the physical and psychological impov-
erishment.

47¢.   Lee Callister and Wendy Jane Carrel, 1973.   25 min.   b/w.
   UCA
A probing study of the relations between the U. S. and the Pit River
Nation and how they feel they have been cheated in a recent land
settlement case.   An award-winning film.

4-BUTTE-1: A LESSON IN ARCHAEOLOGY.   University of California, 1968.   33 min.   color.   UCA
A sensitive film about archaeological findings of a Maidu Indian
village in the Sacramento Valley, California, viewed in terms of
anthropology.

GAME OF STAVES.   University of California, 1962.   (The American Indian Series.)   10 min.   color.   UCA
How California Pomo youths play the game of staves, a variation
of the dice game.

GERONIMO JONES.   Bert Salzman, 1970.   (The Many Americans
   Series.)   21 min.   color.   LEC
A visit with a young Indian boy, a descendant of Apache Chief
Geronimo, as he experiences the joys and pain of contemporary
Indian life.   Filmed at the Papago Indian Reservation in Arizona.
An award-winning film.

GRAND CANYON.   NBC, 1966.   26 min.   color.   UCA
Describes the beauties of the Grand Canyon and the Havasupi people, representing the oldest Native American culture in the U. S. ,
who live near Hoover Dam.   Based on writings of Joseph Wood
Krutch.

HAIDA CARVER.   National Film Board of Canada, 1964.   12 min.
   color.   IFB
How the Haida Indians live on the Queen Charlotte Islands off the
Pacific coast of Canada.   Focuses on one Haida Indian who, in the
traditional way, carves miniature totems from slate.

HASKIE. Jack L. Crowder, 1970. 25 min. color. IND
A Navajo boy wants to become a medicine man but instead is sent
to a boarding school as required by law.

HIGH STEEL. National Film Board of Canada, 1965. 14 min.
    color. ACI
The story of the men who construct the tall skyscrapers in New
York--the Mohawk Indians of Caughnawaga who are employed for
their ease and skill in working at great heights.

THE HOPI INDIAN. Coronet, 1945. 11 min. color. UUT. Al-
    so revised edition. Coronet, 1975. 10 1/2 min. color. COR
The Hopi people of the Southwest are observed in daily routines and
in special celebrations, such as a wedding ceremony.

HOPI INDIAN ARTS AND CRAFTS. Coronet, 1945. 10 min.
    color. UCO, UUT. Also revised edition. Coronet, 1974.
    10 min. color. COR
The weaving, basket making, silversmithing and ceramics crafts
of the Hopi people of the southwest.

HOPI INDIAN VILLAGE LIFE. Coronet, 1956. 10 1/2 min.
    color. COR, UCO, UUT, UWY
The changing character of Hopi daily life observed by following a
family and other villagers through a typical day's routine.

HOPI KACHINAS. ACI, 1961. 10 min. color. ACI
The religion and rituals of an Indian tribe are studied. Discusses
the Kachina dolls of the Hopi people which are used as instructional
aids for religious study.

THE HOPI WAY. Visual Education Centre, n.d. 22 min. color.
    VEC
Discusses the conflict of the Hopi people of Arizona who have lived
in harmony with nature for 1,300 years but who must now contend
with the bad effects of coal mining in the Black Mesa area.

HOW TO BUILD AN IGLOO. National Film Board of Canada, 1949.
    11 min. color. UCO
A demonstration of igloo-building by people of Canada's Far North.

HUNTERS OF THE NORTH POLE. National Film Board of Canada,
    1950. 10 min. b/w. UWY
Follows the life of the Eskimos of Thule in Greenland.

HUPA INDIAN WHITE DEER SKIN DANCE. Arthur Barr, 1958.
    12 min. color. UCA
About the ceremonies and other cultural traditions of the Hupa Indians who live in northwestern California.

I AM THE TZINQUAW. Soundings, 1975. 10 min. color. SOUN
The story of how Tzinquaw the Thunderbird struggled to save the
Cowichan Indians from Quannis the killer whale is told in three

authentic sacred songs and dances of the Cowichan people. Emphasizes the spiritual significance of every detail: face painting, costuming, drumbeat, movement, and word.

IN SEARCH OF A CITY.   KETC, 1961.   (National Parks Series.)
     9 min. color. IND
A visit to Mesa Verde National Park in Southwestern Colorado to
see archeologists uncover Indian cities from ancient times.

INDIAN AMERICA.   Sterling, 1974.   50 min.   color.   SEF
Henry Fonda narrates this study of Native Americans covering
"30,000 years" of their culture and philosophy.

INDIAN ARTISTS OF THE SOUTHWEST.   Encyclopaedia Britannica
     Educational Corporation, 1972.   14 min.   color.   EBEC
A look at the arts and crafts of three Pueblo groups: the Zuni,
Hopi and Navajo peoples.

INDIAN ARTISTS OF THE SOUTHWEST.   John S. Candelario, 1956.
     20 min.   color.   MGH
Written and directed by Arthur Gould.   A comprehensive history of
American Indian paintings.

INDIAN DIALOGUE.   National Film Board of Canada, 1969.   28
     min.   b/w.   NFBC, MGH
Indians of Canada talk about the threat to their culture by white society.

INDIAN FAMILY OF LONG AGO.   Encyclopaedia Britannica Educational Corporation, 1957.   14 min.   color.   EBEC, UCO,
     UUT, UWY
A re-creation of a summer's day in the life of a Sioux family in
the Dakotas of the U. S. , showing the relationship of the Sioux with
the buffalo.

INDIAN FAMILY OF THE CALIFORNIA DESERT.   Educational
     Horizons, 1967.   15 min.   color.   EBEC, UCO
The story of the Cahuilla Indians of the Dakotas as told by a woman
who recalls the past, the skills and the ritual of her people.

INDIAN INFLUENCES IN THE UNITED STATES.   Coronet, 1964.
     10 1/2 min.   color.   COR, UKE, UWY
How foreign settlers in America have been affected by Native American culture.   Includes the Indian heritage in art, music, cookery,
location of roads and cities, language and literature.

INDIAN LAND: THE NATIVE AMERICAN ECOLOGIST.   Herbert
     McCoy, 1972.   21 min.   color.   MAC
Native Americans speak candidly of their traditional veneration of
the earth and their determination to rescue the land from despoliation.

INDIAN MEMENTO. National Film Board of Canada, 1968. 19
    min. color. NFBC
A look at the Indian exhibit at Expo 67's Canadian pavilion, with an
Indian hostess as tour guide.

INDIAN POW-WOW. Avalon Daggett, 1951. 13 min. color.
    UCO
Southwest tribes are shown during a pow-wow, participating in
festivities that include a parade and a carnival.

INDIAN RELOCATION: ELLIOT LAKE, A REPORT. National
    Film Board of Canada, 1967. 30 min. b/w. NFBC, MGH
About a group of Indians moved to Elliot Lake in Northern Ontario
from nearby reservations. Presents interviews with those who
stayed and some who went back, revealing the adjustments to be
faced.

THE INDIAN SPEAKS. National Film Board of Canada, 1969. 41
    min. color. MGH
Canadian Indians talk about their sense of loss as traditions slip
away and what they are doing about their predicament.

INDIANS IN THE AMERICAS. Wayne Mitchell, 1971. 15 1/2 min.
    color. BFA
Traces the first people who came from Asia to America over
20,000 years ago to the development of advanced cultures, such as
the Mayans and the Incas.

INDIANS OF CALIFORNIA, PART 1: VILLAGE LIFE. Arthur
    Barr, 1955. 15 min. color. UCA, UCO, UNE
A simple introduction to the village life of Native American people
in California before the white man came.

INDIANS OF CALIFORNIA, PART 2: FOOD. Arthur Barr, 1964.
    2nd ed. 14 min. color. UCA, UCO, UNE
A detailed but brief account of food habits of early California Indians as they lived before the white man came.

INDIANS OF EARLY AMERICA. Encyclopaedia Britannica Educa-
    tional Corporation, 1957. 22 min. color. EBEC, UCA,
    UCO, UNE, UUT, UWY
Presents the ceremonies, customs and crafts of early North American Indian tribes.

INDIANS OF THE SOUTHWEST. CCM, 1972. 16 min. color.
    MAC
About the history and culture of the Cochise people, the first Native
Americans to give up nomadic life, and their descendants, the
Pueblos, and other groups of the Southwestern United States.

IRON COUNTRY. JYNE, 1969. 11 min. color. UUT
Shows Indian workers in Iron County, Utah who live in poor conditions. Emphasizes what needs to be done to help them.

ISHI IN TWO WORLDS. Richard Tomkins, 1967. 19 min. color.
  MGH, PAR, UCA, UNE
A portrait of the last survivor of the Yahi Indian tribe of California
near Mount Lassen. Based on the book by Theodora Kroeber.

ISLAND OF THE BLUE DOLPHINS. Universal, 1964. 101 min.
  color. Directed by James B. Clark; screenplay by Ted Sherde-
  man and Jane Klove, based on the novel by Scott O'Dell. With
  Celia Kaye, Larry Domasin, George Kennedy, Ann Daniel.
  UNIV, WECF
An orphan Indian girl finds a home on an isolated island, where she
learns to coexist and communicate with the wild animal life there.

ISLAND OF THE BLUE DOLPHINS. Teaching Film Custodians and
  Universal Pictures, 1964. 20 min. color. IND, UCA
An excerpt from the feature film of the same name about a Chumas
Indian girl who remains with her brother to struggle for survival on
an island off the Southern California coast in the early nineteenth
century. Based on Scott O'Dell's prize-winning book.

JIM THORPE, ALL AMERICAN. Warner Bros. , 1951. 107 min.
  b/w. Directed by Michael Curtiz; screenplay by Douglas
  Morrow and Everett Freeman with additional dialogue by Frank
  Davis, based on a story by Vincent X. Flaherty and the biog-
  raphy by Russell J. Birdwell in collaboration with Jim Thorpe.
  With Burt Lancaster, Charles Bickford, Steve Cochran, Phyllis
  Thaxter. BUDG
The life story of a great Indian athlete who was born on a reserva-
tion and later became one of the great track and football stars as
well as an Olympic champion.

JOHNNY FROM FORT APACHE. Encyclopaedia Britannica Educational Corporation, 1971. 15 min. color. UWY, EBEC
A look at members of an Indian tribe as they cope with problems
of moving from the reservation to the city.

KASHIA MEN'S DANCES: SOUTHWESTERN POMO INDIANS. Uni-
  versity of California, 1963. 40 min. color. UCA
The traditional Pomo Indian's dances as performed on tho Kashia
Reservation near Stewart's Point in Northern California.

LAND OF THE LONG DAY, PART I: WINTER AND SPRING. National Film Board of Canada, 1952. 19 min. color. IFB
The life of an Eskimo hunter on Baffin Island in the winter and
spring.

LAND OF THE LONG DAY, PART II: SUMMER AND AUTUMN.
  National Film Board of Canada, 1952. 19 min. color. IFB
The life of an Eskimo hunter on Baffin Island in summer and au-
tumn.

LEGEND. National Film Board of Canada, 1970. 15 min. color.
  PYR

An artistic film treatment of a West Coast Indian legend in which
a vain woman rejects an ugly man only to be punished later by the
Spirit Woman who can change faces. The characters look and act
like contemporary young people in this version.

LIFE IN COLD LANDS. Coronet, 1956. 10 1/2 min. color.
     COR
An account of the Eskimos' life in the cold Alaskan environment.

LITTLE WHITE SALMON INDIAN SETTLEMENT. Tri-Continental,
     1972. 30 min. color. TRI
A report on the Yakima Indians' struggle over fishing rights on
the Columbia River in the U.S. Pacific Northwest. Also gives details of the history of the Yakima people and their life style.

THE LIVING STONE. National Film Board of Canada, 1959. 33
     min. color. MGH
The heritage and life of the Eskimos at Cape Dorset on Baffin Island.

THE LONGHOUSE PEOPLE. National Film Board of Canada, 1950.
     24 min. color. NFBC, MGH
An award-winning film about the life and ritual of the Iroquois people. Includes a rain dance, a healing ceremony, and a celebration
honoring a new chief.

THE LOON'S NECKLACE. Crawley, 1949. 11 min. color. EBEC
How an aged and blind medicine man gave his magical necklace to
the loon as told by a narrator and acted out in pantomime by actors
wearing masks of Native Americans of the British Columbia area.

MATTHEW ALIUK: ESKIMO IN TWO WORLDS. Learning Corpora-
     tion, 1973. (The Many Americans Series.) 18 min. color.
     LEC
About an Eskimo boy who lives in the city of Anchorage but begins
to learn about his hunting heritage from his uncle.

MEET THE SIOUX INDIAN. Murl Deusing, 1948. 11 min. color.
     IFB, UUT
Gives specific details as to how the Sioux Indians lived on the
Western plains: hunting, cooking, setting up tepees; meat preser-
vation, clothing.

MINORITY YOUTH: ADAM. Stuart Roe, 1971. 10 min. color.
     BFA
An American Indian youth talks frankly about his place in society.

MONUMENT VALLEY: LAND OF THE NAVAJOS. Paul Hoeffler,
     1959. 17 min. color. UCO, UUT
How one Navajo lives in the area where Arizona, New Mexico,
Colorado and Utah meet.

NANOOK OF THE NORTH.   Revillon Freres, 1922.   55 min.   b/w.
   silent.   MGH, PAR, UCO, UNE, UWY
About the Eskimos of sub-arctic Canada, particularly Nanook and
his family.   Script, direction, photography by Robert J. Flaherty.
Titles by Carl Stearns Clancy, Robert J. Flaherty.   Also available
with sound track added in 1954.

NAVAJO.   CCM, n.d.   16 min.   color.   MAC
A visit to the Navajo's homeland, the Grand Canyon, where the
survivors of their society still prevail.

NAVAJO.   Fred J. Pain, Jr., 1972.   21 min.   color.   IND
About the Navajo Indian Nation in the Southwestern U.S.:   traditions,
influences, and drastic changes.

NAVAJO: PART 1.   KETC-TV, 1959.   29 min.   b/w.   IMP, IND
A study of a Navajo reservation--its community, the reconciling of
tradition with modern technology.

NAVAJO: PART 2.   KETC-TV, 1959.   29 min.   b/w.   IMP, IND
A visit to Window Rock, Arizona where Navajo Tribes Council
members discuss problems and adaptations made to new social
values and modern science.

NAVAJO: A PEOPLE BETWEEN TWO WORLDS.   Line, 1958.   13
   min.   color.   LINE
The traditional life of the Navajos is contrasted with modern life
in the reservation in northeastern Arizona.

NAVAJO CANYON COUNTRY.   Avalon Daggett, 1954.   13 min.
   color.   UCO, UWY
How the Navajos live with traditional ways in a modern world.

NAVAJO INDIAN LIFE.   Walter P. Lewisohn, 1966.   11 1/2 min.
   color.   COR
Commentary on the plight of the Navajos of the Southwestern U.S.
and their possibilities for the future.   Narration written and spoken
by Carl Carmer.

NAVAJO LIFE.   KETC-TV, 1961.   (National Parks Series.)   9 min.
   color.   IND
The life of Navajos of the Canyon de Chelly in Arizona, their farming, cooking, trading, home construction.

NAVAJO MIGRANT WORKERS.   JYNE, 1969.   11 min.   color.
   UUT
Migrant Navajos are shown in poor living conditions as they work
on the harvests in Utah.   Includes interviews with several workers,
interpreted by a Navajo woman.

NAVAJO NIGHT DANCES.   Walter P. Lewisohn, 1966.   11 1/2
   min.   color.   COR
Follows a Navajo family to a Nine-Day Healing Chant.   Includes
rare scenes of the feast and rituals.

NAVAJO SILVERSMITH.   ACI, 1961.   10 min.   color.   ACI
A report on an Indian silversmith who has developed a productive
life in spite of the limited atmosphere on an Arizona reservation.

NAVAJO: THE LAST RED INDIANS.   BBC and Time-Life, 1972.
   50 min. color.   TL
A detailed study of the Navajos, their language, rituals, including
healing ceremonies, and the problems they face in maintaining cultural identity.

THE NAVAJO WAY.   Robert Northshield, 1974.   54 min.   color.
   FI
A look at the present-day Navajos, many of whom have managed to
preserve the integrity of their culture while living in the white man's
environment.

THE NAVAJOS AND ANNIE WAUNEKA.   CBS, 1965.   25 min.
   b/w.   MAC
A television documentary about a Navajo woman, a Freedom Medal
winner, who has worked with her people under difficult conditions
in the field of public health.

THE NAVAJOS: CHILDREN OF THE GODS.   Disney, 1967.   20
   min. color.   DIS
The Navajo's life style, including his traditional religious outlook.

THE NAVAJOS OF THE 70'S.   Coleman, 1971.   (The North American Indians Today Series.)   15 min.   color.   UUT, CEN
Illustrates the history of the Navajo's loss of lands at the hands of
the U. S. Army in the nineteenth century.   Gives detailed description
of Navajo culture, religious rites, including the puberty ritual.

NOAH.   Basset, 1974.   17 min.   color.   ACI
About an Eskimo who is a master carver.   He is observed carving
a stone figure as he discusses the changes in his people's life style
during his own life at Frobisher Bay on Baffin Island.

NOMADS OF THE NORTH.   Eskimoland, 1955.   (Beyond the Yukon
   Series.)   11 min.   color.   UCO, UUT
An old film that illustrates how Eskimo nomads track reindeer as a
major food staple and resource for the items needed in daily life.

THE NORTH AMERICAN INDIAN: PART I, TREATIES MADE,
   TREATIES BROKEN.   Jay K. Hoffman, 1970.   18 min.   color.
   MGH, UNE
Describes the fishing rights provided in Washington State by the
Treaty of Medicine Creek, which has been disputed by State offi-
cials.   Narrated by Marlon Brando.

THE NORTH AMERICAN INDIAN: PART II, HOW THE WEST WAS
   WON ... AND HONOR LOST.   Jay K. Hoffman, 1970.   25
   min. color.   MGH, UNE
The history of America in terms of how Native Americans were

treated from the landing of Columbus to the defeat of Geronimo in 1886. Narrated by Marlon Brando.

THE NORTH AMERICAN INDIAN: PART III, LAMENT OF THE
    RESERVATION. Jay K. Hoffman, 1971. 24 min. color.
    MGH, UNE
A realistic look at Indian reservation life, replete with poverty and unemployment.

NORTHWEST INDIAN ART. Walter P. Lewisohn, 1966. 9 min.
    color. COR
A look at sophisticated art of Native Americans of the U.S. Northwest. Movement and dance, showing the significance of their double-faced mechanical masks, are also presented.

OBSIDIAN POINT MAKING.   University of California, 1964.
    (American Indian Series.) 13 min. color. UCA
Describes the three known methods of shaping obsidian arrow points used by a Tolowa Indian of Northern California.

OUR TOTEM IS THE RAVEN. King Screen, 1971. (An Indian
    Heritage Film.) 21 min. color. BFA
Chief Dan George portrays a grandfather who gives his urban, fifteen-year-old grandson an understanding of his people's cultural roots.

PAINTING WITH SAND: A NAVAJO CEREMONY. Encyclopaedia
    Britannica Educational Corporation, 1950. 10 min. color.
    UCA, UUT
Shows the way a Navajo medicine man would use the sand painting healing rite to aid the sick--in this case, a sick child.

THE PEOPLE AT DIPPER. National Film Board of Canada, 1967.
    19 min. color. NFBC
A visit with the Chipperwayan people on a reservation in northern Saskatchewan. Presents an Indian who is satisfied with his life because of the sense of community he and others feel.

PEOPLE MIGHT LAUGH AT US. National Film Board of Canada,
    1965. 10 min. color. NFBC, MGH
A study of Micmac Indian children of Quebec who make things out of paper but don't like to be observed doing it.

PEOPLE OF THE BUFFALO. National Film Board of Canada,
    1969. 15 min. color. EBEC, UCO, UWY
An account of the disruption of the natural way of life on the western plains in the U.S. Uses paintings of American Indians and buffalo.

PIKANGIKUM. National Film Board of Canada, 1968. 10 min.
    b/w. NFBC, MGH
Presents an artist's view of an Indian reservation in northern Ontario. Shows grim scenes of hunger and sickness.

PINE NUTS. University of California, 1961. (American Indian
    Series.) 13 min. color. UCA
How the Paviotso, Washo and other Indian groups of Western Nevada adapted to a barren region, using the pine nut as a food staple.

POMO SHAMAN. University of California, 1965. 20 min. b/w.
    UCA
An edited version of a longer documentary on a curing ceremony
held by the Kashia group of the Southwestern Pomo Indians. The
Indian doctor is a 61-year-old woman.

POWWOW AT DUCK LAKE. National Film Board of Canada, 1968.
    15 min. color. NFBC, MGH
Indians and whites gather at Duck Lake, Saskatchewan to discuss
educational opportunities available to Indians and the way in which
schooling limits the Indians' chances for the future.

THE PRIDE AND THE SHAME. BBC, 1969. 30 min. b/w. TL
A close look at the degrading conditions of the Sioux people of North
Dakota's Black Hills.

THE QUILLAYUTE STORY. Olympic, 1951. (Northwest Coast In-
    dians Series.) 25 min. color. UCA
Shows the village life of Pacific Coast Indian groups in modern
times. Illustrates practices gradually changing as the groups move
away from their traditional roots.

RIFF '65. New York University, 1966. 12 min. b/w. NYU,
    UCA
Follows an American Indian boy who belongs to a Harlem gang as
he wanders through an aimless life.

RONNIE. Image, 1968. 26 min. b/w. UCA
About a Canadian Indian who drifts between two worlds, leaves
school, takes a job, regrets his present life.

SEQUOYAH. Anthony Corso, 1974. 15 min. color. DIS
The story of the Cherokee man, a silversmith, who gave his people
a written form of communication.

THE SHADOW CATCHER: EDWARD S. CURTIS AND THE NORTH
    AMERICAN INDIAN. T. C. McLuhan, 1975. 88 min. color.
    PHO
About the ambitious project of Edward S. Curtis, anthropologist
and filmmaker, who made films, recorded songs, took photographs,
and transcribed tales and customs. Uses all of his extant film
footage to convey a feeling of Curtis' actual work. Donald Suther-
land's voice represents Curtis, and Patrick Wilson narrates his
life. Written by T. C. McLuhan and Dennis Wheeler. Directed
by T. C. McLuhan. Cinematography by Robert Fiore.

THE SILENT ENEMY: AN EPIC OF THE AMERICAN INDIAN.
    William Douglas Burden and William C. Chanler, 1929. 60

min. b/w. silent/with musical score. Directed by H. P.
Carver. With Chief Yellow Robe, Chief Long Lance, Chief
Akawansh, Spotted Elk and Cheeka. BLF, ROAF
An early film by Douglas Burden, explorer, about the life of the
Ojibway Indians in Canada before the white man came. Describes
how the Indians had to hunt for food to stave off the silent enemy--
hunger. Shows some elderly Indians performing some of their al-
most lost arts, such as birchbark canoe making. Based on details
in "The Jesuit Relations," a record of Jesuit missionaries in New
France from 1610 to 1791.

THE SINEW-BACKED BOW AND ITS ARROWS. University of
California, 1961. (American Indian Series.) 24 min. color.
UCA
Describes the sinew-backed bow, the finest bow constructed, from
the filling of the yew tree to the painting and stringing.

SNAKETOWN. Emil W. Haury and Helga Trives for the Arizona
State Museum, 1968. 40 min. color. UCA
The study of an excavation site in the Pima Indian reservation in
southern Arizona, a center of the sophisticated Hohokam culture
from 300 B. C. to the 12th century A. D.

SOLDIER BLUE. Harold Loeb and Gabriel Katzka, 1970. 112
min. color. cinemascope. Directed by Ralph Nelson;
screenplay by John Gay, based on the novel "Arrow in the Sun"
by Theodore V. Olsen; photography by Robert Hauser; music
by Roy Budd; songs "Soldier Blue" and "No One Told Me"
written and performed by Buffy Sainte-Marie. With Candice
Bergen, Peter Strauss, Donald Pleasance, John Anderson,
Jorge Rivero. MAC[1]
Story based on the Sand Creek Massacre of 1864 that killed approximately 300 Indian men, women and children. However, for a
change, this film actually reveals white brutality that incited Indian
attacks.

A SONG FOR DEAD WARRIORS. Norma Allen, Michael Anderson,
Larry Janss, Saul Landau, Rebecca Switzer and Bill Yahraus.
25 min. color. TRI
The first film to provide background explaining the occupation of
Wounded Knee in 1973 by Oglala Sioux Indians and members of AIM
(the American Indian Movement). Shows the Indians' plight, their
desire for the U. S. to respect treaty rights and the wish to return
to tribal culture.

SOUTHWEST INDIAN ARTS AND CRAFTS. Running, 1973. 13 1/2
min. color. COR
Present-day Native Americans of the Southwestern U. S. practice
their traditional crafts.

SOUTHWEST INDIANS OF EARLY AMERICA. Running, 1973. 14
min. color. COR
The remains of dwellings, rock paintings and pictographs in northern

Arizona and New Mexico provide clues to the once prospering ancestors of the Hopi, Pima and Papago peoples.

SPIRIT OF STONE. Hamilton-Brown, 1973. 25 min. color.
    EFD
A Canadian production which describes the petroglyphs--prehistoric rock carvings--at Stoney Lake in Canada.

STANDING BUFFALO. National Film Board of Canada, n. d. 23
    min. color. NFBC, MGH
A visit in southern Saskatchewan where Sioux women have formed a rug-making cooperative.

SUCKING DOCTOR. William R. Heick, 1964.   45 min.   b/w.
    UCA
A look at a curing ceremony held by the Kashia group of the Southwestern Pomo Indians in which the patient's pain is located, germs removed, and pain eventually removed by an Indian doctor and spiritual leader--the last remaining "sucking doctor" of the Bole Maru religion.

SUPAI INDIAN. Coronet, 1947. 11 min. b/w.   UCO, UUT
How the Supai Indians of Colorado live. Shows old customs, such as toasting corn.

TAHTONKA. Nauman, 1968. 30 min. color. ACI
A reenactment of the last days of the buffalo herds and the end of a free life for the Great Plains Indians in the American West.

THIS LAND. National Film Board of Canada, 1968. 57 min.
    b/w. NFBC, MGH
Nishga Indian spokesmen in British Columbia protest white people's right to sing "This Land Is Our Land. "

THIS WAS THE TIME. National Film Board of Canada, 1970. 16
    min. color. NFBC, MGH
Haida Indians of Masset in the Queen Charlotte Islands raise a towering totem during a festival in remembrance of colorful life of two generations ago, before missionaries toppled, and the government forbade, their totems.

TO BE INDIAN. Canadian Broadcasting Corporation, n. d.   20
    min. color. VEC
The Indian people from Alberta and the Kootenay district reserves speak frankly about their condition today.

THE TOTEM POLE. University of California, 1964.   (American
    Indian Series.) 27 min. color. UCA, UCO
Describes the sophisticated wood carving art exemplified by the totem pole as demonstrated by the late carver chief of the Kwakiutl, Mungo Martin.

THE TRANSITION.   National Film Board of Canada, n. d.   18 min.
   b/w. NFBC
A film for young Canadian Indians who will need to adjust to city
life.

THE TREASURE.   King Screen, 1970.   (An Indian Heritage Film.)
   13 min. color. BFA
Two Indian brothers reject their traditional ways only to find themselves reconsidering their heritage when their father is arrested
for defending tribal fishing rights.

TRIBE OF THE TURQUOISE WATERS.   Avalon Daggett, 1952.   12
   min. color. UCA
A visit by pack-train to an Indian group that has lived in the Grand
Canyon for hundreds of years.   Includes scenes of basket making,
food preparation and use of sweat lodges.

VISION QUEST.   Montana State College, 1961.   30 min. color.
   MGH
A fourteen-year-old Indian boy searches for a guardian spirit, a
spiritual experience required for acceptance as a man and warrior.
Reenacted by Montana Indians.

VISITING THE INDIANS WITH GEORGE CATLIN.   University of
   Iowa, 1973.   24 min. color. UIO
A view of the Native Americans of the 1830s period as painted by
George Catlin.

WARRIORS AT PEACE.   Avalon Daggett, 1953.   12 min. color.
   UCA
A contrast study of modern Apache homes and life with the Apaches
of earlier days.   Includes the Pollen Blessing Ceremony and the
Devil Dancers.

WASHOE.   Western Artists, 1968.   56 min. b/w. MGH, UNE
About one of America's oldest groups of settlers--the Washoe Indians.   Shows the Pine Nut Ceremony and the Girls Puberty Ceremony
plus details of everyday life.   An award-winning film.   Also available in two parts. Part 1, 31 min.; Part 2, 24 min.

WATER IS SO CLEAR A BLIND MAN COULD SEE.   NET, 1970.
   (Our Vanishing Wilderness Series.)   30 min. color. IMP,
   IND, UNE
The legal plight of New Mexico's Taos Indians who, despite their
concern for the land and reverence for natural life, are slated to
lose their land when their permit expires.

WAY OF OUR FATHERS.   University of California, 1972.   33 min.
   color. PEN, UCA
Studies Northern California Indians who show the unique features of
their culture.   Examines the loss of heritage caused by conventional
white-oriented educational systems and what can be done to reverse
this influence.

WHEN LEGENDS DIE. Twentieth Century-Fox, 1972. 105 min.
    color. Directed by Stuart Miller; screenplay by Robert Dozier.
    With Richard Widmark, Frederick Forest, Luana Anders. FI
A Ute Indian boy comes of age under the guidance of the rough and
tough character portrayed by Richard Widmark. An attempt to
express the frustration and anger of the contemporary Native
American.

WHITE FEATHER. Twentieth Century-Fox, 1955. 100 min. color.
    Directed by Robert Webb; screenplay by Delmer Daves and Leo
    Townsend from a story by John Prebble. With Robert Wagner,
    John Lund, Debra Paget, Jeffrey Junter, Eduard Franz, Hugh
    O'Brien. FI
A film about Indians, in which the characters are not portrayed as
stereotypes, with a story about the final peace treaty in 1877 between Wyoming Territory Indians and the U. S. government forces.
A flawed but sympathetic portrayal of Native Americans as human
beings.

WHO WERE THE ONES? National Film Board of Canada, 1973.
    7 min. color. MAC
Presents a protest song, written, sung, and accompanied by art
work of three Canadian Indians, which describes the generosity to
early European colonists repaid by treachery.

WOODEN BOX: MADE BY STEAMING AND BENDING. University
    of California, 1963. (American Indian Series.) 33 min.
    color. UCA
Shows a specialty of Northwest Coast Indians--cedar wood steaming and bending to shape a box without nails, screws or glue.

WOODLAND INDIANS OF EARLY AMERICA. Coronet, 1958.
    10 1/2 min. color. UCO, UWY
An attempt to reconstruct the life of Native Americans in the eastern Great Lakes regions of the U. S. in the days before the European influence. Follows a Chippewa family through simulated daily
routines.

YOU ARE ON INDIAN LAND. National Film Board of Canada,
    1970. 37 min. b/w. MGH
Uses cinema-vérité to show a confrontation between Mohawk Indians
and the Cornwall, Ontario police.

LATIN AMERICA

Includes: Central America; South America; West Indies; Puerto Rico.

General

EL CHE GUEVARA. Italy, 1968. 98 min. color. Directed by
   Paolo Heusch. With Francisco Rabal, John Ireland, Howard
   Ross. IVY
A feature-length drama about the Latin American guerrilla leader
who rose to fame in Cuba and lost his life in Bolivia.

CIVILIZATIONS OF ANCIENT AMERICA. Visual Education Centre,
   n. d. 24 min. color. VEC
Traces the achievements of the Olmec, Mayan, Aztec and Inca
civilizations and the tragedy of their eventual destruction or decline.

COFFEE PRODUCTION IN LATIN AMERICA. Centron, 1968. 9
   min. color. MGH
A comprehensive documentary on the details and importance of coffee production in Latin America.

DISCOVERING THE MUSIC OF LATIN AMERICA. Bernard Wilets,
   1969. 20 min. color. BFA
The roots of classical and folk music of Latin America are described back to pre-Columbian days.

EARLY AMERICAN CIVILIZATIONS. Coronet, 1957. 12 1/2 min.
   color. COR, UCA
The influences of the highly developed civilizations of the Mayas,
Aztecs, and Incas on the present. Shows artifacts of these cultures.

FOLK ART IN LATIN AMERICA. Jack Stoops, 1971 17 min.
   color. BFA
A discussion of Latin American art in relation to its varying geographical and cultural traditions.

LATIN AMERICA: AN INTRODUCTION. Coronet, 1961. 10 1/2
   min. color. COR, UCO

Introduces the viewer to aspects of history, religious customs and languages that culturally link together the various Latin American nations.

LATIN AMERICA: NEIGHBORS TO THE SOUTH. United World, 1964. 17 min. color. UEVA
A comprehensive view of Latin America's variety in historical, cultural and economic aspects.

LATIN AMERICA, PART 1: ITS COUNTRIES. National Film Board of Canada, 1964. 26 min. b/w. MGH, UCA
Examines the countries and rich resources of Latin America.

LATIN AMERICA, PART 2: ITS HISTORY, ECONOMY AND POLITICS. National Film Board of Canada, 1964. 33 min. b/w. MGH, UCA
A survey of Latin American history with focus on inequality, political unrest, progress.

SKY CHIEF. University of California, 1972. 26 min. color. UCA, UMN
A documentary on Latin America's social and economic conflicts. Gives examples of collusion in an international consortium involving a petroleum operation in Ecuador presented as typical throughout Latin America.

SPANISH CONQUEST OF THE NEW WORLD. Coronet, 1954. 10 min. b/w. UCA
Describes Spain's exploration and colonization in the New World. Includes Cortez, Pizarro, Balboa, De Soto.

Central America

(Includes Costa Rica, El Salvador, Guatemala, Honduras, Nicaragua, Panama. For Mexico see separate section, beginning page 206.)

ANCIENT MAYA INDIANS OF CENTRAL AMERICA. Encyclopaedia Britannica Educational Corporation, 1972. (The Ancient American Indian Civilizations Series.) 9 min. color. EBEC
About the contributions of the Maya civilization to science and the Mayan organization of city-states.

ANCIENT NEW WORLD. Churchill, 1965. 16 min. color. UCA, CHU
Examines the development of Middle American civilizations, including the Mayan and Aztec peoples.

CENTRAL AMERICA. Encyclopaedia Britannica Educational Corporation, 1944. 11 min. b/w. UCO
How Central America looked in the 1940s. Discusses culture, political organization and industrial and agricultural efforts.

CENTRAL AMERICA: CHANGING SOCIAL PATTERN. Barr, 1963.
   16 min. color. UCO
Provides an historical review of Central America plus discussion
of the present and future. Studies the poor, the wealthy, the social and economic changes.

CENTRAL AMERICA: FINDING NEW WAYS. Encyclopaedia Britannica Educational Corporation, n. d. 17 min. color. EBEC
Explains the blending of Spanish and Maya cultures that accounts
for the present large population of mixed blood and the feudal system
of wealthy landowners and poor peasants in Central America's six
republics. Discusses the governments' new programs to develop
the economy and change old ways.

CENTRAL AMERICA: GEOGRAPHY OF THE AMERICAS. Coronet, 1955. 10 1/2 min. color. COR, UCO, UUT
A study of six Central American republics: Guatemala, Honduras,
El Salvador, Nicaragua, Costa Rica and Panama and British Honduras.

CENTRAL AMERICA: THE CROWDED HIGHLANDS. McGraw-
   Hill, 1964. 19 min. color. UCO, UWY
An introduction to the highland areas of Central America and the
people who live there; stresses economic and social patterns.

CHILDREN OF THE WORLD: GUATEMALA. NET, 1968. 28 min.
   color. IND
About two Indian girls of Guatemala's highlands and their way of
life, including starvation in their village.

CHILE AND COSTA RICA, TWO LATIN AMERICAN NEIGHBORS.
   United World, 1964. 17 min. color. UEVA
How the people of Chile and Costa Rica develop their natural re-
sources.

THE COASTAL LOWLANDS OF CENTRAL AMERICA. McGraw-
   Hill, 1964. (Middle America Regional Geography Series.)
   19 min. color. UCO, UWY
Tells about the tropical lowlands of Central America, who lives
there, how the land is used, what ties exist with the U.S., and
why the Panama Canal is vital to ocean transportation.

CORN AND THE ORIGINS OF SETTLED LIFE IN MESOAMERICA.
   Educational Development Center, 1964. In 2 parts. Part 1,
   41 min. color; Part 2, 41 min. color. UCA
A study of the crops of early communities in the Western Hemisphere over 10,000 years ago as determined by "back-breeding" of
modern corn strains. Includes discussion of the significance of
archeological findings of 6,000-year-old corn cobs.

COSTA RICA. Dudley, 1947. 10 min. b/w. UWY
A mid-1940s view of the geography of Costa Rica, its government,
agriculture and recreation.

CROSS SECTION OF CENTRAL AMERICA.   Universal Education
    and Visual Arts, 1948.   20 min.   b/w.   UUT
Focuses on the life style of the Indian people in Guatemala with
comments on effects of altitude on climate, products, and life.
Includes a visit to Guatemala City.

FIESTA! A CENTRAL AMERICAN HOLIDAY.   Pan-American
    World Airways, 1969.   28 min.   color.   ASF, PAN
A travelogue designed to promote tourism in Central America,
featuring Guatemala, Honduras, Costa Rica, Nicaragua, Panama
and El Salvador.

THE GOLDEN ISTHMUS: THE HISTORY OF PANAMA.   BBC,
    1967.   52 min.   color.   TL
The background of the Panama Canal, from the idea of Balboa to
the actual completion of the Canal, and into the present when engi-
neers plan a new canal.

GUATEMALA: NATION OF CENTRAL AMERICA.   Encyclopaedia
    Britannica Educational Corporation, 1961.   17 min.   color.
    EBEC, UCA
Compares Guatemala's tradition-rooted villages with large-scale
plantations geared to the needs of the modern world.

THE ISTHMUS OF PANAMA.   Murl Deusing, 1964.   20 min.
    color.   EFD, IFB, UUT
Studies Panama from its historic, geographic and strategic importance and the contemporary life in the Republic of Panama.

THE LAND OF THE EAGLE.   BBC and Odyssey, 1967.   (Central
    and South America Series.)   25 min.   color.   TL
An account of the conflict experienced by Mayan descendants who
are torn between their ancestors' culture and that of the Spanish.
Narrated by Lowell Thomas.

LOST WORLD OF THE MAYA: THE ANCIENT CIVILIZATIONS OF
    CENTRAL AMERICA.   BBC, 1974.   36 min.   color.   TL
Dr. Eric Thompson, world-renowned authority on Mayan culture,
discusses the characteristics of Mayan life with easy familiarity.

MAYA THROUGH THE AGES.   Willard, 1949.   45 min.   color.
    UCA
Examines the features of Mayan civilization of southern Mexico,
Guatemala and Honduras and studies details of the lost city of
Bonampak discovered by Giles Healey, anthropologist, with help
from the almost extinct tribe, the Lacandons.

THE MAYAS.   Coronet, 1957.   10 1/2 min.   color.   COR, UCO,
    UUT, UWY
Includes first footage of the ruins of Tikal in Guatemala; also follows the Mayas to Uxmal and Chichen Itza.   The former is an example of the Mayas' Old Empire; the latter two sites represent the
New Empire.

MIDDLE AMERICA, THE LAND AND THE PEOPLE. Centron,
   1964. (Middle America Regional Geography Series.) 22 min.
   color. UCO, UWY
Discusses the role of the tourist in the economy of Central America, the economic relationships of Central American countries to
the U.S., the culture, and political situation.

MY COUNTRY OCCUPIED. (MI PATRIA OCUPADA.) Third
   World Newsreel, 1971. 30 min. b/w. TWN
Focuses on a typical Guatemalan woman whose life on the United
Fruit Company plantation was one of exploitation by the company.
Her move, along with her husband, to the city reveals further ex-
ploitation. Discusses her subsequent affiliation with guerrilla
forces. In Spanish and English language versions.

NATIVES OF GUATEMALA. Bailey, 1950. 11 min. color. UCO
How Guatemala's geographic location and its climate are interrelated with the lifo style of the people.

PANAMA. U.S. Department of Defense, 1955. 19 min. b/w.
   NAC
The history of Panama's social, economic and military status as
well as the functioning of the U.S. Armed Forces in the Canal
Zone.

PANAMA. RKO, 1946. 16 min. b/w. UCO
An old film that serves as introduction to the study of Panama, its
importance, the operation of the locks, problems of protection and
maintenance, and scenes of the Canal Zone.

PANAMA CANAL. Coronet, 1958. 10 1/2 min. color. COR
The history and significance of the Panama Canal. Also includes
scenes of how people live in the surrounding cities.

THE PANAMA CANAL, GATEWAY TO THE WORLD. Encyclopaedia
   Britannica Educational Corporation, 1961. 14 min. color.
   EBEC
A brief review of the history, function and operation of the Panama
Canal.

PANAMA, NICARAGUA. Park, 1955. 11 min. color. UCA
Concerning the proposed second canal through Nicaragua and the
operation of the present Panama Canal. Uses animation scenes to
show the operation of the Canal.

THE PATIENT MAYA. University of Utah, School of Medicine,
   1962. (Man and Culture Series.) 29 min. b/w. UUT
Discusses the Maya Indian culture of Yucatan and Central America's
highlands.

REPUBLIC OF GUATEMALA. Pan American Union, 1949. 22
   min. color. IFB
A study of the history, the geography, landmarks and modern life
of Guatemala.

THE REPUBLIC OF PANAMA. United World, 1964. (Our World
    of the 60's Series.) 17 min.   color.   UEVA
An account of contemporary Panamanian life and a trip through
the Panama Canal.

THE TURTLE PEOPLE. B and C, 1973. 26 min. color. PEN
About the Miskito Indians of eastern Nicaragua who pursue sea
turtles for money in a market economy, not for food as they would
have done in the past.

Mexico

THE ADVENTURES OF CHICO.   International Film Bureau, 1938.
    55 min.   b/w.   EFD, TWY
About a boy named Chico and his pet bird who live in a rural part
of Mexico--the central Mexican plateau.

ANCIENT AZTEC INDIANS OF NORTH AMERICA.   Encyclopaedia
    Britannica Educational Corporation, 1972.   8 min.   color.
    EBEC
A brief description of the Aztec invasion of Mexico and their development of a rich civilization.

APPEALS TO SANTIAGO.   Duane Metzger and Carter Wilson for
    University of California, Irvine, 1968.   27 min.   color.   MGH
Follows an eight-day Mayan Indian fiesta in Southern Mexico.

ARTS AND CRAFTS OF MEXICO.   PART I: POTTERY AND
    WEAVING. Rev. ed.   Museo Nacional de Artes e Industrios
    Populares, Mexico City, 1961.   14 min.   color.   EBEC
About Mexico's arts and crafts, especially the ancient arts of pottery making and weaving.

ARTS AND CRAFTS OF MEXICO.   PART II: BASKETRY, STONE,
    WOOD, AND METALS.   Rev. ed.   Museo Nacional de Artes
    e Industrios Populares, Mexico City, 1961.   11 min.   color.
    EBEC
A description of Mexico's many crafts, including onyx carving,
guitar-making, silverwork, making spurs and equipment for horses.

THE AZTECS.   Coronet, 1955.   10 min.   color.   UCA
A view of pre-Aztec and Aztec ruins, artifacts, and religious ceremonies.

BROOMS OF MEXICO.   International Film Bureau, 1971.   25 min.
    color.   EFD
Guitar music accompanies this film study of the inner life of six
Mexicans for whom the broom is an important part of their lives.

CAJITITLAN.   Harry Atwood, 1966.   41 min.   color.   MGH
A close look at the details of a Mexican village where the culture
has remained unchanged for more than one thousand years.   An
award-winning film.

CAPTAIN FROM CASTILE. Twentieth Century-Fox, 1947. 140
   min. color. Directed by Henry King; screenplay by Lamar
   Trotti, from the novel by Samuel Shellabarger. With Tyrone
   Power, Jean Peters, Cesar Romero, Lee J. Cobb, George
   Zucco, Jay Silverheels. FI
A fictional story about a young Spaniard's life from his youth to
his participation in Cortez's expedition to Mexico.

CORTEZ AND MONTEZUMA: CONQUEST OF AN EMPIRE. David
   Wolper, 1974. 52 min. sepia/color. FI
Reconstructs the fateful meeting of Cortez and Aztec Emperor
Montezuma. Written, produced and directed by Robert Guenette.

CORTEZ AND THE LEGEND. ABC, 1967. 52 min. color.
   MGH
An award-winning documentary on the Spanish colonization of Mexi-
co and tho clash between conqueror Cortez and Aztec emperor
Montezuma.

EL. (HE. THIS STRANGE PASSION.) Oscar Dancigers, 1952.
   82 min. b/w. In Spanish with English subtitles. Directed
   by Luis Buñuel; screenplay by Luis Buñuel and Luis Alcoriza,
   based on the novel by Mercedes Pinto; photography by Gabriel
   Figueroa; music by Luis Hernandes Breton. With Arturo de
   Cordova, Delia Garces, Luis Beristain, Aurora Walker.
   MAC[1], AZT
Director Buñuel shows the ruination of an obsessively religious
man, a celibate, who during a religious ceremony becomes equally
obsessed with a beautiful woman. He marries her, then develops
an insane jealousy that threatens her and others. The man's men-
tal breakdown is treated with elements of black humor. A bitter
denunciation of Christianity.

EXCAVATIONS AT LA VENTA. University of California, 1963.
   29 min. color. UCA
Shows the archeological excavations at La Venta, Tabasco, Mexico,
the site of Olmec ruins.

FISHER FOLK OF LAKE PATZCUARO. Classroom Film, 1951.
   18 min. color. UCA
How the Tarascan Indians catch ducks, fish, and barter in the markets of Mexico.

THE FORGOTTEN VILLAGE. Herbert Kline, 1944. 60 min.
   b/w. MAC[1]
About a young peasant boy who, while trying to get help for his sick
brother, meets resistance from many of his people who still use
folk medicine. Eventually he decides to become a doctor. Based
on a story by John Steinbeck. English narration by Burgess Mere-
dith. Also available with Spanish narration, no English subtitles.

HACIENDA LIFE IN OLD MEXICO. (UNA HACIENDA MEXICANA.)
   Dana and Ginger Lamb, 1947. 12 min. color. IFB

How life goes on in the traditional way in the self-sufficient community of San Carlos.

HEART OF MEXICO. Twentieth Century-Fox, 1942. 10 min.
   b/w. IND
About Mexico's geologic and historic past in brief sequences showing the volcano Popocatepetl and remains of Aztec civilization.

HERITAGE FROM TULA, MEXICO. Mexico, 1960. 14 min.
   color. MAC
Written by Mel Fowler with technical assistance by Jorge R. Acosta, discoverer of Tula. Shows examples of magnificent artifacts from Tula, capital of the Toltec nation, destroyed by the Aztecs in 1250 A.D.

INDIAN VILLAGERS IN MEXICO. Films Inc., 1969. 12 min.
   color. FI, VEC
Daily routines of people in Teotitlan del Valle, a village 600 miles from Mexico and near Oaxaca.

INDIANS OF MEXICO: THE TARASCANS. Dan McLaughlin, 1975.
   14 min. color. COR
How the Tarascan people, because of geographic isolation, continue to follow ancient traditions in their farming, fishing, and crafts.

JUAREZ. Warner Bros., 1939. 132 min. b/w. Directed by
   William Dieterle; screenplay by John Huston, Wolfgang Reinhardt and Aeneas MacKenzie; music by Erich Wolfgang Korngold. With Paul Muni, John Garfield, Bette Davis, Claude Rains, Donald Crisp, Brian Aherne, Joseph Calleia, Gilbert Roland. MGH
A biography of Juarez and a study of Hapsburg Emperor Maximilian and Empress Carlotta in Mexico.

LAND AND WATER. W. T. Sander, W. G. Mather, 1961. 25
   min. color. PEN
How human life is interrelated with climatic conditions. Illustrates peasant and plantation agriculture in a Mexican valley.

MACARIO. (ALLEGORY.) Clasi Films Mundiales, 1961. 91 min.
   b/w. In Spanish with English subtitles. Directed by Roberto Gavaldon; screenplay by Emilio Carballido, Roberto Gavaldon, from a story by Bruno Travern; photography by Gabriel Figueroa; music by Raul Lavista. With Ignacio Lopez Tarso, Pina Pellicer, Enrique Lucero, Jose Galvez, Jose Luis Jimenez, Mario Alberto Rodriguez. AZT
A peasant, who meets Death one day in the forest, is thereby given miraculous powers, which, in turn, lead to his torture by robed officers of the Inquisition.

THE MAGNIFICENT MATADOR. Twentieth Century-Fox, 1955.
   94 min. color. Directed by Budd Boetticher; screenplay by Charles Lang. With Maureen O'Hara, Anthony Quinn, Manuel

Rojas, Richard Denning. BUDG, MAC[1], WIL
About a matador who suddenly drops his career when he begins to
fear that his son will be killed if he enters the ring. Shows Mexican villages, cities and ranches.

MARIA CANDELARIA. Clasa, 1944. 90 min. b/w. In Spanish
    with English subtitles. Directed by Emilio Fernandez; screen-
    play by Emilio Fernandez; music by Francisco Dominguez;
    photography by Gabriel Figueroa. With Pedro Armendariz,
    Dolores del Rio, Margarita Cortes, Alberto Galan, Manuel
    Inclan. AZT
A peasant boy tries to aid an Indian girl who is being destroyed by
the gossip of villagers. A view of Indian life in Mexico, particularly Wochimilco. Gabriel Figueroa won the Cannes Festival
Award for best photography.

MAYA FAMILY TODAY. Hartley, 1972. 23 min. color. ACI
Follows an Indian family of Mayan descent who live in Chiapas in
southern Mexico. Stresses the impact of Mayan ancestry.

MAYA OF ANCIENT AND MODERN YUCATAN. 2nd ed. Guy
    Haselton, 1967. 20 min. color. BFA, UCA
Describes the great achievements of the Mayan people in Mexico.
Compares Chichen Itza and Uxmal with the culture of present-day
Mayas in the same region.

THE MAYAN MYSTERY. Hartley, 1970. 18 min. color. ACI
Using music by composer Carlos Chavez, this film examines the
magnificent Mayan ruins in Mexico and raises questions about the
mystery of the Mayan civilization's decline.

MEXICAN BUS RIDE. (ASCENT TO HEAVEN. SUBIDA AL CI-
    ELO.) Manuel Alto Laguirre, 1951. 73 min. b/w. In
    Spanish with English subtitles. Directed by Luis Buñuel;
    screenplay by Luis Buñuel, Juan la Cabado, and Manuel Alto
    Laguirre, from a story by Alto Laguirre; photography by Alex
    Philips; music by Gustavo Pitaluga. With Lilia Pardo, Car-
    melita Gonzales, Esteban Marquez, Manuel Donde, Robert
    Cobo, Ascevez Castenada. MGH, AZT
About the comic misadventures of a young man who takes a bus to
go to the next town to bring a lawyer to his dying mother. A
Cannes Festival award winner.

MEXICAN CERAMICS. Reino Randall and Richard Townsend, 1966.
    18 min. color. BFA
Describes low-fire pottery making by primitive methods which pre-
ceded the potter's wheel.

MEXICAN HANDICRAFT AND FOLK ART. Coronet, 1969. 10 1/2
    min. color. COR
Shows the wide range of Mexico's hand crafts from jewelry to
housewares, and the influence of history on them.

MEXICAN MAIZE. Roger Sandall, 1962. 10 min. color. PEN
Traces the study of Indian life in Western Mexico made by anthropologists from the American Museum of Natural History. Emphasizes the importance of maize to Latin American peasants.

MEXICAN MARKET. ACI, 1971. 10 min. color. ACI
Reveals the activities and appeal of a typical market place outside
Mexico City. Contains a simple Spanish narration which names
the various items shown.

MEXICAN MURALS. Twentieth Century-Fox, 1937. 10 min.
    b/w. IND
Very brief view of the Aztec culture and twentieth century life in
Taxco, Xochimilco and Mexico City as it was in the late 1930s.

MEXICO, A CHANGING LAND. Alfred Higgins, 1972. 21 min.
    color. EFD
A report on present-day Mexico presenting contrasts of old and
new elements, improvements in the standard of living, and industrial growth.

MEXICO BEFORE CORTEZ. Martley, 1970. 14 min. color.
    ACI
A visit to the remains of Mexico's great civilizations that existed
before the conquests by Cortez. Includes Mixtecs, Toltecs, Aztecs and Zapotec Indians.

MEXICO: FOUR VIEWS. Robert Flaxman for Coronet, 1975.
    14 1/2 min. color. COR
Four people give their personal views of Mexico: a truck driver,
a teacher, a farmer, and a building contractor.

MEXICO IN THE '70'S: A CITY FAMILY. Frank Gardonyi, 1971.
    17 1/2 min. color. BFA
How a family lives in Mexico City with increased affluence, the
concomitant of industrialization.

MEXICO IN THE 70'S: HERITAGE AND PROGRESS. Frank Gar-
    donyi, 1971. 11 1/2 min. color. BFA
Three Mexicans, a farmer, a butcher and an architect, provide
an unusual view of Mexico's old and new culture.

MEXICO: THE FROZEN REVOLUTION. Raymundo Gleyzer, 1971.
    60 min. color/b/w. In Spanish with English subtitles. TRI
An underground film, shot in Mexico and completed in Argentina,
about Mexican history and the oppressive political reality of today.

MEXICO: THE LAND AND THE PEOPLE. 2nd ed. Encyclopaedia
    Britannica Educational Corporation, 1961. 20 min. color.
    EBEC, UCO, UUT, UWY
Covers the historical, cultural and economic background of the
Mexican people.

MEXICO'S HISTORY.   Coronet, 1969.   16 min.   color.   COR
With a wide range of materials tells the most important events in
Mexico's history.   Includes the conquest of 1519, the revolt in
1810, the revolt led by Juarez in 1857, and the revolution of 1910.

NAZARIN.   Manuel Barbachano Ponce, 1958.   92 min.   b/w.   In
Spanish with English subtitles.   Directed by Luis Buñuel;
screenplay by Luis Buñuel and Julio Alejandro, based on the
novel by Benito Pérez Galdós; photography by Gabriel Figueroa.
With Francisco Rabal, Rita Maceda, Marga Lopez, Jesus
Fernandez.   MAC1
Here director Luis Buñuel tries to demonstrate that he who tries
to be absolutely pure is condemned to defeat.   Nazarin, a nineteenth century priest, encounters contempt and ridicule for his efforts to be humble and kind.

OLLERO YUCATECO.   (YUCATAN POTTER.)   University of Illinois, 1965.   25 min.   color.   PEN, UIL
About a Yucatan potter at work.   Shows techniques unlike those
used by Americans.

LOS OLVIDADOS.   (THE YOUNG AND THE DAMNED.)   Oscar
Dancigers, 1950.   81 min.   b/w.   In Spanish with English
subtitles.   Directed by Luis Buñuel; screenplay by Luis Buñuel
and Luis Alcoriza; photography by Gabriel Figueroa; music
by Rodolfo Holffter.   With Estela Inda, Miguel Inclan, Roberto
Cobo, Alfonso Mejia, Hector Lopez Portillo, Salvador Quiros.
MAC1, AZT
A realistic portrayal of juvenile delinquents in which even an attempt at reform fails.   The filmmaker integrates extraordinary
imagery with reality.

THE OROZCO MURALS: QUETZALCOATL.   Robert Canton, 1962.
23 min.   color.   MAC
An award-winning film about the mural painted on the walls of
Dartmouth College in 1934 by Mexican artist Orozco.

THE PEARL.   Oscar Dancigers, 1947.   77 min.   b/w.   In English.   Directed by Emilio Fernandez; screenplay by Emilio
Fernandez, John Steinbeck and Jackson Wagner, based on the
novel by John Steinbeck; photography by Gabriel Figueroa; music by Antonio Diaz Conde.   With Pedro Armendariz, Maria
Elena Marquez, Fernando Wagner.   MAC1
A poor fisherman discovers a pearl of great value which could
change the lives of his family, his wife and son.   His greedy neighbors create such trouble and violence, however, that he returns
the pearl to the sea.

A PORTRAIT OF MEXICO.   Radio-Television Bureau, University
of Arizona, 1969.   34 min.   color.   IFB, UUT
An introduction to the history and contemporary life of Mexico.

RACE TO EXTINCTION.   BBC, 1967.   50 min.   b/w.   TL
How the Lacandan Indians, the descendents of Mayan civilization
who live near ancient Mayan ruins, have survived as a "pure" group
and how they may be doomed to extinction through inbreeding.

REED: INSURGENT MEXICO.   Paul Leduc, 1972.   110 min.
    sepia.   In Spanish with English subtitles.   Directed by Paul
    Leduc; based on John Reed's book; photography by Alexis
    Grivas; editors, Rafael Castanedo and Giovanni Korporaal.
    With Claudio Obregon, Eduardo Lopez Rojas, Ernesto Gomez
    Cruz, Juan Angel Martinez.   NYF
An account of the activities in the Mexican Revolution of 1913,
based on the reports of the American radical journalist, John
Reed.

THE ROOTS.   Manuel Barbachano, 1958.   85 min.   b/w.   In
    Spanish and Indian with English subtitles.   Directed by Benito
    Alazraki; based on "El Diosero," a collection of short stories
    by Francisco Gonzales; adapted by Carlos Vejo, Manuel Bar-
    bachano, Maria Elena Lazo, Benito Alazraki, J. M. Garcia
    Ascot and Fernando Espejo.   MAC[1]
Four stories by Francisco Gonzalez.   "The Cows": a mother becomes a wet-nurse to support her family.   "Our Lady": an American anthropologist learns that the Indians she is studying are not
"savages."   "The One-Eyed Boy": a mistreated, almost blind boy
only finds happiness when he becomes totally blind.   "The Filly":
A married archeologist offers a farmer money for his attractive
daughter.   In turn, the Mexican farmer offers much more for the
archeologist's wife.   Made with a non-professional cast.   An award-
winning film.

RUFINO TAMAYO: THE SOURCES OF HIS ART.   Gary Conklin,
    1972.   27 min.   color.   ALCF
John Huston narrates this report on the work of Mexican artist
Rufino Tamayo.

SENTINELS OF SILENCE.   Manuel Arango, 1973.   19 min.   color.
    EBEC
Orson Welles narrates this aerial visit to the pre-Columbian ruins
of ancient Mexico.   Also available in Spanish language version narrated by Ricardo Montalban, CENTINELAS DEL SILENCIO.

SIMON OF THE DESERT.   (SAN SIMEON DEL DESIERTO.)   Luis
    Buñuel, 1965.   43 min.   b/w.   In Spanish with English subti-
    tles.   Directed by Luis Buñuel; written by Luis Buñuel;
    photography by Gabriel Figueroa.   With Silvia Pinal, Claudio
    Brook, Hortensia Sontovana, Jesus Fernandez Martinez.
    MAC[1]
A satiric comedy based on the life of St. Simeon Stylites of the
fifteenth century, the holy man who sat atop a pillar to commune
with God.   Despite the man's good works, the people below him
display all-too-human frailties.   The Devil, played by a woman,
does everything possible to shock or horrify him.

SIQUEIROS: "EL MAESTRO." Encyclopaedia Britannica Educational Corporation, 1969. 14 min. color. EBEC
A visit with Mexican artist David Siqueiros at work and a look at
his unique mural, the largest ever created, "The March of Humanity in Latin America," as an expression of his political and philosophical beliefs.

SPAIN IN THE NEW WORLD. Encyclopaedia Britannica Educational
Corporation, 1963. 13 min. color. EBEC, UCO
The Spanish influence on Mexican culture from the days of Cortez
to the present.

SPANISH CONQUEST IN THE NEW WORLD. Twentieth Century-
Fox, 1947. 16 min. color. IND
Excerpt from THE CAPTAIN FROM CASTILE showing the organiza-
tion of Hernando Cortez' expedition against Mexico.

SPANISH INFLUENCE IN MEXICAN CRAFTS. Gateway, 1947.
10 min. color. UCA
About the contributions of new materials to the Indian craftsmen in
the sixteenth century and the effect of Spanish importation of sheep
and cattle on the manufacture of fine leather.

TEPOZTLAN. Earl Griswold, 1970. 30 min. color. BFA
A description of the traditional life in Tepoztlan, a village only 40
miles from Mexico's capital.

TEPOZTLAN IN TRANSITION. Holt, Rinehart and Winston, 1970.
20 min. color. BFA
The village of Tepztlan viewed as it emerges into the modern world
following the construction of a major road link to Mexico City.

TIME IN THE SUN. Marie Seton, 1939. 60 min. b/w. Narration in English. MAC[1]
The producer Marie Seton and editor Roger Durnford took footage
from the unfinished film QUE VIVA MEXICO! by Sergei Eisenstein
and Gregori Alexandrov and attempted to reconstruct the original
film's intent to depict ancient Yucatan, the arrival of the conquista-
dores and Spanish settlers, Tehuantepec, feudal Mexico, the Revolution and the festival of All Soul's Day.

TO FIND OUR LIFE: THE PEYOTE HUNT OF THE HUICHOLS
OF MEXICO. University of California at Los Angeles, 1969.
60 min. color. PEN, UCLA
About the Huichol Indians led by a shaman to obtain peyote. Includes the hunting and eating of peyote cactus, as well as ritual
ceremonies involving its use for curing the sick.

TORERO! Manuel Barbachano Ponce, 1957. 75 min. b/w. With
English narration. Directed by Carlos Velo; screenplay by
Velo and Hugo Mozo. With Luis Procuna, Manolete, Carlos
Aruzza, Antonio Sevilla. MAC[1]
A staged reenactment of the dramatic return in 1953 of Mexican

bullfighter Luis Procuna to the ring after a premature retirement. Also includes footage of other great bullfighters like Manolete and Carlos Arruza. Luis Procuna portrays himself.

VIVA MEXICO. McGraw-Hill, 1971. 25 min. color. MGH
A cultural visit in Mexico, tracing art, dance, crafts, artifacts to the accompaniment of native folk music.

YANCO. Miguel Gonzalez, 1964. 85 min. b/w. No dialog, music and sound effects only. Directed and written by Servando Gaonzalez; photography by Alex Phillips, Jr.; music by Gustavo C. Carreon. With Ricardo Ancona, Jesus Medina, Maria Bustamente. MAC[1], AZT
A young Indian boy in a village near Mexico City learns to play a home-made violin, nicknamed "Yanco." When the old man who is his teacher dies, the boy is kept from having the violin. However, each night he "borrows" it to play beautiful music, thus frightening the superstitious villagers. Winner of sixteen international awards.

YUCATAN: LAND OF THE MAYA. Paul Hoefler and Disney, 1962. 17 min. color. UCA
The modern life of the Yucatan area in Mexico with its evocations of the great ancient Mayan culture.

South America

General

AMAZON. National Geographic Society, 1968. 52 min. color. FI, VEC
Pierre Gaiseau, filmmaker and explorer, travels to film people and natural life along the Amazon River. Shows groups such as the Jivaro people, mystic rituals, hunts, frightening swamps.

AMAZON LIVES. International Film Foundation, n.d. 19 min. color. IFF
A close-up view of an Amazon family that lives near the common border of Bolivia, Peru, and Brazil. Includes details of daily life as well as methods for collecting latex from rubber trees and processing the rubber for the market.

BOLIVAR, SOUTH AMERICAN LIBERATOR. Coronet, 1962. 11 min. color. COR
The story of Simon Bolivar who liberated five South American countries and dreamed of a United South America. With footage covering Venezuela, Ecuador, Peru and Colombia.

GEOGRAPHY OF SOUTH AMERICA: THE CONTINENT. Coronet, 1961. 14 min. color. COR
Covers the agriculture, industry, culture, and commerce of the major geographic areas of South America--the Andes, the Guiana and Brazilian highlands and the Orinoco, Amazon and Plata-Parana river basins.

PEOPLE OF THE AMAZON.   National Geographic Society, 1968.
2nd ed.   22 min.   color.   FI, VEC
A study of the Indians who live along the Amazon River and the
history of the region, including Machu Picchu and Sao Domingo.

SIMON BOLIVAR.   n. d.   No credits listed.   105 min.   color.
With Maximilian Schell, Rossano Schiaffino.   MAC[1]
The life story of the 19th century liberator who led a revolution to
free northern countries of South America from Spanish control.

SOURCE OF THE AMAZON.   Harry Grubbs, 1947.   11 min.   color.
IFB
Follows the course of the important Amazon River from the mountains through plateaus, across the jungle plains.   Shows the variety
of people who use the river for drinking, washing, or transportation.

SOUTH AMERICA.   International Film Foundation, 1960.   28 min.
color.   IFF, IFP, UCA, UCO, UUT
Shows conflicts of a rising industrial society with traditional folk-
ways and contrasts the wealthy with the poverty-stricken.   With
music based on South American sources.

SOUTH AMERICA.   McGraw-Hill, 1962.   20 min.   b/w.   UCA
A survey of the contrasts--including political aspects--of the various individual countries of South America.

SOUTH AMERICA.   Pan-American World Airways, n. d.   15 min.
color.   ASF, PAN
A travelogue designed to promote tourism in South America.   Shows
highlights of the South American countries.

SOUTH AMERICA: A LAND OF MANY FACES.   McGraw-Hill,
1975.   15 min.   color.   MGH
A survey of the cultural and geographical diversity of South America's various nations.

SOUTH AMERICA: LIFE IN THE CITY.   Art Evans, 1971.   10
min.   color.   BFA
The beauties and blights of some of the world's greatest cities, Rio
de Janeiro, Sao Paulo, Buenos Aires, Caracas, Santiago, and
Lima.

SOUTH AMERICA: MARKET DAY.   Art Evans, 1971.   10 min.
BFA
Reveals the excitement and color of market days all over South
America.

SOUTH AMERICA: OVERVIEW.   Sterling, 1973.   (The Latin
American Series, A Focus on People.)   17 min.   color.   SEF
How South America is changing in the last half of the twentieth
century.

SOUTH AMERICA: THE WIDENING GAP. McGraw-Hill, 1975.
     15 min. color. MGH
A survey of the differences between upper and lower classes and
rural and urban life in South America. Attempts to deal with the
realities of the existing social order, as well as the economy and
natural resources. Advisers for this film: Dr. Nelson Robinson,
University of Tennessee, and Tad Szulc, author and former N. Y.
Times correspondent.

SOUTH AMERICA TODAY. International Film Foundation, 1973.
     25 min. color. EFD, IFF
One of the newest films available on South America. Emphasizes
the diversity and rapid change to be found throughout the continent.

SOUTH AMERICA: VOTES OR VIOLENCE? NET, 1965. 60 min.
     b/w. UCA
A study of Bolivia, Brazil and Chile to determine what type of
governmental system would work best in Latin America.

STATE OF SIEGE. Cinema 10 and Reggane, 1973. 119 min.
     color. In French with English subtitles. Directed by Costa-
     Gavras; written by Franco Solinas; music by Mikis Theodora-
     kis. With Yves Montand, Renato Salvatori, O. E. Hasse, and
     Jean-Luc Bideau. CF
Somewhere in South America a U. S. official is kidnapped for poli-
tical reasons. Based on an actual incident in 1970 in Montivideo,
Uruguay. By the director of Z and the writer of THE BATTLE OF
ALGIERS.

Argentina

ALLIANCE FOR PROGRESS. Julio Luduena, 1972. 108 min.
     b/w. In Spanish with English subtitles. Directed by Julio
     Luduena; written by Julio Luduena; photography by Juan Carlos
     Ciravegna; edited by Jorge Valencia. With Roberto Carnagui,
     Carlos Del Burgo and Juana De Manet. TRI
A satiric allegory about warfare between Revolutionary forces and
the Establishment. Among the various stereotyped characters are
Miss Middle Class and the Artist who have to adjust to changing
situations. Suggests an outcome of a new social order.

ARAUCANIANS OF RUCA CHOROY. Jorge Preloran, 1974. 50
     min. color. PHO
A document of one Araucanian Indian man's life in the valley of
Ruca Choroy in Argentina. Traces his parents' arrival in Argentina
and the history of the Indians' flight through the Andes from the
Spaniards. Includes candid scenes of villagers commenting on their
views and concerns, plus a good look at the extraordinary terrain.

ARGENTINA. McGraw-Hill, 1963. (Our Latin American Neighbors
     Series.) 16 min. color. MGH
Shows the capital, Buenos Aires, and Cordoba, plus the major

regions of Argentina--sheep ranches, the pampas, foothills. Spanish language version also available.

ARGENTINA, COUNTRY AT THE CROSSROADS. Hearst, 1962.
    8 min. b/w. UCO
A history of Argentina with emphasis on Peron's regime from 1946 until 1955. Also covers subsequent struggles for power.

ARGENTINA: PEOPLE OF THE PAMPA. Encyclopaedia Britannica Educational Corporation, 1957. 2nd ed. 16 min. color.
    EBEC, UCA, UCO, UUT, UWY
Presents the important features of the Argentinian economy and how the people live in both rural and urban settings.

ARGENTINA, THE PORT CITY AND THE PAMPA. United World, 1967. 20 min. color. UEVA
A description of Argentina's contrasts--the busy city life of Buenos Aires and the flat, fertile Pampas with its agricultural culture.

CHILE AND ARGENTINA. Sterling, 1973. (The Latin American Series. A Focus on People.) 19 min. color. SEF
A report on the two countries with the highest standard of living in South America. Studies Argentina's social problems that result from aspirations not matched by productivity. Discusses Chile's Marxist government and its crises stemming from the move to nationalization.

THE EAVES DROPPER. Paul M. Heller, 1966. 90 min. b/w.
    Directed by Leopold Torre Nilsson; screenplay by Leopold Torre Nilsson, Beatriz Guido, et al. In Spanish with English subtitles. With Stathis Giallelis, Janet Margolin. COLU
The story concerns the spying of a wealthy Fascist terrorist who hides out in a fancy hotel occupied by Spanish refugees. His continual snooping leads to problems in his love life and politics.

END OF INNOCENCE. (LA CASA DEL ANGEL.) Torre Nilsson, 1957. 76 min. b/w. In Spanish with English subtitles. Directed by Leopold Torre Nilsson; screenplay by Torre Nilsson and Beatriz Guido, based on the novel by Guido. With Elsa Daniel, Lautaro Murua, Guillermo Battaglia. MAC[1]
Director Torre Nilsson's first film to win international acclaim about a young girl from a puritanical home who is seduced but unable to overcome her guilt feelings.

EVA PERON. David Wolper, 1965. 27 min. b/w. SEF
An account of the actress who rose to controlling power and fame in Argentina and whose impact is still felt many years after her death.

THE FALL. (LA CAIDA.) Leopold Torre Nilsson, 1961. 86 min.
    b/w. In Spanish with English subtitles. Directed by Leopold Torre Nilsson; screenplay by Torre Nilsson and Beatriz Guido, based on the novel by Guido; photography by Anibal Gonzalez

Paz. With Elsa Daniel, Lautaro Murua, Duilio Marzio. MAC[1]
A prudish young girl, living as a boarder with a disturbed household, has several love affairs which upset her moral values.

GEOGRAPHY OF SOUTH AMERICA: ARGENTINA, PARAGUAY,
  URUGUAY. Coronet, 1961. 10 1/2 min. color. COR, UCO
The geographic factors, achievements and problems of three coun-
tries located on the Plata-Parana river system.

HAND IN THE TRAP. Leopold Torre Nilsson, 1961. 90 min.
  b/w. In Spanish with English subtitles. Directed by Leopold
  Torre Nilsson; screenplay by Torre Nilsson, Beatriz Guido,
  Ricardo Luna. With Elsa Daniel, Francisco Rabal, Leonardo
  Favio. MAC[1]
A young girl interferes in her aunt's affairs and brings about a
tragedy.

THE HOUR OF THE FURNACES. Grupo Cine Liberacion, 1968.
  PART I, 95 min. b/w.; PART II, 120 min. b/w.; PART III,
  45 min. b/w. In Spanish with English subtitles. Directed by
  Fernando Solanas and Octavio Getino. TRI
Produced clandestinely as a report on the struggle for liberation
in Latin America, with Argentina as a model for background.
This much-awarded film is in three parts. PART I: NEW
COLONIALISM AND VIOLENCE consists of an analysis of the Ar-
gentine situation, its history, geography and economy. PART II:
AN ACT FOR LIBERATION is a two-part study of Peronism,
Peron's ten-year reign and the activities during the decade follow-
ing his fall from power. PART III: VIOLENCE AND LIBERATION
examines the role of violence in the national liberation movement.

IMAGINERO. Jorge Preloran, Robert Gardner, 1971. 52 min.
  color. PHO
A look at a local religious artisan who sees his art as a way of
honoring God. Explains his work, his life style and gives examples
of his cactus wood crucifixes, shrines, paintings and church decora-
tions.

IT HAPPENED IN HUALFIN. Raymundo Gleyzer and Jorge Preloran, 1969. PART I, 15 min. b/w.; PART II, 15 min. b/w.;
  PART III, 20 min. color. In Spanish with English subtitles.
  TRI
A three-part story made by Raymundo Gleyzer and Jorge Preloran.
PART I: WHEN THE WIND IS SILENT tells the life of an old man
who worked for years in the canefields. PART II: THE CLAY is
about the old man's sister-in-law who is a potter in Hualfin. She
reflects on issues such as poverty, pottery. PART III: ELINDA
OF THE VALLEY is the story of the woman potter's daughter who
weaves blankets for sale and seems to be trapped in the life of
poverty, despite her potential for other work.

LIFE IN GRASSLANDS. Coronet, 1961. 10 1/2 min. color.
  COR

A visit with a family living in the Argentine pampas, a grassland region rich in food crops, cattle and sheep.

NEW HORIZONS: ARGENTINA. Pan-American World Airways, n. d. 13 min. color. ASF, PAN
A travelogue designed to promote tourism in Argentina. Shows the major scenic features of the country.

LAS OLLAS POPULARES. Gerardo Vallejo, 1968. 5 min. b/w. TRI
Tells the plight of the cane-cutters of Tucuman in northern Argentina, who are jobless when the sugar harvest ends each year and must survive with the help of the "popular pots" (las ollas populares) that stave off hunger.

LA PAZ. 1968. 5 min. b/w. In Spanish. TRI
An anonymous Argentinian film about military and police repression of students and workers.

PERON AND EVITA. CBS, 1958. 26 min. b/w. MAC
The story of Juan Peron and the woman who helped him rule Argentina.

RANCHERO AND GAUCHOS IN ARGENTINA. Films Inc., 1969. 17 min. color. FI, VEC
A successful meat broker-rancher flies to the interior of Argentina to supervise the activities on his ranch. Shows gauchos at work in their semi-feudal community.

THE RETURN OF JUAN PERON. Hearst, n. d. 20 min. color. HMN
Traces the political career of Juan Peron who first became president of Argentina in 1946. Examines his commitment to being a dictator.

SOUTH AMERICA: ESTANCIA IN ARGENTINA. Art Evans, 1969. 21 min. color. BFA
A look at the feudal life on the large ranches (estancias) of Argentina's fertile plains (pampas).

SUMMERSKIN. Leopold Torre Nilsson, 1961. 96 min. b/w.
In Spanish with English subtitles. Directed by Leopold Torre Nilsson; screenplay by Torre Nilsson and Beatriz Guido; photography by Oscar Melli. With Graciela Borges, Alfredo Alcon, Franca Boni. MAC[1]
A dying young man recovers, only to discover that his girlfriend had been promised a reward for her friendship upon his death.

THE TRAITORS. Grupo Cine de la Base, 1973. 114 min. color.
In Spanish with English subtitles. TRI
An interweaving of documentary, fictional and surrealistic sequences in the dramatic portrayal of a trade union leader's life in Argentina for the past two decades. A study in corruption of the labor

movement. Indicates how American unions work with international
corporations and the CIA to buy off Latin American union leaders.

Bolivia

AMAZON FAMILY. International Film Foundation, 1961. 19 min.
color. EFD, IFF
The simple life of a village people who live in Bolivia, 2,500 miles
up the Amazon River.

ANDEAN WOMEN. Norman N. Miller, n. d. (Faces of Change
Series.) 19 min. color. FF
How Aymará women actually perform vital tasks even though they
view themselves as "helpers" to men.

ARTICLE 55. United Nations, 1952. 10 min. b/w. UUT
Includes a brief overview of Bolivia's history and resources, along
with a report on the U. N. 's response to Bolivia's request for technical aid.

BLOOD OF THE CONDOR. Ukamau Group, 1969. 85 min. b/w.
In Quechua and Spanish with English subtitles. Directed by
Jorge Sanjines; written by Oscar Soria and Jorge Sanjines;
photographed by Antonio Eguino. With Marcelino-Yanahuaya,
Vicente Salinas, Benedicta Huanca and the population of the
Kaata rural community. TRI
A strong political statement and an example of cinematic art in this
dramatic reenactment of an incident involving the sterilization of
Quechuan Indian women without consent by the Peace Corps. A re-
flection of Latin American attitudes to the U. S. aid programs.
Bolivia's first feature film.

BOLIVIA. Herbert Millington, 1966. 15 min. color. MGH
Explores Bolivia's struggle to attain economic prosperity and the
geographic problems that act as obstacles.

BOLIVIA, PERU AND ECUADOR. Sterling, 1973. (The Latin
American Series: A Focus on People.) 19 min. color. SEF
The culture of the three countries and the reforms and political
changes now taking place.

THE CHILDREN KNOW. Norman N. Miller, n. d. (Faces of
Change Series.) 33 min. color. FF
A study of discrimination in Bolivia's Andean society, the conflict
between the rural and towns people and its effect on the children.

THE COURAGE OF THE PEOPLE. Radio Televisione and the
Ukumau Group, 1971. 90 min. color. In Spanish with Eng-
lish subtitles. Directed by Jorge Sanjines; written by Oscar
Soria; photography by Antonio Eguino; edited by Carlos Macias
and Sergio Buzi; music by Nilo Soruco. With Federico Vallejo,
Felicidad Coca, Domitila Chungara and Eusebio Gironda. TRI

Actual survivors of the Bolivian army massacre of miners in 1967 participated in this reconstruction of the events and conditions leading to the massacre. Also documents the earlier history of repression beginning in 1942. An example of the structure of exploitation and of the new revolutionary cinema which attempts to reveal that structure.

THE CRY OF THE PEOPLE. Grupo Tercer Cine, 1972. 65 min. color. In Spanish with English subtitles. Directed by Humberto Rios; written by Humberto Rios, Hebe Serebrisky, and Jorge Honig; photographed by Mario Diez; edited by Juan Carlos Macias. TRI
A disturbing documentary on the physical and political realities of Bolivia, citing the hunger, the death rate, the illness, the depression, the economic status and the revolutions. Uses newsreel footage as well as interviews and commentary to analyze Bolivia's problems.

GEOGRAPHY OF SOUTH AMERICA: COUNTRIES OF THE ANDES. Coronet, 1961. 10 1/2 min. color. COR, UCO
Bolivia, Ecuador, Chile, and Peru are the Andean countries covered in this survey of their geographical and cultural aspects.

HASTA LA VICTORIA SIEMPRE. Cuba, 1967. 20 min. b/w. TWN
A Cuban film made as tribute to Ché Guevara with emphasis on his last work with the guerrilla struggle in Bolivia.

MAGIC AND CATHOLICISM. Norman N. Miller, 1974. (Faces of Change Series.) 34 min. color. FF
The interface of the ancestors and conquerors with the religions in everyday life in the Bolivian highlands.

MINERS OF BOLIVIA. Films Inc., 1969. 15 min. color. FI, PEN, VEC
A brief overview of tin miners working in ancient mines of the Bolivian highlands and living in Potosi and Catavi. Shows the squalor in which they live.

POTATO PLANTERS. Norman N. Miller, 1974. (Faces of Change Series.) 19 min. color. FF
An intimate portrait of a typical Aymará family filmed with understanding.

THE SPIRIT POSSESSION OF ALEJANDRO MAMANI. Norman N. Miller, 1974. (Faces of Change Series.) 27 min. color. FF
How an elderly Bolivian faces the end of a long life, despairing his lack of spiritual contentment.

VIRACOCHA. Norman N. Miller, 1974. (Faces of Change Series.) 30 min. color. FF
A study of various racial and social strata, the mestizos, the compesinos, the Aymará and Quechua.

Brazil

THE ALIENIST.   Nelson Pereira dos Santos, 1970. 80 min. color.
In Portuguese with English subtitles.   Directed by Nelson Pereira dos Santos; screenplay by Mr. dos Santos, based on the
novel by Machado De Assis; photography by Dib Lutfi; music
by Guicherme Magalhaes Vaz.   With Nildo Pareate, Isabel
Riberio, Leija Diniz.   NYF
What happens to a small Brazilian town in the early 19th century
when a young priest decides to study lunacy in order to relate it
to reason.

THE AMAZON: PEOPLE AND RESOURCES OF NORTHERN BRA-
ZIL.   Encyclopaedia Britannica Educational Corporation, 1957.
22 min.   color.   EBEC, UCA, UCO, UNE, UUT, UWY
How the people of the swampland, jungle, villages, farms, towns,
and harbor cities live in Brazil.

ANTONIO DAS MORTES.   Claude-Anotine, Mapa and Glauber
Rocha, 1969. 100 min.   color.   In Portuguese with English
subtitles.   Directed by Glauber Rocha; screenplay by Glauber
Rocha; photography by Alfonso Beato; music by Marios Nobre.
GRO
A guerrilla film and a folk-epic with revolutionary and operatic
overtones.   Antonio is a landlord's hired assassin assigned to kill
a group of peasant rebels.   Instead he joins them.   Rocha re-
ceived the Best Director Award in the 1969 Cannes Film Festival
for this film, which has itself been much awarded.

ARROW GAME.   T. Asch, N. Chagnon, 1975. 7 min.   color.
PEN
A group of boys from the Yanamomo people, who live where Brazil
and Venezuela meet, shoot blunt arrows at each other in order to
practice dodging and shooting.

BARRAVENTO.   (THE TURNING WIND.)   Glauber Rocha, 1962.
76 min.   b/w.   In Portuguese with English subtitles.   Directed
by Glauber Rocha.   NYF
Rocha's first feature film and one of the early cinema novo films
acclaimed internationally.   A story about the subjugation of Bahian
fishermen through superstition and an account of macumba, an
African and Christian ritualistic mix.

BARREN LIVES.   (VIDAS SECAS.)   Luis Carlos Barreto, Herbert
Richers, Darulo Trellers, 1963. 115 min.   b/w.   In Portu-
guese with English subtitles.   Directed and written by Nelson
Pereira Dos Santos; based on Gaciliano Ramos' novel "Vidas
Sêcas"; photographed by Luiz Carlos Barreto.   With Athila
Iorio, Maria Riberio, Jofre Soares.   MGH, ACB
A disturbing film about the poor of Brazil who are slaves to the
landowners.   With a cast of nonprofessional actors, except for one
person.   An example of cinema novo.

BERIMBAU.   Tony Talbot.   12 min.   b/w.   NYF
Nana, black musician, performs traditional music and his own im-
provisations on the berimbau, a one-stringed bow instrument
brought by slaves from Angola to Brazil.   With English narration.

THE BIG CITY.   (GRANDE CIDADE.)   Carlos Diegues, 1966.   80
    min.   b/w.   In Portuguese with English subtitles.   Directed
    by Carlos Diegues.   With Leonardo Vilar, Anecy Rocha, An-
    tonio Pitanga.   HCW, NYF
A young girl comes to Rio de Janeiro to find her fiancé and dis-
covers he is a hunted criminal.   An example of Cinema Novo
Brasil.

BLACK GOD, WHITE DEVIL.   Glauber Rocha, 1963.   120 min.
    b/w.   In Portuguese with English subtitles.   Directed by
    Glauber Rocha.   With Geraldo Del Ray, Othon Bastos, Yona
    Magalhaes.   HCW
Explores the plight of the poor people of Brazil who search for
something to transform their lives.

BLACK ORPHEUS.   (OREFEU NEGRO.)   Sacha Gordine, 1960.
    103 min.   color.   In Portuguese with English subtitles.   Di-
    rected by Marcel Camus; screenplay by Jacques Viot, based
    on the play "Orfeu da Conceicao!" by Vinicius de Moraes.
    With Marpessa Dawn, Breno Melo, Lourdes de Oliveira, Lea
    Garcia.   NC, JAN
A modern and Brazilian version of the Orpheus and Euridice story
set in the black section of Rio de Janeiro.   In this case Eurydice
is a country girl and Orpheus, a streetcar conductor.

BLOWGUN.   International Film Foundation, 1971.   (Indians of the
    Orinoco Series.)   13 min.   color.   EFD, IFF
Shows Makiritare Indian men of the Orinoco River area in Brazil
and Venezuela making blowguns.

BRASILIA.   George Tamarski, 1961.   13 min.   color.   EFD,
    IFB, UCA
A study of the building of Brazil's new capital from advance planning to construction and use.

BRAZIL.   Centron, 1961.   (Our Latin American Neighbor Series.)
    20 min.   b/w.   MGH
About the geography, the crops, the resources of Brazil.   Shows
the Amazon, Rio de Janeiro, Brasilia and Sao Paulo, Belo Hori-
zante.

BRAZIL: A REPORT ON TORTURE.   Saul Landau and Haskell
    Wexler, 1971.   60 min.   color.   In Portuguese with English
    subtitles.   NYF
A report made in Chile about the testimony of torture by a group
of Brazilian political prisoners recently freed in exchange for the
release of the Swiss Ambassador to Brazil.   Their descriptions of
depraved acts are explicit and presumably typical of conditions now

endured by an estimated 20,000 persons still located in Brazilian
prisons.

BRAZIL: CHANGE COMES TO THE RAIN FOREST. Universal
    Education and Visual Arts, 1967. 20 min. color. UMI
Shows the life of a boy in the tropical rain forest of Brazil in the
Amazon area. Gives contrast of manganese mining with life on the
river bank.

BRAZIL: NO TIME FOR TEARS. University of Chile, 1971. 40
    min. b/w. In Portuguese with English subtitles. TRI
A chilling account of the climate of terror, imprisonment and torture that has existed after the 1964 coup d'état in Brazil. Told by
nine recently released prisoners now in Chile, who recount details
of torture and killing which have involved an estimated 50,000 Bra-
zilians. Directed by Pedro Chaskel and Luis Alberto Sanz.

BRAZIL: PEOPLE OF THE FRONTIER. Coronet, 1969. 15 min.
    color. COR
A view of the pioneering people of Colinas de Goias, a frontier in
the Brazilian interior.

BRAZIL: PEOPLE OF THE HIGHLANDS. Encyclopaedia Britannica
    Educational Corporation, 1961. Rev. 2nd ed. 17 min. color.
    EBEC, UCO, UUT, UWY
Studies the life styles of four families of various socio-economic
levels, on farms and in a factory in Sao Paulo.

BRAZIL: THE GATHERING MILLIONS. NET, 1965. 60 min.
    b/w. UCA; IND has 30 min. version.
Describes Brazil's lowered death rate, increasing population figures
and the rural movement to the cities.

BRAZIL: THE RUDE AWAKENING. CBS, 1961. 54 min. b/w.
    MGH
Discusses the growing social unrest in Brazil, its causes and possible future course.

BRAZIL: THE TAKE-OFF POINT. NET, 1964. 60 min. b/w.
    IND
An exploration of Brazil's major problems and efforts taken to
cope with them.

BRAZIL: THE TROUBLED LAND. ABC, 1964. MGH
A film documentary made for TV about the starving people of Brazil and their political status, including their inclination toward
communism.

BRAZIL: THE VANISHING NEGRO. NET, 1965. 30 min. b/w.
    IND, UCA, UCO
About the racial intermixing in Brazil that accounts for the disap-
pearance of the Negro in a country whose port city Salvador was
once the New World's largest port of entry for slaves.

CANGACEIRO. Vera Cruz, 1954. 92 min. b/w. In Portuguese
with English subtitles. Directed and written by Lima Barreto.
With Milton Ribeiro, Alberto Ruschel, Marisa Prado. MAC[1]
Scenes of violent bandits' fury such as are seldom seen in films.
They roam the ranges of Brazil pillaging, playing Robin Hood, and
even when they relax, the passion and wildness of their rhythms
"make the blood run cold."

CHILDREN OF THE WORLD: BRAZIL. NET, 1968. 28 min.
color. IND
Describes a thirteen-year-old Brazilian boy who travels across
Brazil to search for his father, learning about his country's heritage along the way.

CHILDREN'S MAGICAL DEATH. T. Asch, N. Chagnon, 1975.
8 min. color. PEN
Some young boys are seen pretending to be shamans in imitation of
their fathers.

CLIMBING THE PEACH PALM. T. Asch, N. Chagnon, 1975 9
min. color. PEN
A young Yanomamo man ascends a peach palm tree to harvest the
fruit.

CONTACT WITH A HOSTILE TRIBE. BBC and Odyssey, 1967.
(Central and South America Series.) 25 min. color.
Two men try to befriend an isolated people, the Txicaos Indians of
central Brazil. Narrated by Lowell Thomas.

CRAFTSMAN. International Film Foundation, 1971. (Indians of
the Orinoco Series.) 12 min. color. EFD, IFF
Studies the crafts of the Makiritare Indian who lives near the
borders of Brazil and Venezuela.

EARTH ENTRANCED. Mapa, 1967. 110 min. color. In Portu-
guese with English subtitles. Directed and written by Glauber
Rocha; photography by Luiz Carlos Barreto; music by Sergio
Ricardo. With Jardel Filho, Paulo Autran, Jose Lewgoy,
Glauce Rocha, Paulo Gracindo, Danuza Leao. NYF
About a young poet who gradually becomes radicalized in an en-
vironment of upper class decadence contrasted with poetic poverty.

A FATHER WASHES HIS CHILDREN. T. Asch, N. Chagnon,
1975. 13 min. color. PEN
The shaman and headman of a Yanomamo village takes his young
children to the river to wash them with care and patience.

FAVELA: LIFE OF POVERTY. Institut für Film und Bild, 1974.
17 min. color. FI
Based on Carolina Maria de Jesus book, "Diary of Poverty," describing her poverty and misery in a favela of Sao Paulo.

THE FEAST. T. Asch, N. Chagnon, 1968. 29 min. color.
PEN, NAC
Discusses an alliance between hostile Yanomamo villages of northern
Brazil and southern Venezuela, formed through feasting, trading,
dancing, and chanting. Without narration.

FIREWOOD. T. Asch, N. Chagnon, 1975. 10 min. color. PEN
Shows a woman doing her daily wood collecting. A description of
typical life in a Yanomamo Indian community.

FLAVIO. Elektra, 1964. 12 min. b/w. MGH
Black American photographer and filmmaker Gordon Parks directed,
wrote and photographed this account of slum life in Rio de Janeiro
as seen through the eyes of a twelve-year-old boy.

FOOD GATHERING. International Film Foundation, 1971. 11 min.
    color. EFD, IFF
Shows how the Waika and Makiritare Indians of the Orinoco River
area gather food.

GANGA ZUMBA. Carlos Diegues and Jarbas Barbosa, 1963. 99
    min. b/w. In Portuguese with English subtitles. Directed
    by Carlos Diegues; adapted by Leoppoldo Seran, Rubem Rocha
    Filho and Carlos Diegues, from the novel by Joao Felicio dos
    Santos; photography by Fernando Duarte; music by M. Santos.
    With Antonio Pilango, Leo Garcia, Eliazer Gomes. NYF
How black slaves escaped from the sugar plantations in 1641 to
establish an independent state, a symbol of freedom, that survived
for fifty years. Drawn from legend and historical fact.

GEOGRAPHY OF SOUTH AMERICA: BRAZIL. Coronet, 1961. 13
    min. color. COR
A survey of the rich resources, plantations and big cities of Brazil.

THE GIVEN WORD. (KEEPER OF PROMISES.) Oswaldo Massaini,
    1962. 98 min. b/w. In Portuguese with English subtitles.
    Directed by Anselmo Duarte; written by Anselmo Duarte, based
    on the play "O Pagador de Promessas" by Dias Gomes; photog-
    raphy by Chick Fowle; music by Gabriel Migliori. With Leo-
    nardo Vilar, Gloria Menezes, Dionizio Azevedo. MAC[1]
About a simple peasant who carries an enormous cross to the
church door as offering in gratitude for the recovery of his injured
donkey but is denied permission to enter because he made the
pledge of his offering at a voodoo ritual.

THE GODS AND THE DEAD. (OS DEUSES E OS MORTOS.) Ruy
    Guerra, 1971. 97 min. color. In Portuguese with English
    subtitles. Directed by Ruy Guerra; screenplay by Ruy Guerra,
    Flavio Imperior, Paulo Jose; photography by Dib Lutfi; music
    by Milton Nascimento; produced by Freddy Rozenburg. With
    Othon Bastos, Norma Bengell, Ruy Polanah, Itala Nandl, Nelson
    Xavier. NYF
Two rival plantation owners fight for power but are doomed by exporters and an economic depression. Although filled with violence,
this is a powerful statement about poverty and corruption.

HOW TASTY WAS MY LITTLE FRENCHMAN. (COMO ERA GOS-
TOSO O MEU FRANCES.) Nelso Pereira dos Santos, 1971.
80 min. color. In Tupi Indian dialect with English subtitles.
Directed by Nelson Pereira dos Santos; screenplay by dos
Santos and Luis Carlos Barreio. With Arduino Colasanti,
Ana Maria Magalhaes, Ital Natur. NYF
The tale of a Frenchman captured by a tribe of naked Brazilian In-
dians in the sixteenth century. He tries to help them in the rivalry
between the tribes but is eventually eaten. A comic allegory and
an anthropological reconstruction.

HUNGER FOR LOVE. (FOME DE AMOR.) Herbert Richers and
Paulo Porto, 1969. 75 min. b/w. In Portuguese with English subtitles. Directed by Nelson Pereira dos Santos; photography by Dib Lutfi. With Leila Diniz, Irene Stefania, Arduino
Colasanti and Paula Porto. MGH
A cinema novo film describing the frustration of political life in
contemporary Brazil in a story about a marriage, an attempted
murder, and escape.

INCIDENT IN THE MATTO GROSSO. BBC and Odyssey, 1967.
(Central and South America series.) 25 min. color. TL
The ceremonies and problems of central Brazil's Indians. Narrated
by Lowell Thomas.

JOURNEY TO CHINALE. Willard Baldwin, 1970. 25 min. color.
MGH
Follows an Indian family, the only survivors of an epidemic, in
their travels from their Brazilian village to Surinam where more
of their people, the Oyanas, live.

JOURNEY TO THE MAKIRITARE. International Film Foundation,
1971. (Indians of the Orinoco: The Makiritare Series.) 9
min. color. EFD, IFF
Shows the cameramen's adventurous trip up the Orinoco and Padamo
Rivers to the area where the Makiritare Indians live--a region that
includes part of Brazil and Venezuela.

JUNGLE FARMING. International Film Foundation, 1971. (Indians
of the Orinoco: The Makiritare Series.) 10 min. color.
EFD, IFF
A description of the Makiritare Indians of the Orinoco region that
includes part of Brazil and Venezuela and how they do their farming.

THE KINGDOM IN THE JUNGLE. Adrian Cowell, n.d. 30 min.
color. ITC
The true story of two brothers who for 25 years have helped Indians
from Brazil's primitive jungles to cope with the contemporary world
outside.

THE LAND BURNS. Raymundo Gleyzer, 1968. 12 min. b/w.
English narration. TRI

A story of a family that settled on an abandoned ranch in the ser-
tao, the northeastern drought region of Brazil where the average
life expectancy is 27 years. Now several years later, with seven
children gone and only four left, the family decides to go to the
city where they hope life will be better.

LAND IN ANGUISH. Glauber Rocha, 1967. 115 min. b/w. Di-
    rected by Glauber Rocha. With Jardel Filho, Paulo Autran,
    Jose Lewgoy, Glauce Rocha. HCW
Set in a mythical South American country during a political campaign, the story concerns a poet-journalist who is shot down by
the police and, as he lies dying, reflects on the oppressive past.

LIFELINE AMAZON. ACI, 1970. 10 min. color. ACI
A strip along the Amazon River shows the hard life of the people
who reside by the river. Shows the town of Manaus, Brazil,
2,000 miles up the river, that serves as the key market for the
people's products.

MACUMBA. NBC, n.d. 15 min. b/w. SEF
About the many spiritist cults and practices in Brazil.

A MAN AND HIS WIFE MAKE A HAMMOCK. T. Asch, N. Chag-
    non, 1975. 9 min. color. PEN
The headman of a Yanomamo village, in the area of southern Venezuela and northern Brazil where the Yanomamo people live, is
shown weaving a hammock while his family watches.

MATRAGA. Roberto Santos, 1966. 110 min. b/w. In Portu-
    guese with English subtitles. Directed by Roberto Santos; based
    on a novel by Joao Soares, Maria Ribeiro. With Leonardo
    Vilar, Jofre Soares, Maria Ribeiro. HCW
About a violent man who is degraded by his enemies but eventually
is redeemed through religion.

MEMORIES OF HELEN. (MEMORIAS DE HELENA.) David Neves,
    1971. 75 min. color. In Portuguese with English subtitles.
    Directed by David Neves. NYF
In Rio a girl shows her boy friend home movies of her girlhood in
a town in Minas Garais. Like old snapshots, the movies provide
a framework for this romantic story of the girl's once comfortable
but limited world which is destroyed by a disillusioning love affair.

MEMORIES OF THE CANGACO. Thomas Farkas, Documentaries
    Cinema E. Television, 1965. 26 min. b/w. Directed by
    Paulo Gil Soares. NYF
"Cangaco" is the traditional death by violence performed by the
cangaceiros, the bandits of northeastern Brazil. This is the story
of the famous cangaceiro, Limpiao, as revealed through song,
legend and interviews.

NEW HORIZONS: BRAZIL. Pan-American World Airways, n.d.
    22 min. color. ASF, PAN

A travelogue designed to promote tourism in Brazil. Shows scenic highlights.

OS FUZIS. (THE GUNS.) Ruy Guerra, 1963. 109 min. b/w.
  In Portuguese with English subtitles. Directed by Ruy Guerra.
  NYF
The first cinema novo film shown outside of Brazil, a prize-winning effort that describes the barren northeastern section of Brazil.
A powerful merchant convinces the government that troops should be sent to maintain order among the starving peasants who are suffering from a recent drought. A peasant is shot and loads of food are carted away. Finally the people attack the Sacred Ox in a religious procession for food.

PLANTATION BOY. (MENINO DE ENGENHO.) Walter Lima,
  Jr., 1965. 85 min. b/w. Directed by Walter Lima, Jr.
  Rest of credits and cast unlisted. NYF
Based on Jose lins do Rego's novel about industrialization of the northeast area of Brazil as seen from a child's viewpoint. Includes frank treatment of sexual discovery among children.

PROPHET OF HUNGER. Maurice Capouilla, 1970. 93 min.
  b/w. In Portuguese with English subtitles. Directed by
  Maurice Capouilla. Rest of credits and cast unlisted. TRI
An allegory about a circus performer who, despite his variety of tricks, finds audiences bored. When he has himself nailed to a cross to attract attention, he is jailed for the sacrilege of imitating Christ. Finally he goes 100 days without food, breaking all records to become "World Hunger Champion."

THE RAFT. Sluizer, 1973. 29 min. color. PHO
The raft is the means of transportation on the Parnaiba River in Brazil. Follows the trip of one household down the River to sell homemade earthenware and other goods along the way.

TERRA EM TRANSE. Glauber Rocha, n.d. 115 min. b/w.
  In Portuguese with English subtitles. Directed by Glauber
  Rocha. With Jardel Filho, Paulo Autran, Jose Lewgoy,
  Glauce Rocha. ICW
Brazilian director Glauber Rocha's film is set in a mythical South American country. An aristocratic intellectual ponders his life as he lies dying, shot by the oppressive police.

THREE DAYS RESPITE. Sluizer, 1974. 15 min. color. PHO
A carnival celebration in northeast Brazil with three days of relief from daily problems for rich and poor alike.

THE TRIBE THAT HIDES FROM MAN. NET, 1973. 62 min.
  color. IND
Brazilian explorers Orlando and Claudio Villas Boas are seen hunting for an Indian tribe of the Amazon jungles, who kill on sight, to rescue them from the new "Civilization" of hunters and prospectors.

TROPICI. (TROPICS.) Italian TV, 1969. 87 min. b/w. In
  Portuguese with English subtitles. Directed by Gianni Amico.
  With Joel Barcelos, Janira Santiago. NYF
The story of an impoverished family's trip from Brazil's northeast
to Sao Paulo. Contrasts life in a shanty with the father's eventual
job--construction work on a Hilton hotel.

VILLAGE LIFE. International Film Foundation, 1971. (Indians of
  the Orinoco: The Makiritare Series.) 12 min. color. EFD,
  IFF
About the village life of the Makiritare Indians, a group whose life
style is described as but a "step from the Stone Age." Emphasizes
values that urban man has lost.

WOODWINDS AND DANCE. International Film Foundation, 1971.
  (Indians of the Orinoco: The Makiritare Series.) 10 min.
  color. EFD, IFF
Shows Makiritare Indians making musical instruments.

THE XINGUANA: ABORIGINES OF SOUTH AMERICA. Vision,
  1971. 29 min. color. MGH
A study of the Xinguana people of Central Brazil who live untouched
by outside influences in the jungle area of the Xingu River.

YANOMAMO: A MULTI-DISCIPLINARY STUDY. T. Asch, N.
  Chagnon, J. Neel, 1970. 45 min. color. PEN, NAC
A study of the Yanomamo Indians of southern Venezuela and north-
ern Brazil from the biologist's and anthropologist's points of view.

ZECA. Sluizer, 1974. 19 min. color. PHO
Focuses on a cowherd (vaqueiro) or cowboy, of Northeastern Brazil,
his work, social life and family. Pictures him as a product of his
environment.

Chile

A VALPARAISO. Argos, 1963. 30 min. b/w. In French with
  English subtitles. MGH
Director Joris Ivens' award-winning film about the Chilean port, a
city of poverty and prosperity.

THE ANDES: CHILE'S BARRIER. Harry Grubbs, 1947. 11 min.
  color. EFD, IFB
How the climate and topography affect the life of the people of
Chile.

ATACAMA DESERT. U.S. National Audiovisual Center, 1943. 18
  min. b/w. UCO, UWY
About the hot, dry desert area of Chile, the people who live and
work there, and the mining methods of the 1940s used to produce
nitrate.

CAMPAMENTO.   Avram Nowak, 1973.   26 min.   color.   IMP,
   TRI
The Chilean Socialist Revolution as seen through the eyes of the
determined residents of a Santiago slum.   An award-winning film.

CHILE.   McGraw-Hill, 1965.   15 min.   color.   MGH, UMN
Examines daily life of a boy in Santiago, Chile with attention to
background of urban and rural life, agricultural resources.

CHILE AND ARGENTINA.   Sterling, 1973.   (The Latin American
   Series: A Focus on People.)   19 min.   color.   SEF
A report on the two countries with the highest standard of living in
South America.   Discusses Chile's Marxist government and its
crises stemming from the move to nationalization.

CHILE AND COSTA RICA, TWO LATIN AMERICAN NEIGHBORS.
   United World, 1964.   17 min.   color.   UEVA
How the people of Chile and Costa Rica develop their natural re-
sources.

CHILE PUTS ON LONG PANTS.   NET, 1971.   30 min.   color.
   IMP
A study of modern Chile in which Marxist President Allende takes
over copper mines, industry is nationalized, the peasants form cooperatives, and the Congress modifies Chile's constitution.

CHILE WITH POEMS AND GUNS.   Lucha Educational Films Collective and the Los Angeles Group for Latin American Solidarity,
   1973.   55 min.   b/w.   In Spanish and English with English
   subtitles.   TRI
About the military coup that cast out Salvador Allende's Popular
Unity government in 1973.   Attempts to correct distorted versions
of what actually happened as provided in the news media.   Includes
interviews with North American experts on Chile, workers who discuss their own observations in Chile, and reports by survivors of
the coup.

COMPANERO.   Stanley Foreman, 1974.   60 min.   color.   NYF
Tells through an interview with his widow the story of the folk
singer, Victor Jara, who was killed in Chile's military coup in
1973.

COMPANERO PRESIDENTE.   1971.   70 min.   b/w.   English narration.   IMP
An interview with leaders of different points of view--Regis De-
bray, proponent of guerrilla warfare and Marxist president, Salvador Allende.

GEOGRAPHY OF SOUTH AMERICA: COUNTRIES OF THE ANDES.
   Coronet, 1961.   10 1/2 min.   color.   COR, UCO
Bolivia, Ecuador, Chile, and Peru are the countries covered in this
survey of their geographical and cultural aspects.

HOMMAGE TO NICANOR PARRA.   Jaime Barrios, 1968.   44 min.
    b/w.   In Spanish; no subtitles.   FMCO
Chilean filmmaker Jaime Barrios, who now resides in New York,
made this film about Chilean poet Nicanor Parra reading his poetry
during the latter's visit to New York.

HOUSES OR SHIT.   (CASA O MIERDA.)   Carlos Flores and Guil-
    lermo Cahn.   18 min.   b/w.   In Spanish.   TRI
The Mapuche Indians in their struggle for housing seize land and
set up a camp as demonstration of the tactics proposed by Chile's
Revolutionary Movement of the Left.

I AM PABLO NERUDA.   Harold Mantell, 1967.   28 min.   b/w.
    MGH
Pablo Neruda, Chilean poet, is discussed in regard to his life and
work.   Anthony Quayle provides the narration.

INTERVIEW WITH PRESIDENT SALVADOR ALLENDE.   Dove,
    1971.   31 min.   color.   IMP, NYF
An interview with Allende, the Marxist elected president of Chile
in 1970 and the antithesis of typical revolutionary leaders.

INTRODUCTION TO CHILE.   Chile/ICAIC, 1972.   60 min.   b/w.
    In Spanish with English subtitles and narration.   TRI
A Chilean-Cuban co-production which reports the accomplishments
of the three years of Salvador Allende's Popular Unity government.
Directed by Miguel Torres.

THE JACKAL OF NAHUELTORO.   Cine Experimental de la Uni-
    versidad de Chile and Cinematografica Tercer Mundo, 1969.
    95 min.   b/w.   In Spanish with English subtitles.   Directed
    and written by Miguel Littin; photographed by Hector Rios;
    edited by Pedro Chaskel; music by Sergio Ortega.   With Nel-
    son Villagra, Shenda Roman and Marcelo Romo.   TRI
This is Chilean director Miguel Littin's first feature film, a reenactment of a murder case of 1963 in which a poor drunken peasant murdered a woman and her five children, was tried and executed.   The film realistically reveals the social horrors which led
to the tragedy.

LOS MAPUCHI.   (THE MAPUCHE.)   Carlos Flores and Guillermo
    Cahn, 1971.   20 min.   b/w.   In Spanish.   TRI
Using a popular Indian song as background, this film retraces the
white man's arrival in Chile and his subsequent seizure of Mapuche
Indian land.   Describes the present-day practices of the Indians to
retrieve their land.

PABLO NERUDA: POET.   Douglas Harris and Dr. Eugenia Neves,
    1972.   30 min.   b/w.   In Spanish and English versions.   TRI
An interview with Latin America's renowned poet made shortly before his death.   Includes poetry readings and commentary tracing
his artistic development.

PEOPLE OF CHILE. Harry Grubbs, 1947. 22 min. color. IFB,
    UCA
A comprehensive study of the Chilean people, their background,
customs, problems, resources. One of the few surveys of Chile
available on film.

THE PROMISED LAND. Miguel Littin, 1973. 110 min. color.
    In Spanish with English subtitles. No credits listed. TRI
This is Chile's first widescreen color epic--a story based on actual
events of the 1930s, a time of social and economic upheaval in
Chile. Using myth, music, and spectacle, the film shows how a
group of peasants and workers are massacred after they occupy
some unused government land and try to spread their revolution to
a nearby town. Directed by Miguel Littin.

QUE HACER. Loboc, 1972. 90 min. color. In Spanish and
    English versions. Directed by Saul Landau, Nina Serrano,
    Raul Ruiz; music by Country Joe McDonald. With Sandra
    Archer, Anibal Reyna, Richard Stahl, Lucho Alarcon, Pablo
    de la Barra, Jorge Yanez. IMP
A feature film that documents the Chilean political situation. Includes a scene in which Salvador Allende, then President of Chile,
addresses a rally and talks to the filmmakers.

SOUTH CHILE. U.S. National Audiovisual Center, 1945. 21 min.
    b/w. UCO
One of the few films that describes the region at the southern tip
of South America--Patagonia. Includes scenes of agricultural
work.

VALPARAISO MI AMOR. Cine Nuevo, 1970. 85 min. b/w. In
    Spanish with English subtitles. Directed and written by Aldo
    Francia; photographed by Diego Bonacina; edited by Carlos
    Piaggio; music by Gustavo Becerra. With Hugo Carcamo, Sara
    Astica, Rigoberto Rojo, Liliana Cabrera, and Pedro Alvarez.
    TRI
A grim, neo-realist story and social indictment against Chile's
legal system--a poor slum family's plight after the father is arrested for stealing food.

VENCEREMOS! Pedro Chaskel, 1970. 20 min. b/w. In Spanish
    with English subtitles. TRI
A collage of sequences that reports the contrast between the poor
and the rich of Chilean society and the joyful demonstrations after
Salvador Allende's election in 1970.

WHEN THE PEOPLE AWAKE. Tricontinental, 1972/73. 60 min.
    color. In Spanish with English subtitles and narration. TRI
A Chilean documentary which reviews the country's social history
and then examines the political dynamics and technological developments of today in relation to the popular election of Salvador Allende, the first Marxist President in Latin America.

Colombia

CAMILO TORRES.   Tricontinental, 1965.   10 min.   b/w.   In
    Spanish.   TRI
The last interview made in Colombia by Father Camilo Torres before joining the guerrilla movement.   He explains why he made
his decision and why the revolution is not anti-Christian.

COLOMBIA.   Centron, 1964.   18 min.   color.   MGH
A look at Colombia through the eyes of one family, and a camera
tour of the capital city, other industrial and agricultural centers,
and the important seaport of Barranquilla.

COLOMBIA.   United World, n. d.   16 min.   color.   UEVA
Examines Bogota and gives a comprehensive view of Colombia.

COLOMBIA AND VENEZUELA.   Encyclopaedia Britannica Educa-
    tional Corporation, 1961.   2nd ed.   19 min.   color.   EBEC,
    UCO
Shows the respective lives of a Colombian coffee grower, a Venezuelan professor, and a Lake Maracaibo oil worker in the geographical settings where they live.

COLOMBIA, CROSSROADS OF THE AMERICAS.   Julian Bryan,
    1942.   27 min.   b/w.   UCO
Life in Colombia as seen in the 1940s.   Features the home of a
foremost family in Bogota.

COLOMBIA 70.   Tricontinental, 1970.   5 min.   b/w.   In Spanish
    with English subtitles.   TRI
Shows a poor woman dying in Bota surrounded by a world of wealth.

GEOGRAPHY OF SOUTH AMERICA: FIVE NORTHERN COUN-
    TRIES.   Coronet, 1972.   10 1/2 min.   color.   COR, UCO
A look at the people, their way of life, and the physical aspects of
Colombia, Venezuela, Guyana, Surinam, and French Guiana.

GOLPEANDO EN LA SELVA.   Santiago Alvarez, 1967.   15 min.
    b/w.   TWN
Cuban filmmaker Santiago Alvarez' report on the urban poor and the
guerrilla struggle in Colombia.   With soundtrack of music and
some narration.

ONE DAY I ASKED.   Julia Alvarez, 1970.   9 min.   b/w.   In
    Spanish with English subtitles.   TRI
A study of the religious alienation of exploited people.   With revolutionary songs as background.

A PROBLEM OF POWER.   National Council of Churches, 1970.
    45 min.   color.   NACC
Presents interviews with peasants and landowners about the socio-
economic problems in Colombia.

QUEST FOR ELDORADO. Francisco Norden, n. d. 18 min. color.
MAC[1]
Shows the Andes Indians' gold works of art and stone monoliths
found near Bogota against a background of Colombian mountains.

REPUBLIC OF COLOMBIA. Pan-American World Airways, 1954.
11 min. color. IFB, UMN
Shows cities, geographic features, resources, agriculture with economic, historic and cultural background.

SOUTH AMERICA: CARTAGENA, A COLONIAL CITY. Art Evans,
1969. 17 min. color. BFA
Follows a boy of Cartagena, Colombia through a typical day revealing unique aspects of South American life.

WHAT IS DEMOCRACY? Carlos Alvarez, 1971. 42 min. b/w.
In Spanish with English subtitles. TRI
Evaluates Colombia's special brand of democracy as practiced over
the past forty years. A critical view punctuated with cartoons,
newsreels, and photographs.

WOMANPOWER: THE PEOPLE'S CHOICE. United Nations, 1974.
28 min. color. UN
Shows three women running for election in Colombia--one wants to
be president, another a senator, and the third a member of the
Bogota City Council.

Ecuador

BOLIVIA, PERU AND ECUADOR. Sterling, 1973. (The Latin
American Series: A Focus on People.) 19 min. color. SEF
The culture of the three countries, reforms and political changes
now taking place.

ECUADOR. Frederik Lek, 1963. 16 min. color. MGH
Ecuador is presented as a country of contrasts with its equatorial
region, Andes Mountains, humid as well as cool areas, and a wide
range of cultures from sophisticated cities to primitive villages.

ECUADOR: LAND OF THE EQUATOR. LeMont, 1965. 17 min.
color. LMF
Describes Ecuador's Spanish and Indian heritage and gives views of
the city of Quito as well as industries and crafts.

GEOGRAPHY OF SOUTH AMERICA: COUNTRIES OF THE ANDES.
Coronet, 1961. 10 1/2 min. color. COR, UCO
Bolivia, Ecuador, Chile and Peru are the Andean countries covered
in this survey of their geographical and cultural aspects.

OVER THE ANDES IN ECUADOR. Films Inc. , 1969. 18 min.
color. FI, UMN
Follows a crate of machine parts from Guayaquil to Quito, over the
mountains to the Amazon while studying the people along the way.

THE SOUND OF RUSHING WATER.   Ricardo Tankamash and Bruce
    Horowitz, 1973.   40 min.   color.   In Spanish and Shuar with
    English subtitles and narration.   TRI
The Shuar people (the Jivaro or "headhunter" Indians) relate their
history of struggle against the Inca and Spanish Empires.   They also
tell of present efforts to keep their cultural identity and traditions.
With authentic Shuar music.

VALLEY OF THE OLD ONES.   Gene Ayers, 1974.   26 min.   color.
    TL
The incredible story of a small community of people in Vilcabamba,
Ecuador who have lived to be over 100 years of age.   Explores
their way of life and their future as civilization creeps nearer.

Guiana
(includes Dutch Guiana [Surinam], French Guiana)

GEOGRAPHY OF SOUTH AMERICA: FIVE NORTHERN COUN-
    TRIES.   Coronet, 1972.   10 1/2 min.   color.   COR, UCO
A look at the people, their way of life, and the physical aspects
of Colombia, Venezuela, Guyana, Surinam, and French Guiana.

GUYANA: NATION BUILDING.   NET, 1971.   20 min.   color.
    IND
Reveals recent political and economic developments in Guyana.
Includes conversations with Prime Minister Forbes.

GUYANA: SOUTH AMERICA'S NEWEST NATION.   Maritime Col-
    lege, New York, 1969.   18 min.   color.   MGH, UUT
An analytical look at Guyana, the people and environment of an undeveloped nation of rich resources.

LEENYA, DAUGHTER OF THE NOBLE BLACKS OF SURINAM.
    International Film Bureau, 1973.   11 min.   color.   EFD, IFB
A black girl of Surinam tells her personal view of her people, her
family, her land, and her own life and hopes for the future.

SURINAM, A SONG OF DEMOCRACY.   Educational Film, n. d.   28
    min.   color.   EFD
A report on the Dutch commonwealth in northeastern South America,
including its diverse peoples: Chinese, Javanese, Hindus, Africans, Europeans, American Indians, and Creoles.   Each group
tells its story of why its members came to Surinam.

WE PEOPLE OF SURINAM.   Netherlands Government, n. d.   26
    min.   color.   UUT
Surinam (Dutch Guiana) is presented in terms of cultural and racial
intermingling, efforts to improve education, industry and government.

Paraguay

CUARAHY OHECHA. D. Dubosc, 1968. 26 min. b/w. PEN
Typical daily life of a Paraguayan peasant family with scenes of
work at home, with the crops, at play, and eating a midday meal.

GEOGRAPHY OF SOUTH AMERICA: ARGENTINA, PARAGUAY,
URUGUAY. Coronet, 1961. 10 1/2 min. color. COR, UCO
The geographic factors, achievements and problems of three coun-
tries located on the Plata-Parana River system.

PARAGUAY: A NEW FRONTIER. Hoefler-Disney, 1958. 20 min.
color. UCA
A look at the many nationalities of people in the wild Chaco of
Paraguay.

PARAGUAY AND URUGUAY: CONTRAST ON THE PLATA. Herbert Millington, 1967. (Our Latin American Neighbors Series.)
17 min. color. MGH
Shows the people and physical characteristics of the two South
American countries and discusses the progress now being made in
Paraguay at the same time that Uruguay tries to maintain its high
standard of living.

Peru

AGUA SALADA. (BITTER WATERS.) Arturo Sinclair F., 1974.
12 min. b/w. TEX
A talented Peruvian filmmaker has created a contemporary Passion
in a story about two fishermen, a father and son, involved in a
tragedy. Uses Johann Sebastian Bach's "Passion According to St.
John" as a dramatic musical parallel to the powerful visual images.

AMAHUACA: A TROPICAL FOREST SOCIETY IN SOUTHEASTERN
PERU. G. Dole, 1973. 25 min. color. PEN
Studies the daily routines and ritual of an unacculturated group of
Amahuaca people in the eastern uplands of Peru. Gives details of
maize cultivation and processing.

ANCIENT INCA INDIANS OF SOUTH AMERICA. Encyclopaedia
Britannica Educational Corporation, 1972. 8 min. color.
EBEC
About the achievements of the largest empire in the ancient world
of the Western Hemisphere.

THE ANCIENT PERUVIAN. International Film Foundation, 1968.
29 min. color. EFD, IFF, UCA, UCO, UUT
An account of Peru's ancient civilizations including those of the
Chavin, Paracas, Nasca, Mochica, Tiahuanaco, and Inca peoples.
Live action photography intercut with animation by Gerald McDer-
mott.

ANTHROPOLOGY: THE STUDY OF PEOPLE. Wayne Mitchell,
      1971. 16 1/2 min. color. BFA
The methods of anthropologists are studied in this close-up view of
Peru's Indian people. Shows the relationship between their sophisticated pre-Columbian ancestors and the present-day descendants who
live a life of poverty.

BOLIVIA, PERU AND ECUADOR. Sterling, 1973. (The Latin
      American Series: A Focus on People.) 19 min. color. SEF
The culture of the three countries, the reforms and political changes
now taking place.

BROTHERS OF THE SUN. BBC and Odyssey, 1967. (Central and
      South America Series.) 25 min. color. TL
A view of the lost city of Machu Picchu and a climbing trip to the
summit of the Andes. Narrated by Lowell Thomas.

CUZCO ... IN THE VALLEY OF THE INCAS. Tom Schroeppel,
      1974. 20 min. color. SCHR
Shows sites of the surviving landmarks of the Inca Empire where
rituals were performed and scenes of present-day descendants at
work and in religious ceremonies.

EMPIRE OF THE SUN. CCM, n.d. 90 min. color. MAC
A documentary about the hard life of the Incas' descendants who
live amid the ruins of the once-great civilization.

FAMILY OF THE MOUNTAINS: A PERUVIAN VILLAGE. McGraw-
      Hill and Pan American World Airways with Vision Associates,
      1971. 12 min. color. MGH
Follows the children of a Peruvian village family who live in the
Andes. Peruvian music serves as background to this life portrait.

FARMERS OF THE ANDES. Harry Grubbs, 1947. 11 min. color.
      IFB
How the Incas survive at 10,000 to 15,000 feet in an agricultural
community.

GEOGRAPHY OF SOUTH AMERICA: COUNTRIES OF THE ANDES.
      Coronet, 1961. 10 1/2 min. color. COR, UCO
Bolivia, Ecuador, Chile and Peru are the Andean countries covered
in this survey of their geographical and cultural aspects.

THE GREEN WALL. Amaru, 1970. 110 min. color. In Spanish
      with English subtitles. Directed and written by Armando
      Robles Godoy; photographed by Mario Robles Godoy. With
      Julio Aleman, Sandra Riva, Raul Martin. MAC[1]
Acclaimed best picture in four international film festivals, one of
the most honored Latin American films ever made. This is the
director's autobiographical story about a family who leave their life
in Lima for a new home in the lush Peruvian jungle.

HIGHLAND INDIANS OF PERU.   Films Inc. , 1969.   18 min.   color.
   FI, VEC
Questions the relative merits of life in the highlands versus the
city, Lima, as a suitable habitat for Peru's Indians.

INCAS.   Coronet, 1961.   10 1/2 min.   color.   COR
With footage made in existing Peruvian villages and at sites of
archeological remains, this film discusses the Incas' government
and economy as well as their cultural life.   Includes a reenactment
of worship to the sun-god.

THE INCAS: ANCIENTS OF THE ANDES.   Harry Grubbs, 1947.
   10 min.   color.   EFD, IFB
A brief survey of the Incas' life before Spanish colonization.   Presents rare views of ancient settlements never discovered by the
conquerors.

LIFE AROUND LAKE TITICACA.   Hartley, 1970.   14 min.   color.
   ACI
About the topography, Indian culture, and economic factors of the
Lake Titicaca region between Bolivia and Peru.

LIFE IN THE HIGH ANDES.   Coronet, 1961.   10 1/2 min.   color.
   COR
A visit with an Indian family who live in a Peruvian mountain valley.
Shows influences of the ancient Incan civilization and a modern
market day in a village.

THE LOST CITY IN THE ANDES.   Simmel Meservey, 1954.   14
   min.   color.   UUT
Tells the story of Machu Picchu, lost since the Pizarro conquest
and rediscovered in 1911.   Shows the extraordinary architectural
features.

PEOPLE OF PERU.   Harry Grubbs, 1947.   11 min.   color.   IFB
About the city people, the plateau and jungle dwellers, and the effect of the geography on their life style.

PERU.   McGraw-Hill, 1964.   17 min.   color.   MGH
Contrasts between the rich and the poor; the life of a shepherd boy
of the Andes; Cuzco; Machu Picchu; Lima.

PERU: INCA HERITAGE.   Hartley, 1970.   18 min.   color.   ACI
An award-winning film that examines the Peruvian Indians of today
in relation to their Inca roots, the remains of which are now in
ruins.   Presents a good look at Machu Picchu and other great cultural contributions of the Indians.

PERU: PEOPLE OF THE ANDES.   Encyclopaedia Britannica Edu-
   cational Corporation, 1959.   2nd ed.   16 min.   color.   EBEC,
   UCO, UUT, UWY
How people now live in the Chincheros Valley, former center of the
Inca empire, the tenant farmers and Indian village dwellers.

PERU: UPPER AMAZON REGION.   Hoefler-Disney, 1957.   17
    min.   color.   UCA
About an American and his family who live in an isolated village
near the rain forest of Eastern Peru where he studies crop development.

PERUVIAN ARCHAEOLOGY.   Pan American Union, 1954.   10 min.
    color.   UCA
Shows Peruvian artifacts and the Inca Temple of the Sun and Machu
Picchu.

SO THAT MEN ARE FREE.   CBS, 1963.   27 min.   b/w.   MGH,
    UCA
Describes how the Incas' descendants, the Viconsinos, have lived
for 400 years on a hacienda until recent times when a university
grant made it possible to prepare them for twentieth century life
and freedom.

SOUTH AMERICA: INDIANS OF THE ANDES.   Art Evans, 1970.
    20 1/2 min.   color.   BFA
The daily life of an Inca family in the Andes Mountains far from
contemporary urban society's influences.

EL VISITANTE.   (THE VISITATION.)   Arturo Sinclair F. , 1975.
    9 min.   b/w.   TEX
An example of film art used to express the emotions of a contem-
porary woman.   Without dialogue; uses only sounds and images.
Made by a Mexican filmmaker who now resides in Peru.

WEALTH OF THE ANDES.   Du Art, 1943.   19 min.   color.   UUT
A visit to the Cerro de Pasco mining district deep in the Andes
Mountains of Peru.   Includes glimpses of the Central Railway sys-
tem.

Uruguay

EL PROBLEMA DE LA CARNE.   Third World Cinematheque, 1968.
    21 min.   b/w.   In Spanish.   TRI
A discussion of the problem of the meat industry in Uruguay which
analyzes its history and development as well as the reasons for its
decline partly due to foreign interests.   Shows a strike by slaughter-
house workers to keep their company from closing.   Directed by
Mario Handler in cooperation with the Third World Cinematheque.

GEOGRAPHY OF SOUTH AMERICA: ARGENTINA, PARAGUAY,
    URUGUAY.   Coronet, 1961.   10 1/2 min.   color.   COR, UCO
The geographic factors, achievements and problems of three countries on the Plata-Parana River system.

IN THE JUNGLE THERE IS LOTS TO DO.   Tricontinental, 1972.
    17 min.   color.   In Spanish with English narration.   TRI
An animated film based on a letter from a Uruguayan political

prisoner to his daughter in which he tries to explain why he has been imprisoned in such a way as to get his message past the prison censor. His solution is an imaginative allegory about jungle animals who are captured by a hunter, taken to the zoo and locked up in cages. An unusual description of repressive political regimes.

NEW HORIZONS: URUGUAY.   Pan-American World Airways, n. d. 13 min.   color.   ASF, PAN
A travelogue designed to promote tourism in Uruguay.   Contains highlights of scenic locations.

PARAGUAY AND URUGUAY: CONTRAST ON THE PLATA.   Herbert Millington, 1967.   (Our Latin American Neighbors Series.) 17 min.   color.   MGH
Shows the people and physical characteristics of the two South American countries and discusses the progress now being made in Paraguay at the same time that Uruguay tries to maintain its high standard of living.

TUPAMAROS! Jan Lindqvist in cooperation with the National Liberation Movement, Tupamaros, 1972.   50 min.   color.   In Spanish with English subtitles.   TRI
A rare look inside the renowned urban guerrilla organization, Uruguay's National Liberation Movement (MLN), made by Swedish filmmaker Jan Lindqvist and smuggled out of Uruguay with the help of the Tupamaro guerrillas.   A Tupamaro leader is interviewed as are several kidnapped officials.

URUGUAY.   Julian Bryan, 1945.   20 min.   b/w.   UCO, UUT
An old film descriptive of the life of people in Uruguay as compared with that in the U. S.

URUGUAY: NUTRITION SURVEY FILM.   Walter Reed Army Institute of Research, 1964.   30 min.   color.   WRAI
Indicates how the nutrition survey was conducted.   Describes living conditions as well as agriculture and food processing practices.

Venezuela

ARROW GAME.   T. Asch, N. Chagnon, 1975.   7 min.   color. PEN
A group of boys from the Yanomamo people, who live where Brazil and Venezuela meet, shoot blunt arrows at each other in order to practice dodging and shooting.

ASSIGNMENT: VENEZUELA.   Creole Petroleum, 1957.   25 min. b/w.   UUT
A visit with an employee of the Creole Petroleum Corporation assigned to the Maracaibo oil fields in Venezuela.   Shows major cities and the community integration project attempted by the Corporation.

BLOWGUN. International Film Foundation, 1971. (Indians of the
    Orinoco Series.) 13 min. color. EFD, IFF
Shows Makiritare Indian men of the Orinoco River area in Brazil
and Venezuela making blowguns.

CHILDREN'S MAGICAL DEATH. T. Asch, N. Chagnon, 1975. 8
    min. color. PEN
Some young boys are seen pretending to be shamans in imitation of
their fathers.

CLIMBING THE PEACH PALM. T. Asch, N. Chagnon, 1975. 9
    min. color. PEN
A young Yanomamo man ascends a peach palm tree to harvest the
fruit.

COLOMBIA AND VENEZUELA. Encyclopaedia Britannica Educa-
    tional Corporation, 1961. 2nd ed. 19 min. color. EBEC,
    UCO
Shows the respective lives of a Colombian coffee grower, a Venezuelan professor, and a Lake Maracaibo oil worker in the geographical settings where they live.

CRAFTSMAN. International Film Foundation, 1971. (Indians of
    the Orinoco Series.) 12 min. color. EFD, IFF
Studies the crafts of the Makiritare Indian who lives near the borders of Brazil and Venezuela.

F. A. L. N. Dawn, 1965. 30 min. b/w. TWN
About the F. A. L. N. , the armed National Liberation Front of Venezuela, and what led to its growth in the Venezuelan political scene.

A FATHER WASHES HIS CHILDREN. T. Asch, N. Chagnon, 1975.
    13 min. color. PEN
The shaman and headman of a Yanomamo village takes his young
children to the river to wash them with care and patience.

THE FEAST. T. Asch, N. Chagnon, 1968. 29 min. color.
    PEN, NAC
Discusses an alliance between hostile Yanomamo villages of northern
Brazil and southern Venezuela formed through feasting, trading,
dancing, and chanting. Without narration.

FIREWOOD. T. Asch, N. Chagnon, 1975. 10 min. color. PEN
Shows a woman doing her daily wood collecting. A description of
typical life in a Yanomamo Indian community.

FOOD GATHERING. International Film Foundation, 1971. 11 min.
    color. EFD, IFF
Shows how the Waika and Makiritare Indians of the Orinoco River
area gather food.

GEOGRAPHY OF SOUTH AMERICA: FIVE NORTHERN COUNTRIES.
    Coronet, 1972. 10 1/2 min. color. COR, UCO

A look at the people, their way of life, and the physical aspects of Colombia, Venezuela, Guyana, Surinam, and French Guiana.

JOURNEY TO THE MAKIRITARE. International Film Foundation, 1971. (Indians of the Orinoco: The Makiritare Series.) 9 min. color. EFD, IFF
Shows the cameramen's adventurous trip up the Orinoco and Padamo Rivers to the area where the Makiritare Indians live--a region that includes part of Brazil and Venezuela.

JUNGLE FARMING. International Film Foundation, 1971. (Indians of the Orinoco: The Makiritare Series.) 10 min. color. EFD, IFF
A description of the Makiritare Indians of the Orinoco region that includes part of Brazil and Venezuela and how they do their farming.

MAGICAL DEATH. Documentary Educational Resources, 1973. 29 min. color. PEN
Reveals the intertwined political and religious roles of the shamans of the Yanomamo Indian people.

A MAN AND HIS WIFE MAKE A HAMMOCK. T. Asch, N. Chagnon, 1075. 9 min. color. PEN
The headman of a Yanomamo village, in the area of southern Venezuela and northern Brazil where the Yanomamo people live, is shown weaving a hammock while his family watches.

A MAN CALLED BEE: STUDYING THE YANOMAMO. N. A. Chagnon, T. Asch, 1974. 42 min. color. DOCE, PEN
Follows anthropologist Napoleon Chagnon as he studies the Yanomamo Indians of Southern Venezuela.

MOSORI MONIKA. McGraw-Hill, 1972. 20 min. color. MGH
About the cultural clash that occurred when in 1945 Spanish Franciscan missionaries went to Venezuela to work with the Warao Indians of the Orinoco River.

OCAMO IS MY TOWN. T. Asch, N. Chagnon, 1975. 22 min. color. PEN
Studies the work of a Salesian priest who has been working for many years to slow down the effect of outer civilization on a Yanomamo village on the Ocamo River, Venezuela.

PEOPLE AND PETROLEUM. Standard Oil, 1959. 27 min. b/w. UCO, UUT, UWY
Presents the oil industry of Venezuela, its history and impact on the people.

VENEZUELA. Centron, 1961. 16 min. color. MGH
A visit with people in the city of Caracas used to make a contrast with the farmer's life--a bare subsistence--in an area with sparse or nonexistent rainfall. Also includes scenes of great oil wealth and iron riches as examples of Venezuela's potential.

VENEZUELA. Films Inc., 1970. 14 min. color. FI, VEC
Pictures modern Venezuela as a nation of extreme contrasts. Presents arguments for and against nationalization of oil production.

VENEZUELA: LAST CHANCE FOR DEMOCRACY. NET, 1966.
    60 min. b/w. IND
Discusses the strains on the Venezuelan government to fulfill the
people's needs and, at the same time, maintain a democratic system.

VENEZUELA: MARIO'S JOURNEY. Universal Education, 1967.
    21 min. color. UEVA
A lagoon village and a thriving town near a rich oil field are compared. Follows a boy whose family works to produce oil, copra,
and dried coconut with traditional methods.

VENEZUELA: OIL BUILDS A NATION. Sleeping Giant, 1972.
    17 min. color. EBEC
How oil-rich Venezuela plans to build up its economy by developing
the mineral-rich jungle.

VENEZUELA: THE MAKING OF A GOVERNMENT. NET, 1963.
    59 min. b/w. IND
An account of Venezuela's development of democratic government
with interviews involving Past President Betancourt and President-
Elect Leoni.

VILLAGE LIFE. International Film Foundation, 1971. (Indians of
    the Orinoco: The Makiritare Series.) 12 min. color. EFD,
    IFF
About the village life of the Makiritare Indians, a group whose life
style is described as but a "step from the Stone Age." Emphasizes
values that urban man has lost.

WINGS TO VENEZUELA. Pan-American World Airways, 1967.
    15 min. color. ASF, PAN
A travelogue designed to promote tourism in Venezuela. Features
scenic highlights of the country.

WOODWINDS AND DANCE. International Film Foundation, 1971.
    (Indians of the Orinoco: The Makiritare Series.) 10 min.
    color. EFD, IFF
Shows Makiritare Indians making musical instruments.

YANOMAMO: A MULTI-DISCIPLINARY STUDY. T. Asch, N.
    Chagnon, J. Neel, 1970. 45 min. color. PEN, NAC
A study of the Yanomamo Indians of southern Venezuela and northern Brazil from the biologist's and anthropologist's points of view.

West Indies

(Includes Haiti, Dominican Republic, Jamaica, Trinidad, Tobago, Barbados. Cuba covered in separate section, see p. 247.)

ADELAIDE VILLAGE. National Film Board of Canada, 1974. 15
min. color. PHO
An animated film which describes the changing life style of the native people of the Caribbean area. Directed by Montreal artist
Pierre L'Amare whose sketches reflect the vitality of the people of
a Bahama village.

BACKGROUND TO FEDERATION. National Film Board of Canada,
1958. (New Nation in the West Indies Series.) 30 min. b/w.
UCO
An introduction to the Federation of the West Indies formed by
Caribbean states.

BERMUDA, THE ISLAND NOBODY WANTED. Bermuda Trade Development Board, 1968. 28 min. color. BTDB
Mark Twain's thoughts about Bermuda are used in this examination
of that island's history.

THE CARIBBEAN: ANTIGUA, BARBADOS, MARTINIQUE, TRINIDAD, TOBAGO AND JAMAICA. United World, 1966. 17 min.
color. UEVA
A close view of the Caribbean people--their culture, agriculture,
tourism.

THE EIGHTH CONTINENT. Pan-American World Airways, n.d.
13 min. color. ASF, PAN
A tourist travelogue about Latin American islands Grenada, St.
Thomas, Puerto Rico and Martinique.

ETHNIC DANCE: ROUNDTRIP TO TRINIDAD. WGBH-TV, 1960.
(A Time to Dance Series.) 29 min. b/w. IND
Shows a variety of West Indian dances and explains their derivations.
Features Geoffrey Holder and Carmen de Lavallade.

HAITI. National Film Board of Canada, 1957. 30 min. b/w.
UWY
Presents typical scenes of daily life and the unusual trade and language relationship between Haiti and Canada.

INTRODUCTION TO HAITI. U.S. Office of Inter-American Affairs,
1942. 10 min. color. UUT
A tourist film which describes the history and daily life of Haiti.
Shows Port au Prince, Cap-Haitien and Henri Christophe's palace.

ISLANDS OF THE WEST INDIES. Columbia, 1941. 11 min. b/w.
IND
A brief travelogue covering Curaçao, Martinique and Trinidad.

JAMAICA, HAITI, AND THE LESSER ANTILLES.   McGraw-Hill,
   1964.   20 min.   color.   UCO, UWY
Studies the European and African influences on the life of these islands.   Compares the geographic and economic features of the various islands.

JOJOLO.   Grove, 1968.   12 min.   b/w.   UCA
When a Haitian woman goes to work in Paris, her background affects her experiences in the city.

MUSIC FROM OIL DRUMS.   Pete and Toshi Seeger, 1958.   15
   min.   b/w.   MAC[1]
How steel drums are made, tuned and played in Trinidad.

POCOMANIA: A LITTLE MADNESS.   BBC, 1968.   22 min.   b/w.
   TL
Observations of a Jamaican cult, named Pocomania hundreds of
years ago by the Spaniards, their secret ritual, "speaking in
tongues," their performance of a small miracle.

REGGAE.   Horace Ové, 1970.   60 min.   color.   IMP
Based on the 1970 Caribbean Music Festival in England which brought
together some of the leading exponents of reggae music, a type of
Jamaican music.   Shows the impact of reggae on the English working class.

THE RICHES OF THE INDIES.   National Film Board of Canada,
   1958.   (New Nation in the West Indies Series.)   30 min.   b/w.
   UCO
A report on the economic status of the British West Indies in the
year of federation.

SHANGO.   Fritz Henle, 1953.   10 min.   color.   MAC[1]
Geoffrey Holder and his troupe perform authentic dances of Africa
that have become part of the Trinidad musical heritage.   Includes
ritual dance in which a chicken is sacrificed.

THREE BROTHERS IN HAITI.   Visual Education Centre, n. d.
   17 min.   color.   VEC
Tells the story of three brothers who inherit land but, because of
the land's small size, one leaves and the others remain to farm
the land.   Later a United Nations official helps teach the farmers
new techniques.

VOODOO ISLAND.   BBC and Odyssey, 1967.   (Central and South
   America Series.)   25 min.   color.   TL
The role of voodoo in Haiti.   Includes an authentic ceremony.   Nar-
rated by Lowell Thomas.

THE WEST INDIES.   Encyclopaedia Britannica Educational Corporation, 1965.   2nd ed.   22 min.   color.   EBEC, UWY
A view of the West Indies scenic beauty contrasted with below-
standard living conditions for the inhabitants.

WEST INDIES: GEOGRAPHY OF THE AMERICAS. Coronet, 1958.
11 min. color. UWY
A geographic introduction with emphasis on economic development,
resources.

WEST INDIES: TRINIDAD TRAILS. NBC, 1969. 18 min. color.
FI
Records the life of a family living in Point-à-Pierre, an oil well
area in Trinidad.

WINGS TO THE CARIBBEAN. Pan-American World Airways, 1968.
28 min. color. ASF, PAN
A travelogue designed to promote tourism in the Dominican Republic, Antigua, St. Thomas, Tobago, Trinidad, Curaçao, Martinique,
Puerto Rico and Jamaica.

WITCH DOCTOR. Ritter-Young-Lerner Associates, 1952. 9 min.
b/w. MAC[1]
Dancer Jean Leon Destiné dances an impression of a voodoo rite
of a Haitian witch doctor. Original story and choreography by
Jean Leon Destiné.

Cuba

BAY OF PIGS. ICAIC, 1973. 110 min. b/w. In Spanish with
English subtitles. Cinemascope. TRI
A reconstruction of the Bay of Pigs assault by Cuban exile troops
in 1961. Uses interviews with participants, reenactments, documentary footage and photographs. Directed by Manuel Herrera.

LA CAMPANA DE LA ALFABETIZACION. Sergio Nunez Martinez,
1961. 55 min. b/w. In Spanish. TRI
How in 1960 Cuba successfully sponsored a nationwide literacy campaign to go out into the countryside to teach the peasants and workers to read.

CASTRO VS. BATISTA. Metromedia, 1965. 25 min. b/w. VEC
Tells the story of Batista's rise to power in the 1930s, his rule,
and the takeover by Castro and his revolutionary army.

CERRO PELADO. ICAIC, 1967. 60 min. b/w. TWN
About the Pan American Games held in Puerto Rico in 1967 at
which the Cuban athletic team won victories despite efforts to block
their participation. Shows scenes en route aboard the "Cerro
Pelado."

COMPAÑERAS AND COMPAÑEROS. Barbara Stone, David C.
Stone, and Adolfas Mekas, 1970. 80 min. color. In Spanish.
Directed and written by Barbara Stone, David C. Stone and
Adolfas Mekas; photographed by Robert Machover and Robert
Lucativa. MONF
A documentary which explores the consciousness of various Cuban

people: the student, the worker, peasant, soldier, and others.
Shows discussions of guerrilla warfare and efforts toward building
a new world.

CUBA. Kerry Feltham, n. d. 30 min. color/b. w. GRO
Starting with the opening scene at a mass meeting where Fidel
Castro announced Ché Guevara's death, the filmmaker reveals the
moods and points of view of the Cuban people. Presents interviews
and footage contrasting the Batista and Castro regimes.

CUBA: ART AND REVOLUTION. BBC, 1971. 46 min. color.
     TL
Examines the artistic revolution in Cuba, the new film industry,
ballet, and three theatre companies. Also presents leading writers.

CUBA: BATTLE OF THE 10,000,000. Chris Marker, 1970. 60
     min. b/w. NYF
A report on the 1970 period when an anticipated harvest of over
10,000,000 tons failed to materialize. With dialogue between Castro and the Cuban people, including critics.

CUBA: BAY OF PIGS. NBC, n. d. 29 min. b/w. VEC
Includes on-the-spot photography to tell the story of the Bay of
Pigs attempted invasion in terms of its historical significance.

CUBA: THE LAND AND THE PEOPLE. Coronet, 1966. 2nd
     ed. 10 1/2 min. color. COR
Follows a 700-mile trip from Havana to Santiago to show the varied
heritage of the people and the relationship of the island to the U. S.

CUBA: THE MISSILE CRISIS. NBC, 1965. 52 min. b/w. UCA,
     UNE
About the fifteen days in October 1972 when a nuclear conflict over
Cuba was avoided by negotiations of President Kennedy and Premier
Khrushchev.

CUBA TODAY. NBC, 1974. 11 min. color. FI
A look at the economic and educational progress of Cuba.

CUBA VA! Felix Greene, 1971. 76 min. color. IMP
A look at present-day Cuba after the Revolution. Includes an interview with Fidel Castro.

CYCLONE. Santiago Alvarez, n. d. 20 min. b/w. TWN
A documentary about the effects of hurricane and floods as Cuban
people mobilize to save lives and possessions.

DIALOGO CON CHE: CHE IS ALIVE. Jose Rodriguez-Soltero,
     1968. 53 min. b/w. In Spanish. Directed by Jose Rodri-
     guez-Soltero; music by Carlos Gandel. With Rolando Pena,
     Taylor Mead, Ana Maria Fuensalida, Joseph Aliaga, Salvador
     Cruz, Cesar Vallejo Carlos Anduze, Raymond Pinero, Santos
     Negron. FMCO

The first film to deal with the death of Ernesto "Ché" Guevara.
The filmmaker has chosen not to attempt a reenactment of Ché's
life but to have an actor representing him read about his work and
thought.

FIDEL. Saul Landau, 1969. 95 min. color. NYF
Filmmaker Saul Landau and his crew traveled with Fidel Castro on
a five-day tour of Oriente province. The result is a unique portrait of Castro. Also includes interviews with anti-Castro Cubans.

FIDEL CASTRO. David Wolper, 1964. 26 min. b/w. MGH
The life story of Castro and an account of his rise to power in
Cuba.

THE FIDEL CASTRO STORY. Hearst, 1959. 6 min. b/w. UCO
A report on the Cuban revolutionary who overthrew the Batista regime.

FIRST CHANGE OF THE MACHETE. (LA PRIMERA CARGA AL
    MACHETE.) Instituto Cubano del Arte e Industria Cinemato-
    graficos, 1974. 84 min. b/w. In Spanish with English sub-
    titles. Directed by Manuel Octavio Gomez; screenplay Julio
    Garcia Espinosa, Alfredo De Cuelo, Jorge Herrera, and Octa-
    vio Gomez; photography by Jorge Herrera; edited by Nelson
    Rodriguez; music by Leo Brower and Pablo Milanes. With
    Rogoberto Agulia, Idalia Andreus, Miguel Benavides, Carlos
    Bermudez. TRI
A re-creation of October 1868 when Cubans rebelled against Spanish
colonialism. Uses camera techniques to simulate the photographic
work of the mid-nineteenth century.

FOR THE FIRST TIME. ICAIC, 1967. 12 min. b/w. In Spanish
    with English subtitles. TRI
An account of how the Cuban Film Institute took informational and
entertainment films to the remotest villages of Cuba in order to
give everyone exposure to the education and culture formerly re-
served for the privileged people of the large cities.

HISTORIA DE UNA BATALLA. Cuba, 1962. 40 min. b/w. TWN
Uses newsreel footage to show two simultaneous battles--one the
Bay of Pigs invasion effort and the young people's struggle to end
illiteracy among Cuba's rural population. With English soundtrack.

ISLE OF YOUTH. Third World Newsreel, 1969. 15 min. b/w.
    TWN
A report on young Cubans working to convert the Isle of Pines, a
prison site, to an Isle of Youth suited for work, recreation and
education. With Cuban music.

LUCIA. ICAIC, 1969. 160 min. b/w. In Spanish with English
    subtitles. Directed by Humberto Solas. With Raquel Revuelta,
    Adela Legra. TRI
A much acclaimed film, sometimes cited as Cuba's "Gone with the

Wind," about three separate Cuban women named Lucia and three periods in the Cuban struggle for liberation: 1895, Cuba's war for independence from Spain; the 1933 overthrow of the dictator Machado, and in 1960, when a woman learns to read and confronts her husband's macho attitudes.

MEMORIES OF UNDERDEVELOPMENT. Instituto Cubano del Arte e Industria Cinematograficos, 1968. 96 min. b/w. In Spanish with English subtitles. Directed by Tomas Gutierrez Alea; screenplay by Tomas Gutierrez Alea; photographed by Ramon Suarez; edited by Nelson Rodriguez; music by Leo Brouwer. With Sergio Corrieri, Daisy Grandos, Eslinda Nunez, and Beatriz Ponchara. TRI
This is the first post-revolutionary Cuban feature film available in the U. S. --a story about the alienation of an intellectual caught in the fast changing world of revolutionary Cuba. Based on the novel, "Inconsolable Memories," by Edmundo Desnoes.

A MESSAGE FROM GARCIA. Teaching Film Custodians, 1955. (Calvacade of America Series.) 20 min. b/w. IND
The story of the American Lieutenant who, risking his life to gather information about Cuban forces from their General Garcia, managed successfully to bring Garcia's message through in time for the American landing and liberation of Cuba.

REPORT FROM CUBA. NET, 1967. 57 min. b/w. IND
The status of Cuba is reflected in speeches by Castro, scenes of experimental communities, carnivals and other events.

THREE CUBANS. Robert Cohen, 1969. Part I. THE EXILE. 27 min. color; Part II. THE REVOLUTIONARY, THE WORKER. 30 min. color. UCO
Three views of Cuba after the 1959 revolution: one from an upper middle class exile; the second from a Castro supporter and manager of a cigarette factory; the third from a worker.

VENCEREMOS BRIGADE. Sergio Nunez Martinez, 1970. 20 min. b/w. In English and Spanish versions. TRI
A report on the efforts of Americans who went to Cuba to help with the cane harvest of 1970.

WHY MONCADA? Sergio Nunez Martinez, 1969. 20 min. b/w. In Spanish with English prologue. TRI
A fast-paced collage on the history of events, including the attack on the Moncada garrison in 1953, that led to the Cuban revolution.

Puerto Rico

CASALS CONDUCTS: 1964. Encyclopaedia Britannica Educational Corporation, 1967. 17 min. b/w. UCA
An Academy Award-winning film that shows the Festival Casals in Puerto Rico featuring the famous cellist, composer, and conductor, Pablo Casals.

CULEBRA: THE BEGINNING. Diego de la Texera, 1970-71. 20
     min. color. In Spanish with English subtitles. TRI
Expresses the growing concerns of the residents of Culebra, an island off the coast of Puerto Rico where the U.S. military forces
have practiced bombing and shooting almost daily since 1936.

THE EIGHTH CONTINENT. Pan-American World Airways, n. d.
     13 min. color. ASF, PAN
A tourist travelogue about Latin American islands, Grenada, St.
Thomas, Puerto Rico and Martinique.

FESTIVAL IN PUERTO RICO. National Film Board of Canada,
     1961. 28 min. b/w. MGH
The annual Festival Casals, held in Puerto Rico and founded by
Spanish cellist Pablo Casals. This festival features contralto
Maureen Forester.

THE NATIONALISTS: PATRIOTISM IS VALOR AND SACRIFICE.
     Jose Garcia for National Educational Television, 1973. 28
     min. color. In Spanish with English subtitles. TRI
A study of the Puerto Rican independence movement traced from
the 1950s. Presents interviews with important leaders of the
movement.

PUERTO RICO. Dudley, 1952. (This World of Ours Series.) 9
     min. color. UUT
Presents the outstanding historical, geographical and scenic features
of Puerto Rico. Includes tourist attractions.

PUERTO RICO AND THE VIRGIN ISLANDS. Coronet, 1964. 10
     1/2 min. b/w. COR
A cultural, geographical and historical view of Puerto Rico with
emphasis on its economic program.

PUERTO RICO: HOMELAND. Sterling, 1973. (The Latin Ameri-
     can Series: A Focus on People.) 9 min. color. SEF
Illustrates the mountain villages and big cities of Puerto Rico along
with the rural economy and big business found there. Also available with Spanish narration.

PUERTO RICO, ISLAND IN THE SUN. United World, 1961. 18
     min. color. UEVA
About some efforts to improve the education and cultural activities
in Puerto Rico.

PUERTO RICO: ITS PAST, PRESENT AND PROMISE. Encyclo-
     paedia Britannica Educational Corporation, 1965. 20 min.
     color. EBEC, UCA, UCO
An account of the partnership between the U. S. and Puerto Rico in
"Operation Bootstrap" that has helped a once-starving economy.

PUERTO RICO: MIGRATION. Sterling, 1973. (The Latin Ameri-
     can Series: A Focus on People.) 11 min. color. SEF

A report on the migration of Puerto Rican families and their problems of adjustment to big cities. Also available with Spanish narration.

PUERTO RICO, MORE OR LESS. U. S. Department of the Army,
    1972. 22 min. color. MAC
Shows the natural beauty of Puerto Rico and the efforts of the Institute of Tropical Forestry and others to improve the forests.

PUERTO RICO: OPERATION BOOTSTRAP. United World, 1963.
    (Our World of the 60's Series.) 17 min. color. UEVA
A study of Puerto Rico's standard of living. Shows construction of housing and attempts to attract industry.

PUERTO RICO: PAIS COLONIZADO. Jon Alpert, Carlos Dias,
    Keiko Tsuno and Yoko Maruyama, 1972. 30 min. b/w. In
    Spanish. TRI
Probes the question as to whether or not Puerto Rico is a colony of the U. S.

PUERTO RICO: THE CARIBBEAN AMERICANS. ABC, 1970. 22
    min. color. EFD, IFB, UUT
A television documentary that traces the past and contemporary life of Puerto Rico through the eyes of one Puerto Rican who went to the United States and decided to return to his homeland.

PUERTO RICO: THE PEACEFUL REVOLUTION. CBS, 1962. 27
    min. b/w. MGH, UCO
Governor Luis Muños Marin of Puerto Rico discusses how his island has managed to overcome the problems of poverty and dense population.

QUE PUERTO RICO! Tibor Hirsch, 1963. 16 min. color. MGH
Tibor Hirsch directed this film which reflects his artistic view of Puerto Rico.

REPORT ON PUERTO RICO. Emerson Yorke, 1955. 20 min. b/w.
    UUT
The economic and educational status of the Commonwealth of Puerto Rico in the mid-1950s.

VISIT TO PUERTO RICO. International Film Bureau, 1962. 17
    min. color. IFB
About the culture, the geography and recent developments in Puerto Rico. Spanish language version also available.

WINGS TO THE CARIBBEAN. Pan-American World Airways, 1968.
    28 min. color. ASF, PAN
A travelogue designed to promote tourism in the Dominican Republic, Antigua, St. Thomas, Tobago, Trinidad, Curaçao, Martinique, Puerto Rico and Jamaica.

THE THIRD WORLD IN EUROPE

This section offers a few film titles that reflect either a
European view of Third World people or Third World experiences in Europe. Titles selected are limited to films
available for distribution in the U. S. and Canada.

ALI: FEAR EATS THE SOUL. (ANGST ESSEN SEELE AUF.)
Tango und Film verlag der Autorn, 1974. 94 min. color.
In German with English subtitles. Directed by Rainer Werner
Fassbinder; photography by Jurgen Jurges. With Brigitte
Mira, El Hedi Ben Salem, Irm Hermann. NYF
A film about two lonely people who meet and fall in love; he is an
Arab, she a German floorwasher about twenty years his senior.
Although the emphasis is on the characters and their interrelation-
ship with the society in which they live, the story also turns out
to be concerned with racial prejudice in contemporary Germany.

BLACK GIRL. (LA NOIRE DE ...) Films Domirev, 1969. 60
min. b/w. In French with English subtitles. Directed by
Ousmane Sembene; based on Ousmane Sembene's novel "La
Noire de ..." With Mbissine Therese Diop, Anne-Marie
Jelinck, Robert Fontaine. NYF
A young girl from Dakar is maneuvered into working for a typical
middle-class French family. A virtual prisoner, she commits suicide. This is Ousmane Sembene's first feature film and the first
black African feature-length film. Sembene won a Prix Jean Vigo
for Best Direction with this film.

LA CHINOISE. Productions de la Gueville, 1967. 95 min. color.
NYF
In Paris five pro-Chinese students discuss how to bring about a
cultural revolution in the West, similar to the one in China, through
terrorism. Directed and written by Jean-Luc Godard.

HEAVENS ABOVE. Roy Boulting, 1963. 118 min. color. Directed by John Boulting; music by Richard Rodney Bennett.
With Peter Sellers, Cecil Parker, Isabel Jeans, Brock Peters,
Ian Carmichael, Bernard Miles. MAC[1], ROAF, TWY
A social satire in which Peter Sellers portrays a minister who is
assigned to a new vicarage. He turns out to be a rare sort of
religious man, one who actually practices the life he preaches,

including taking on a black dustman (garbageman) as a church em-
ployee--an act which startles his middle class parish. Although
this film is not primarily concerned with Third World issues, it
provides an example of the roles played by black actors in English
films.

IF THERE WEREN'T ANY BLACKS YOU'D HAVE TO INVENT
     THEM. London Weekend Television, 1969. 52 min. b/w.
     IMP, PAR
A bizarre story of the slaying of various sacred cows, such as religion, militarism, medicine, class. Various factions, in their
need for a scapegoat, bootblack the skin of an arrogant white man
and arrange to kill him despite his protests that he is not black.
Written by Johnny Speight for London Weekend Television.

JAMAICANS IN LONDON. Derrick Knight, 1970. 30 min. b/w.
     MGH
The son of an anti-black family and a daughter of an immigrant
black Jamaican family meet and explore their London neighborhood,
including a condemned house from which they must later be rescued
by their two fathers.

JOANNA. Twentieth Century-Fox, 1968. 107 min. color. ana-
     morphic. Directed by Michael Sarne; written by Michael Sarne;
     produced by Michael S. Laughlin. With Genevieve Waite,
     Glenna Forster-Jones, Calvin Lockhart. FI
A swinging London art student falls in love with a black nightclub
owner.

JOJOLO. Grove, 1968. 12 min. b/w. UCA
How the background of a Haitian woman, who goes to Paris to
work, affects her experiences in the city.

THE L-SHAPED ROOM. Romulus, 1963. 124 min. b/w. Di-
     rected by Bryan Forbes; screenplay by Bryan Forbes, based
     on an original novel by Lynne Reid Banks. With Leslie Caron,
     Tom Bell, Brock Peters. COLU
A French woman, an expectant mother of an illegitimate child, falls
in love with a struggling young writer. But her lover becomes upset when he learns of her condition, and Brock Peters, who plays
a black jazz musician residing in the same shabby rooming house,
finds that his friendship for the two is torn.

MANGROVE NINE. Monument, 1973. 40 min. color. ODEO
A British film about seven black men and two women arrested on
riot and assault charges after a demonstration to protest police
harassment of their social center, the Mangrove Restaurant in the
Notting Hill Gate area. The film intends to expose the hypocrisy
of the bourgeois system.

THE PASSENGERS. Centre Algerien de Documentation d'Informa-
     tion, 1968-71. 90 min. b/w. In French with English subti-
     tles. TRI

Follows a young Algerian from his departure from Algeria through his two-year stay in Metropolitan Paris to his return home.   Gives a probing examination to the problems of language, culture, racism, and oppressive regulations barring job training and access to certain jobs.   Directed by Annie Tresgot.

SANDERS OF THE RIVER.   Alexander Korda, 1935.   80 min.   b/
  w.   Directed by Zoltan Korda; adapted from Edgar Wallace's short stories; screenplay by Lajos Biro and Jeffrey Dell; lyrics by Arthur Wimperis; music by Michael Spolianski.   With Paul Robeson, Leslie Banks, Robert Cochrane.   BUDG
A not-too-successful film about Africa but important for the fact that it provided a starring role for American black actor Paul Robeson, who found similar opportunities for non-stereotyped roles in the U. S. quite scarce.   Robeson portrays a native chieftain who remains faithful to the British despite the rebellion that is stirring among African tribes.

SAPPHIRE.   Rank, 1959.   92 min.   b/w.   Directed by Basil Dearden; screenplay by Janet Green; produced by Michael Relph.
  With Nigel Patrick, Yvonne Mitchell, Bernard Miles, Gordon Heath, Yvonne Buckingham.   AST
A combination murder mystery and study of racial issues.   Sapphire's body is found in Hampstead Heath and later it is learned that she was engaged to a white student architect, was pregnant, and was also a "lily-skin" (a black passing for white).   The prime detective in the case must cope with bigotry and suspicion among his colleagues.

SOLEIL-O.   Med Hondo, 1972.   106 min.   b/w.   In French with English subtitles.   Directed by Med Hondo.   Credits and cast unlisted.   NYF
The first feature film by a black Mauritanean--the story of a black African seeking work and acceptance in Paris.

THE STORY OF A THREE-DAY PASS.   Sigma III, 1968.   87 min.
  b/w.   In French with English subtitles.   Directed by Melvin Van Peebles; screenplay by Melvin Van Peebles.   With Harry Baird, Nicole Berger.   MAC[1]
This was Melvin Van Peebles' first effort as a director.   The story, filmed in France, is based on his novel about an interracial love affair between a black soldier and a white French girl.

PART II
FILM DISTRIBUTORS

AAI   African-American Institute
           833 United Nations Plaza, New York, N. Y. 10017

ACB   Art Cinema Booking Service
           1501 Broadway, New York, N. Y. 10036

ACI   ACI Films, Inc.
           35 West 45th Street, New York, N. Y. 10036

ACW   Amalgamated Clothing Workers of America, AFL-CIO
           15 Union Square, New York, N. Y. 1003

AEF   American Educational Films
           132 Lasky Drive, Beverly Hills, Calif. 90212

AFGR   Afrographis
           P. O. Box 8361, Los Angeles, Calif. 90008

AFR   Afram Associates, Inc.
           68-72 East 131st Street, New York, N. Y. 10037

AIM   Association Instructional Films (A Division of Associa-
                tion Films)
           866 Third Avenue, New York, N. Y. 10022

ALCF   Alcon Films
           90 Mar Vista, Pasadena, Calif. 91106

ALD   Alden Films
           5113 Sixteenth Avenue, Brooklyn, N. Y. 11204

ALM   Almanac Films
           915 Broadway, New York, N. Y. 10010

ART   Artscope, Ltd.
           310 West 53rd Street, New York, N. Y. 10019

ASF   Association-Sterling Films
           600 Grand Avenue, Ridgefield, N. J. 07657

AST   Astral Films, Ltd.
           224 Davenport Road, Toronto, Ontario M5R 1J7,
                Canada

ATL   Atlantis Productions, Inc.
           850 Thousand Oaks Boulevard, Thousand Oaks, Calif.
                91360

AVE   AV-ED Films
           7934 Santa Monica Boulevard, Hollywood, Calif. 90046

AZT   Azteca Films, Inc.
           132 West 43rd Street, New York, N. Y. 10036

BARR   Barr Films
            P. O. Box 7-C, 1029 North Allen Avenue, Pasadena,
            Calif. 91104

BBC   The British Broadcasting Corporation
            P. O. Box 500, Toronto, Ontario M5W 1E6, Canada

BEF   Benchmark Films, Inc.
            145 Scarborough Road, Briarcliff Manor, N. Y. 10510

BFA   BFA Educational Media
            2211 Michigan Avenue, Santa Monica, Calif. 90404
            [for Canada see SAC]

BLF   Blackhawk Films
            Eastin Phelan Distributing Corporation, P. O. Box
            4528, Davenport, Iowa 52808

BOSU   Boston University
            Abraham Krasker Memorial Film Library, 765 Com-
            monwealth Ave., Boston, Mass. 02215

BTDB   Bermuda Trade Development Board
            620 Fifth Avenue, New York, N. Y. 10020

BUDG   Budget Films
            4590 Santa Monica Boulevard, Los Angeles, Calif.
            90029

CAPC   Capital Cities Communications
            24 East 51st Street, New York, N. Y. 10022

CAR   Carousel Films Inc.
            1501 Broadway, New York, N. Y. 10036

CCRC   Cine-Craft Company
            1720 West Marshall, Portland, Ore. 97209

CEMC   Center for Mass Communication of Columbia University
            Press
            136 South Broadway, Irvington, N. Y. 10533

CEN   Centron Educational Films
            1621 West Ninth Street, Lawrence, Kan. 66044
                              and
            International Tele-Film Enterprises
            221 Victoria Street, Toronto, Ontario, Canada

CF   Cinema Five
            595 Madison Avenue, New York, N. Y. 10022

CGJ   Consulate General of Japan
            235 East 42nd Street, New York, N. Y. 10017

CHAR   Charard Motion Pictures
            2110 East 24th Street, Brooklyn, N. Y. 11229

CHU   Churchill Films
            662 North Robertson Boulevard, Los Angeles, Calif.
              90069

CIN   Cintec Productions
            611 West Pacific Coast Highway, Long Beach, Calif.
              90806

CINL   Cinemedia, Ltd.
            P. O. Box 332, Agincourt, Ontario M1S 3B9, Canada

CIPI   Cine-Pic Hawaii
            1847 Pacific Heights Road, Honolulu, Hawaii 96813

COLU   Columbia Cinemateque
            711 Fifth Avenue, New York, N. Y. 10022

COM   Communetics, Inc.
            485 Madison Avenue, New York, N. Y. 10022

COR   Coronet Instructional Media
            65 East South Water Street, Chicago, Ill. 60601
                                  and
            Coronet Instructional Media Ltd.
            2 Thorncliffe Park Drive, Toronto, Ontario M4H 1H2,
              Canada

CPC   Columbia Pictures of Canada
            72 Carlton Street, Toronto, Ontario, Canada

CRA   Crawley Films Ltd.
            Distribution Division, 409 King Street West, Toronto,
              Ontario M5V 1K1, Canada

DANA   Dana Productions
            A Division of Saparoff Films, Inc. , 6249 Babcock
              Avenue, North Hollywood, California 91606

DAV   Tom Davenport Films
            Pearlstone, Dept. DM, Delaplane, Va. 22025

DIBD   Dibie-Dash Productions
            4949 Hollywood Boulevard, Suite 217, Los Angeles,
              Calif. 90027

DIS   Walt Disney Educational Media Company
            800 Sonora Avenue, Glendale, California 91201

DOCE   Documentary Educational Resources
            24 Dane Street, Somerville, Mass. 02143

DOU   Doubleday Multimedia
             P. O. Box 11607, Santa Ana, Calif. 92705

DOUG   Neil Douglas Productions
             3030 Iroquois Street, Detroit, Mich. 48214

EAG   Arnold Eagle Productions
             41 West 47th Street, New York, N. Y. 10036

EBEC   Encyclopaedia Britannica Educational Corporation
             425 North Michigan Avenue, Chicago, Ill. 60611
             [for Canada see VEC]

EDC   Education Development Center
             39 Chapel Street, Newton, Mass. 02160

EFD   Educational Film Distributors Ltd.
             285 Lesmill Road, Don Mills, Ontario M3B 2V1,
             Canada

ETS   Educational Testing Service
             Cooperative Test Division, 20 Nassau Street, Prince-
             ton, N. J. 08540

EYR   EYR Campus Programs
             78 East 56th Street, New York, N. Y. 10022

FAU   Film Australia
             c/o Australian Information Service, 636 Fifth Avenue,
             New York, N. Y. 10020

FF   Fieldstaff Films
             American Universities Field Staff, 3 Lebanon Street,
             Hanover, New Hampshire 03755

FFTH   Films For The Humanities
             P. O. Box 378, Princeton, N. J. 08540

FI   Films Incorporated
             4420 Oakton Street, Skokie, Ill. 60076
                                 and
             440 Park Avenue South, New York, N. Y. 10016
                                 and
             5625 Hollywood Boulevard, Hollywood, Calif. 90028
                                 and
             5589 New Peachtree Road, Atlanta, Georgia 30341

FICE   Film-Classic Exchange
             1926 South Vermont Avenue, Los Angeles, Calif. 90007

FIF   Film Forum, Inc.
             2070 Business Center Drive, Irvine, Calif. 92664

FLOF   Flower Films
            11305 Q-Ranch Road, Austin, Texas 78757

FMCO   Film-Makers' Cooperative
            175 Lexington Avenue, New York, N. Y. 10016

GRE   William Greaves Productions, Inc.
            1776 Broadway, New York, N. Y. 10019

GRO   Grove Press Film Division
            53 East 11th Street, New York, N. Y. 10003

GRP   Golden Reel Productions
            2311 Brewster Avenue, P. O. Box 122, Redwood City,
                Calif. 94062

HAD   Hadassah, The Women's Zionist
            Organization of America, 470 Park Avenue South,
                New York, N. Y. 10016

HARP   Hartley Productions, Inc.
            Cat Rock Road, Cos Cob, Connecticut 06807

HCW   Hurlock Cine-World
            13 Arcadia Road, Old Greenwich, Conn. 06870

HFC   Handel Film Corporation
            8730 Sunset Boulevard, West Hollywood, Calif. 90069

HFE   Hollywood Film Enterprises, Inc.
            6060 Sunset Boulevard, Hollywood, Calif. 90028

HMN   Hearst Metrotone News
            235 East 45th Street, New York, N. Y. 10017

IFB   International Film Bureau
            332 South Michigan Avenue, Chicago, Ill. 60604
                [for Canada see EFD]

IFF   International Film Foundation
            475 Fifth Avenue, Suite 916, New York, N. Y. 10017

IFP   Independent Film Producers Company
            P. O. Box 501, Pasadena, Calif. 91102

IMP   Impact Films
            144 Bleecker Street, New York, N. Y. 10012

IND   Indiana University Audio-Visual Center
            Bloomington, Indiana 47401

INTF   International Film Distributors
            20 Bloor Street West, Toronto, Ontario M4W 1C8,
                Canada

ITC   Independent Television Corporation
555 Madison Avenue, New York, N. Y. 10022

IVY   IVY Film
165 West 46th Street, New York, N. Y. 10036

JAN   Janus Films
745 Fifth Avenue, New York, N. Y. 10022

JAS   Jason Films
2621 Palisade Avenue, Riverdale, N. Y. 10463

JNF   Jewish National Fund
Youth and Educational Department, JNF House, 42
   West 69th Street, New York, N. Y. 10021

KING   Martin Luther King Foundation
309 East 90th Street, New York, N. Y. 10028

LEC   Learning Corporation of America
1350 Avenue of the Americas, New York, N. Y. 10019
[for Canada see MAR]

LINE   Line Films
P. O. Box 328, Capistrano Beach, Calif. 92672

LMF   Le Mont Films
P. O. Box 63, 17622 Willard Street, Northridge,
   Calif. 91324

LUTH   Lutheran Film Library
315 Park Avenue South, New York, N. Y. 10010

LYM   Charles Lyman
c/o Columbia College, 540 North Lakeshore, Chicago,
   Ill. 60614

MAC   Macmillan Films, Inc.
34 MacQuesten Parkway So. , Mt. Vernon, N. Y. 10550

MAC[1]   Macmillan Audio Brandon
34 MacQuesten Parkway So. , Mt. Vernon, N. Y. 10550
             and
1619 North Cherokee, Los Angeles, Calif. 90028
             and
3868 Piedmont Avenue, Oakland, Calif. 94611
             and
8400 Brookfield Avenue, Brookfield, Ill. 60513
             and
8615 Directors Row, Dallas, Texas 75247

MAR   Marlin Motion Pictures Ltd.
47 Lakeshore Road, East, Port Credit, Ontario L5G
   1C9, Canada

MAY   Harold Mayer Productions
               155 West 72nd Street, New York, N. Y. 10023

MEN   A-V Department
               Mennonite Central Committee, Akron, Pa. 17501
                                     and
               Winnipeg, Manitoba R3T 2C8, Canada

MGH   McGraw-Hill Films
               1221 Avenue of the Americas, New York, N. Y. 10020

MIR   Miramar Film Library
               19 Cornell Street, Newton Lower Falls, Mass. 02162

MLA   Modern Learning Aids
               Division of Ward's Natural Science, P. O. Box 302,
                   Rochester, N. Y. 14603

MOGU   Mogull's
               235 West 46th Street, New York, N. Y. 10036

MONF   Monument Film Corporation
               267 West 25th Street, New York, N. Y. 10001

MOSP   Modern Sound Pictures
               1402 Howard Street, Omaha, Nebraska 68102

MUND   Munday and Collins
               270 Willow Street, San Jose, Calif. 95150

NAC   National Audiovisual Center
               Sales Branch or Rental Branch
               Washington, D. C. 20409

NACC   Broadcasting and Film Commission
               National Council of Churches, 475 Riverside Drive,
                   New York, N. Y. 10027

NC   New Cinema
               35 Britain Street, Toronto, Ontario M5A 1R7, Canada

NEF   New Film Company, Inc.
               331 Newbury Street, Boston, Mass. 02115

NFBC   National Film Board of Canada
               P. O. Box 6100, Station A, Montreal, Quebec H3C
                   3H5, Canada

NGS   National Geographic Society
               Dept. 1347, Washington, D. C. 20036
                                     and
               National Geographic Educational Services
               151 Carlingview Drive, Unit No. 5, Rexdale, Ontario

M9W 5E7, Canada
or
Rental
c/o Modern Film Rentals
1145 North McCadden Place, Los Angeles, Calif. 90038
or
1687 Elmhurst Road, Elk Grove Village, Ill. 60007
or
412 West Peachtree Street, N. W., Atlanta, Georgia
30308
or
315 Springfield Avenue, Summit, N. J. 07901
or
1875 Leslie Street, Don Mills, Ontario M3B 2M6

NLC   New Line Cinema
        853 Broadway, New York, N. Y. 10003

NYF   New Yorker Films
        43 West 61st Street, New York, N. Y. 10023

NYU   New York University Film Library
        41 Press Annex, Washington Square, New York, N. Y.
        10003

OBE   Vaughn Obern
        704 Santa Monica Boulevard, Santa Monica, Calif.
        90403

ODEO   Odeon Films, Inc.
        1619 Broadway, New York, N. Y. 10019

OXF   Oxford Films (or Paramount Oxford Films)
        5451 Marathon Street, Hollywood, Calif. 90038

PAN   Pan Am Film Sales
        600 Grand Avenue, Ridgefield, N. J. 07657

PAR   Kit Parker
        Box 227, Carmel Valley, Calif. 93924

PARD   Paradigm Film Productions
        6305 Yucca Street, Los Angeles, Calif. 90028

PAUL   Paulist Productions
        P. O. Box 1057, Pacific Palisades, Calif. 90272

PEN   Psychological Cinema Register
        Audio-Visual Services, The Pennsylvania State Univer-
        sity, University Park, Pa. 16802

PER   Perennial Education, Inc.
        P. O. Box 236, 1825 Willow Road, Northfield, Ill.
        60093

PFS   Paramount Film Service Ltd.
            Toronto Star Building, One Yonge Street, Toronto,
              Ontario M5E 1E9, Canada
                           and
            Canfilm Screen Services
            956 Richards Street, Vancouver, British Columbia,
              Canada
                           and
            Canfilm Screen Services
            522 - 11th Avenue S.W., Calgary, Alberta, Canada

PHO   Phoenix Films
            470 Park Avenue South, New York, N.Y. 10016
              [for Canada see NC]

PIC   Pictura Film Distribution Corporation
            43 West 16th Street, New York, N.Y. 10011

PPC   Paramount Pictures Corporation
            1 Gulf and Western Plaza, New York, N.Y. 10023
              [see also PFS]

PSFC   Pacific Street Film Collective
            280 Clinton Street, Brooklyn, N.Y. 11201

PYR   Pyramid Films
            Box 1048, Santa Monica, Calif. 90406

RAD   Radim/ Film Images
            17 West 60th Street, New York, N.Y. 10023
                           and
            1034 Lake Street, Oak Park, Ill. 60301

RAY   Bruce Raymond Studios
            2264 Lakeshore Boulevard W., Toronto, Ontario M8V
              1A9, Canada

READ   Walter Reade Organization, Inc.
            241 East 34th Street, New York, N.Y. 10016

REI   Max Reid Films
            533 Bienveneda Avenue, Pacific Palisades, Calif. 90272

RFSV   Reaction Films
            Steck-Vaughn Company, P. O. Box 2028, Austin, Texas
              78767

RIT   George Ritter Films Ltd.
            2264 Lakeshore Boulevard West, Toronto, Ontario
              M8V 1A9

ROAF   Roa's Films
            1696 North Astor Street, Milwaukee, Wisconsin 53202

ROE   Stuart Roe
           1135 South Sage Court, Sunnyvale, Calif. 94087

ROT   Rothschild Film Corporation
           1046 East 18th Street, Brooklyn, New York 11230

SAC   William Sacherek
           559 Austin Avenue, Coquitlam, British Columbia V3K
              3M6, Canada

SCHP   Tom Schroeppel
           241 South Royal Poinciana, Miami Springs, Fla. 33166

SEF   Sterling Educational Films
           241 East 34th Street, New York, N.Y. 10016

SERB   Serious Business Company
           1609 Jaynes Street, Berkeley, Calif. 94703

SFL   Shell Film Library
           450 North Meridian Street, Indianapolis, Indiana 46204

SIM   Sim Productions, Inc.
           Weston, Conn. 06880

SNY   Robert Snyder
           8455 Beverly Boulevard, Suite 506, Los Angeles,
              Calif. 90048

SOH   Soho Cinema Ltd.
           508 Broadway, New York, N.Y. 10012

SOL   Solfilm International
           R.R. No. 1, Box 30, Kapaa, Kauai, Hawaii 96746

SOUN   Soundings
           2193 Concord Boulevard, Concord, Calif. 94520

STA   Statens Filmcentralen
           The Danish Government Film Office, 27, Vestergarde -
              DK 1456, Copenhagen K, Denmark

STAN   Stanton Films
           7934 Santa Monica Boulevard, Los Angeles, Calif.
              90046

STD   Standard Film Service
           14710 West Warren Avenue, Dearborn, Mich. 48126

SUM   Summit Films, Inc.
           2145 South Platte River Dr., Denver, Colo. 80223

SWA   Swank Motion Pictures
     201 South Jefferson Avenue, St. Louis, Mo. 63166

SYR   Syracuse University
     Film Rental Center, 1455 East Colvin Street, Syra-
      cuse, N. Y. 13210

TEX   Texture Films
     1600 Broadway, New York, N. Y. 10019

TFC   Trend Films Corporation
     P. O. Box 69680, Los Angeles, Calif. 90069

THUN   Thunderbird Films
     P. O. Box 4081, Los Angeles, Calif. 90054

TL   Time-Life Films
     100 Eisenhower Drive, Paramus, N. J. 07652
     [for BBC productions in Canada see BBC]

TMOC   The Movie Center
     57 Baldwin Street, Charlestown, Mass. 02129

TOH   Toho International, Inc.
     1501 Broadway, New York, N. Y. 10036

TRI   Tricontinental Film Center
     333 Avenue of the Americas, New York, N. Y. 10014
           and
     P. O. Box 4430, Berkeley, Calif. 94704

TWF   Trans-World Films
     322 South Michigan Avenue, Chicago, Ill. 60604

TWN   Third World Newsreel
     26 West 20th Street, New York, N. Y. 10011

TWY   Twyman Films
     329 Salem Avenue, Dayton, Ohio 45401

UAR   University of Arizona
     Bureau of Audiovisual Services, Tucson, Arizona 85721

UCA   University of California
     Extension Media Center, 2223 Fulton Street, Berkeley,
      Calif. 94720

UCLA   University of California at Los Angeles
     405 Hilgard Avenue, Los Angeles, Calif. 90024

UCO   University of Colorado
     Bureau of Audiovisual Instruction, Stadium Building,
      Boulder, Colo. 80302

UEVA   Universal Education and Visual Arts
            221 Park Avenue, South, New York, N. Y. 10003

UIA   United Israel Appeal
            515 Park Avenue, New York, N. Y. 10022

UIL   University of Illinois
            223 Administration Bldg. , Champaign, Ill. 61801

UIO   Iowa Films
            c/o Audiovisual Center, Media Library, C-5 East
            Hall, University of Iowa, Iowa City, Iowa 52242

UKE   AV Services
            University of Kentucky, Scott Street Building, Lexing-
            ton, Kentucky 40506

UMIC   AV Education Center
            University of Michigan, 416 - 4th Street, Ann Arbor,
            Mich. 48103

UMN   University of Minnesota
            Audio-Visual Library Service, 3300 University Avenue
            S. E. , Minneapolis, Minn. 55414

UN   United Nations
            Radio and Visual Service, OPI, New York, N. Y. 10017

UNAR   United Artists 16
            729 Seventh Avenue, New York, N. Y. 10019

UNE   University of Nevada
            Audiovisual Communication Center, Reno, Nevada 89507

UNIV   Universal 16
            445 Park Avenue, New York, N. Y. 10022

USC   University of Southern California
            Division of Cinema, University Park, Los Angeles,
            Calif. 90007

UUT   University of Utah
            Education Media Center, Milton Bennion Hall 207,
            Salt Lake City, Utah 84110

UWAP   University of Washington Press
            1416 NE 41st Street, Seattle, Washington 98105

UWI   University of Wisconsin
            South Asian Area Center, 1242 Van Hise Hall, Madison,
            Wisc. 53706

UWY   University of Wyoming
               Audiovisual Services, Laramie, Wyoming 82070

VEC   Visual Education Centre
               115 Berkeley Street, Toronto, Ontario M5A 2W8,
                  Canada

WARB   Warner Brothers
               Non-Theatrical Division, 4000 Warner Boulevard,
                  Burbank, Calif. 91503

WECF   Westcoast Films
               25 Lusk Street, San Francisco, Calif. 94107

WGTV   WGTV
               University of Georgia, Georgia Center for Continuing
                  Education, Athens, Georgia 30602

WHF   World Horizon Films
               Pinesbridge Road, Maryknoll, N. Y. 10545

WIL   Willoughby-Peerless
               110 West 32nd Street, New York, N. Y. 10001

WJZ   WJZ-TV
               Channel 13, Television Hill, Baltimore, Md. 21211

WRAI   Walter Reed Army Institute of Research
               Rt. 1, Box 284, Yorktown Heights, N. Y.

XER   Xerox Films
               245 Long Hill Road, Middletown, Conn. 06457

ZIP   Zipporah Films
               54 Lewis Wharf, Boston, Mass. 02110

PART III

LIST OF DIRECTORS, CINEMATOGRAPHERS,
SCENARISTS, AND COMPOSERS

A PARTIAL LIST OF DIRECTORS, CINEMATOGRAPHERS, SCENARISTS, AND COMPOSERS CREDITED FOR WORK ON FEATURE-LENGTH FILMS CITED IN THIS BOOK

Directors

K. A. Abbas
    MUNNA

Benito Alazraki
    THE ROOTS

Tomas Gutierrez Alea
    MEMORIES OF UNDERDE-
    VELOPMENT

Gianni Amico
    TROPICI

Leonard Anderson
    JIVIN IN BE BOP

Robert Alan Aurther
    THE LOST MAN

Souhel Ben Barka
    A THOUSAND AND ONE
    HANDS

Lima Barreto
    CANGACEIRO

Jean-Louis Bertucelli
    RAMPARTS OF CLAY

Herbert Biberman
    SALT OF THE EARTH
    SLAVES

Stig Bjorkman
    GEORGIA, GEORGIA

James Blue
    THE OLIVE TREES OF JUS-
    TICE

Budd Boetticher
    THE MAGNIFICENT MATA-
    DOR

John Boulting
    HEAVENS ABOVE

Luis Buñuel
    EL
    MEXICAN BUS RIDE
    NAZARIN
    LOS OLVIDADOS
    SIMON OF THE DESERT

Marcel Camus
    BLACK ORPHEUS

Maurice Capouilla
    PROPHET OF HUNGER

Frank Capra
    BATTLE OF CHINA

Rick Carrier
    STRANGERS IN THE CITY

H. P. Carver
    THE SILENT ENEMY: AN
    EPIC OF THE AMERICAN
    INDIAN

John Cassavetes
SHADOWS

James B. Clark
ISLAND OF THE BLUE
DOLPHINS

Shirley Clarke
THE COOL WORLD

Walter Colmes
THE BURNING CROSS

Costa-Gavras
STATE OF SIEGE

Michael Curtiz
JIM THORPE, ALL AMER-
ICAN

Herbert Danska
SWEET LOVE, BITTER

Jules Dassin
UP TIGHT

Ossie Davis
COTTON COMES TO HAR-
LEM

Michael Dearden
SAPPHIRE

Benie Deswarte
KASHIMA PARADISE

Carlos Diegues
THE BIG CITY
GANGA ZUMBA

William Dieterle
JUAREZ

Robert Downey
PUTNEY SWOPE

Arthur Dreifuss
MURDER ON LENOX
AVENUE

Anselmo Duarte
THE GIVEN WORD

Ilan Eldad
THE DYBBUK

Cy Endfield
ZULU

Rainer Werner Fassbinder
ALI: FEAR EATS THE SOUL

Emilio Fernandez
THE PEARL
MARIA CANDELARIA

Robert J. Flaherty
NANOOK OF THE NORTH

Bryan Forbes
THE L-SHAPED ROOM

John Ford
CHEYENNE AUTUMN

Aldo Francia
VALPARAISO MI AMOR

Sidney Franklin
THE GOOD EARTH

Harry Fraser
SPIRIT OF YOUTH

Thornton Freeland
JERICHO

Roberto Galvedon
MACARIO

Octavio Getino
THE HOUR OF THE FUR-
NACES

Jean-Luc Godard
LA CHINOISE

Armando Robles Godoy
THE GREEN WALL

Martin Goldman
THE LEGEND OF NIGGER
CHARLEY

James Goldstone
BROTHER JOHN

Manuel Octavio Gomez
FIRST CHARGE OF THE
MACHETE

Servando Gonzalez
YANCO

Robert Gordon
THE JOE LOUIS STORY

Alfred E. Green
THE JACKIE ROBINSON
STORY

Felix Greene
CHINA!
CUBA VA!

Ruy Guerra
OS FUZIS
THE GODS AND THE DEAD

Susumu Hani
BAD BOYS
BWANA TOSHI
SHE AND HE

Anthony Harvey
DUTCHMAN

Paolo Heusch
EL CHE GUEVARA

Med Hondo
SOLEIL-O

Kon Ichikawa
THE BURMESE HARP

Tadashi Imai
MUDDY WATERS

Hiroshi Inagaki
SAMURAI

James Ivory
AUTOBIOGRAPHY OF A
PRINCESS
BOMBAY TALKIE

Alex Joffe
IMPOSSIBLE ON SATURDAY

Aejay Kardar
DAY SHALL DAWN

Jeff Kenew
BLACK RODEO

Henry King
CAPTAIN FROM CASTILE

Teinosuke Kinugasa
GATE OF HELL

Ephraim Kishon
SALLAH

Zoltan Korda
CRY, THE BELOVED COUN-
TRY
SANDERS OF THE RIVER

John Korty
THE AUTOBIOGRAPHY OF
MISS JANE PITTMAN

Joseph Krumgold
AND NOW MIGUEL

Akira Kurosawa
THE BAD SLEEP WELL
DODES'KA-DEN
DRUNKEN ANGEL
THE MEN WHO TREAD ON
THE TIGER'S TAIL
RASHOMON
RED BEARD
SANJURO
SEVEN SAMURAI
STRAY DOG
YOJIMBO

Saul Landau
FIDEL
QUE HACER

David Lean
LAWRENCE OF ARABIA

Paul Leduc
REED: INSURGENT MEXICO

Ivan Lengyel
CLOUDS OVER ISRAEL

Carl Lerner
BLACK LIKE ME

Walter Lima, Jr.
PLANTATION BOY

Jan Lindqvist
TUPAMAROS!

Miguel Littin
THE JACKAL OF NAHUEL-
TORO
THE PROMISED LAND

Carlo Lizzani
BEHIND THE GREAT
WALL OF CHINA

Julio Luduena
ALLIANCE FOR PROGRESS

Kent MacKenzie
THE EXILES

T. C. McLuhan
THE SHADOW CATCHER:
EDWARD S. CURTIS
AND THE NORTH AMER-
ICAN INDIAN

Sarah Maldoror
SAMBIZANGA

Louis Malle
PHANTOM INDIA

Joseph L. Mankiewicz
NO WAY OUT

Chris Marker
CUBA: BATTLE OF THE
10,000,000

Yanh Le Masson
KASHIMA PARADISE

Yasuzo Masumura
HOODLUM SOLDIER

Gerald Mayer
BRIGHT ROAD

Adolfas Mekas
COMPAÑERAS AND COM-
PAÑEROS

Sidney Meyers
THE QUIET ONE

Robert Ellis Miller
THE HEART IS A LONELY
HUNTER

Stuart Miller
WHEN LEGENDS DIE

Vincente Minnelli
CABIN IN THE SKY

Kenji Misumi
BUDDHA

Kenji Mizoguchi
THE BAILIFF
THE LIFE OF O-HARU
PRINCESS YANG KWEI FEI
SAGA OF THE CRUCIFIED
LOVERS
STREET OF SHAME
TALES OF THE TAIRA CLAN
UGETSU

Dudley Murphy
EMPEROR JONES

Ralph Nelson
SOLDIER BLUE

David Neves
MEMORIES OF HELEN

Shinsuke Ogawa
PEASANTS OF THE SECOND
FORTRESS

Shin San Okk
SPRING FRAGRANCE

Nagisa Oshima
BOY
DEATH BY HANGING

Yasujiro Ozu
AN AUTUMN AFTERNOON
LATE AUTUMN

LATE SPRING
OHAYO
RECORD OF A TENEMENT
    GENTLEMAN
TOKYO STORY
UKIGUSA

Gordon Parks
    THE LEARNING TREE
    SHAFT
    SHAFT'S BIG SCORE

Melvin Van Peebles
    THE STORY OF A THREE-
        DAY PASS
    WATERMELON MAN

Larry Peerce
    ONE POTATO, TWO PO-
        TATO

Jean Pelegri
    THE OLIVE TREES OF
        JUSTICE

Leo Penn
    A MAN CALLED ADAM

Daniel Petrie
    A RAISIN IN THE SUN

Sidney Poitier
    BUCK AND THE PREACHER

Barry Pollack
    COME BACK CHARLESTON
        BLUE

Bud Pollard
    THE BLACK KING

Gillo Pontecorvo
    BATTLE OF ALGIERS

Otto Preminger
    CARMEN JONES

George Randol
    RHYTHM RODEO

Satyajit Ray
    THE ADVENTURES OF
        GOOPY AND BAGHA

THE ADVERSARY
APARAJITO
CHARULATA, THE LONELY
    WIFE
DAYS AND NIGHTS IN THE
    FOREST
DEVI
DISTANT THUNDER
KANCHENJUNGHA
MAHANAGAR
THE MUSIC ROOM
NAYAK, THE HERO
PATHER PANCHALI
TAGORE
THE WORLD OF APU

Allen Reisner
    ST. LOUIS BLUES

Alain Resnais
    HIROSHIMA, MON AMOUR

Humberto Rios
    THE CRY OF THE PEOPLE

Martin Ritt
    THE GREAT WHITE HOPE

Mark Robson
    HOME OF THE BRAVE

Glauber Rocha
    ANTONIO DAS MORTES
    BARRAVENTO
    BLACK GOD, WHITE DEVIL
    EARTH ENTRANCED
    LAND IN ANGUISH
    LION HAS SEVEN HEADS
    TERRA EM TRANSE

Jose Rodriguez-Soltero
    DIALOGO CON CHE: CHE
        IS ALIVE

Nicholas Roeg
    WALKABOUT

Lionel Rogosin
    COME BACK, AFRICA

Raul Ruiz
    QUE HACER

Jorge Sanjines
  BLOOD OF THE CONDOR
  THE COURAGE OF THE
    PEOPLE

Nelson Pereira dos Santos
  THE ALIENIST
  BARREN LIVES
  HOW TASTY WAS MY
    FRENCHMAN
  HUNGER FOR LOVE

Roberto Santos
  MATRAGA

Michael Sarne
  JOANNA

Michael A. Schultz
  TO BE YOUNG, GIFTED
    AND BLACK

Joseph Seiden
  PARADISE IN HARLEM

Ousmane Sembene
  BLACK GIRL
  EMITAI
  MANDABI
  XALA

Nina Serrano
  QUE HACER

Melville Shavelson
  CAST A GIANT SHADOW

Mashiro Shinoda
  CAPTIVE'S ISLAND

Paulo Gil Soares
  MEMORIES OF THE CAN-
    GACO

Fernando Solanas
  THE HOUR OF THE FUR-
    NACES

Humberto Solas
  LUCIA

John Stahl
  IMITATION OF LIFE

Josef von Sternberg
  THE SAGA OF ANTAHAN

Andrew Stone
  STORMY WEATHER

Barbara Stone
  COMPANERAS AND COM-
    PANEROS

David C. Stone
  COMPANERAS AND COM-
    PANEROS

Arne Sucksdorff
  THE FLUTE AND THE AR-
    ROW

Hiroshi Teshigahara
  WOMAN IN THE DUNES

Leopold Torre Nilsson
  THE EAVES DROPPER
  END OF INNOCENCE
  THE FALL
  HAND IN THE TRAP
  SUMMERSKIN

Mahama Traore
  REOU-TAKH

Annie Tresgot
  THE PASSENGERS

Jesus Trevino
  YO SOY CHICANO

Jamie Ulys
  DINGAKA

Kamar Vasudev
  AT FIVE PAST FIVE

Carlos Velo
  TORERO!

Mark Warren
  COME BACK CHARLESTON
    BLUE

Harry Watt
  THE OVERLANDERS

Robert Webb
WHITE FEATHER

Nicholas Webster
GONE ARE THE DAYS

Alfred L. Werder
LOST BOUNDARIES

Spencer Williams

BLOOD OF JESUS

J. Elder Wills
SONG OF FREEDOM

Robert Wise
ODDS AGAINST TOMORROW

Sam Zebba
FINCHO

Cinematographers

Yuzuru Aizawa
THE BAD SLEEP WELL

Ernst Artaria
COME BACK, AFRICA

Yushun Atsuta
LATE AUTUMN
LATE SPRING
OHAYO

Luiz Carlos Barreto
BARREN LIVES
EARTH ENTRANCED

Alfonso Beato
ANTONIO DAS MORTES

Andreas Bellis
GEORGIA, GEORGIA

Diego Bonacina
VALPARAISO MI AMOR

Kamal Bose
AT FIVE PAST FIVE

Rick Carter
STRANGERS IN THE CITY

William Clothier
CHEYENNE AUTUMN

Erik Daarstad
THE EXILES

Stephen Dade
ZULU

Robert De Grasse
HOME OF THE BRAVE

Mario Diez
THE CRY OF THE PEOPLE

Fernando Duarte
GANGA ZUMBA

Antonio Eguino
BLOOD OF THE CONDOR
THE COURAGE OF THE
PEOPLE

Gabriel Figueroa
EL
MARIA CANDELARIA
NAZARIN
LOS OLVIDADOS
THE PEARL
SIMON OF THE DESERT

Robert J. Flaherty
NANOOK OF THE NORTH

Chick Fowle
THE GIVEN WORD

Yasumichi Fukuzawa
DODES'KA-DEN

Marcello Gatti
BATTLE OF ALGIERS

Mario Robles Godoy
THE GREEN WALL

Paul Goldsmith

TO BE YOUNG, GIFTED AND
  BLACK

Burnett Griffey
  THE GREAT WHITE HOPE

Alexis Grivas
  REED: INSURGENT MEXICO

Robert Hauser
  SOLDIER BLUE

Jorge Herrera
  FIRST CHARGE OF THE
    MACHETE

Yoshimi Hirano
  THE LIFE OF O-HARU

Gerald Hirschfeld
  COTTON COMES TO HARLEM

Takeo Ito
  DRUNKEN ANGEL
  THE MEN WHO TREAD ON
    THE TIGER'S TAIL

Jurgen Jurges
  ALI: FEAR EATS THE SOUL

Monji Kanou
  BAD BOYS
  BWANA TOSHI

Emil Knebel
  COME BACK, AFRICA

Setsuo Kobayashi
  HOODLUM SOLDIER

Dick Kratina
  COME BACK CHARLESTON
    BLUE

Walter Lasally
  DAY SHALL DAWN

Charles Lawton, Jr.
  A RAISIN IN THE SUN

Robert Lucativa
  COMPANERAS AND COM-
    PANEROS

Dib Lutfi
  THE ALIENIST
  THE GODS AND THE DEAD
  HUNGER FOR LOVE

Robert Machover
  COMPANERAS AND COM-
    PANEROS

Yanh Le Masson
  KASHIMA PARADISE

Oscar Melli
  SUMMERSKIN

Subrata Mitra
  APARAJITO
  BOMBAY TALKIE
  CHARULATA, THE LONELY
    WIFE
  KANCHENJUNGHA
  MANANAGAR
  THE MUSIC ROOM
  NAYAK, THE HERO
  PATHER PANCHALI
  THE WORLD OF APU

Kazuo Miyogawa
  THE BAILIFF
  SAGA OF THE CRUCIFIED
    LOVERS
  TALES OF THE TAIRA CLAN
  UKIGUSA
  YOJIMBO

Juichi Nagano
  SHE AND HE

Asaichi Nakai
  SEVEN SAMURAI

Shunichiro Nakao
  MUDDY WATERS

Goetz Neumann
  THE DYDBUK

Anibal Gonzalez Paz
  THE FALL

Alex Phillips, Jr.
  BUCK AND THE PREACHER
  MEXICAN BUS RIDE
  YANCO

Soumendu Ray
  THE ADVERSARY

Hector Rios
  THE JACKAL OF NAHUEL-
    TORO

Soumendu Roy
  DAYS AND NIGHTS IN THE
    FOREST
  DISTANT THUNDER
  TAGORE

Takao Saito
  DODES'KA-DEN
  RED BEARD

Baidy Sow
  REOU-TAKH

Josef von Sternberg
  THE SAGA OF ANATAHAN

Ramon Suarez
  MEMORIES OF UNDERDE-
    VELOPMENT

Arne Sucksdorff
  THE FLUTE AND THE ARROW

Tatsuo Suzuki
  CAPTIVE'S ISLAND

Michio Takahashi
  HIROSHIMA, MON AMOUR

Masaki Tamura
  PEASANTS OF THE
    SECOND FORTRESS

Sacha Vierny
  HIROSHIMA, MON AMOUR

Andreas Winding
  RAMPARTS OF CLAY

Jun Yasumoto
  SAMURAI

Minoru Yokoyama
  THE BURMESE HARP

Yasuhiro Yoshioka
  DEATH BY HANGING

Scenarists

Kobo Abe
  WOMAN IN THE DUNES

Luis Alcoriza
  EL
  LOS OLVIDADOS

Tomas Gutierrez Alea
  MEMORIES OF UNDERDE-
    VELOPMENT

Julio Alejandro
  NAZARIN

Manuel Altolaguirre
  MEXICAN BUS RIDE

Gianni Amico
  THE LION HAS SEVEN
    HEADS

Maya Angelou
  GEORGIA, GEORGIA

George Barraud
  JERICHO

Robert Alan Aurther
  THE LOST MAN

Lima Barreto
  CANGACEIRO

Herbert J. Biberman
  SLAVES

Lajos Biro
  SANDERS OF THE RIVER

Robert Bolt
  LAWRENCE OF ARABIA

Edward Bond
  WALKABOUT

Luis Buñuel
  EL

MEXICAN BUS RIDE
NAZARIN
LOS OLVIDADOS
SIMON OF THE DESERT

Juan la Cabado
MEXICAN BUS RIDE

Emilio Carballido
MACARIO

To Chin
PRINCESS YANG KWEI
FEI

Shirley Clarke
THE COOL WORLD

Alfredo De Cuelo
FIRST CHARGE OF THE
MACHETE

Herbert Danska
SWEET LOVE, BITTER

Jules Dassin
UP TIGHT

Delmar Daves
WHITE FEATHER

Ruby Dee
UP TIGHT

Jeffrey Dell
SANDERS OF THE RIVER

Pathe Diagne
REOU-TAKH

Robert Downey
PUTNEY SWOPE

Robert Dozier
WHEN LEGENDS DIE

Anselmo Duarte
THE GIVEN WORD

Marguerite Dumas
HIROSHIMA, MON AMOUR

Jean Duvignaud
RAMPARTS OF CLAY

Peggy Elliott
COME BACK CHARLESTON
BLUE

Cy Endfield
ZULU

Julio Garcia Espinosa
FIRST CHARGE OF THE
MACHETE

Emilio Fernandez
THE PEARL
MARIA CANDELARIA

Jean Ferry
IMPOSSIBLE ON SATURDAY

Bryan Forbes
THE L-SHAPED ROOM

Carl Foreman
HOME OF THE BRAVE

Aldo Francia
VALPARAISO MI AMOR

Everett Freeman
JIM THORPE, ALL AMER-
ICAN

Shraga Friedman
THE DYBBUK

Roberto Galvadon
MACARIO

John Gay
SOLDIER BLUE

Armando Robles Godoy
THE GREEN WALL

Martin Goldman
THE LEGEND OF NIGGER
CHARLEY

Octavio Gomez
FIRST CHARGE OF THE
MACHETE

Servando Gonzalez
  YANCO

Ruy Guerra
  THE GODS AND THE
    DEAD

Beatriz Guido
  THE EAVES DROPPER
  END OF INNOCENCE
  THE FALL
  HAND IN THE TRAP
  SUMMERSKIN

Moshe Hadar
  CLOUDS OVER ISRAEL

Orville H. Hampton
  ONE POTATO, TWO
    POTATO

Susumu Hani
  BAD BOYS
  BWANA TOSHI

Lorraine Hansberry
  A RAISIN IN THE SUN

Shinobu Hashimoto
  RASHOMON

Raphael Hayes
  ONE POTATO, TWO
    POTATO

Du Bose Hayward
  EMPEROR JONES

Jorge Herrera
  FIRST CHARGE OF THE
    MACHETE

Eijiro Hisaita
  THE BAD SLEEP WELL

Shinobu Hashimoto
  THE BAD SLEEP WELL
  DODES'KA-DEN

Jorge Honig
  THE CRY OF THE PEOPLE

John Huston
  JUAREZ

Masato Ide
  RED BEARD

Flavio Imperior
  THE GODS AND THE DEAD

Hiroshi Inagaki
  SAMURAI

John Ireland
  THE OVERLANDERS

Shintaro Ishihara
  CAPTIVE'S ISLAND

James Ivory
  BOMBAY TALKIE

Frederick Jackson
  STORMY WEATHER

Lewis Jacobs
  SWEET LOVE, BITTER

Im Hi Jai
  SPRING FRAGRANCE

Talbot Jennings
  THE GOOD EARTH

Ruth Prawer Jhabvala
  AUTOBIOGRAPHY OF A
    PRINCESS
  BOMBAY TALKIE

Alex Joffe
  IMPOSSIBLE ON SATURDAY

LeRoi Jones
  DUTCHMAN

Quincy Jones
  BROTHER JOHN

Jyung Yoon Joo
  SPRING FRAGRANCE

Paulo Jose
  THE GODS AND THE DEAD

Matsutaro Kawaguchi
  PRINCESS YANG KWEI FEI
  UGETSU

Ryuzo Kikushima
  THE BAD SLEEP WELL
  HOODLUM SOLDIER
  RED BEARD
  SANJURO
  STRAY DOG
  YOJIMBO

John O. Killens
  SLAVES

Ernest Kinoy
  BUCK AND THE PREACH-
  ER

Teinosuke Kinugasa
  GATE OF HELL

Ephraim Kishon
  SALLAH

Harry Kleiner
  CARMEN JONES

Jane Kloue
  ISLAND OF THE BLUE
  DOLPHINS

Ted Koehler
  STORMY WEATHER

Akira Kurosawa
  THE BAD SLEEP WELL
  DODES'KA-DEN
  DRUNKEN ANGEL
  THE MAN WHO TREAD ON
  THE TIGER'S TAIL
  RASHOMON
  RED BEARD
  YOJIMBO

Masutaro Kwaguchi
  SAGA OF THE CRUCIFIED
  LOVERS

Charles Lang
  THE MAGNIFICENT MATA-
  DOR

Emmet Lavery
  BRIGHT ROAD

Carl Lee
  THE COOL WORLD

Pierre Levy-Corti
  IMPOSSIBLE ON SATURDAY

Eugene Ling
  LOST BOUNDARIES

Julio Luduena
  ALLIANCE FOR PROGRESS

Ricardo Luna
  HAND IN THE TRAP

Aeneas MacKenzie
  JUAREZ

Joseph Mankiewicz
  NO WAY OUT

Arthur Mann
  THE JACKIE ROBINSON
  STORY

Julian Mayfield
  UP TIGHT

Adolfas Mekas
  COMPANERAS AND COM-
  PANEROS

Kenji Mizoguchi
  THE LIFE OF O-HARU

Bloke Modisane
  COME BACK, AFRICA

Douglas Morrow
  JIM THORPE, ALL AMERI-
  CAN

Masashige Narusawa
  PRINCESS YANG KWEI FEI
  STREET OF SHAME
  TALES OF THE TAIRA CLAN

Lewis N'Kosi
  COME BACK, AFRICA

Kogo Noda
AN AUTUMN AFTERNOON
LATE AUTUMN
LATE SPRING
OHAYO
TOKYO STORY
UKIGUSA

Hideo Oguni
THE BAD SLEEP WELL
DODES'KA-DEN
RED BEARD
SANJURO
YOJIMBO

Yasujiro Ozu
AN AUTUMN AFTERNOON
LATE AUTUMN
LATE SPRING
OHAYO
TOKYO STORY
UKIGUSA

Gordon Parks
THE LEARNING TREE

Alan Paton
CRY, THE BELOVED
COUNTRY

Melvin Van Peebles
THE STORY OF A THREE-
DAY PASS

Les Pine
A MAN CALLED ADAM

Barry Pollack
COME BACK CHARLESTON
BLUE

Maurice Pons
SAMBIZANGA

John Prebble
ZULU

Satyajit Ray
THE ADVENTURES OF
GOOPY AND BAGHA
THE ADVERSARY
APARAJITO
CHARULATA, THE LOVELY

WIFE
DAYS AND NIGHTS IN THE
FOREST
DEVI
DISTANT THUNDER
KANCHENJUNGHA
MAHANAGAR
THE MUSIC ROOM
NAYAK, THE HERO
PATHER PANCHALI
TAGORE
THE WORLD OF APU

Wolfgang Reinhardt
JUAREZ

Humberto Rios
THE CRY OF THE PEOPLE

Glauber Rocha
ANTONIO DAS MORTES
EARTH ENTRANCED
THE LION HAS SEVEN
HEADS

Lionel Rogosin
COME BACK, AFRICA

Tina Rome
A MAN CALLED ADAM

Thomas C. Ryan
THE HEART IS A LONELY
HUNTER

Howard Sackler
THE GREAT WHITE HOPE

Lesser Samuels
NO WAY OUT

Jorge Sanjines
BLOOD OF THE CONDOR

Nelson Pereira dos Santos
THE ALIENIST
BARREN LIVES

Michael Sarne
JOANNA

Joseph Schrank
CABIN IN THE SKY

Bontche Schweig
COME BACK CHARLESTON
BLUE

Toru Segawa
WOMAN IN THE DUNES

Ousmane Sembene
BLACK GIRL

Hebe Serebrisky
THE CRY OF THE PEOPLE

Virginia Shaler
LOST BOUNDARIES

Ted Shardeman
ISLAND OF THE BLUE
DOLPHINS
ST. LOUIS BLUES

Melville Shavelson
CAST A GIANT SHADOW

Shebati-Tevet
IMPOSSIBLE ON SATUR-
DAY

Alida Sherman
SLAVES

Kunio Shimzu
BWANA TOSHI

Tess Slesinger
THE GOOD EARTH

Robert Smith
ST. LOUIS BLUES

Franco Solinas
BATTLE OF ALGIERS
STATE OF SIEGE

Oscar Soria
BLOOD OF THE CONDOR
THE COURAGE OF THE
PEOPLE

Larry Spangler
THE LEGEND OF NIGGER
CHARLEY

John Steinbeck
THE PEARL

Josef von Sternberg
THE SAGA OF ANATHAN

Barbara Stone
COMPANERAS AND COM-
PANEROS

David Stone
COMPANERAS AND COM-
PANEROS

Robert Sylvester
THE JOE LOUIS STORY

Tsutomo Tamura
BOY

Lawrence Taylor
THE JACKIE ROBINSON
STORY

Leopold Torre Nilsson
THE EAVES DROPPER
END OF INNOCENCE
THE FALL
HAND IN THE TRAP
SUMMERSKIN

Leo Townsend
WHITE FEATHER

Mahama Traore
REOU-TAKH

Lamar Trotti
CAPTAIN FROM CASTILE

Kyuichi Tsuji
TALES OF THE TAIRA CLAN

Jamie Ulys
DINGAKA

Kamar Vasudev
AT FIVE PAST FIVE

Keinosuke Vegusa
DRUNKEN ANGEL

Jacques Viot
  BLACK ORPHEUS

Natto Wada
  THE BURMESE HARP

Tokuhei Wakao
  SAMURAI

Harry Watt
  THE OVERLANDERS

James Webb
  CHEYENNE AUTUMN

Claudine West
  THE GOOD EARTH

Michael Wilson

SALT OF THE EARTH

Aubrey Wisberg
  THE BURNING CROSS

Fuji Yahiro
  BUDDHA

Juli Yahiro
  THE BAILIFF

Yoshikata Yoda
  THE BAILIFF
  THE LIFE OF O-HARU
  PRINCESS YANG KWEI FEI
  SAGA OF THE CRUCIFIED
    LOVERS
  TALES OF THE TAIRA CLAN
  UGETSU

Composers

Taos Amrouche
  RAMPARTS OF CLAY

Maya Angelou
  GEORGIA, GEORGIA

Richard Rodney Bennett
  HEAVENS ABOVE

Gustavo Becerra
  VALPARAISO MI AMOR

Anil Biswas
  MUNNA

Georges Bizet
  CARMEN JONES

Luis Hernades Breton
  EL

Leo Brower
  FIRST CHARGE OF THE
    MACHETE
  MEMORIES OF UNDERDE-
    VELOPMENT

Lucy Brown
  COME BACK, AFRICA

Roy Budd
  SOLDIER BLUE

Gustavo C. Carreon
  YANCO

Benny Carter
  BUCK AND THE PREACHER

Antonio Diaz Conde
  THE PEARL

Charley Cuva
  PUTNEY SWOPE

Ikuma Dan
  MUDDY WATERS
  SAMURAI

Georges Delerue
  HIROSHIMA, MON AMOUR

Vasent Desai
  AT FIVE PAST FIVE

Francisco Dominguez
  MARIA CANDELARIA

Vernon Duke
  CABIN IN THE SKY

Giovanni Fusco
  HIROSHIMA, MON AMOUR

Carlos Gandel
  DIALOGO CON CHE: CHE
    IS ALIVE

Iyotirindra Gangophyay
  TAGORE

Akira Hakube
  THE SAGA OF ANATAHAN

Hirashi Hara
  KASHIMA PARADISE

Donny Hathaway
  COME BACK CHARLESTON
    BLUE

Tadasha Hattori
  THE MEN WHO TREAD ON
    THE TIGER'S TAIL

Fumio Hayasaka
  THE BAILIFF
  DRUNKEN ANGEL
  SEVEN SAMURAI
  STRAY DOG
  TALES OF THE TAIRA
    CLAN

Hikaru Hayashi
  DEATH BY HANGING

Donald Heywood
  MURDER ON LENOX
    AVENUE

Roldfo Holffter
  LOS OLVIDADOS

Akira Ifukube
  THE BURMESE HARP

Maurice Jarre
  THE OLIVE TREES OF
    JUSTICE

Sol Kaplan
  SALT OF THE EARTH

Erich Wolfgang Korngold
  JUAREZ

Alexander Laszlo
  FINCHO

Raul Lavista
  MACARIO

Galt MacDermot
  COTTON COMES TO HAR-
    LEM

Country Joe McDonald
  QUE HACER

Gabriel Migliori
  THE GIVEN WORD

Pablo Milanes
  FIRST CHARGE OF THE
    MACHETE

Ennio Morricone
  BATTLE OF ALGIERS

Milton Nascimento
  THE GODS AND THE DEAD

Marios Nobre
  ANTONIO DAS MORTES

Alex North
  CHEYENNE AUTUMN

Sergio Ortega
  THE JACKAL OF NAHUEL-
    TORO

Gordon Parks
  THE LEARNING TREE

Melvin Van Peebles
  WATERMELON MAN

Gustavo Pitaluga
  MEXICAN BUS RIDE

Gillo Pontecorvo
  BATTLE OF ALGIERS

Bob Prince
  STRANGERS IN THE CITY

Lloyd Price
 THE LEGEND OF NIGGER
  CHARLEY

Timir Bahan Rahat
 DAY SHALL DAWN

Satyajit Ray
 THE ADVERSARY
 CHARULATA, THE LONELY
  WIFE
 DAYS AND NIGHTS IN THE
  FOREST
 DISTANT THUNDER
 NAYAK, THE HERO

Sergio Ricardo
 EARTH ENTRANCED

Laurence Rosenthal
 A RAISIN IN THE SUN

Buffy Sainte-Marie
 SOLDIER BLUE

Takanobu Saito
 LATE AUTUMN
 UKIGUSA

M. Santos
 GANGA ZUMBA

Masaru Sato
 THE BAD SLEEP WELL
 RED BEARD
 SANJURO
 YOJIMBO

Ravi Shankar
 APARAJITO
 THE FLUTE AND THE
  ARROW
 KANCHENJUNGHA
 MAHANAGAR
 PATHER PANCHALI
 THE WORLD OF APU

Noam Sheriff
 THE DYBBUK

Nilo Soruco
 THE COURAGE OF THE
  PEOPLE

Michael Spolianski
 SANDERS OF THE RIVER

Toru Takemitsu
 BAD BOYS
 BWANA TOSHI
 CAPTIVE'S ISLAND
 DODES'KA-DEN
 SHE AND HE

Nauman Taseer
 DAY SHALL DAWN

Mikis Theodorakis
 STATE OF SIEGE

Dimitri Tiomkin
 HOME OF THE BRAVE

Naozumi Yamamoto
 HOODLUM SOLDIER

Daniel Valdez
 YO SOY CHICANO

Magalhaes Guicherme Vaz
 THE ALIENIST

Sven Olaf Waldorf
 GEORGIA, GEORGIA

PART IV

INDEX OF FILM TITLES

TITLE INDEX

291

N